When Histories Collide

When Histories Collide

The Development and Impact of Individualistic Capitalism

RAYMOND D. CROTTY

ALTAMIRA
PRESS
A Division of
ROWMAN & LITTLEFIELD PUBLISHERS, INC.
Walnut Creek • Lanham • New York • Oxford

ALTAMIRA PRESS
A Division of Rowman & Littlefield Publishers, Inc.
1630 North Main Street, #367
Walnut Creek, CA 94596
www.altamirapress.com

Rowman & Littlefield Publishers, Inc.
4720 Boston Way
Lanham, MD 20706

12 Hid's Copse Road
Cumnor Hill, Oxford OX2 9JJ, England

British Library Cataloguing in Publication Information Available

Library of Congress Cataloging-in-Publication Data

Crotty, Raymond D.
 When histories collide : the development and impact of individualistic capitalism /
Raymond D. Crotty.
  p. cm.
 Includes bibliographical references and index.
 ISBN 0-7591-0157-4 (cloth : alk. paper) — ISBN 0-7591-0158-2 (pbk. : alk. paper)
  1. Europe—Economic conditions. 2. Capitalism—Europe—History. 3. Developing
countries—Dependency on foreign countries. I. Title.

HC240 .C758 2001
330.12'2—dc21

                                                        2001033498

Printed in the United States of America

♾™ The paper used in this publication meets the minimum requirements of American
National Standard for Information Sciences—Permanence of Paper for Printed Library
Materials, ANSI/NISO Z39.48–1992.

Contents

Tables

Foreword: Raymond Crotty's World History

Lars Mjøset

Raymond Crotty (1925–1994) was an Irish intellectual inspired by Georgist and Third World populist viewpoints. His book *When Histories Collide,* published here for the first time, provides perspectives on world history that are fascinating and original. Through eight chapters, the reader is taken from the neolithic revolution up to the end of the twentieth century. On the way, Crotty invites us to share his explanations of the role of pastoral migrations, India's holy cows, the decline of the Roman empire, feudalism, slavery, the rise of the West, the specificities of Britain's early modern development, the patterns of Western colonization, the lack of socioeconomic development in former capitalist colonies today (including a case study of Ireland), and the recent development success of Japan and China.

Seldom have so many of the cultural problems addressed by world historians been dealt with in one single volume. It is all the more impressive that all these topics are discussed within a single social scientific framework. The framework is multidisciplinary, combining elements of agricultural economics, nutritional science, development studies, economic geography, economic anthropology, demography, and history. Nonetheless, it forms a comprehensive framework for assessing the evolution of the human condition. It is also empirically founded, relying not only on empirical information drawn from a variety of secondary historical sources, but also on skillful use of statistical indicators as well as reasoning based on agronomic considerations applied to prehistorical and early historical periods.

Although the notion of theory is often hazy in social science, Crotty's framework really deserves the label *theory*. True, it is not a collection of laws on the natural science model. Although elements of evolutionary biology are invoked at certain points of the argument, the method is not based on deduction from a collection of laws. The framework has strong elements of conventional economics (which, together with statistics, was Crotty's academic background), but these elements are not brought together in decontextualized models based on very strong behavioral assumptions, typical of most rational choice approaches in present social science.

When Histories Collide is a work with a meticulous architecture. It is one of those rare cases of a social science work that can be read with great excitement. Crotty provides a framework of quite general preconceptions that are combined in order to explain various historical trajectories and their interaction. His world historical scheme is constructed via turning points and "collisions," with the use of comparative analysis to trace the specificity of the developments that are of specific interest. In particular, he studies the collision between western individualist capitalism, and the collectivist "Third World" societies that became the food-producing colonies of the "First World."

In fact, a main implication of Crotty's approach is the questioning of any simple distinction between the First and the Third Worlds. To deal with contemporary development problems, he suggests another dichotomy, namely between the former capitalist colonies and the rest of the world's countries. The first group, he holds, is locked into a situation in which they do not develop, they *undevelop*.[1] The rest all develop, but they consist of many different constellations, from the original group of capitalist colonial countries, to groups of settler capitalist countries, autocratic capitalist countries in eastern Europe, and collectivist capitalist countries in east Asia. The latter cases started their development later than the first group, but they have all developed.

Crotty's preconceptions do not form a set of factors determining world history. He has place for unique conjunctures. His most fundamental conjuncture is the emergence of what he terms individual capitalism by the migration of lactose tolerant pastoralists into the dense central-western European forests around 2000 BC (chapter 3).[2] His explanations are always sensitive to the ecological and historical context. This sensitivity emerges above all in his thorough use of comparative reasoning. Cases that have been analyzed in preceding chapters are used in the following chapters to help specify the new contexts considered. For instance, the analysis of Mediterranean slavery (37–41) is used to trace the specificities of later Caribbean (42) and antebellum U.S. slavery (43, 118–21). Such a procedure matches what has been termed *grounded theory* in social science.[3] Still, Crotty's analysis also relies on his set of quite general preconceptions. This makes his approach very rich on interesting implications; it generates a host of new perspectives and surprising questions.

Last, but not least, Crotty's framework is a theory in the classical sense of forming an answer (in the form of a set of explanations) to questions of great existential concern to the social scientist and the community to which he belonged. Crotty's main cultural problem is how the undevelopment of former capitalist colonies can be overcome. In order to address that problem, he analyzes world history in order to spell out how individualist capitalism emerged and how it came to colonize—besides Ireland—huge fertile and populous areas in Asia, Africa, and Latin America.

In the following, we first provide the most brief and synthetic restatement of Crotty's framework. We then show how his approach to world history was intimately connected to his own experiences as an Irish farmer who wondered about his fate, went into social science, gained a lot of additional experience as a consultant to several poor countries struggling to overcome undevelopment, and then returned to Ireland with a specific political program that he pursued while also writing up his account of Irish and world history in several books, out of which this came to be the last, unfinished one.

General Preconceptions

Let us first list a number of general preconceptions that inform Crotty's analysis throughout this and his earlier books.

I. Human Survival

In any context where members of human society relate to the environment in a struggle to survive, one out of the three factors of production—land, labor, capital—will play a limiting role. Crotty takes care to specify the context in ecological terms. In his focus on man's interchange with nature, he emphasizes geoclimatic conditions, the balance of production factors, innovations that contribute to "state of the art" knowledge, and properties acquired by humans and domesticated animals. The latter may be among his most original contributions, as can be seen in his analysis of lactose tolerance (14–16, 44–46, 62–63) and the difference between the *Bos Taurus* and *Bos Indicus* breeds of cattle (62–63, 100).

II. Development

When struggling to survive, human beings interact in societies based on socioeconomic structures. These societies are said to *develop* to the extent that "more people are better off today than in the past and that fewer people are as badly off as was the case hitherto" (1). If either of these criteria is not satisfied, the society in question is said to *undevelop*.

III. Collectivism

In the early history of mankind, production for a living was always land-limited. A member of society could not contribute anything to production by means of his individual efforts. The marginal product of the individual was zero. Population was the dependent variable. Even in modern history, such land-limited, collectivist societies exist.

IV. Evolution

According to Crotty, the progress of humanity was marked by natural selection.

This evolution favored groups that were able to adapt and adopt appropriate technologies and institutions. As crucial instances, he mentions the innovation of using food to produce future food, rather than using it for immediate consumption. More would survive and the pace of innovation and adaptation accelerated. As groups increase in number, they tend to expand and colonize. Crotty sees life as a "colonizing process," and man "has been the most successful colonizer" (115).

V. Individualism

Historical conjunctures can be specified in which individual effort makes a difference. In contexts where arable land is unlimited, production is limited by either labor or capital. In such contexts, the institution of individual property is established in the form of a title to the limiting resource. This and related institutions secure the efficiency of production. They emerge autochthonously, that is, they are established by the people originally living in that area, they are not established by external imposition.

VI. Georgism

There is an even more specific conjuncture in which even property in land emerges. The specific feature of property in land is that it gives no efficiency gain. The supply of land is fixed; such basic geoclimatic conditions cannot be created by individuals.

VII. Dependence

If an institution is forcibly imposed in a context in which it would not have emerged autochthonously—that is, it is imposed out of context—then production is determined by concerns external to the producing community and this causes undevelopment.

Combining preconceptions II, III, V, VI, and VII, we arrive at Crotty's most crucial claim: The undevelopment (II) of the (presently former) capitalist colonies is the result of the forcible imposition (VII) of institutions evolved in connection with individualist capitalism (V and VI) on to collectivist societies (III).

The Naked Scheme of Crotty's World History

As such, these preconceptions could have been the start of a deductive exercise in economic modeling, but Crotty turns them into something quite different, namely a synthetic view of world history. This view defines the plot of *When Histories Collide,* and we shall here only present the most stripped down version. Most detailed arguments that would be needed for a causal account are omitted in order to present the naked scheme in thirteen steps. We get a sequence starting at the point where human history gets a substance different from natural history.

(1) The starting point is a world inhabited by hunter-gatherers, living "like animals" by harvesting food that is immediately available. At the most, such hunter-gatherers would engage in swidden farming, that is, burning down parts of nature in order to "provoke" the local ecosystem to recover in ways that gave a higher nutritional yield than before. The hunter-gatherer situation can be modified in two ways: pastoralism, domesticating some of the animals (mostly ruminants) earlier hunted; and settled agriculture, permanently modifying the ecosystems to improve food supply (chapter 2).

(2) The innovation of settled agriculture (the neolithic revolution)—the first sowing of a grain by a person willing to wait for the crop to mature—occurred in the most fertile belt of the planet (12). Here, all land was cultivated, and the land yielded a surplus large enough to allow the emergence of a civilization with a population higher than what would be needed to produce food. These economies were land-limited; the marginal product of the individual was zero.

(3) The pastoralists were nomads in environments where domesticated animals could be left on the pastureland (13–16). Among some of the pastoralists, the mutation of lactose tolerance spread. These people did not get sick from the lactose contained in the milk they could get from their domesticated ruminants. This implied an advantage in terms of food supply (milk and milk products), so these pastoralists produced a population surplus. However, suitable land remained the limiting factor of production; the marginal product of the individual remained zero.

(4) This population surplus led to invasions by lactose tolerant pastoralists into the fertile, crop-growing areas of Eurasia. Recurrent invasions into China produced no synthesis. Invasions into India produced a quite stable constellation based on holy cows, a ban on eating beef, and a caste system. Invasions into the Near East simply destroyed these old cradles of civilization (24). Invasions into Europe, in contrast, created *individualist* constellations, in which the institutions of individual property emerged (chapter 3). In such economies capital was the constraining factor, and the marginal product of the individual was non-zero; the individual actually made a separate, identifiable contribution to the total product.

(5) Invasions into southern Europe created individualist slavery, based on property in slaves (37–41). Mediterranean production conditions were such that the individual could produce sufficient food to maintain himself, but not to reproduce. Only by extracting the surplus to maintenance of his slaves could the individual reproduce himself. Moreover, the individual slaveholder with his slaves increased the total product, so Europe's Mediterranean civilization expanded rapidly and aggressively in a race for slaves. During the Roman empire expansion was in the end forced toward the North, where ecological conditions were such that the slavery-based economy was undermined.

(6) Invasions into central-western Europe created individualist capitalism (chapter 4), defined by Crotty as an economy based on the savings and resulting investments of individual peasants relying on cattle, cultivating food and winter

fodder, and building shelter for the harsh winter. In this very general definition, capitalism has existed since about 2000 BC. (This is obviously a definition very different from the Marxist one, which refers specifically to the historical phase in which wage labor emerges.) In the European agrarian economy, the institution of property rights in capital (cattle, shelter, crops, food) developed. Gradually, this constellation proved highly dynamic. Savings and investments led to surges of technological innovations, spilling over into innovations in instruments of warfare, due to the tense relationships among Europe's feudal states.

(7) Thanks to innovations in shipping, mercantile capitalism could expand *overseas*—outside Eurasia—from about 1450 onward. In areas where hunter-gatherers prevailed, the natives were marginalized and/or exterminated, and settler capitalism was established (107–10).

(8) In some coastal areas, however, capitalist colonialism was established by Spanish and Portuguese expeditions in the mercantilist age (110–12). The colonizers were not after land; they needed labor to extract spices (to conserve European food stored for the winter) and precious metals (needed to spur trade given the metal-based currency system). As the Caribbean case shows, the colonialists produced sugar using slaves imported from Africa.

(9) In the course of this competition among the European states, in Europe and abroad, an exceptional constellation emerged as England's Tudor monarchy established property rights in land (89–97). In the wake of this development, and also helped by the stimulus to Europe from the first surge of capitalist colonialism, factory capitalism developed, England being the pioneer that the other European and settler capitalist countries emulated.

(10) Factory capitalism revolutionized transport further (steam engines on iron ships and railways), and made possible a second surge of capitalist colonization in which the land of the remaining non-European areas was put to use to produce metropolitan profits, securing Europe's food supply (112–15). There was a huge expansion of cultivated land in the settler capitalist countries and in the eastern European areas. Here, however, the ecological conditions were such that individualist capitalism fit the context, either individualist capitalism as in the settler colonies (147–50) or what Crotty terms "autocratic capitalism" (87). It was otherwise in the huge land-limited, labor-rich inland areas that were opened up by the steam and rail technologies—especially the rice economies of India and Indonesia, but also other southeast Asian as well as African areas. In these areas Western institutions and technologies were applied: in the case of plantations, property in land was imposed. In Africa, for instance, property in cattle was strengthened, and veterinary science influenced animal husbandry. These institutions, legal systems, and technologies were forcibly imposed onto conditions where they would not have emerged autochthonously. Production was for the profit of metropoles, to serve the markets of the richer parts of the world. The natives were displaced to marginal lands, and often hired to serve as laborers on the now privately owned land. Thus, these cases were very different from the settler capitalist cases, as Crotty's comparison of North and Latin America demonstrates (147–50). Undevelopment (as defined in preconception

II) resulted from "the forcible superimposition on the peoples of these countries of an alien, individualist, capitalist culture" (9). Crotty's work provides many examples of this mechanism, but one of the strongest emerges from his combined analysis of Ireland's Great Famine and antebellum North American slavery. In the 1840s, one million Irish people starved to death, while profit from Irish land increased. At the same time, the U.S. slave population recorded an annual increase of 2.5 percent. U.S. property in men served even the American slaves better than Anglo-Irish property in land served the Irish people, in the specific sense that the starving Irish agricultural underclass (coolies) would clearly have preferred to be slaves.[4]

(11) Europe's overseas empire lasted from 1500 to 1900; then it declined. But unlike all other empires it did not decline due to external and internal pressures that brought down the empire itself (chapter 7). Europe and the Western world continued to prosper even though their former colonies gained sovereignty through processes of decolonization. In these processes, the postcolonial elites always gained the upper hand. These elites maintained the social order that had brought them to power, an order originally imposed by the colonial rulers. This was also why Latin America, which had won sovereignty as far back as in the early nineteenth century, remained haunted by the effect of Western institutions imposed out of context (150). This is why, in Crotty's terms, the "capitalist colonies" and the "former capitalist colonies" refer to the same group of countries. These countries are the "wretched of the earth," hurt not by capitalism, but by its extension via colonialism to food- and raw-materials-producing areas where land was the limiting factor of production. It follows from this that Crotty is not a critic of capitalism; he is a critic of the forced imposition of the institutions of individualist capitalism out of context, in areas where land was the limiting resource. The result of this intrusion is that the land and raw materials are no longer used with reference to collective needs. The detailed case study of Ireland shows how the use of Irish land shifted periodically in four phases from 1601 to 1920 (169–79).

(12) Still, some areas did not fall under the control of capitalist colonization. The most important cases were Japan and China. It is interesting to note that these countries have industrialized in a way which has retained important collectivist institutional features. In Crotty's understanding, capitalism (saving and investing) may well be developed within a collectivist framework. But in the capitalist colonies that are caught in the trap of undevelopment, the turn to such a framework has so far never been seen.

(13) For the study of capitalist colonization, Ireland plays a special role. It was the first country to be exposed to such colonization (chapters 8–10). It is also the colony that was closest to the metropoles. Ireland had in fact been settled by the same lactose tolerant pastoralists who created individualist capitalism when they invaded central western Europe. Given Ireland's dual character, Crotty holds that it could serve as an example for other former capitalist colonies: it could be the first country to dethrone the postcolonial elites who maintain the institutions imposed by the colonizers. This vision defined Crotty's poli-

tics.

Now, how could an Irish farmer come to develop such a reconstruction of world history?

An Irish Farmer Becomes a World Historian: Crotty's Personal Background

In his partly autobiographical book, *A Radical's Response,* Crotty recounts how during World war II he joined the Irish "back to the land" movement, leaving the town (Kilkenny) in which he grew up to work a farm in 1942. He took a year on an agricultural college, sharecropped for a further year, and then bought a farm in Dunbell in 1945. He wanted to run the farm in a modern way. Against local advice, he invested in a tractor and other capital goods, ploughing all his pastureland in 1945. Such a strategy was in line with the strategy of capital-intensive farming introduced in most of western Europe in the postwar period, inspired by the U.S. interwar experience. Retrospectively, Crotty compared his choice with the advice of the World Bank expert who had "never grown a crop or raised an animal in his life": it was a strategy "that conflicted with the local wisdom painfully achieved over the ages."[5] Two bad years followed, and the idealistic young farmer was heavily in debt. The situation stabilized somewhat in a few years. But every day Crotty could observe his neighbor, who left the cattle to grass and to live off their fat through the short, dormant winter season. This neighbor invested very little, but still it seems that he earned about as much as Crotty did, despite the higher productivity (eight times as high output per acre) of the capital-intensive farm.[6]

After ten years of farming Crotty had understood that under Irish conditions, successful farmers did the opposite of what he had done: they held operating costs to a minimum, and invested spare resources in land. "Acquiring additional land to operate on a low-cost/low-output basis made sense given that the cost of holding that land was virtually zero."[7] Government policy supported this approach by taxing everything except land.

In the early 1950s, Crotty agreed to contribute to a small column in the *Irish Farmers Journal.* The absence of a land tax was one of the topics he dealt with. He argued that quite in contradiction to the government's objective of increasing Ireland's agricultural output, its tax policy depressed output, by increasing the cost of capital to agriculture. Crotty received a reply which noted that such a land tax had traditionally been proposed by the Georgist movement. Reading Henry George's writings, Crotty writes, "all the bits and pieces with which I had struggled so painfully and ponderously seemed now to fall so easily and neatly into place."[8] He proceeded to read classical economics. "I wanted to understand further why government, while saying it wanted agricultural output to expand, pursued policies that were directly contrary to that objective."[9]

By 1955, Crotty had investigated into the conditions for taking a B.Sc.

(Econ.) at the University of London by correspondence. He reorganized his farm, firing five out of six men, selling two out of three tractors, buying sixty in-calf heifers, and starting to produce milk. Inputs would be minimized, output would not be maximized. He began to study in 1956. His wife and one farm-worker worked the farm. While studying, he was earning more than he had ear-lier, maintaining a family with five children. He was very relieved because studying was a great contrast to the "endless disappointments" of trying to suc-ceed doing capital-intensive farming in Ireland.[10]

Crotty finished his economics B.Sc. in 1959, specializing in mathematical economics, and proceeded with graduate studies in London, earning an M.Sc. in 1961. He then lectured in agricultural economics at University College Wales, Aberystwyth. There he wrote *Irish Agricultural Production,* which is today ac-cepted as a major revisionist interpretation of Ireland's agricultural develop-ment.[11] That book's central proposal was to tax away the value of land. Crotty was now firmly committed to the Georgist idea that property in land could not be defended.

In *Progress and Poverty,* Henry George had written: "Vice and misery, poverty and pauperism, are not the legitimate results of increase of population and industrial development; they only follow increase of population and indus-trial development because land is treated as private property—they are the direct and necessary results of the violation of the supreme law of justice, involved in giving to some men the exclusive possession of that which nature provides for all men."[12] The value of land, argued George, expresses land monopoly, it is not created by the individual who owns it. It can be taxed to the advantage of the community without any reduction in the production of wealth. Even if all land rent is taxed away, there will be no price increases on any commodities, and production will in no way be impaired.[13] We shall return to Crotty's relationship to Georgism below.

Our short resume should be sufficient to indicate the unity between Crotty's world historical scheme and his own life history. Since colonization, completed in 1601, the output of Irish land had been regulated not according to the interests of the people, but according to the interests of the colonizers (step 10).[14] The postcolonial Irish state reproduced the institutional and legal arrangements im-ported by colonial authorities (step 11), and property in land was a prime ex-pression of this.

Given his Georgist conviction, Crotty sold off his farm. Between 1966 and 1974 he lived in Kilkenny, Ireland, but worked as an economic advisor to vari-ous development agencies, including the World Bank. He first worked in Ma-laysia, also gaining insight into South Asian conditions more generally. Then he worked in the Caribbean and Latin America, and finally in India and Africa. He had a specific niche among economic advisors to the Third World. This was, as he wrote himself, largely based on the fortuitous circumstances that made him "(a) a farmer with practical experience from livestock farming; (b) an economist with a special interest in the economic relationships between people and their livestock; and (c) an observer of all the major livestock keeping systems of the world."[15]

In 1976, Crotty received a fellowship to visit the Institute of Development Studies at the University of Sussex.[16] There he wrote *Cattle, Economics and Development*, which synthesized his knowledge of the world's cattle-keeping systems, writing about how the two main breeds of cows differ with respect to lactation, systematizing the geography of lactose tolerance, and explaining Third World undevelopment with reference to the imposition of Western institutions and technologies regardless of their local impact.[17] A measure of the disruption caused by the West is that the Third World pastoral resources are yielding much less than those of the wealthiest countries (although Third World cropland yields more): if the Western interest could be curbed, and Third World pastureland improved, it would alleviate some of the world's food problem.[18]

In 1982, Crotty returned to Ireland, working as a statistics lecturer at Trinity College, Dublin. Again, he actively intervened in Irish public debates. In the late 1960s, he had experienced the start of Ireland's deficit-financed, Keynesian offensive for economic development. He now diagnosed an approaching crisis of the Irish economy. Published in 1986, *Ireland in Crisis* was mainly a book on Ireland, but in contrast to the 1966 book on Irish agriculture, the country's development was now analyzed in light of Crotty's broad experience with undevelopment in other former capitalist colonies.[19] Thus, the book contains three astonishing appendices, occupying about a third of the book, giving the first compact sketch of his world historical scheme. This is the scheme expanded on in the present book, and now it is Ireland that has been put last (chapters 8–9).

It followed from Crotty's analysis that Irish postcolonial sovereignty had so far been fictitious. His political strategy was to make it real by a national strategy based on the land tax. He saw EU membership as a step in the wrong direction, since the EU consisted of all the original capitalist colonizing countries. Crotty's most famous act of political intervention was when he took part in the movement which challenged the Irish government's support for the EU's Single European Act in 1986, bringing the case to the Supreme Court which ruled the act unconstitutional. A referendum had to be conducted in May 1987 to amend the Irish Constitution. The Single European Act was delayed, but the amendment was accepted. Summing up this phase of activism, Crotty wrote *A Radical's Response*, published in 1988, linking together his biography, his politics, and his world historical scheme.[20]

Crotty worked on the present manuscript since the late 1980s. A first draft version was ready in 1992. He worked further on it until his death in January 1994, assisted through the last months by his son, Raymond J. Crotty. In the late 1990s, the manuscript was circulated to several world historians and macrosociologists, but for strange reasons it got turned down by several British publishers. One reason for these problems was probably Crotty's wish that the analysis of Irish developments should still play a crucial role, despite the fact that the main topic was world history. We have already (step 13 above) noted the crucial role of Ireland in Crotty's analysis, but a few more comments will further illuminate this point.

The Standpoint of the Third-World Farmer

In the first paragraph of his autobiography, Crotty notes that he appears "to be the only economist who has earned a living for a prolonged period—from 1942 to 1961—solely from farming in a former capitalist colony." Being such a farmer is also "the sole occupation of perhaps as much as one third of the world's workforce."[21] This occupation implies "the way of life still practiced by almost half the world's population" (10).

This point is not unrelated to Crotty's account of world history. In fact, all social science theories that deal with real-life problems are related to specific perspectives on society. These perspectives are related to social movements, as in Marx's special relation to the labor movement of the nineteenth century, or in feminist social scientists' relation to the women's movement of the postwar period. Other perspectives may be related to social problems defined by the state or other bureaucracies, but these may again be seen as either institutionalized results of the successful efforts of earlier social movements, or as related to specific social movements or interest groups.

A major claim in feminist social science is that the standpoint of women as mothers and caregivers gives them a specific advantage in gaining insight into the mechanisms of patriarchy. Similarly, we find in Crotty a claim that his standpoint, his ability to look at both world history and the present from the point of view of the Third World farmer, gives him a special advantage in gaining insight into the mechanisms and effects of colonial and postcolonial dominance.[22]

Living in Ireland made it easier to give voice to these insights: Crotty had an urban background, and when he quit farming, he could get a first class university education in the educational institutions of the neighboring colonizer, England. Ireland, says Crotty, belongs both to the individualist West and to the colonial world. In geographical location and also ethnically, it belongs to the West. But it is unique in the West in being a food-producing country where individualist capitalism did not develop autochthonously. This is Crotty's notion of a land-limited, collectivist context. Due to Ireland's status as "neighbor and colony," analyzing it would give insight into both the nature of capitalist colonialism and its impact on the Third World (9). It is a case for close comparison, allowing the specification of the exact criteria for the emergence of individualist capitalism.

Reaching back to the example of feminist social science, there are now more women working as social scientists than when feminist approaches were first launched. But social science is concentrated in the West, and those who practice it lead a middle-class lifestyle insulated from the daily routines of surviving on small plots of agricultural land in former capitalist colonies. Crotty's ambition of giving voice to the standpoint of the masses living in the food-producing, former colonial countries should thus be taken seriously. Just as the worker's standpoint gradually gained legitimacy through the nineteenth and

twentieth centuries and women's standpoint gained legitimacy through the postwar period, the legitimacy of the standpoint of the poor masses is hard to dis-
pute: their interest in a better life situation is a universal interest!

Crotty's Contribution in the Light of Other Approaches to World History

Crotty's reflections on world history grew from his experiences as an Irish
farmer, his education as an economist, and his work as a consultant in many
parts of the Third World. From about the late 1970s he occasionally referred to
other approaches to world history, but not in any extensive or systematic way.
This section thus offers a very brief overview of some academic specializations
in this field—mainly world history, comparative historical sociology, macrosociological development theory, and microeconomic rational choice history—
with the aim of tracing some of the distinctive features of Crotty's approach.[23] It
is a service for all those middle class social scientists (by one of them), who
need to relate new contributions to established research in the field.

In Western thought, there is a long tradition of speculative philosophy of
history. This tradition was criticized by modern historical science, which was
established as a discipline in conjunction with the nationalist phase in nineteenth
century Europe. But despite their rejection of the attempts to attribute some kind
of teleological meaning to world developments, the nationalist historians created
other myths by projecting "national" histories far back in time.

In the second half of the nineteenth century, particularly inspired by the ex-
plosive success of popularized Darwinism, various evolutionist schemes represented a departure from the nationalist histories. Marx's materialistic conception
of how modes of production had evolved was an early case, as was the evolu-
tionism of Herbert Spencer. These and later approaches did not return to speculative philosophy of history, but rather linked social development to selected
secular imperatives, be it the struggle between classes (Marx), the anarchy of
states in the state system (geopolitics), or racial tensions (social Darwinism).
Despite many weaknesses, we find among these studies both the first attempts at
fully secularized, "materialist" accounts of historical developments, and also the
first attempts to trace developments spanning the whole globe, particularly with
the geopolitical models, in which the Eurasian continent played a particularly
important role.

In the tense early twentieth century, marked by two Europe-based world
wars, there was a growing impact of cultural pessimism on world historians. In
the wake of Nietzsche, world history was analyzed with reference to the rise,
fall, and struggle between civilizations. Such approaches reached back to a
speculative concern, now formulated as the problem of the loss of meaning in
the modern secularized world. Most of these approaches looked at the rise of
Western civilization from a culturalist perspective.[24] They would judge the pre-

sent in the light of nostalgic ideals derived from idealized accounts of earlier historical epochs, religious communities, or other types of organically integrated societies. A main point of departure was the Hegelian schemes of Oswald Spengler, followed by Arnold Toynbee's monumental work on cyclical patterns in world history, published in six volumes in 1933 and 1939, and another six in the 1950s until 1961. To the same tradition we can count Pitrim Sorokin, Lewis Mumford, and William McNeill. The latter is particularly interesting in our context, since he retains a focus on secular progress, being less committed to explanations only in terms of ideas, culture, and knowledge than most other representatives of this tradition.[25]

The whole tradition of spiritual world historians strove to define the uniqueness of the Western civilization. This is a point of convergence with the other main tradition that emerged at the time of World War I. Weber's comparative historical sociology was committed to a multidimensional explanatory approach. There are similarities with the world historians: Weber compared the West with parallels such as the Chinese, Indian, and Judaic civilizations. He paid special attention to the meaning of the Protestant ethic in the emergence of Western capitalism, and lamented the "iron cage" of contemporary rationality. But organizing his huge, unfinished treatise, *Economy and Society,* he conducted comparisons within several dimensions, ranging from economic and legal factors, to the development of power, science, and religious beliefs. Among the world historians, only McNeill has a similar ideal of explanation. McNeill is much less Eurocentric than his predecessors, and unlike them, he balances his emphasis on diffusion of cultural, technological, and institutional factors with thorough comparative reasoning.

In a broader view, we can also count branches of the Durkheimian school in France (Simiand, Bloch, the Annales school) to the tradition of comparative historical sociology. The distinct feature here is the focus on the material ways of life that mark various historical regions, while the focus on Western uniqueness is less marked.

Like both the spiritual and the Weberian traditions covered so far, Crotty's world history focuses on the uniqueness of the West. But his approach is more heavily materialistic. Even Weberian multidimensional explanatory schemes are too flexible for him. While Weber emphasized the conjuncture of factors relating to science, law, economics, the state, and religion, Crotty was preoccupied with the material ways of life, in a way that was more tied to conventional economic theory than the Annales school. He saw institutions as adaptations to distinct ways of life in specific ecological, geoclimatic contexts.

There are, however, Weberian studies with a materialist leaning. In particular, E. L. Jones's interpretation is a useful contrast to Crotty's scheme, since both are strongly focused on agrarian topics.[26] Jones starts his account about 1500 AD, and his four privileged explanatory factors are low birthrates, few natural disasters, rich and varied natural environment, and a balance of political powers. In Crotty's view these factors are either not specific to Europe or they merit further explanation. Jones does not explain the low birthrates; he does not take into consideration that disasters spur growth and development, nor the fact that political units were fragmented elsewhere too (e.g., in Africa). Finally, Crotty emphasizes that central western Europe's natural environment was much harsher than Jones claims. In response to this environment, the advantages of Europe had been building up slowly but consistently since 2000 BC. As Jones's account of Europe's "miracle" starts in 1500 AD, he has no chance of grasping the deep roots of Europe's peculiar development.[27] We see here how Crotty insists on his very long term perspective on the development of capitalism.

Returning to the postwar period, the tradition of comparative historical sociology took a turn towards more specific problems within the Western world, notably the victory of fascism and the continued opposition of democracy and dictatorship in the Cold War. These experiences inspired the classic postwar works of Gerschenkron, Bendix, Moore, Rokkan, and Skocpol. Somewhat later, a group of British scholars worked further along these lines fusing neo-Marxist and neo-Weberian elements: Anderson covered questions of Europe's unique development and in particular the question of feudalism and the comparison with Japan.[28] Mann provides a history of power that goes back to the earliest civilizations.[29] Crotty relates to the two scholars, but only in quite specific questions. The analysis of feudalism and the state is one case of convergence.[30]

The more specific cultural problems relating to the West's internal political developments were distant in the Irish setting. The problem of economic development was the most burning one. Crotty's background as an Irish radical and an economist brought him close to two other traditions. First, we can see parallels to dependency theory in development studies, historicized in world systems theory. Second, there are points of convergence with the property rights approach, which derives from the strong influence exerted by neoclassical economic models in the postwar period. We consider these two in turn.

In the postwar period, the Western capitalist countries lost their colonial possessions (step 11). In the 1950s, modernization theory provided an optimistic assessment of the Third World's future: poor countries would pass through a take-off to enjoy the same kind of development and wealth-creation as the countries of the First World. But Latin American economists (the ECLA-school), soon backed by other economists in the UN circuit (such as Gunnar Myrdal), realized that the Latin American countries encountered much greater development problems in the liberalized trade regime of the postwar period than under the more closed and import-substitution oriented interwar and wartime periods.

Crotty had the same experience. Just like in Latin America, economic problems in Ireland reached crisis proportions in the late 1950s. This was a paradox for modernization theory, and dependency theory aimed to explain it. Although later adopted by radical Western economists, dependency theory was probably the earliest economic theory to emerge outside the Western world. The main criticism was that modernization theory ignored the impact of asymmetries in the international division of labor. These asymmetries would lead to polarization rather than convergence, working to the disadvantage of raw materials- and food-producing countries of the periphery. Dependency theory was given a historical foundation in Immanuel Wallerstein's world systems theory.[31] This approach is macrosociological, departing from the Weberian comparative views, instead seeking overarching and materialist explanations.

Crotty's work shows parallels with the world systems approach: patterns of interaction between the metropoles and the food- and raw materials-producing satellites, are always at the core of his analysis. But he departs from it in certain crucial respects. While world systems theory is strongly focused on trade and patterns of international division of labor, Crotty is much more oriented towards production and towards the impact of the institutions imposed by colonialism. As noted in step 10, Crotty deals with both institutions and technologies, but as we shall discuss further in the last section of this introduction, his analysis of technologies is restricted to specific elements, such as veterinary science. Thus, the impact of institutions is the most decisive feature of Crotty's analysis.

The roots of undevelopment is not at all trade, but institutional transfer with economic effects that strangle collectivist forms of economic organization. Thus, unlike world systems theory, Crotty's main distinction is not between core and periphery in a trading system. For world systems and dependency theorists, even countries that were never colonized by the West would be analyzed as peripheries. Since these theorists describe the fate of the periphery as *underdevelopment,* Crotty avoids this term, using *undevelopment* instead.[32] For Crotty, the real periphery is only those countries that have been exposed to the colonization by Western powers and then to decolonization led by postcolonial elites. In this focus on the concrete effects on the poorest, he is close to Wolf's focus on the effects of Western colonialism on the Third World masses in the mercantilist and industrial phases, but Wolf relies on a neo-Marxist and world systems analysis, and also limits his analysis to the period from 1400 and onwards.[33]

This point was also a political concern for Crotty: his experience in Ireland was that postcolonial elites would gladly blame undevelopment on "neocolonial" trade patterns and too low prices for raw materials and foodstuffs. Thereby, they would deflect attention from their own preference for the old social order, continuing to blame the old colonial powers for any development problem. Thus, integral to Crotty's diagnosis of undevelopment was an understanding of the postcolonial state. In fact, for a time he used *Our Enemy the State* as a working title of his last manuscript.[34] World systems theory also implies a theory of the state, but the focus is on the peripheral state, which is seen as an organization that helps reproduce a system of asymmetric trade patterns by enforcing systems of labor organization that fits the prevailing international division of labor. Crotty's focus on the postcolonial state involves a stronger focus on the particular institutions imposed.

World systems theory has developed in different ways. Wallerstein's study of cycles and secular trends has been limited to the modern world from about 1450 onwards,[35] but in Frank's work, an Afro-Eurasian world system is analyzed from about the same starting point as Crotty's capitalism, that is 2700 BC.[36] The focus here is on a universal drive for capital accumulation: it is claimed that each world region has a hegemonic center with a dependent periphery and a distant hinterland. Among the regions there may be relations of superhegemony. Elites in one region can acquire parts of the surplus extracted by the elites of other regions, and they may even also involve elites of a third region. The cycles of this world system are expansion and contraction over four to five centuries. Expansive periods tend to produce superhegemons, while contractive periods makes a region vulnerable to invasions. This leads to a heroic exercise in fitting historical information to abstract cyclical patterns, and it leads away from comparative analysis.

Crotty's approach is highly distinct from such attempts to project world system cycles backwards. It is not at all cyclical at the world level. He emphasizes that the collectivist land-limited societies displayed cycles before they were colonized, but never seems interested in studying the links between these on a world level before the various transport and infrastructural revolutions of early modern history. Crotty's explanations are materialist, but with an emphasis on conjunctures and path dependencies, much in contrast to the search for recurrent patterns over 5000 years of world history. While Crotty's explanations are less multidimensional than most Weberian explanations, his interest in turning points is a point of convergence with the Weberian tradition. With the European individualist constellation the pace of change is altered: there is the rapid expansion of the Mediterranean empires (step 5), and the long slow emergence of the West (step 6), which, however, leads to a spurt when the technological impact of savings and investments is unleashed (steps 7 and 10).

In Crotty's focus on the state, there is a parallel with the fourth tradition we shall here relate to: the rational choice-based economic history that was developed in the postwar period. Neoclassical economics emerged in this period as the most prestigious and influential branch of social science. The program of rational choice theory extended the highly abstract, decontextualized, and mathematized principles of neoclassical economics to all the social sciences. Economic historian Douglass North developed a theory of institutions on this basis, emphasizing how scarcity or abundance of factors of production led to the constitution of property rights in these factors. This led North to develop a theory of the state, since the state came to be the institution that establishes and maintains property rights. In 1973, these ideas were brought to bear on the question of the uniqueness of Western developments.[37]

Although he never refers to this tradition, we have already seen that Crotty, with his background in just this kind of economics, thinks in parallel ways. But as in the case of world systems theory, closer inspection shows Crotty's position to be distinct. We have already noted that his approach is contextualized in terms of world regions and processes of diffusion between these. North's rational choice history has few considerations of developments prior to the early Middle Ages, while Crotty studies what he terms a capitalist savings/investment dynamic in Western agriculture since about 2000 BC.

An even more striking difference from North is that Crotty always relates the institutions of individual property rights to a specific ecological context (cf. preconception I). This is the core of his analysis of the Mediterranean and central western Europe (steps 5–6). He then claims that the extension of such institutions into food-producing societies colonized by the West lock these societies into the trap of undevelopment (step 10). The analysis of the Western kind of postcolonial state that maintains "out of context" institutions follows from this (step 11). Rational choice theory, in contrast, sees efficiency-promoting institutions all over, with no distinction between ecological contexts.

In this connection, we can also emphasize Crotty's unique contribution to Georgism. We quoted George's main claim above. In the present book, Crotty echoes George: "Property, as perceived here, is the recognition by society, in society's superior interest, of the exclusive enjoyment by individuals of particular assets in order to secure an increase in the supply of the assets in question. Property in land cannot increase its supply, if that supply is fixed. Exclusive title to land in a land-based society is in inherent conflict with society's interest. It cannot benefit society. It can be exercised only in spite of, and not with the consent of, society. It is, in that sense, the antithesis of property. An exclusive title to land in a land-based society, established by force or otherwise, disrupts society" (48).

George saw property in land as a general problem, as the key single factor root of all problems of poverty. Crotty, in contrast, sees no problems with individualist capitalism as long as it evolves within its own ecological context. The problem of poverty only emerges when its principles are applied "out of context" to settings in which land is scarce. The reference to land-based economies is the crucial difference when we compare the quote from Crotty with the quote from George above. To Crotty, Georgist mobilization would be irrelevant in central western Europe, and also in the settler capitalist countries, since they had unlimited land (35–37, 118–21). For Crotty, mobilization with reference to Georgist arguments is only relevant in the case of (former) colonized food-producing countries with huge native populations.

While George's criticism of property in land derived from a Christian conception of the "supreme law of justice," Crotty rather paid due attention to the historically unprecedented emergence in Tudor England of a class enjoying exclusive property in land, creating a society dichotomized into the landed and the landless. His analysis (89–97) involves the economic history of relative price changes after the Black Death, England's specific geoclimatic and geopolitical conditions, the emergence of absolutist rule in England 200 years before continental Europe, and the specific constellation that made it imperative for the absolutist Tudor rulers to break with Catholic Rome.[38] Again using his comparative method of contrasting to the closest case (Britain versus Continental Europe, France in particular), Crotty concludes that Tudor Britain, confined to its island, with a polarized society, and an economy specialized in wool production, was the condition of Britain's ascent to world hegemony in the seventeenth and eighteenth centuries. Continental European countries needed their farmers as soldiers while England could largely depopulate its countryside (sheep replaced men).

Thus, England had the means to construct, provision, and crew a navy that provided defense and served as a tool of empire, both in military and commercial respects (ships were used for both trade and battles). This is one of the most penetrating special case-studies of the book, perhaps because this was also the constellation in which Ireland was colonized. Britain needed to control Ireland as a geopolitical barrier against the Catholic continent. When Ireland was colonized, it was exposed to the property institution as developed in Britain, and so the Irish economy became a functional appendage to the British wool economy. The British wool economy was again a crucial factor behind the transformation of the British textile industry, a precondition for its move into cotton-spinning and weaving in the Industrial Revolution.[39]

We have so far considered Crotty's contribution in the light of four important approaches to the history of the West. In addition, a couple of more specific approaches deserve mention. Crotty's background in agricultural economics brings him close to a recent addition to world history, the ecological imperialism literature, which has extended the study of colonization by means of closer interdisciplinary exchange with the life sciences. Alfred Crosby pioneered this inclusion of a more ecological perspective.[40] However, these studies have focused on the first phase of colonialism (step 7), that is on the settler capitalist countries, spelling out, for example, how besides military factors, there were also epidemic factors behind the extermination/marginalization of the natives. They have argued that the fact that the Eurasian invaders were much more resistant to diseases such as measles, smallpox, etc. than the natives of the new world, was in part due to the domestication of cattle, pigs, and sheep, which had only taken place in Eurasia.[41] The latter point supports Crotty's emphasis on the importance of cattle in world history, but Crotty takes the extermination of natives by European imperialists as a given historical fact which explains how the settler colonies were open to the unhindered application of individualist capitalist principles. Crotty's main focus, however, is on the second phase of imperialist expansion, the inclusion of the food-producing economies and the mismatch between institutions and various ecological settings. In any case it seems obvious that Crotty's analysis of the world historical importance of lactose tolerance for Europe's dynamic development is something that the ecological imperialism research tradition will have to take up and evaluate within their own framework for world history.

In the 1990s, a tradition of postcolonial studies has emerged as an integral part of the post-structuralist wave in the social sciences, anthropology in particular. As we noted, Crotty's world history is written from the standpoint of a Third World farmer. In that sense, he could be counted as a pioneer in such a tradition of postcolonial studies. However, most postcolonial studies are based on an interdisciplinary mix between the humanities and the social sciences. Edward Said, for instance, one of the pioneers of this tradition, critically deconstructs conventional civilizational studies, questioning the idea that the "Great books" will—through interpretation—display the inner nature of the civilization in question.[42]

Crotty would obviously agree that there are no civilizational essences

(East/West, traditional/modern). As noted, his analysis in fact contributes to the dissolution of the First/Third World dichotomy. But it is also clear that at certain points, his analysis has interesting implications for cultural studies. His analysis of Mediterranean slave civilization clearly give clues for the understanding of Greek philosophy and legal thought (37–44). Crotty would, however, stick to his materialist approach and his interdisciplinary stance between the social sciences and the life sciences. He would not follow postcolonial studies into the kind of constructivist and relativist culturalism, which has moved from the deconstruction of the norm of Western civilization into the celebration of a multitude of local identities that are seen as equally legitimate standpoints. Although not a Christian idealist as Henry George, Crotty sticks to a firm ethical standpoint defined with reference to the collectives whose life chances are impaired by the institutions of colonial capitalism.

To finish this survey, we need to return to the Weberian tradition of comparative historical sociology. Only one branch of this tradition has systematically addressed the question of development and barriers to development. In the 1970s and 1980s, Dieter Senghaas led a major German research project which accumulated case-studies of both failed and successful development.[43] The project aimed to draw lessons for the poorest countries from countries with a successful development record, with specific attention to the historical experience of small countries—for example, the Nordic ones—that had developed despite a strong peripherization pressure from close-by metropoles. The project yielded a list of factors that could be combined in various ways to explain cases of successful development.

Development was defined in terms of structural homogeneity between economic sectors. This implied a balanced development of export-production (food or raw materials) and up-to-date manufacturing production for domestic mass markets, generating a virtuous circle of development in which productivity growth interacted with increasing real wages. This latter criteria is close to Crotty's formula: that more people are better off and fewer people are worse off than before. Undevelopment, on the other hand, would be defined by "structural heterogeneity," implying a huge plantation or raw materials extracting sector with very few linkages to the domestic market, organized exclusively with reference to the needs (profitability, food, and raw materials supplies) of the metropoles and their collaborators in the periphery.[44]

Despite this convergence in definition of the basic concepts, there are differences. Senghaas is ambivalent as to whether any particular factor deserves to be seen as more basic than others, but sometimes he—like Gunnar Myrdal—regards the egalitarian distribution of land and income as a "deep structure" conducive to development. To the extent that Senghaas emphasizes a conjunction of factors, Crotty differs in the same way as with respect to other Weberians. To the extent that Senghaas turns to distribution as a deep structure, Crotty would wish to go further: not the distribution, but the private holding of land in the (former) colonies is the main problem, and the problem is specific to the food-producing areas which were exposed to capitalist colonization.[45] Thus,

Senghaas's preferred comparative strategy of contrasting non-European peripheral countries with European ones—as in his famous comparative sketch of
Denmark and Uruguay—misses what is Crotty's main point: that the Nordic
countries developed their institutions in context, while in Latin America, "alien"
institutions were imposed.

Furthermore, the finding that has been promoted as a main lesson from
Senghaas's project, namely the parallels between the recent East Asian development successes (South Korea, Taiwan) and the development patterns of the
Nordic countries, would be no surprise to Crotty. To him, both were cases of
institutions developing in context. The fact that the Nordic countries had limitless land and were open to individualism, while the East Asian cases were land
limited and collectivist, matters less, since in the absence of exposure to colonialism, individualist capitalism may develop in several ways. Furthermore, for
the Nordic countries, colonization (e.g., Norway under Danish rule for 300
years) made no difference, since both contexts allowed individualist capitalism.

Crotty's views have been well known in Irish public debates, but in that
context, attention has been paid only to the political implications he promoted.
Relating his broader analysis of world history to comparable approaches, we see
that he has provided us with a rich addition to that field of research, one that is
bound to be discussed as the knowledge in this field accumulates. It now only
remains to take a closer look at Crotty's analysis of present development problems and the case of Ireland in particular.

Crotty's Diagnosis of the Present

The wish to diagnose the present led Crotty back into world history, and his
world history led him back to his overall cultural problem: how can former capitalist colonies escape the vicious cycle of undevelopment?

He finds that none of the former capitalist colonized countries have yet
made the transition from undevelopment to development. In the debates on development problems since the 1980s, the success of the East Asian "tigers" has
often been quoted as evidence of a transition into growth and development. But
such a conclusion assumes that the label "Third World" as commonly used refers to a homogenous group of countries. In Crotty's view it does not, since the
successful countries quoted turn out to be those that were never capitalist colonized.

Japan, South Korea, and Taiwan were never colonized by the West. Attempts at colonizing China never fully succeeded. Hong Kong and Singapore—
two other "tigers"—were trade entrepots and settler societies, not capitalist
colonized, so institutions, technology, and law were not imposed on a huge native population, and they had no agrarian sectors. Finally, Thailand was not
colonized, since it served as a buffer between French and British possessions.
Then there are exceptions to Crotty's criteria: former capitalist colonies that in

fact have both more people better off and fewer worse off. For the period considered by Crotty, these are Kuwait, Oman, Saudi Arabia, United Arab Emirates, Botswana, and Malaysia. These exceptions, he holds, are due to great natural wealth (7–8). They are not referred to as development successes either.

Ireland was the point of departure for Crotty's analysis, and it is also the end point. His idea, namely, is that Ireland is best placed to be the first country to break the spell of undevelopment. Crotty, as we know, defines capitalism in a "neutral" way: it is simply savings and investment. Given that capitalism has emerged and developed, any economy can be managed with emphasis on savings and investments. But in the land-limited economies of the former capitalist colonies, the institutions of individualist capitalism have created undevelopment. However, these countries can in principle develop capitalism within a different institutional framework. Capitalism is then coupled with institutions that retain the collectivist orientation of these land-limited economies.

Capitalism in Crotty's sense has developed in a collectivist setting. This is proved by the development of East Asian cases such as Japan. But both the cases of autocratic and collectivist capitalism have developed without a former influence of capitalist colonization. A change towards collectivist institutions in the former *capitalist colonized* countries is very difficult given the vested interests of the postcolonial elites. This is such a crucial difference that Crotty seems to hold that there are few lessons to be learned.[46] But if Ireland could make the transition, there might be lessons.

The crucial criterion is that the basic interests of the collective are taken into account. This requires social and political mobilization. A new alliance of social forces could make even Irish savings and investments generate development. There is a link back to his early experience as a farmer. If Irish institutions had been favorable to Crotty's capital-intensive agriculture, supporting it by means of a land tax and related concrete measures (chapter 10), the yields of the land would be available for the whole collective, and various structural changes would have enabled Ireland to gain from the huge postwar boom. In Senghaas's terms we would have a transition from structural heterogeneity to structural homogeneity.

It is clear that in the 1980s, Crotty did not regard the ruling class in Ireland as capable of managing a transition from undevelopment to development. Judging from their economic policies, Crotty regarded the Irish ruling elite as equal to any other postcolonial elites. He was highly critical of their deficit-financed, export-oriented strategy of industrialization and their belief that foreign multinationals with enormous support and tax-relief would be a stable basis for the upgrading of the Irish economy.

Crotty hoped that the mobilization against Irish support for EU's Single European Act could develop into an alliance against these misguided policies. A broad anti-EU alliance could influence Irish policy-making, and Ireland could set an example for other former capitalist colonies. Irish mobilization against EU membership was considerable, but, as already noted, the referendum on the Single European Act was lost.

At the time, since the end of the 1980s, economic transformation gained pace. Throughout the 1990s, the Irish economy showed persistent high growth rates. Just at the time of Crotty's death in 1994, the business press began to write about the "Celtic tiger," breaking into the league of development states, following in the wake of the East Asian tigers. This would be very much against Crotty's diagnosis. If this was a real transition from undevelopment to development, it would be a transition triggered by the elites that Crotty saw as no different from other postcolonial elites. Let us briefly discuss whether Ireland's success in the 1990s undermines Crotty's diagnosis.

First, Ireland's economic success is not a success on every count. The GNP (gross national product) measure is inflated by profits that are repatriated by foreign firms; thus the growth of GDP (gross domestic product) has been much lower than GNP growth. There is also a major discussion of whether Ireland's economic sectors are linked together in a structurally homogenous way. Some analysts claim that the large share of U.S. multinational companies in certain growth branches spells structural problems in the longer term. Furthermore, unemployment remains high, and employment growth and participation rates (especially for women) do not develop as favorably as in many other countries relevant for comparison.

If, however, we update Crotty's calculation of the number of people better and worse off, finding that the Irish 1990s boom has been really substantial, another counterargument can be mobilized. Crotty argues, with respect to the setback of former USSR, that a reversal of the fortune of an area is possible, but that in the long term, the deep structural forces will assert themselves. In the longer term, we will observe development in Russia and undevelopment in Ireland.

If we find this defense to be weak, we would have to ask the more serious question: If Crotty's diagnosis of the Irish case is refuted on empirical grounds, what is the consequence for his world historical scheme? Only a brief discussion can be given of this topic.

While rejecting the First/Third World dichotomy, Crotty still ends up with a dichotomy between two worlds: one is the former capitalist colonized countries (imposed on land limited collectivist economies), the other is the countries where institutions and technologies developed autochthonously. Let us see how thorough Crotty's analysis of the two worlds is.

In his definition, capitalism simply means savings and investment. The special reference to individualism simply explains all innovation, both in military and industrial technologies (114–115). There is no attention to cyclical developments, economic crises, and the like. The closer we get to our own times, the more general is his analysis. There is a distinction between agrarian, mercantilist, and factory capitalism, as well as a rudimentary distinction between the original individual capitalism "settler capitalism" (United States), "autocratic capitalism" (eastern Europe/Russia), and "collectivist capitalism" (East Asia).

Crotty's notion of autocratic capitalism merits further attention. He claims that in eastern Europe capitalism did not develop in agriculture. Instead, capitalist institutions and technologies were, he writes, imposed by indigenous elites. The only difference to capitalist colonialism here is that the imposition was not by foreign elites. Eastern Europe also contrasts with the settler capitalist countries: there, the natives were marginalized, whereas in eastern Europe and Russia they were not. The marginalization of natives is a similarity between settler capitalism and capitalist colonization, but as Crotty emphasizes in his contrasting of capitalist colonized Latin America with settler capitalist North America (148–50), the masses of the capitalist colonized countries were significantly weakened before postcolonial rule was established.[47] A similar weakening of the masses would not be typical of eastern Europe's autocratic capitalism. The consequence for that type, we must assume, has been that the elites imposing Western institutions and technologies were forced to be more attentive to the way the masses were organized. In addition, these masses were not so numerous that land became a limiting factor; in that respect the eastern European case was open to individualist capitalist principles. These are similarities between eastern Europe and the settler capitalist countries.

Now, clearly, the depth of analysis must be related to the specific question asked, and Crotty's main concern is how the undevelopment of former capitalist colonies came about and how it can be overcome, not the differentiation of the various noncolonized countries. But the lack of differentiation becomes a problem as soon as the question arises of whether a former capitalist colony today can emulate processes of industrialization.

We noted above that former capitalist colonies must be restructured in accordance with the broad collective interests of the masses. Originally these interests were displaced by the imposition of "alien" individual capitalist institutions. But surprisingly, Crotty writes that even individualist capitalism can be an option for Ireland (260). We shall relate this paradox to two topics: first, weaknesses in his analysis of technology, and second, the question of Irish specificity.

Crotty's analysis is at its strongest when he relates to institutions (such as property in land), while his considerations on technology only refer to certain special fields, such as veterinary science. A more comprehensive study of the relation between capitalist and technological development must relate to the neo-Schumpeterian analysis of techno-economic paradigms: the periodical emergence of radical technologies within capitalism (cotton textile technologies, steam power/railways, electrical/chemical products and technologies, the automobile complex and the present information and communication technologies). This development has always been rooted in the original individualist capitalist countries, with addition in the twentieth century of settler capitalist United States and collectivist-capitalist Japan. It has been claimed that each new cluster of radical technologies opens new options for countries that want to catch up with the leading industrial countries.[48]

Such an analysis may be weak in that it does not sufficiently consider institutional legacies of colonialism in the countries that undevelop. Crotty would argue that the emerging techno-economic paradigms can most easily be utilized

by countries that do not carry the colonial burden via the postcolonial state. But
to the extent that also the poor countries—even in some limited respect—
succeed in extending manufacturing and services based on the new technological clusters, the more the economy in question evolves with relative autonomy
from land-limitations. As non-agricultural sectors become increasingly important, the state's strategy with respect to land ownership becomes less important,
and a greater number of development options should be possible.

Crotty's perspective is strongly wedded to economies that are predominantly agrarian. This point can be linked to the topic of Ireland's specificities.
Among the former capitalist countries, Ireland probably has the largest share of
its labor force in industry and services. Although it lagged in comparison to
other industrialized countries, structural change has been considerable. Roughly
20 percent of the Irish labor force was occupied in agriculture in 1980, and by
2000 this had declined to about 10 percent. The share of the labor force in manufacturing increased from just under 20 percent to about 30 percent, while services increased from just above 40 percent to nearly 60 percent of the labor
force. Via industrialization, the vested interests of agriculture, a major basis for
the postcolonial elites, have been gradually weakened.

Let us pursue the question of Irish specificities further by turning to
Crotty's treatment of the group of former capitalist colonies. His research program requires a thorough comparative study of former capitalist colonies. But in
When Histories Collide, he provides only yet another case study of Ireland, the
case which he knew best. He claims, however, that Ireland "illustrates the general process that applied in all the capitalist colonies." Indian, Asian, and African cases are briefly discussed (157–60) to indicate that the Irish experience is
general. But he leaves it "to students with greater knowledge in these other areas
to complete the individual country by country analysis" (141). We must certainly accept these limits to his capacity, but we may still ask whether it is also
interesting to focus on features specific to Ireland.

It is certainly true that many of the former capitalist colonies are still overwhelmingly agrarian. Among the world's poorest countries today we can even
find really vicious processes of destruction of whatever small industries there
once were, and a regression to a more exclusively agrarian economy. The consolidation of industrialized agriculture in the richer countries increasingly puts
pressure on small scale agriculture in poor countries. The difference in labor
productivity between manual and mechanized agriculture has increased from
1:10 at the beginning to 1:500 at the end of the twentieth century![49]

Crotty's perspective on postcolonial inertia may work better with reference
to the poor African and Asian countries than with respect to Latin America.
Latin America, namely, was to some extent depopulated by colonialism and thus
has regions of land-abundance. The subcontinent is much more urbanized than
Africa and Asia, and thus the main development questions are as much linked to
urban as to rural developments. In Brazil, for instance, the Sao Paolo region has
been an enclave marked by considerable industrialization. Thus, it seems that,
also within the group of former capitalist colonies, distinctions are necessary. In

particular, the distinction between development states and predatory states, which has been an influential recent addition to neo-Weberian development studies, might turn out helpful.[50] One can argue that, at least in cases with some industrial development, domestic patterns of interest group formation and collective action will lead to struggles for influence on the state, thus challenging the traditional postcolonial elites.

The various countries trapped in undevelopment also face different external situations. Here we can return to the question of Irish specificities. As Crotty noted, Ireland is both Western and non-Western. Thus its undevelopment has a profile different from all the other former capitalist colonies. Like countries that develop, Ireland has "fewer people as badly off as formerly." But this can still not be counted as development, since Ireland does not have "more people better off than formerly." For a former capitalist colony, Ireland has very high living standards, but for fewer and fewer people. The decisive background factor is Ireland's enormous emigration: so many of the people born in Ireland since the Great Famine of the mid-nineteenth century have had to leave the country to find work. A crucial question for Crotty's analysis of Ireland is thus whether the high emigration numbers are drying up permanently, or whether the return migration of the 1990s will again turn to high emigration in the next economic slump.

In this connection, Crotty's classification of Ireland can be questioned. Maybe Ireland is basically Western, so that the individualist institutions fit even that case. Crotty's classification can be defended with reference to Ireland's longer term history, but the context of rising living standard (thanks to emigration) and recent industrial transformations may have made Ireland a *sui generis* case among the former capitalist colonies.

Ireland is also special in being located in the midst of the West. In the postwar "American century," Ireland is right between England and the United States, and with most of its diaspora living in these two countries. Concerning the spectacular Irish growth rates of the 1990s, analysts debate whether Ireland in the age of information and communication technologies has been integrated into a thriving Atlantic economy, mainly powered by the enormous U.S. boom of the 1990s. It has been claimed that in the present world economic constellation, the coming of microelectronics—and a successful constellation of circumstances, relating to educational policy, among other things—has enabled the Irish economy to hook on to world economic developments in quite a different way than in the "Fordist" era of 1945–75.

This analysis is certainly sketchy. No detailed analysis of the Irish situation in comparison with that of other former capitalist colonized countries can be given here. But even if our sketchy objections to Crotty's diagnosis of Ireland turn out to be confirmed by further studies, we can draw an interesting conclusion. The weaknesses we point to are not related to Crotty's world historical scheme as such. They are related to the fact that, to understand the present world, we must basically study processes of capitalist industrialization.

Crotty's major competence was in agrarian economics, and although he was good at spelling out the macroeconomics of his Irish reform-proposals, the analysis of industrial transformations was never his strength. It is tempting to conclude that the more agrarian the society, the sharper Crotty's analysis.[51] Crotty's world historical schemes relate to periods of overwhelming agrarian dominance in world development. Thus, they stand as his strongest contribution to world history. *When Histories Collide* is the only book in which the presentation of Crotty's world historical scheme plays the main part, while Ireland is relegated to the role of a case. Seven years after his death, it is now published, and world historians and historical macrosociologists can judge.

*   *   *

Lars Mjøset is Professor of Sociology at the University of Oslo, Norway and Director of the Oslo Summer School of Comparative Social Science Studies at the Social Science Faculty, University of Oslo. He has published extensively on social science theory, international relations and comparative socioeconomic development, including *The Irish Economy in a Comparative Institutional Perspective,* (Dublin, 1992).

Preface

My father had substantially completed this book when he died, in January 1994. The task of taking the book to publication fell to me and I have made two contributions. First, I have tried to complete the endnotes—a troublesome business for me. Although I have verified the great majority of the references that my father left, my lack of deep familiarity with the material, with his private system of abbreviations and, it must be said, with his dreadful handwriting means that I cannot claim that all of the footnotes are absolutely correct. Second, I have altered the overall structure of the book by largely separating out the Irish material from the world history theme. The original manuscript interwove insights from the Irish experience into the larger world history in a much more continuous and subtle manner than this version. But it needed editing and, because I lack my father's familiarity with the way in which the two themes interact, I did not feel confident to edit the manuscript as it stood. The result of this is that the book is rather more blocky than he had intended. Chapters 1 through 7 contain the world history material; Ireland is presented separately in chapters 8 and 9. Chapter 10 draws the two major themes back together and contains the outline of my father's prognosis and recommendations.

It would be inappropriate to put into my father's mouth words of acknowledgment or thanks to the many colleagues and sparring partners who through his life helped him to hone the ideas contained in this book. I must, however, thank all those who have helped me in getting the work to this point. They include my father's colleagues and the research and secretarial staff at Trinity College Dublin, Professor Joe Lee of University College Cork, Professor Wynne Godley of the Jerome Levy Institute of Bard College and University of Cambridge, Professor Alan Matthews of Trinity College Dublin, and particularly Tony Coughlan, a longtime friend and companion in battle of my father's. Above all, I would like to thank Lars Mjøset of the University of Oslo for his enduring support and assistance throughout.

At a more personal level, I thank my brothers and sisters, all of whom helped to proof various drafts of the book and provided continuous encouragement of the sort only siblings can. My wife, Martha, has helped us through the whole thing with enormous patience and wise humor. At the end of the day though, this has been my way of honoring a great man. To have had a father who was heroic, inspirational, loving, and compassionate was the greatest joy and privilege.

Ray Crotty
Twickenham, England, December 2000

Chapter 1

Introduction and Background

The world today is a Western place. It is dominated and largely shaped by Western assumptions, Western modes of thought, and Western institutions. We, in the West at least, tend to accept this, to regard it as being somehow the natural way of things. After all, there is no doubt that, for us, the formula—whatever that might mean—has worked. We have unquestionably developed socioeconomically in the sense both that more people are better off today than in the past and that fewer people are as badly off as was the case hitherto.[1] And, with a few more or less heroic assumptions, there seems to be no reason why the formula should not continue to work for us into the foreseeable future.

So why does it not seem to work for the 2.9 billion people of the 140 or so countries that make up the Third World? The answer lies in the fact that each of the countries that currently make up the Third World, at some stage in its past, was subjected to what is here defined as *individualist capitalist colonialism* by one or other of the major European powers. In this process the institutions, technologies, and legal systems of individualist capitalism, as these had evolved in central western Europe, were forcibly imposed, for metropolitan profit, on food producing societies that had, throughout their previous histories, been nonindividualist and noncapitalist.

Countries which have experienced this process invariably undergo socioeconomic retrogression. That is to say, not that they develop less rapidly than others, that they are underdevelopers; on the contrary they actually retrogress, or undevelop. This state of affairs is described in more detail in the following section. For present purposes it is sufficient to realize that, in these countries now, more people are experiencing worse poverty than ever before and all the indications are that they will continue to do so.

The main purpose of this book is to explain the term "individualist capitalism": its origins and development; its unique dynamic character as a source of socioeconomic impetus; and, above all, its initial and enduring impact on the indigenous societies of what we call the Third World.

Individualist capitalism is a socioeconomic institution that developed in Europe and only in Europe. It is the defining feature of European history. To begin to understand it therefore we have to go back four or five thousand years, to the origins of the peoples who created Europe. In terms of the overall time-scale of human existence, however, individualist capitalism is a relative new-comer; nonindividualist, noncapitalist modes of production predated it by at least ten thousand years. To complete the picture, to provide a reasonable com-parative analysis, we must therefore push our horizon back to the very origins of human civilization.

The overall scope of the book thus spans the entire history of mankind, and its general structure is chronological. However, in the more recent part of the story, an additional dimension that will help illuminate the general picture is also introduced. This is the case of the Republic of Ireland.

We are accustomed to the classification of the countries of South and Southeast Asia, of most of Africa and of Latin America as constituting what we call the Third World. Certainly these are what are described here as being unde-veloping countries in that they have more people worse off than before. How-ever, if we go back to Myrdal's definition of development—fewer people worse off *and* more people better off—Ireland very clearly falls into the category of undeveloping countries. Ireland today, admittedly, has fewer people worse off than in the past; so in that sense it can be said to have developed. But crucially, Ireland today does not have more people better off. The Irish economy today supports far fewer people than it has in the past. For the last 170 years, since the era of mercantile capitalism, virtually every second person born there has failed to secure a livelihood in Ireland. Since 1848, net emigration from the country has stood at about 40 percent of the birthrate.

I have written elsewhere on the persistent failure of Irish socioeconomic in-stitutions.[2] Ireland's failure is attributable to precisely the same forces, the same collision of histories, that caused and perpetuates undevelopment in the Third World. Ireland was the first nonindividualist, noncapitalist society to be sub-jected to European individualist capitalist colonization. It was in every sense the prototype capitalist colony.

The purpose of introducing the Irish case in this book is twofold. First is be-cause of the subtle but quite profound manner in which it can be used to chal-lenge assumptions about socioeconomic history. Ireland, in most peoples' eyes and despite its problems, is considered a very European country. (For a short time the Island of Saints and Scholars was considered the main repository of all that was precious in European thinking.) However if, even only hypothetically, we suspend our skepticism and accept the concept of Ireland's being part of the undeveloped world, we undergo an immediate dislocation, a doubt-provoking shift of perspective which can be very useful in discussions such as this. The second, more pragmatic reason for invoking the Irish case is because of the wealth of reasonably reliable information that is available on Ireland. Though specific to Ireland, this information can often be used very effectively to illumi-nate more global arguments.

Undevelopment in the Third World

Socioeconomic failure in the Third World is manifested above all by a widening, deepening morass of poverty. There are, in almost every Third World country, more people experiencing worse poverty now than at any time in the past.

Average annual income per head in 1990 of the 3.0 billion or so people in the Third World—which here excludes China for reasons given presently—was estimated as US$1,000 by the World Bank.[3] The same source estimated the average income per head, in the same year, of the 777 million people in the countries of the "West," or of the Organization of Economic Co-operation and Development, to be over twenty times greater, or $20,170.

The low incomes of the Third World are attributable, in part at least, to rapid population growth. Population has increased as in table 1.1 in the twentieth century.

Table 1.1. World Population Annual Rates of Change

	Third World		Rest of World		Total	
	Millions	**Percent ***	**Millions**	**Percent***	**Millions**	**Percent***
1900	613		1012		1625	
1950	1080	1.14	1420	0.68	2500	0.87
1980	2254	2.48	2194	1.46	4448	1.94
1990	2871	2.45	2423	1.00	5294	1.76

Sources: P. Bairoch, *The Economic Development of the Third World Since 1900* (London: Methuen, 1975), Table 1.
UNCTAD, *Handbook of International Trade and Development Statistics 1992* (New York: United Nations, 1993), Table 6.1.
*Adjusted to exclude China from Third World.

Not only has the poor population of the Third World been increasing, but it did so up to the 1980s at an accelerating rate, as table 1.1 indicates. The rate of population growth continues to rise in most Third World countries. It was higher in the 1980s than previously in fifty-one out of the eighty-one Third World countries with populations over one million for which the World Bank publishes the relevant data. It was lower in twenty-eight and unchanged in ten countries. Slight decreases in the rate of population growth in five large countries—Bangladesh, Brazil, India, Indonesia, and Mexico—account for most of the small overall decline in the rate of growth of the Third World's population in the 1980s.[4] Rapid growth of poor populations, which implies the existence of more people living at declining living standards, is here perceived as the most important manifestation of socioeconomic retrogression in the Third World.

It is true that Gross National Product per person is rising in many Third World countries. It did so during the 1980s in twenty-four of the sixty-nine countries for which the World Bank gives the relevant data, which was fewer than in the earlier period, 1965–1980, when average GNP per head increased in forty-nine of those countries. But as the countries with rising GNP per head in the 1980s, for the most part, had larger populations, they accounted for slightly over 70 percent of the total population of the sixty-nine countries. That still meant that, in countries containing over 800 million people, average incomes declined during the 1980s. Even in those countries where average incomes were rising, the number of the very poor almost certainly increased. India, which has the largest population in the Third World and the second largest after China in the whole world, is a case in point.

India's population increased by an annual average of 2.2 percent between 1965 and 1989, growing from slightly under 500 million to almost 840 million.[5] Its GNP per head increased on average by 1.8 percent annually over the same period.[6] It rose, from the equivalent in terms of U.S. dollars of 1989 purchasing power, from $220 in 1965 to $340 in 1989.[7] In 1965, 80 percent of India's population, or almost 400 million people, had incomes below the average of $220.[8] Assuming, as is indicated by Sundrum, that a similar income distribution obtains now in India as in 1965, about 55 percent of its present population of 840 million, or around 450 million people, continue to have incomes below the $220 level.[9] Thus, despite India's expanded economy and higher average income per head, it has now more very poor people than it had twenty-five years ago.

Few Third World countries have performed nearly as well economically as India during this period. Both FAO and World Bank data suggest that the numbers of chronically malnourished in the countries of the Third World increased absolutely over this period.[10] In virtually all of them, there are now more very poor people than formerly.

Undevelopment in Ireland

Ireland's failure is that for the last 170 years, or throughout the era of factory capitalism, of virtually every second person born there to secure a livelihood in the country. In the first decades of the period in question, that failure caused a swelling mass of population to experience declining incomes, in a manner very similar to that of the Third World now. A crisis occurred 150 years ago when the exotic potato crop, on which the population had become virtually totally dependent, failed.[11] Within five years, one million people, or one-eighth of the total, starved to death or died of famine-related diseases; and another million emigrated.[12]

The floodgates of emigration, thus opened by the Great Famine of 1845–1848, have remained open. The rate of net emigration (i.e., gross emigration less immigration, which includes returning emigrants) has, since the famine, been about 40 percent of the birthrate. Between 1864, when the compulsory registration of births and deaths was introduced, and the most recent census year, 1991, 9,442,000 people were born in the Republic, and there have been 3,905,000 net emigrants from it.[13] During the most recent intercensal period, 1986–1991, 277,546 people were born in the Republic and there were 136,170 net emigrants.[14]

Emigration on this scale has caused the Republic's population to decline from 6,529,000 in 1841, shortly before the Great Famine and when the country's first definitive census was taken, to 3,536,000 in 1991, or by 46 percent.[15] The decline in the number of people gainfully employed in the Republic has been even more remarkable; in the 1991 census it was 1,091,155. The number in the first census taken after the state's foundation, in 1926, was 1,220,000. The number recorded as gainfully occupied in the 1841 census was 2,715,000.[16] Assuming an unchanged dependency ratio prior to 1841, it is necessary to go back to the 1770s, when the island's estimated population was around 3,800,000,[17] to reach a time when the number of people gainfully employed was as low as it is now, with 1,085,000 at work in the Republic and some 600,000 at work in Northern Ireland.[18]

The world's gainfully employed population increased by 34 percent between 1975 and 1990, or by almost 2 percent annually.[19] No country, other than Ireland, appears to have fewer people getting a livelihood now than in the past. Certainly no other country has fewer getting a livelihood now than seventy years ago, when the Irish State was established and when 12 percent more people were at work than now. Since 1841, when Ireland's gainfully occupied population has declined by two-thirds, the world's total population, and presumably its gainfully employed population, has increased nearly sixfold. Since the 1770s, when the number of people getting a livelihood was last as low in Ireland as it is now, the world's total population, and presumably its gainfully employed population, has increased almost ninefold.[20] So this fact, the failure of almost half those born there to secure a livelihood in Ireland, which has persisted for some 170 years, is the most important manifestation of socioeconomic failure in the Irish case.

Development Elsewhere

Ireland and the countries of the Third World share the common, unique experience of having been capitalist colonized. All of them, within the past 500 years, have been conquered and had sovereignty exercised over their indigenous populations by one or another of nine European countries. Those nine countries, together with Greece, Luxembourg, and Ireland, comprise the European Union, or EU. Capitalist colonization is the process whereby the institutions, technology, and legal systems of individualist capitalism, as these evolved in central, western Europe, were forcibly superimposed, for metropolitan profit, on food producing societies that were nonindividualist and noncapitalist.

Ireland and the countries of the Third World, which have experienced this process, undergo socioeconomic retrogression. They do not develop less rapidly, or "under develop"; they retrogress or undevelop. Ireland retrogresses in that it has provided a livelihood for a diminishing number of people for 150 years, and seems likely to continue to do so. The countries of the Third World retrogress in that they now have more people experiencing worse poverty than ever before;

and again, all the indications are that this process of retrogression will persist in the Third World.

Countries that have not been capitalist colonized, by contrast, develop. All of them have more people who are better off than formerly and fewer who are as badly off. Ireland, while fulfilling the first of these conditions, fails to fulfill the second; it does not have more people at work and better off now than formerly. The countries of the Third World, on the other hand, while in most cases fulfilling the first condition—India, for example, now has more people with French income levels, or higher, than there are in France—fail to fulfill the second. For these reasons, Ireland and the countries of the Third World are here said to retrogress, or undevelop.

The conditions, which are defined here as socioeconomic development, patently obtain in all the countries of western Europe, apart from Ireland, where the nine capitalist colonizing countries are located. They also obtain in the "settler" colonies of North America and Oceania, where the indigenes were hunter-gatherers and not food producers, and could not therefore be "squeezed" for metropolitan profit. They were instead exterminated or confined to reservations by settlers from Europe whose economies now develop.

It may not be so clear that the countries of eastern Europe and of the former USSR develop. Yet their average GNP per head has risen for many decades;[21] and their annual population growth is slow: less than 0.5 percent in the eastern European countries and less than 1 percent in the former USSR.[22] It is hardly conceivable, therefore, that they have not fulfilled the two conditions for development specified here: viz., more people having high incomes *and* fewer having low incomes than formerly. Long-term development is consistent with periods of short-term retrogression when, due to political turmoil, output declines and incomes fall. That may be occurring in eastern Europe and the former USSR now (1993). It certainly occurred there during the Second World War, as it also did in many other countries that have developed over the long term.

The so-called Five Tigers of the East, Japan, Korea, Taiwan, Hong Kong, and Singapore, develop. The first three of these were not colonized by the West, but the others were. However, Hong Kong and Singapore were *settler* and not *capitalist* colonies, in the sense that the islands were occupied as entrepots, and not for the purpose of imposing the institutions, technology, and laws of the West on the islands' indigenes. The handful of natives on both islands had minimal impact on their history subsequent to their settlement by Britain, as was the case with the original inhabitants of North America and Oceania.

All these countries fall unambiguously into one or other of the two categories: those that have been capitalist colonized and undevelop, and those that have not been capitalist colonized and develop. There are, however, some countries that do not fit so readily into either category. China, with one-fifth of the world's total and the country with the largest population in the world, is one of these. It was deeply penetrated by the West's colonizing powers at the end of the nineteenth and in the early decades of the twentieth century. It also then displayed the most distinctive characteristic of socioeconomic retrogression: rapid growth of a population experiencing declining incomes. But China never lost sovereignty to the intrusive powers. A Chinese government has operated throughout modern times, even if not always effectively. Unlike in the Third World and Ireland, Western sovereignty was never exercised over the Chinese people. When China's latter day invaders withdrew, that government extended its rule and brought back under its rule whichever territory and sections of its population had temporarily fallen under foreign control. This process, which began millennia ago with the invasions and subsequent withdrawals of the pastoralists from Asia's steppes, was indeed part of the Chinese way of life. The Western, no less than the pastoral, invaders, affected that way of life; but neither set of invaders succeeded in replacing the indigenous culture and institutions with alien ones.

China, therefore, was not capitalist colonized. While it did seem to undevelop in the past, it seems now to have ceased to do so. Its real GNP has grown on average by 10.5 percent annually throughout the 1980s, which is much faster growth than has been achieved by any other major economy. Its annual population growth rate has been reduced from 2.2 percent previously to 1.4 percent in the 1980s.[23] Its government aims to end population growth by the end of this century and thereafter to reduce China's population, which now exceeds one billion, to 700 million in the course of the twenty-first century. Almost certainly then China, which was not capitalist colonized, is developing in the sense of having more people who are better off and fewer who are as badly off as in the past.[24]

Thailand, like China, came under the influence of imperial European powers. But it was suffered by the French and British to survive as a buffer between their colonies in French Indo-China and Burma and Malaya. Its sovereignty, though greatly compromised, was never quite lost; a Thai monarchic government survived throughout. Like China, Thailand also seemed to undevelop for many decades of rapid population and slow economic growth. That situation may have now changed. Its economy is growing rapidly while its population growth has slowed, though, at 1.9 percent per annum, it is still above the world average. Average annual GNP per head growth of 4.2 percent between 1965 and 1989 may have reduced the number of Thais living in poverty. Thailand therefore, which like China was not capitalist colonized, may also, like China, be developing.[25]

There are, finally, six countries that have high and/or rapidly rising incomes, but which were capitalist colonized. These are Kuwait, Oman, Saudi Arabia, and the United Arab Emirates (UAE) in the Middle East, Botswana in southern Africa, and Malaysia in Southeast Asia. In 1990, Malaysia's population was 18 million; Saudi Arabia's was 14 million; and the average size of the other four countries' population was 1.6 million.[26] Kuwait, Oman, Saudi Arabia, the UAE, and Botswana all have, relative to their small populations, very great natural wealth: oil in the case of the Middle Eastern countries, and diamonds in the case of Botswana. Their average incomes are high and/or rising rapidly because of their natural wealth.[27] They thus diverge from the generalization that countries that have been capitalist colonized undevelop. But they do so only for the fortuitous reason of having great natural wealth relative to small populations to defend that wealth, and having that wealth defended for them by Western powers in this postcolonial era. Meanwhile, they retain the characteristic that is otherwise closely associated with declining incomes and socioeconomic retrogression, viz., rapid population growth rates. These range from 3.3 percent annually in Botswana to 4.9 percent in the UAE and average 4.2 percent.[28]

Malaysia too has great natural wealth in its tin and petroleum deposits. The former caused it to experience something like a double colonization in the nineteenth century. The first was by emigrant Chinese who came to operate the Malay peninsula's tin deposits. Britain, which already occupied, as entrepots, the islands of Penang and Singapore and the port of Malacca, was invited by Malaya's sultans to take control of the peninsula, largely for the purpose of protecting the interests of the indigenous Malay people against the thrusting and occasionally violent, Chinese immigrants. Subsequent British rule in Malaya, while concerned to protect and preserve indigenous Malay interests, tended rather to treat the Chinese as a law unto themselves. While, for example, employment conditions were controlled for Malays and immigrant Indians working on rubber estates, Chinese workers, on both European and Chinese owned rubber estates, were excluded from these controls. The immigrant Chinese, who can never be said to have been capitalist colonized, have, since Malaysian independence in 1956, provided the principal thrust to economic growth. The indigenous Malays, under the constitutional arrangements made at the time of Britain's withdrawal, have, by contrast, had a virtual monopoly of political power in Malaysia. Successive Malay-dominated governments have sought, most notably through the Bumi-Putra initiative and other programs, to redistribute the wealth generated by the Chinese to the Malays. Notwithstanding these actions, incomes of rural Malays have remained low and probably declined.[29] In Southwest Perak state, one of the longest settled and most fertile parts of peninsular Malaysia, it was observed in 1975 that "it is likely that smallholder incomes in the study area are substantially lower now than they were seven years ago."[30] While birthrates among the noncapitalist-colonized Chinese Malaysians have dropped and their population has stabilized, the Malay birthrate remains well above the crude death rate and the population of Malays continues to increase rapidly in the normal Third World manner.

Book Outline

The continuing undevelopment of former capitalist colonies is a long-standing and worldwide phenomenon. Argentina, the first capitalist colony to become independent, continues to undevelop more than 180 year later. Zimbabwe, the most recently independent capitalist colony, undevelops rapidly. The process affects some 140 countries, with populations of size ranging from India's almost 850 million to that of St. Kitts and Nevis in the Caribbean, which is some

40,000. About fifty of these countries have populations of less than one million; but in total the 140 or so countries contain almost three billion people, or over half the world's total. This undevelopment is the result of the forcible superimposition on the peoples of these countries of an alien, individualist, capitalist culture. It is necessary, in order to understand this process, to appreciate the distinctive features of both individualist capitalism and of the nonindividualist, noncapitalist cultures of the societies that were capitalist colonized. That appreciation cannot be acquired without considering, however briefly and inadequately, the origins of human society, before it became differentiated into individualist and nonindividualist. That is the topic of chapter 2.

Chapters 3 and 4 examine the nature of individualism and its emergence uniquely in Europe; the record of individualist slavery in the ancient Mediterranean; and the record of individualist capitalism in central western Europe. Chapter 5 treats of the operation of individualist capitalism in Europe's main regions and of its failure to emerge in Ireland. At this point the book bifurcates. The main stream of the general argument is pursued through chapters 6 and 7 while the particular, more detailed analysis of the Irish experience is followed through chapters 8 and 9.

Thus, chapter 6 examines the chronological spread of individualist capitalism through the non-European world and analyzes the impact of this spread on the nonindividualist, noncapitalist indigenous societies which were colonized by Europe. And chapter 8 deals in more detail with the course of capitalist colonialism in Ireland and with its effects on Irish society. Chapter 7 examines decolonization as the final stage of capitalist colonial undevelopment, while chapter 9 reviews the ending of colonialism in Ireland and the particular experience of Irish society in the postcolonial era.

In chapter 10 the two streams of discussion are re-united in consideration of how the mold of capitalist colonial undevelopment might be shattered to allow of socioeconomic development. This is done in relation to the specific case of Ireland, which is perceived as thereby providing the precedent, now lacking, for a former capitalist colony to transform undevelopment into development.

Perspectives

The link between the study of Ireland and the study of the Third World is that Ireland uniquely belongs to two worlds. It is geographically and ethnically part of the individualist West, which capitalist colonized the Third World. It is also bound by history to the Third World, being alone of the food-producing countries of Europe, from the steppes to the Atlantic, where an autochthonic individualism did not develop; and alone of European countries to have been capitalist colonized. Ireland has been both neighbor and colony; located within sight of Britain, the premier capitalist colonial power, it has been capitalist colonized for longer and more thoroughly than any other country.

Ireland's unique dual status of neighbor and colony is, in a sense, like the

Rosetta Stone, which was inscribed in both ancient Egyptian hieroglyphics and classical Greek. It was possible, by combining both scripts, to secure an understanding of the previously indecipherable Egyptian script. Likewise, the unique status of Ireland as neighbor and colony provides otherwise unattainable insights into the nature of capitalist colonialism and how it has impacted, and continues to impact, both Ireland and the Third World.

But that is not all. Because Ireland was the only part of food-producing Europe, from the steppe to the Atlantic, where individualism did not emerge, and is separated from England, regarded by many as "the cradle and nursery of capitalism,"[31] only by the narrow Irish Sea, consideration of its case helps critically to define the conditions that made possible the emergence of individualism, in Europe alone; and more specifically the emergence of individualist capitalism which followed from that; and the modern world, which was ultimately created by individualist capitalism. That is why Irish history and Irish current events can only be understood within the context of global capitalist colonialism; why knowledge of the Irish experience is crucial to understanding the phenomena of capitalist colonizing and Third World undevelopment; and why, indeed, consideration of the Irish experience provides otherwise unattainable insights into the character of the modern world itself.

A work that attempts to overview vast tracts of human experience, as this one does, must of its nature be mainly one of synthesis. Little of what is presented here represents original research; the work relies for the most part on secondary sources. The content that is original stems largely from field work in a literal sense. The author, for several years in early adulthood, derived a living solely from farming in Ireland. That experience provided many insights into the way of life still practiced by almost half the world's population,[32] a way of life that was practiced by virtually all the world's population up to a couple of centuries ago, but from which latter day social scientists, by the very nature of their occupation, have become increasingly remote. Those original insights, derived from earning a living by farming in Ireland, were subsequently broadened and enriched by being able to observe farming, at first hand, in a variety of consulting roles, in a score of other former capitalist colonies in South and Southeast Asia, in Africa, South America, and the Caribbean. Those insights are the principal basis of this work which, it is hoped, contains enough that is both new and true to outweigh that which is not new, is not true, and is neither new nor true.

Chapter 2

Early Agriculture

Though informed by reason, the individual's relationship with society has, in most societies, been dominated by necessity. The available resources and the technology to exploit them at any time have shaped political relationships. For almost all of man's two million or so years of archaeologically recorded existence, that technology was concerned with hunting and gathering the produce of occupied land.

Population expanded to consume the food available at the most critical time. This normally, and especially among hunter-gatherers, occurred seasonally. The interstices between troughs in the food supply are now, and presumably were in the past, characterized for hunter-gatherers by conditions of leisure and relative abundance.[1] At critical periods, however, vulnerable groups like infants, children, pregnant and parturient women, and the aged, came under pressure and would have been the first to die. Seasonal food shortages, with their correspondingly heavy toll on vulnerable sections of populations, resulted in a long term balance between the crude death rate and a biologically determined birthrate for humans of around fifty per 1000 per annum. These high death rates were consistent with most people at most times securing adequate nutrition without being subjected to undue stress.

An increased food supply, which could have resulted from improved technology, climatic amelioration, or the colonization of new territories, and which relaxed seasonal shortages, reduced mortality rates. Sheratt among others makes the same point: "It was a small initial change in feeding habits, associated with opportunities opened up by the reduction in forests, that created a situation in which more far-reaching changes could occur."[2] Mortality rates remained low until population expanded sufficiently to absorb the additional food at the old level of nutrition and mortality, which latter approximated the biologically determined birthrate. The human population was around 4 million 12,000 years ago;[3] it was about 500 million 500 years ago.[4] The long term, average annual rate of population growth was, therefore, 0.3 per 1000. That is, the death rate, over the long term, did not diverge by more than 0.3 per 1,000 from the biologically determined birthrate of around 50 per 1000 per annum. Had death rates fallen by more than 0.3 per 1000 below the birthrate, population would have grown more rapidly than it did. It would have encountered more serious food shortages, especially of a seasonal character. Mortality among vulnerable sections especially would have been higher, which would have choked off the excessive population growth.

Throughout human history, until recent times in the developed West, population has been a dependent variable. Population has expanded, or contracted, in line with the resources available to sustain it. Those resources, in turn, have been determined by the natural endowment and the state of the art. Those vulnerable sections of the population who were most responsive to the availability of resources were the ones least able to exert pressure to effect change. Population pressure as a force for development is a figment of the imagination of commentators and not a historical reality.

Early Settled Agriculture

Well before the first people reached the far west of Europe, the first man—or almost certainly more correctly, the first woman—had taken the momentous step from hunting and gathering to producing food. Some twelve thousand years ago, in the Fertile Crescent of the Middle East, an individual took the major, unprecedented step of deliberately consigning back to the earth, instead of consuming or storing, some of the gathered wild seed in the hope of being able to reap manifold at a later season. There too, at around the same time, another person deliberately mated, instead of eating, a mature, feral female goat, sheep, or auroch (wild cow), with a view to securing progeny subsequently. The production of food, as distinct from hunting and gathering it, has made it possible for 5,000 million food-producing people to secure a livelihood where for eons previously there had been only 12 million hunters and gatherers.

The tremendous innovation of using food that had already been gathered or hunted for the production of future food, rather than to satisfy immediate wants, is only likely to have occurred under conditions where those immediate wants were already adequately met. The seed-gathering woman who first deliberately consigned some of her gathered seeds back to the earth, in the highly speculative hope of garnering many more seeds of the same type in the same place a year later, must already have gathered sufficient seeds to satisfy her immediate needs. Likewise the hunter who had corralled some wild sheep or goats must already have had sufficient meat before he deliberately allowed two animals to mate in the hope that they would produce offspring which would yield meat a year or more later. Only the absence of pressure of population on the means of subsistence would have made possible these tremendous innovations.

This is directly opposite to the view of those who suggest that pressure of population forced people to change from hunting gathering, which normally requires only about three hours of effort daily to procure sufficient food, to the much more laborious business of food production. Thus: "Probably hunting and gathering depends upon low population, and therefore ultimately upon the exposure of children. As hunters and gatherers failed historically to control their population, the adoption of agriculture became necessary."[5] But it is inconceivable that persons suffering from food shortage would have consigned part of their small stock, as seed or breeding animals, back into the highly speculative process of food production. However, once the increase in population made possible by the transition had been achieved, there was no possibility for the larger population of reverting to the more leisurely life of hunting-gathering.

The circumstantial evidence is that, 12,000 years ago, in the fertile crescent of the Anatolian foothills, where the transition from hunter-gatherer to food producer was first effected, conditions were indeed unusually felicitous. Following the ending of the last Ice Age, the climate had ameliorated, with less frost and more rain in that area. The region itself contained an exceptionally rich endowment of flora and fauna, which included the precursors of the modern cereals, wheat and barley, as well as feral sheep, goats, cattle (aurochs), and pigs.[6]

Food production, during the succeeding millennia, developed principally in the alluvial riverine valleys located between the tropics of Cancer and Capricorn. These rich, well watered, warm soils produced, for relatively little human effort, the food that supported most of the human population. They sustained all the great civilizations of the ancient world: Sumeria, Egypt, the Indus valley, the Yellow River valley in China, and the Aztec and Inca civilizations of America. Cultivators in these areas produced more than was sufficient to maintain and to reproduce themselves. Populations were surplus to the numbers required to cultivate all the available arable land. Surplus labor was used to build massive monuments like the pyramids of Egypt and Central America; or to extend the arable area through enormously labor-intensive drainage and irrigation systems; or to build the Great Wall of China.

Another—"swidden"[7]—or slash-and-burn form of crop-growing occurred more extensively. This was rain-fed and less productive. The crops were normally insufficient to maintain and reproduce its cultivators, without supplementation from hunting and gathering or from grazed livestock. Otherwise population would have expanded to occupy all the arable land under swidden agriculture, as was all the irrigated land of the riverine valleys. This continues to be the case with this type of farming now in Africa, Latin America, and Southeast Asia. The amount of the surplus available from complementing hunting, gathering, or livestock grazing usually determined the extent of the "swidden" crop growing that was practiced. An exception may have been the cultivation of limited areas of exceptionally fertile, rained soils, located in regions of high rainfall and high mean temperature, like the volcanic soils in parts of Indonesia, those around Lake Victoria in Africa, and those around Lake Titicaca in South America. These areas may have supported cropgrowers without supplementation from hunting gathering or grazing, as was the case also with classical irrigated agriculture. But swidden farming, including that on the most productive soils, did not support any of the great civilizations of the ancient world.

The Emergence of Pastoralism and Lactose Tolerance

A third, purely pastoral form of food production also evolved. This occurred on land that was non-arable. Land is non-arable if, at the state of the art, it yields less than the seed to sow it, plus the grazing which the uncultivated land would have given.

Most of the land of Egypt, beyond the narrow strip of black alluvium in the floodplain, was of this nature. Sowing seed on this land would simply waste the seed. But while cropgrowing was impossible, the other, livestock, branch of food production was possible on much of this non-arable land.

It is unclear, and immaterial for present purposes, how the neolithic revolution spread into non-arable regions from its origin in the riverine valleys of the Middle East. Elements of the riverine population may have migrated into the desert, taking with them as much of the new food producing technology as could survive in the desert; or hunting-gathering desert denizens may have learned by observing the cultivators and borrowing from them as much of their technology as could work outside the riverine valleys.

A specialist livestock husbandry spread into the non-arable areas adjacent to the great riverine societies of the Middle East. It spread northwards beyond the Caucasus, where it was too cold for crop-growing. It spread out into the desert that lay eastwards and leeward of the Lebanese mountains where, except on the banks of the Euphrates and Tigris rivers and in oases, it was too dry to grow crops. The neolithic revolution spread southwest of the Nile Valley into the Sahel, which stretches across Africa from the Nile to the Atlantic and which again was too dry to support crop-growing.

The northern Eurasian pastoralists (who included both the Indo-European groups and the Mongols), the Bedouin pastoralists of the Middle East, and the Nilo-Hamites of the Sahel all effected an important genetic change that greatly adapted them to their non-crop-growing environments. All three groups of pastoralists acquired the genetic mutation of *lactose tolerance*.

It is characteristic of the order Mammalia that while mother's milk is essential in infancy, later, due to enzymatic change in the digestive system, milk becomes less digestible, causes nausea and, in some cases, induces vomiting and diarrhea. This clinical condition, which appears to be common to all members of the order Mammalia, is referred to as lactose malabsorption.[8] It is presumably a device of nature to ensure that mothers, having fulfilled the essential role of feeding their offspring in infancy, are then set free to re-engage in their primary function of reproduction.

Mutations occur that are lactose tolerant, perhaps in 1 percent of populations that are normally lactose malabsorbent. These mutants have the capacity to drink milk and to gain nourishment from it beyond infancy. That capacity, in a situation where people have domesticated ruminants but could not grow crops, conferred major advantages.

The use of domesticated ruminants solely for meat provides little more nutrition for the husbandmen than the same grazing area might yield to hunters. This is illustrated, for example, by observation of the nutrition obtained from hunting reindeer in Greenland.[9] The persistence of hunting rather than husbandry among the Lapps of northern Europe also suggests that the latter form of exploitation has no overwhelming advantages for a predominantly lactose malabsorbent people, as the Lapps are. Likewise in Southern Africa, the survival in the past in the same area of both the Khoikhoi, who had cattle, and the Sen, the latter of whom are purely hunter-gatherers, but both of whom are lactose malabsorbent, supports the point that the use of domesticated ruminants for meat yields little if any more nutrition than hunting from a given grazing area.[10]

The acquisition of lactose tolerance and the ability to drink the milk of domesticated ruminants transforms this situation. The advantage of lactose tolerance under these conditions may be illustrated as follows. Very roughly, the same pastoral resources will, in a year, produce 400 gallons of milk (the yield from a mediocre cow) or 250 lbs. liveweight gain from a bullock, or ox.

The milk, which weighs roughly 10 lbs. per gallon and has about 12 percent dry matter content, gives $400 \times 10 \times 0.12 = 480$ lbs. of digestible dry matter. The bullock liveweight gain will convert into carcass at around 55 lbs. carcass per 100 lbs. liveweight. The carcass has about 70 percent meat and fat (the balance being inedible bone), of which the dry matter content is about 50 percent. The bullock liveweight gain gives therefore $250 \times 0.55 \times 0.70 \times 0.5 = 48$ lbs. (approx.) of digestible dry matter.

Thus the acquisition through natural selection under these crop-less circumstances of the ability to consume milk from other species beyond infancy and, indeed, as in the case of the Tutsi in Rwanda, to live on an almost exclusively milk diet,[11] made it possible for more people, and therefore more efficient and powerful people, to live on given pastoral resources.

The genetic mutation of lactose tolerance had no advantage on arable land, either for riverine cropgrowers or swidden farmers. This was because the use of limited pastoral resources to sustain milch animals would have reduced the amount of these resources available to sustain draught animals. Where a choice was available between using cattle for milk or draught, less food was normally produced by milch animals. That smaller amount of food would have supported a smaller population with less division of labor, which would therefore also have been less efficient and less powerful.

The evolution of races of people who were almost genetically pure for lactose tolerance was a genetic adaptation, by natural selection, to a situation of having domesticated ruminants on non-arable land. Three major groups of people acquired this "freak" condition. One was the Bedouin of the Middle East and North Africa. The second was the peoples of Africa's Sahel, including such as the Fulani, Masai, and Karamojong. The third group was the inhabitants of northern Eurasia, who included the Mongols in the east, the Celts in the west, and all the races of Tatars, Huns, Goths, Turks, and others in between.

Lactose tolerance is not acquired through usage. Individuals are born lactose tolerant or lactose malabsorbent, and remain so. Thus, for example, the increased use of dairy produce in today's affluent east Asia will not increase the incidence of lactose tolerance there. Rather it is likely to make it even scarcer. This is because those rare mutants in the modern, affluent, east Asian population who indulge their genetic capacity to consume dairy produce without discomfort, are, unlike the population of the steppe, likely to die young. The animal fat in dairy produce, under modern, sedentary living conditions, is likely to increase the incidence of coronary disease, causing a higher than average mortality rate among dairy produce consumers. The increased incidence of lactose tolerance among populations in the past was due either to natural selection or crossbreeding.

Pastoral Migrations—Introduction

The tenor of the riverine, settled way of life was disrupted, but not ended, in most parts of the Old World by the pastoral irruptions that commenced around 4,000–5,000 years ago. The acquisition of lactose tolerance, which made it possible for more pastoralists, and therefore more efficient pastoralists, to subsist on given pastoral resources, shifted the balance of power away from the occupants of the arable regions, in favor of those in the non-arable regions where lactose tolerance emerged. Perhaps the most important theme in all subsequent history has been the efforts of the pastoralists to move in from the non-arable regions and to secure a place—or perhaps to recover a place given up by their migrating forebears—in the better watered or warmer, arable regions. The migrations of the three separate groups of pastoralists, in Africa's Sahel, in the Middle East, and in northern Eurasia, followed quite different courses.

None of those courses led to the New World of the Americas or Oceania. The land bridges that had joined these continents to Asia and that had made possible migrations from Asia were inundated by the rising waters of the oceans as the icecap melted with the ending of the last Ice Age. Though the idea of food production may have spanned the gap between Asia and the Americas—though not that between Asia and Oceania—the domesticated ruminants of the Old World did not. They did not reach the New World until recent, Colombian times.

African Pastoralists

The Nilo-Hamite pastoralists of the Sahel were restricted on the west by the Atlantic Ocean. Expansion northwards was blocked by the desertification of the parklands that were once the Sahara Desert. The narrow route down the Nile valley was easily blocked to the pastoralists by forts, the maintenance and manning of which were a primary defense charge on the crop-growing Egyptians.[12]

Expansion eastwards was blocked by the Ethiopian massif, wherein dwelt a people who have ever been more Asian than African. The Ethiopians embraced Asia Minor monotheism, in the form of Christianity, centuries before any other part of Sub-Saharan Africa accepted Islamic monotheism. The Ethiopians grow cereals on their plateau and not the tubers and bananas of lower-land, frost-free Africa. To grow those cereals, they have perforce had to use their cattle for draught, which no other Sub-Saharan people have done. Understandably, because they use their cattle for draught, the Ethiopians have not milked them and so are almost entirely lactose malabsorbent.[13] Neither have they used their cattle as bridewealth to acquire wives, as is the norm everywhere else in Sub-Saharan Africa. Instead women in Ethiopia, as generally in Eurasia, have paid dowries on getting married.[14]

The spread of Nilo-Hamitic influences southwards was almost as constrained as it was to the west, north, or east. The African rainforest and the lighter bush and scrub of the east African plateau, south of the Sahel, stretched from the Atlantic to the Indian Ocean. All of this was infested with the trypanosomiasis-bearing tsetse fly. Because cattle, like the other domesticated ruminants, are not indigenous to Africa but were introduced from Eurasia 4,000–5,000 years ago, they do not share the natural immunity of the indigenous species and die quickly from trypanosomiasis. The spread of pastoral influences in Africa, south of the Sahel, therefore was not achieved by the pastoral, lactose tolerant Nilo-Hamites. Instead, that influence was spread southwards by the very different Bantu races, who are primarily cropgrowers with a small incidence of lactose tolerance.[15]

The Bantus, originating in the present day Cameroon, found themselves some 2,000 years ago possessed of three important assets. They had by then acquired the art of iron making from the Middle East; high yielding yams and bananas from Southeast Asia; and cattle from the Nilo-Hamites of the Sahel. Drawing on this combination of resources, they penetrated, in the remarkably short time of some 1,500 years, the whole of sub-Sahelian Africa as far as the savannah lands south of the Limpopo river and west of the Drackensberg mountains.[16] With iron they cleared the forest and on the cleared land they grew yams and bananas. The clearing of forest for crop-growing also removed the trypanosomiasis-bearing tsetse fly. Cattle were then able to follow the crops and in this way percolated through the east African tsetse fly belt. The Bantus, who did not use their cattle for draught and who for the most part remained lactose malabsorbent so that they could not get the fullest nutritional value from their cattle, were unable to wrest the southwestern savannah of Africa from the indigenous, predominately hunting-gathering, but cattle-keeping Khoikhoi.[17]

Innumerable taboos and restrictions pertaining to the milking of cows and the consumption of cow's milk among the Bantu races seem to be a consequence of their relatively recent introduction to this food. Thus among the Gogo, and typical of a host of similar constraints on the use of milk by Bantus that have been noted by ethnographers: "Milk is drunk fresh, but mostly by children

. . . cattle are milked by married women who are the heads of the houses to which they are allocated."[18] Or: "Cows' milk is drunk fresh or eaten with millet porridge (by the Nuer) . . . the whey is drunk by women and boys. The milk of sheep and goats is used only by children."[19]

The lactose malabsorption of the Bantus is attested, apart from the clinical evidence, by their remarkable omission to milk their goats, which are their most numerous livestock and are regularly milked by true pastoralists. Over 150 million goats, or a quarter of the world's total, are located in Sub-Saharan Africa (see table 3.1); yet none of these Bantu-owned goats is milked. The South African Bantu peoples also prefer sour milk to fresh milk, because the acid in the former makes it more digestible for lactose malabsorbent people. There is also etymological evidence for the comparative novelty of cows' milk among the Bantu races. "It is a fact of the greatest historical interest that proto-Bantu, before its dispersal from the cradle land, was already quite clearly a language of food producers. Among domestic animals it included words for dog, goat, pig, chicken and probably also a word for cow, although there were no special words for cows' milk or for the art of milking."[20]

The combination of swidden cropgrowing, with cattle-keeping in cleared areas, gave rise to a distinctive Bantu way of life. Cropgrowing tied people to the locations where the crops were grown. It made them less mobile, and therefore less gregarious, than the Nilo-Hamite pastoralists of the non-arable Sahel or the Golden Hordes of the steppes. The cropgrowing Bantus were necessarily fragmented into small groups, each attached to a particular area of cropland. And their cattle were held in the open to avoid the trypanosomiasis-bearing tsetse fly. Each group's exposed cattle were vulnerable to attack by neighboring groups, whose cattle were likewise exposed and vulnerable. The fragmented Bantu tribes of necessity therefore spent much time and energy defending their own cattle against attacks by neighbors, or in attacking their neighbors' similarly exposed cattle. Typically, males spent their time herding and defending their cattle or raiding their neighbors, while the women grew crops of tubers, bananas, plantain, and millet.

Cattle have not been traditionally used for draught in Africa, alone among the Old World's arable regions. The explanation appears to be threefold. First, cattle could not be introduced into the uncleared bushland, where most crops were grown. Second, even without draught animals, crops of tubers and bananas could be grown on Africa's warm soils that were sufficient to maintain the women growers and even yield a surplus. That surplus gave value to African women, which is reflected in the payment of "brideprice," a practice that is ubiquitous in, but—with an exception mentioned below—peculiar to, Sub-Saharan Africa. The third factor that uniquely precluded the use of cattle for draught on Africa's arable land was the preoccupation of the men on the grazing land with defending their own, or raiding their neighbors', cattle.

The combination of arable land, cattle, and trypanosomiasis was probably the principal factor that imposed on Africa a way of life that had two distinctive, though contradictory, characteristics. These were, on the one hand, a notable lack of cultural variation and, on the other, an extreme degree of political fragmentation. Innskeep observed: "a continent as large as Africa, with such varied environments, inhabited by 350 million people, could be expected to show greater variety than it does. Even at the height of enthusiasm for racial classification, only half a dozen major groups were distinguished."[21] Yet simultaneously the combination of cropgrowing, cattle, and trypanosomiasis caused great political fragmentation among a population that was forced to spend much of its time and energy raiding and counter-raiding. The multiplicity of languages and dialects in Africa is a measure of that fragmentation. Middleton notes "there are some 3,000 languages and dialects in Africa." These were spoken by a pre-colonial African population of some 46 million, giving an average of some 15,000 people per language/dialect spoken.[22]

Two conditions appear to have halted the remarkably rapid spread of the cattle keeping, cropgrowing Bantus on the line of the Limpopo river and the Drakensberg mountains. The first of these was that the hunting-gathering Khoikhoi indigenes of the territory beyond had also cattle. They presumably got these from the Bantus, as the latter had got them much earlier from the Nilo-Hamites. Other hunter-gatherers in the Sub-Sahelian bush also presumably had acquired cattle, but could not retain and exploit them, because of the prevalence there of the tsetse fly. Only the cropgrowing Bantus could have retained cattle in Africa's tsetse belt, by first clearing part of the bush for cropping. But in the more arid area south of the tsetse belt, the non-cropgrowing, hunting-gathering Khoikhoi could keep and profit from cattle, like the Bantus.

The second condition which probably prevented the further spread of the Bantus was the arid and non-arable nature of the land beyond the Limpopo river and Drakensberg mountains. Hoe cultivation of yams and plantains is possible only in warm, moist areas. It is not feasible on the drier lands of southern Africa, which require either draught animals or tractors for their cultivation for cereal production. As the Bantus had not adapted their cattle for draught, they were unable to cultivate these drier lands. Without crops and without lactose tolerance, they had no advantage over the indigenous Khoikhoi, who also had cattle as well as the advantages of prior occupancy. The latter were therefore able to hold up for centuries what up to then had been the remarkably rapid expansion of the Bantus. The Khoikhoi retained their land until it was taken from them by another race who arrived by sea, were lactose tolerant, and used their cattle for draught to cultivate the semi-arid land.

The Bedouin

The predominantly sheep- and goat-herding pastoralists of the Middle East were more diffused and thinly spread on the sparse pastures of the region than were the predominantly cattle-keeping pastoralists to the north and south (table 3.1). With their sheep, they were less mobile than the cattle-keepers, and so could less easily mass to influence the course of history. Normally they offered little threat to the cropgrowers on the oases and on the rivers of the region.[23] It took the fanaticism induced in a primitive, unlettered people by a monotheism that derived from the sophisticated Judaic and Christian religions of Asia Minor to weld these scattered, impotent, poor, and unsophisticated shepherds and goatherds into an effective force. Even then their effectiveness was dependent on the void left by the collapse of Rome and the ancient Mediterranean society. In that moment of history, when the word of Allah was revealed to the primitive Bedouin of the Middle East and when the Mediterranean world was in turmoil, Islam swept to dominance. Though control did not long remain with the Bedouin, Islam, which originated among the pastoralists of the arid lands of the Middle East, has remained a dominant world force. Its adherents control much of the world, in a broad belt stretching from Morocco in the west to the Philippines in the east.

Northern Pastoralists

The northern pastoralists have been the most successful in moving in from the wilds. This was in no small measure because of their success in domesticating the horse, which was indigenous to the Eurasian steppes and which greatly increased the mobility of the Golden Hordes.[24] These northern pastoralists have been the dominant influence in world history ever since, 5,000 or so years ago, the Hittites swept in from the steppes. Four distinct flows of northern pastoralists from the Eurasian steppes are noted: into East Asia, into Central Asia, into Southwest Asia, and into Europe.

East Asia

Pastoral influence was largely negative in character in East Asia, where it provoked an instinctive resistance by the riverine crop-growing peoples of the region. The Great Wall of China, possibly man's single greatest structure, part of it built 3,000 years ago and stretching 4,000 miles from its origin on the Yellow River into the heart of Asia, is a palpable, enduring monument to the resistance of the civilized cropgrowers to the barbaric pastoralists.[25] Time after time in the long course of Chinese history, at periods of exceptional leadership among the barbarians, or when dynasties were in decline in China, and especially when both of these coincided, the pastoralists broke through, plundered, and devastated the ricefields of China. But once the accumulated wealth of the cropgrowers was dissipated and their complex hydraulic systems were broken down, all that remained was famine, for the invading pastoralists no less than for the indigenous cropgrowers. The pastoralists perforce withdrew back to the more extensive northern grazing lands; and the people of China set about repairing the dykes, filling the breaches in the Great Wall, tilling their ricefields, accumulating wealth, and waiting for the next onslaught.

The most complete and enduring of these pastoral invasions and conquests of China was by the Mongols in the thirteenth century. China then was incorporated into a much more extensive Mongolian pastoralists' empire that, at its zenith in the fourteenth century, was the most extensive that the world has ever seen, stretching from modern Vietnam on the South China Sea, in a great arc westwards, to modern Yugoslavia on the Adriatic Sea. Not until the end of the fourteenth century did China manage to drive out the barbarians and establish the Ming dynasty.

Even then, at the height of their influence in East Asia, the pastoralists never subdued Japan. Two invasions were attempted, in 1274 and 1281, but both were repulsed. The second was destroyed in part by an unexpected storm—a heaven-sent storm, or "Kami-Kaze" in the Japanese view. Japan in this respect had the best of both worlds. It had, like the other societies of the Old World, the benefit of domesticated ruminants for its crop-growing; and like the New World, but unlike any other extensive area of the Old World, it was spared invasion and conquest by marauding pastoralists. That immunity from pastoral invasion would seem to account in large measure for modern Japan's remarkable sense of national identity and exclusiveness.

Chinese crop-growing and Eurasian pastoralism were elements so alien to one another that synthesis was impossible. Time after time, China rejected the foreign pastoral influence. Even when, as happened also in the case of South Africa, that influence came by a devious sea route, China resisted invasion and indoctrination from the outside. Though invaded, it was never conquered and colonized by the West. Chinese governments, however ineffectually, continued to govern at all times. More recently, China mobilized its resources under the foreign flag of Marxist-Leninism, and under the leadership of Mao Tse Tung cast off Western influences. But more recently still, in a manner entirely consistent with the millennia-old resistance of the riverine cropgrowers to the barbarous pastoralists from the north, the Chinese appear to have discarded the intellectual imperialism of Marxist-Leninism together with the tutelage of its Russian proponents, who are the ancient, northern barbarians in modern guise.

South Asia

No mass breakthrough to the south was possible by the pastoralists in Central Asia. Penetration instead occurred by the percolation of pastoralists through the passes in the great central Asian mountain massif. The pastoralists came mainly through the Hindu Kush and roundabout through Afghanistan.

With cultivation more diffuse (49 percent of India's surface is cropped compared to 11 percent of China's) and crop yields lower (Indian yields are less than half those of China),[26] India's relative surplus has been less and the area over which it had to be exercised is more extensive than in the more typical riverine societies of China or Egypt. The dominance of society over the individual has been less complete and more diffused. Centralized political power has always been weaker. Maharajahs have contested with maharajahs, rajahs with rajahs. India has rarely been ruled by the all-powerful, all-centralizing rulers of the more typical riverine societies of China or Egypt. In the absence of powerful central rule, India has rarely been able to mount an effective defense against invasion, especially by the pastoralists. There was no centralized Indian state to maintain a string of forts, as Egypt did on the Upper Nile, nor a great defensive wall, as the Chinese emperors did. India instead has forever played the role its cartographical outline suggests: a net into which the flotsam and jetsam of Eurasia flowed, was held, and merged, to create a unique Indian culture.

The alien pastoral influences from the northern steppes within that net acted on, and reacted with, the indigenous crop-growing culture in a manner that was altogether different from the transient, traumatic interactions of pastoralism and crop-growing in China. Out of the interaction of pastoralism with the indigenous crop-growing cultures, two distinctively Indian societal adaptations evolved. These adaptations continue to be dominant influences in Indian society in the atomic age. The first of these most durable and powerful adaptations was caste which, though originally color-based, was more durable than a color-bar inasmuch as the progeny of a couple from different castes do not acquire the caste of the upper caste partner. The institution of caste thus enabled the minority of paler-skinned, pastoral, Aryan invaders, who comprised the upper caste, to have a range of economic, social, and sexual relationships with the indigenous, wealth-producing, Dravidian cropgrowers without becoming absorbed into, and losing their privileged status to, the mass of indigenes.[27]

The second major societal adaptation was the apotheosis of the cow. The exercise of the conqueror's power of access to the women of the invaded territory meant the implantation and spread of the genetic characteristic of lactose tolerance in crop-growing India. The incidence of lactose tolerance, which the invaders brought with them from the Eurasian steppes, now spreads from a peak of almost 100 percent tolerance in northwest India to virtually 100 percent lactose malabsorption in East Bengal and in Kerala in south India, reflecting the declining genetic influence of the invading pastoralists over distance from the point of entry in the northwest.[28]

Lactose tolerant, milk-consuming stockowners breed their stock as frequently as possible in order to induce lactation and milk production. Lactose malabsorbent crop-growers, on the other hand, breed their stock, which they use as draught animals, only in order to secure replacements, in the same way as, in the pre-tractor West, farmers bred their working mares about once in ten years on average to secure replacement horses. For example, in Ireland in the 1930s, there were about 430,000 horses altogether, of which presumably half were male and half female. The number of horses under-one-year was about 20,000, or one-tenth the total number of female horses.[29] If female bovines are bred regularly to induce lactation, as Indian cows and female buffaloes are, they are unavailable for draught purposes, as Indian female bovines—unlike those of East Asia—are.

Moreover, all the cows of lactose tolerant, milk-consuming pastoralists who graze their animals communally are of the *Bos indicus* type. Cows of this type lactate only in the presence of their live calves. The failure of *Bos indicus* cows to let down their milk, except when they are stimulated by the presence of their live calves, is presumably a consequence of natural selection. Lactose tolerant pastoralists, existing at a subsistence level, would have been irresistibly tempted to draw all the milk they could from their stock. Strains of animals that let down their milk freely would have become extinct under these circumstances and only those strains that withheld their milk for their offspring would have survived. Throughout Asia and Africa, lactose tolerant people therefore not merely breed their animals as frequently as possible; but, willy-nilly, they divert much of the milk to keeping the progeny alive as long as the dams lactate, as part of the price of inducing them to do so. The progeny of the invading, lactose tolerant pastoralists and of the indigenous, lactose malabsorbent Indian cropgrowers, therefore, got from their cows not only milk which, for the most part being lactose tolerant, they relished, but calves which perforce were reared through the normal six to nine months of their dams' lactation. It would not have been surprising if, under the circumstances, India's pastoral resources were, like those of northern Eurasia, diverted into milk and beef production for a small pastoral population. Something of this sort occurred in Africa, where cattle are used exclusively for milk and meat and where, on almost eight times as much land, only a little more than half as many people are supported, at a generally lower level of nutrition, as on the subcontinent of India, Pakistan, and Bangladesh.

The apotheosis of the cow, which appears to have occurred no more than 2,000 years ago,[30] prevented India from being transformed into a sparsely populated cattle walk, its people leading a crude and barbarous existence. Presumably whatever sect first tabooed beef-eating found itself with an abundant supply of young male cattle, which had to be reared to induce their *Bos indicus* dams to lactate and which provided draught power to cultivate India's relatively extensive croplands; and, with the resultant crops, they were able to support a more numerous, and therefore on average also a more efficient, population. More populous and efficient, non-beef-eating, cropgrowing sects would in time have forced out people who continued to use India's limited pastoral resources for milk and beef production and, as a result, failed to grow sufficient crops. The overwhelming advantage in food output, secured among a lactose tolerant people with *Bos indicus* cattle, of apotheosizing cattle would seem to account for the continued centrality of cow-worship today in India where, side by side with atomic power and earth-satellite television broadcasting, cow slaughter is prohibited by laws which it is proposed to reinforce and entrench by constitutional amendment.[31]

But why, it may be asked, did not some sect of Africans similarly apotheosize the cow with similarly beneficial effects on cropgrowing and food production? Or alternatively, why, as in Africa, did not Indians who, like Sub-Sahelian Africans, were both cattle keepers and cropgrowers, exhaust themselves in perpetual raiding and counter-raiding? One possible explanation is that the great riverine surplus produced by the Indus and Ganges rivers supported a central power that was sufficiently strong to dominate much, and to influence all, of the subcontinent. No similar riverine power existed in Sub-Sahelian Africa which might have prevented the continent's wealth being dissipated in unceasing tribal warfare. Another possible explanation is the prevalence in Africa, but absence in

India, of trypanosomiasis which, in the first instance, necessitated the keeping of cattle in the open in Africa, thus forcing cattle keepers to spend their time defending their own and raiding their neighbors' cattle, and which also precluded the use of cattle to cultivate the tsetse-fly infested bush, where African crops were grown.

Southwest Asia

Further west, the horse-mounted, Indo-European pastoralists flowed with little hindrance through the gaps between the southwest Asian chain of inland seas: the Azov, the Caspian, and the Black seas. They were attracted mainly by the wealth of crop-growing Mesopotamia. Mesopotamia, though the cradle of civilization, was peculiarly vulnerable to the power realized by the acquisition of lactose tolerance by the pastoralists of the Eurasian steppes. The vital water supply of the Mesopotamian plain was more precarious than that of any other major riverine culture. It depended, in the first instance, on moisture from the Atlantic carried over the whole length of the Mediterranean before the prevailing west winds deposited it as rain and snow on the Taurus mountains of Anatolia. Even the timing and the amount of water-flow into Mesopotamia depended on the spring thaw in the mountains. If that were late or incomplete, the rivers too flowed late or inadequately.

The twin rivers, Euphrates and Tigris, flowing slowly through the broad Iraq plain, deposited their silt on the way. Many cities grew along the banks of the rivers and in the area between them. Centralized government came slowly and was incomplete, by contrast with nearby Egypt, where the more regularly flowing Nile deposited its greater wealth in a narrower, more fertile strip.[32] The larger Egyptian surplus provided the means to support a more powerful state which, because of its narrower bounds, could in any case be more easily ruled and defended. Government in the Middle East was therefore even less able than in India to defend the crop-growing territory against successive pastoral invasions; and these, in order to reach their Mesopotamian quarry, had not to surmount or circumvent any natural barrier at all comparable to the Himalayan mountains.[33]

Moreover, Mesopotamia, as well as being less protected against invading pastoralists, was more vulnerable to the havoc they created. The rivers, as they meandered through the plain depositing silt, in many places caused the river bed, confined by flood banks, to rise above the surrounding land. Mesopotamian civilization was, therefore, peculiarly dependent on the maintenance of these banks. Once they were breached by the invaders, or through neglect by harassed and war-torn cropgrowers, the basis of the world's oldest civilization was destroyed. Unsurprisingly therefore, following invasion by the Indo-European pastoralists, many of the oldest cities in the world sank back into the Mesopotamian alluvium from which they had arisen, acquiring in time a covering of herbage on which the Bedouin sheep, goats, and camels grazed. Many of these most ancient cities have been rescued from oblivion by recent archaeological excavations, and many continue to be so rescued.[34] The entire region, which was once the most densely populated part of the world, retrogressed for millennia. It contained, 2,000 years ago, when already the most severe damage had been done by the invading pastoralists, 12 percent of the world's population. By 1,800 AD its share of the world's population had declined to 1.5 percent.[35]

The indigenous Semitic peoples of the Middle East, both the lactose malabsorbent cropgrowers of Mesopotamia, Israel, and the oases and the lactose tolerant Bedouin shepherds and goatherds of the deserts, have continued to occupy the lower, more arid lands that were too hot and too dry for permanent occupation by the cattle-owning, Indo-European pastoralists from the steppes. These latter, over the long term, have remained in the cooler, better watered uplands of Anatolia and Iran, though from time to time extending their imperial sway over the Semitic lowlanders. The unceasing conflict between lactose tolerant Indo-European pastoralists and predominantly lactose malabsorbent Semitic cropgrowers has caused the Middle East to retrogress for millennia.

The Significance of the Combination of Lactose Tolerance and Arable Land

The migration of pastoralists from the non-arable regions where they had acquired lactose tolerance, into arable regions, where that genetic characteristic could not have become dominant, created a wholly new situation: the combination of lactose tolerance and arable land. That situation had a distinctive potential. That was to use the much greater surplus which lactose tolerant pastoralists secured from pastoral resources to extend the cultivation of arable land. Relatively little of that land could be cultivated in the absence of lactose tolerant pastoralists. Cultivation was restricted, in the first instance, to the tiny proportion of arable land located in tropical riverine valleys where, at the state of the art, the cultivators could secure sufficient for their reproduction. Outside that limited area, only the small surplus from hunting, gathering, or an unproductive pastoralism practiced by lactose malabsorbent people could be used to complement the product of swidden cropgrowing. That, except in rare cases, yielded insufficient to maintain and reproduce the cultivators. Most of the arable land of the world was therefore uncultivated prior to the eruptions of the pastoralists. The potential of the pastoralist migrations centered on the extent and manner in which that land was brought into cultivation and production.

The migrating pastoralists achieved little in eastern Asia, where they failed to influence permanently China's large, complex riverine society. Their influence in Sumeria, the cradle of civilization, to which they had ready access, was entirely destructive. Through a synthesis with the cropgrowing Dravidian indigenes which involved the distinctive societal adaptations of caste and the apotheosis of the cow, Aryan pastoralists created a remarkably well-adapted society in India. A measure of the success of that adaptation is that 20 percent of the world's population can live on the 3 percent of the world's land that comprises the Indian subcontinent. The combination of pastoralism and arable land in sub-

Sahelian Africa, by contrast, has been singularly unproductive. It generated conflict and failed to free the continent from dependence on hoe-based, swidden cropgrowing. A measure of that failure lies in the fact that today, Africa, with 23 percent of the world's land, supports only 11 percent of the world's population at levels of nutrition that are lower, on average, than in any other continent.[36]

The potential implicit in a combination of lactose tolerance and abundant arable land was most fully realized in Europe. The conditions responsible for that, and the manner in which the potential was realized, are the subject of the next chapter.

Chapter 3

The Emergence of Individualism in Europe

The significance of the lactose tolerant Indo-European pastoralists as a generally destructive force in the histories of Sumeria, India, and China was introduced in chapter 2. Their crucial role—effectively as the architects of the modern world—in the development of Europe is described and explained in this chapter. The chapter begins with an account of the role and status of the individual in pre-European societies. The uniqueness of European geographic conditions is outlined, and the origins of European individualism are then explained, in terms of the conditions of production that prevailed at the entry of the migrating pastoralists into Europe. The two dramatically different manifestations of individualism—individualist slavery and individualist capitalism—are discussed, compared, and contrasted.

The Status of the Individual in Pre-European Societies

The human progress noted to this point was societal. Progress, as measured especially by the size of the population supported, depended on the evolution of technology and on the natural resource base available. The latter included the amount of land under command for irrigation. Progress depended too on such societal adaptations as the emergence, by natural selection, of races of lactose tolerant peoples in non-arable regions.

The individual's role was minimal in all of these pre-European societies. The amount of food available, which was determined by the state of the art and by the natural resource base, in turn determined the size of the population supported. Only rarely and fortuitously was all of the population required to procure or to produce the food. The individual was unable to expand the supply of food available at the seasonal low points which determined the number surviving into periods of greater supply. The population of Ptolemaic Egypt, which is here taken as representative of conditions in riverine societies, was three times as great as was needed to cultivate fully every square inch of the black soil of the valley, out to where the red earth of the desert commenced and where the sown seed did not germinate.[1] Two-thirds of the Egyptian population was superfluous to food production needs; it could make no contribution to the total amount of food produced. This was determined solely by the extent of black, alluvial land available and by the state of the art of cropgrowing. And nothing could be done with that food other than maintain and reproduce an economically superfluous population. A similar situation obtained in Mesopotamia, India, China, and Mezzo-America where, up to a few centuries ago, the bulk of the human population was located.

Most of the rest of the ancient world's population consisted of lactose tolerant pastoralists. Their number was determined by the amount of livestock that could be carried through the dormant season on the communally grazed pastures. If one person, by exceptional skill or by good fortune, had more stock on the dormant season pasture, less grazing was available for the stock of others. The total stock surviving the dormant season was unchanged by individual effort or fortune.

The situation was not dissimilar for swidden farmers and for hunter-gatherers. The number of the former was determined by the food secured from complementing hunting-gathering, and of the latter by hunting-gathering solely. That, in turn, was determined by the fertility of the land and by the state of the art. Individuals could not affect it.

Population was the dependent variable in all cases. Because individuals could not affect total output, they were subordinate to society, on the assets of which individuals were totally dependent. The degree of subordination of the individual or of dominance by society was determined by two factors in particular. The first was the amount of surplus output relative to what was required to maintain and reproduce those who acquired or produced it. If there was none, society had no resources with which to dominate individuals. Where the surplus was large relative to maintenance and reproduction needs, it was available to society, as personified in its rulers, to dominate individuals.

Social dominance could be exercised more readily over confined individuals. Where, as in Egypt, China, and other riverine agricultural societies, populations were confined into narrow river valleys that were highly productive, the large surplus could be used to dominate completely the confined populations. The dominance of the Golden Hordes over individuals on the steppe may have been no less complete. The surplus over the reproduction needs of the small number of necessary producers on most pastures was large. Mobile hordes could have applied that surplus easily to enforce compliance on individuals.

Swidden agriculture produced no surplus; and political power, the power of society, was correspondingly weak. Society could exercise little if any control over individuals who could diffuse over the abundant land that was suitable for that form of food production. Only to the extent that people were dependent on access to common hunting or grazing lands to supplement the inadequate product of swidden farming did they become dependent also on society. Hunting gathering societies rarely had much surplus over the reproduction needs of the hunters and gatherers. Society therefore had few resources with which to dominate its members, who could in most cases have fairly easily broken away to form new groups.

Hunter-gatherers and swidden farmers occupied one end of a spectrum of degrees of society dominance. Society dominance, in their case, was largely a matter of compliance with accepted norms. The penalty for noncompliance was exclusion from the territory over which the group exercised control. The excluded person then depended on getting access to the territory of a neighboring group. Dense populations of riverine cropgrowers, like those on the Nile and Yellow rivers, occupied the other end of the spectrum of society dominance. The large surplus which accrued to society, in the form of taxes that accounted for up to two-thirds of total product, enabled it to exercise absolute control over populations who were confined to the narrow areas under command for irrigation.

Individuals in all cases were absolutely dependent on the socially controlled natural resource base and on what that produced at the state of the art. The individual was powerless to increase the total product available from the group's hunting and gathering territory, from its grazing lands, or from the restricted area under command for irrigation.

The individual hunter-gatherer, the individual on the communally grazed pastures and in the over-crowded riverine valleys, was powerless to add to production; on the contrary, by his presence he reduced the amount available to all the other members of society. His economic insignificance was mirrored by his political insignificance. In Egypt, "the Pharaoh, son of Ra, (was) a god upon earth whose words laid down the law."[2] In Persia, "all the subjects, without exception, up to the highest dignitaries, including ministers and generals, were considered to be the slaves (bandaka) of the king."[3] In the Ottoman empire, "subjects, especially non-Moslems, were in reality what they were in name, Raya (Arabic: ra'ayah, herd) a human flock to be shepherded, milked and fleeced."[4] China was unified, centralized and ruled "by the universal pre-eminence of the Son of Heaven . . . whole system of administration was monolithic."[5] The neighboring Japanese "ideally saw the feudal bond as committing the inferior to absolute obedience and loyalty and granting the superior unlimited authority."[6] The Inca in Peru was divine, like the Egyptian pharaoh.[7] And so on.

Evolution and change within these society-dominant societies were the result of slowly evolving social adaptation. Such were the gradual improvements in hunting-gathering techniques; the planting of seeds and the controlled breeding rather than slaughter of livestock; and the emergence of lactose tolerance. Life proceeded in cycles that were caused by such sequences as the rise and decline of dynasties of rulers or the expansion of flocks and herds, followed by their decimation by disease or starvation when their expanded numbers pressed upon dormant season grazing that might have been made more than usually scarce by exceptionally unfavorable weather. There was little change between the same points on succeeding cycles, though these might have been separated by centuries or even millennia. Cook makes this point: "Ancient Egyptian civilization remained more or less uniform for two and a half millennia. . . . The Hyksos invaded, took over and finally were expelled. . . . Egypt was a prize colony of the Roman Empire, but Rome did little to change the Egyptians. . . . It was not until the Arab invaders of 639 AD that the turning point arrived."[8]

Toynbee makes the same point: "The Sumero-Akkadian and Egyptian civilizations had accomplished most of their great creative achievements in all fields of human activity before the close of the third millennium BC."[9] Thereafter, he suggests, there were just repeated cycles. Lambert erroneously attributes this homeostasis to the proliferation of parasitic worms in warm, moist environments, "which stagnated the cradles of civilization."[10] As Barth notes, "The Baseri, far away from a "warm, moist environment," graze the parched lands of south Persia and lead there a life that is very little different from that of their forebears of 4,000 years ago."[11] And so it goes.

The Unique Circumstances Encountered by Pastoralists in Europe

At the immigration of the lactose tolerant, Indo-European pastoralists, Europe was in many respects the least promising and most uninviting of the continents. Furthest from the equator of the inhabited continents, it received less of the sun's heat, the source of all energy and—ultimately—all progress. Its population some 4,000–5,000 years ago, may well have been below what it had been 20,000 years earlier, during the last Ice Age. Following the retreat of the ice, deciduous forest, from the Atlantic to the Vistula river, encroached on the tundra and forced it, and the reindeer which lived on it, northwards.[12] The Lapps, who hunted them, and whose forebears may well have painted the remarkable pictures on the walls of the Lascaux caves in southern France 17,000 years ago, perforce had to follow the reindeer, abandoning central western Europe to the dark, unproductive forest.[13] Nevertheless, the migrating pastoralists encountered in Europe circumstances that made it possible to realize there more fully than elsewhere the potential inherent in the conjunction of lactose tolerance and available arable land.

A unique combination of four circumstances existed in Europe:

(1) Because of its distance from the equator, Europe alone of the major continents, had no indigenous, riverine, cropgrowing society. Nor, because of the forest which encroached after the Ice Age, had it any indigenous pastoralism. Its swidden agriculture must have been exceptionally difficult and cannot have supported many people. This was because of low temperatures in northern and central Europe and because of the rainfall pattern in the south on the Mediterranean littoral. The rainfall occurs

there in wintertime, when it is of least value for crop growth, while the summers are hot and arid. The immigrating pastoralists consequently were more free than in Asia or Africa from existing, local human influences in adjusting to the new condition of having available arable land.

(2) The immigrating pastoralists were peculiarly well insulated from external, non-European influences also. The Mediterranean and the Bosphorus precluded major incursions in the south by the riverine societies of Mesopotamia or Egypt. Farther north, the forest was an even more effective shield against the Golden Hordes of the steppe. These latter could enter Europe's heartland only by percolating through the forest, a process that transformed the hordes into migrating pastoralist bands.

(3) These percolating bands of pastoralists were forced to settle in Europe in small, disparate groups, because of conditions that are dealt with more fully in following sections.

(4) The immigrating pastoralists had more ready access to arable land in Europe than in the other continents. Though farther from the equator and therefore naturally less well placed to convert the sun's energy into consumable crops, Europe now cultivates a larger proportion of its land than any other continent: 30 percent, compared to 17 percent of Asia's, the next most intensively cropped continent, and compared to 11 percent for the non-European world as a whole.[14]

The numerous, disparate bands of immigrating, lactose tolerant pastoralists therefore secured more readily in Europe than elsewhere available arable land. The numerous, disparate bands who encountered this land were able to respond in different ways to this new circumstance, free from the influence of any major indigenous culture and from interference by any major, non-European culture. This set of conditions, which was peculiar to Europe, provided a more favorable environment than anywhere else for the realization of the potential that lay in the conjunction of lactose tolerance and arable land.

That potential lay in the use of the large surplus available to lactose tolerant pastoralists to extend the area of cultivated land. That surplus was much greater than the surplus available from hunting-gathering, or from livestock held by lactose malabsorbent stockholders. The realization of that potential was a matter of societal adjustment to the new conditions created by the migration of pastoralists from non-arable regions—where alone they could have acquired lactose tolerance—into arable areas.

Similar adjustments occurred wherever and whenever lactose tolerant pastoralists reached arable land. The form the adjustment took was determined by local conditions (see chapter 2). The particular conditions that governed the form of societal adjustment that occurred in Europe were, to repeat, (i) the absence of any major indigenous food production; (ii) insulation from external influences; (iii) the need to settle in many disparate groups; and (iv) the availability of abundant arable land, though only of the poorer sort which, at the state of the art, did not yield sufficient for the cultivator's reproduction.

Once that necessary adjustment was successfully accomplished in Europe, land, for the first time in human experience, ceased to be a constraint on production. There was effectively limitless arable land available; only societal adaptation was required by lactose tolerant pastoralists to bring it into production. As the area of land cultivated was extended, more people were supported. Other things being equal, an increase in population raises efficiency and increases total product disproportionately, because of greater division of labor and the realization of scale and external economies.

That had been the case on the steppe, where natural selection for lactose tolerance made it possible for more people to subsist. Extending the cultivated area by hydraulic development also enabled more people to exist in cropgrowing riverine valleys. But total output, in these latter cases, continued to be limited by the natural resource base: by the amount of winter grazing on the steppe, or by the amount of land under command for irrigation in the riverine valleys. At those limits, more people added nothing to production, but merely shared a total product that was determined by the natural resource base and the state of the art. People in natural resource based, land limiting economies, at the margin, were dependent on society and on its total product. More people reduced the average amount available per person toward the minimum necessary to prevent death rates rising above biologically determined birthrates.

Not land but human ingenuity and adaptiveness limited production in Europe, once the transformation initiated by the conjunction of lactose tolerance and arable land commenced there. People, by the exercise of these qualities, could extend the area of cultivated land effectively without limit. In doing so, through scale and external economies, they added to the total product over and above their own share of it. More people, under European conditions of production where land ceased to constrain output, so far from reducing the portion of a fixed total amount available to others in the society, increased that portion. The more people who were supported on Europe's effectively limitlessly available arable land, the better off and the more secure were those already there. The normal human relationship between the individual and society was thus transformed in Europe. In non-European economies, where land and the state of the art determined output, individuals were totally dependent on society for a share of that output; in Europe where land was non-limiting, society was dependent on the scale and external economies secured by individuals adding to the total product by extending the cultivated part of the limitlessly available arable land.

That transformation in the relationship between individuals and society, which occurred in Europe following the immigration of the lactose tolerant, Indo-European pastoralists, is here referred to as individualism. It is a distinctively European phenomenon. It occurred nowhere outside Europe. It derived from the peculiar circumstances under which lactose tolerant pastoralists came into contact with limitlessly available arable land in Europe, which provided there uniquely the necessary and sufficient conditions for the emergence of individualism.

Individualism in South and Middle Europe

Europe, though the smallest in extent of the five major continents, is more heterogeneous in environment and culture than any of the others. A particular dichotomy of circumstances faced the immigrating Indo-European pastoralists. The circumstances described in the previous section applied to all groups of pastoralists moving into Europe. But three sets of local factors gave rise to profound differences between the way in which the southward-moving pastoralists adapted to their surroundings and the adaptations undertaken by those who moved more directly westward.

These were: the local conditions for grazing, the local conditions for crop growing, and the indigenous peoples encountered in the south and middle of Europe.

Grazing Conditions—Choice of Livestock

Moving westward from the steppe, the pastoralists found only dense forest, in which grazing, because of heavier rainfall, was more suitable for cattle than sheep. Sheep in any case would have been difficult to manage in the forest, where their wool would have tangled with the undergrowth, imprisoning them, preventing their movement, and eventually causing their starvation. The pastoralists, as they migrated westwards, probably shed their sheep and concentrated on cattle. Central western Europe today has only half as many sheep per 100 cattle as the USSR, from where Europe's pastoralists emigrated (table 3.1).

The pastoralists who moved southwestwards, towards the Mediterranean, encountered quite different grazing. Because the rainfall was less and fell mainly in the winter, when it is least conducive to growth, the natural flora was less abundant. Shrub and light grazing predominated, which was suitable for sheep grazing. The Mediterranean region today has 338 sheep per 100 cattle, compared to central western Europe's 61 and the USSR's 130 (table 3.1).

Table 3.1. Composition of Grazing Stock by Region

	Sheep and Goats Per 100 Cattle	Goats Per 100 Cattle
World	126	41
Africa [a]	156	120
Middle East [b]	564	39
Mediterranean [c]	338	29
CW Europe [d]	61	3
USSR	130	4

Source: FAO, *Production Yearbook* (Rome: FAO, 1979)
Notes:
   a.) Africa, excluding Morocco, Algeria, Tunisia, Libya, Egypt, South Africa.
   b.) Afghanistan, Iran, Iraq, Jordan, Saudi Arabia, Yemen, Syria, Turkey.
   c.) Morocco, Algeria, Tunisia, Libya, Egypt, Israel, Lebanon, Greece, Albania, Yugoslavia, Italy, Spain.
   d.) Austria, Belgium, Luxemburg, Czechoslovakia, Denmark, France, Germany, (East and West), Ireland, Netherlands, Switzerland, United Kingdom.

Cropgrowing—Yield Levels

The cereal crops, which are descended from the original wild grasses of the Middle East, yielded less in central western Europe than in the Mediterranean region, where the climate was more akin to that of the original home of the cereals. Some 2000 years ago, a grain of cereal planted in central western Europe returned on average two.[15] One planted near Rome yielded four.[16] A grain planted on the warm, watered alluvium of Ptolemaic Egypt yielded ten.[17] Netting out the seed, the returns from planting a given quantity of grain were in the proportions of 1:3:9.

The Mediterranean littoral contained limitless amounts of arable land. "Arable land" is defined as being land which, when cultivated with the existing technology produces a yield, Y, which is greater than the seed (s) required to plant it; plus the grazing (g) that it would afford if not cultivated; plus the energy (e) expended by the cultivator. That is, land is arable if:

   $Y > s + g + e$.

If M denotes the amount of nutrition required to maintain the cultivator and R that required to maintain and reproduce him, three grades of arable land may be identified:

$Yr > s + g + R$	Yield allows for the cultivator's maintenance and reproduction
$s + g + M < Ym < s + g + R$	Yield sufficient for maintenance but not reproduction
$s + g + e < Ye < s + g + M$	Yield is insufficient even for the cultivator's maintenance needs

R is approximately equal to three times M. A crop grower's maintenance needs were roughly one-third of his reproduction needs. This is because in poor, less developed populations producers account for only about one-third of the total. The proportion is nearer to half in modern, wealthier countries.[18] The "non-producing" two-thirds comprise the young, the old, the sick, the heavily pregnant, and that large section who spend most of their time preparing and cooking the food grown by the "producers."

Conditions in Ptolemaic Egypt may be considered representative of the great riverine systems. Riverine land in the tropics and sub-tropics, in Sumeria, Egypt, the Indus valley, and the Yellow River valley in China supported and produced more than enough people to cultivate all of the land in the confined valley areas. One half or more of all the people supported and reproduced by the produce from these fertile, well-watered, warm lands were surplus, in the sense of having no land to cultivate. Thus "Egyptian peasants of the third millennium may have been able to produce three times as much as their domestic needs,"[19] and "Certainly not less, and perhaps more than half" the Egyptian cultivator's output was appropriated by the Pharaonic state in taxes and used to support the population who were not required as cultivators.[20] The half of the crop left to the cultivator was sufficient normally for his maintenance and reproduction.

From this we can deduce that Yr, the return net of seed to the Egyptian (Riverine) cultivator, was about 2R. That is $Yr = 2R$. The comparable return to the Roman cultivator, Ym, was about a third of that of the Egyptian; or $Ym = 2R/3$. And as $R = 3M$, we can conclude that $Ym = 2M$. That is, yields in the area of the Mediterranean littoral were about twice maintenance needs, but crucially, less than reproduction needs.

The observable agricultural development of the Mediterranean area supports this hypothesis for, had Mediterranean land at the state of the art yielded cultivators their reproduction needs, all the arable land, like that of Egypt, Sumeria, China, Mexico, or Peru, would have been cultivated. In fact, at the most developed stage of the ancient Mediterranean, which was the height of the Roman empire, only a tenth of the land was cultivated.[21]

Further north, in central western Europe, where the net returns to grain growing were only one-third as much as on the Mediterranean ($Ye = Ym/3 = 2M/3$) and only one-ninth as much as in the Nile valley, cultivators, at the state of the art, could not secure even a maintenance. This was a critical difference in the circumstances encountered by the immigrating pastoralists: southwards, on the Mediterranean littoral and at the state of the art, a maintenance, though not reproduction, could be obtained from cropgrowing; westwards, in central western Europe, not even a maintenance could be obtained, at the state of the art, from cultivating the region's abundant arable land.

Indigenous Peoples Encountered by the Pastoralists

Finally, the immigrating pastoralists encountered different indigenes in the two parts of Europe. The seagoing Phoenician indigenes on the Mediterranean probably supplemented their returns from swidden farming with the proceeds of trade by sea with the rich cropgrowers of Egypt, through the Nile delta, and with those of Mesopotamia, through the headwaters of the Euphrates, which rose close to the Lebanese coast. The Phoenicians were able to exchange for the grain that grew abundantly in Egypt and Mesopotamia the tree products that grew well on the stony soils, in the hot and arid Mediterranean summers. These included timber itself, wine, and olive oil. They blended with the forerunners of the Indo-European pastoralists and contributed philologically and physiologically to modern Mediterranean society.

Their philological contribution is that in the Greek language, while most roots are of Indo-European origin, those pertaining to the sea and to commerce are mainly of Phoenician origin, indicating a blend between the indigenous seafarers and traders and the newcomer pastoralists.[22] The physiological evidence is the predominance of lactose malabsorption among those Mediterranean peoples on the southernmost extremes of the northern littoral and especially those in the islands, from Sicily to Crete. Lactose tolerance becomes increasingly dominant farther inland from the shore.[23] These phenomena indicate the survival of a strong Phoenician influence close to the Mediterranean shore where the original blend between immigrating Indo-Europeans and indigenous Phoenicians occurred. A somewhat similar interaction occurred between the immigrant, lactose tolerant Aryans and the indigenous, lactose malabsorbent Dravidians in India. There, under different circumstances, the result was India's caste system and its sacred cows.

Life for the original lactose malabsorbent, swidden agriculturists in the forests of central western Europe must have been exceptionally difficult. Crop yields, as noted, were low. There were particular problems for cattle-keeping in the northern forest (to be enlarged upon below) so that the contribution of cattle, in draught services and meat, must have been slight. Slight too must have been the fruits of hunting and gathering in the northern forest, from which the Lapps had earlier been forced to depart. It was in the words of Tacitus: "a country that is thankless to till and dismal to behold for anyone who was not born and bred there. . . . It is covered either by bristling forests or by foul swamps."[24] It is significant that the principal archaeological remains of these pre-Indo-European peoples are located in Britain and Ireland, where the forest was less dense, the winters less severe, and the grass grew more abundantly. At locations like Stonehenge in southern England and Newgrange in Ireland, less forest, better grass, and milder winters probably made existence less difficult than on the continent, and generated a surplus for substantial monument building. Further west, in County Mayo, where the climate is still milder and the grass competed still better with the forest, the Ceide Fields promise to yield evidence of a still more developed society than those located at Stonehenge or Newgrange. The fields, which are now being excavated archaeologically, extend over some 2,500 acres, divided into regularly shaped lots of some fifteen acres each, and were probably used for the rotational winter grazing of cattle some 5,000 years ago.[25] Swidden farming in the rest of Europe must, however, have been a very marginal affair, incapable of resistance to, or influencing the behavior of, the incoming lactose tolerant pastoralists. The Basques and Lapps are probably the only survivors of these swidden farmers of pre-Indo-European Europe .

The unique combination of abundantly available arable land, the absence of major indigenous food-producing societies, insulation from external intervention, and the need for a multiplicity of nuclear, disparate settlements which the immigrant, lactose tolerant Indo-European pastoralists encountered in Europe, and alone in Europe, were the necessary and sufficient conditions for the emergence in Europe, and only in Europe, of individualism. The differences in the circumstances between southern and central western Europe caused that individualism to take two very different forms: individualist slavery in southern Europe and individualist capitalism in central western Europe.

Individualist Slavery

The Origins of Individualist Slavery

The society of the ancient Mediterranean was the product of mingling two remarkably innovative peoples. One of these were shepherds who had reached the Mediterranean from the distant steppe and who, in their migrations, had adjusted the composition of their livestock to the changing pasturage. They changed from the cattle-dominant stocking of the steppe to the sheep-dominant stocking of the Mediterranean littoral. The lighter sheep could graze more efficiently than cattle the sparse pasture of the Mediterranean; but being small animals, they could travel less far than the longer legged cattle. Their shepherd owners therefore had little option, on arrival at the Mediterranean, but to divide along with their flocks, into numerous different groups along the littoral. These disparate groups of lactose tolerant, Indo-European shepherds, it may be supposed, encountered similarly disparate groups of lactose malabsorbent, Phoenician cropgrowers, located close to the sea from which, through trade and fishing, they supplemented the sparse produce of the crops.

The lactose tolerant progeny of the synthesis could use their pastoral surplus to cultivate some of the available arable land. That would have produced more food, which would have enabled more people to survive the dormant season dearth. It would have been a simple extension of that process to capture later waves of immigrating shepherds and to force them, in a life of work, punishment, and food, to cultivate more of the available arable land.

The potential once realized of enslaving later arriving barbarian pastoralists and forcing them to cultivate the abundant second class arable land on the Mediterranean was fuelled by successive waves of migrating barbarians. These, in a sense, represented the pastoral surplus of the steppe, which stretched from the Carpathian mountains to the distant Pacific ocean. The steppe could support many more lactose tolerant people than were required to tend the stock. Some at least of the economically surplus population, with a low or zero marginal productivity, migrated. They left production unaffected, but raised consumption levels for the residual, reduced population. Some of these pastoral emigrants fuelled the glory that was Greece and Rome.

A unique combination of lactose tolerance, sheep-grazing, and limitless arable land that, at the state of the art, produced above maintenance, but below reproduction for the needs of its cultivators occurred on the Mediterranean littoral 3,000–4,000 years ago. That combination permitted the evolution of a distinctive, slave-based, individualist economy. The economy was slave-based in the sense that the supply of slaves alone restricted output and the population which it supported. There was limitlessly available arable land on the Mediterranean littoral from which the slave labor of pastoralists could extract a surplus over maintenance; the total amount of that surplus depended solely on the number of captured pastoralists.

The spread of slavery in the ancient Mediterranean was irresistible once its profitability was established. Slavery allowed the reproduction of larger populations of citizens who individually, as a result of greater division of labor and economies of scale, were also more efficient. Larger, more efficient groups, whose wealth and numbers were restricted only by the supply of slaves, could enslave other, smaller, less efficient groups. The underlying, basic social rule was: enslave or be enslaved. Those groups dominated who, by good fortune, a favorable location, or better adaptation of their institutions to the requirements of the circumstances, acquired the most slaves and made the best use of them. The rest, if not enslaved like the barbarian pastoralists, became the clients and dependants of the dominant group.

Improved, more appropriate institutional adjustment for an individualist society based on slavery would have included maximizing the incentive for individuals to capture and to extract the maximum surplus from slaves, and, by corollary, maximizing also the deterrent for failing to do so; and it would have included maximizing the attraction for outsiders with slaves to join the group and by their presence to add more than proportionately to the product and security of the receiving group; and also by corollary minimizing the incentive for group members with slaves to depart and to join other, welcoming groups. Those results were most likely to be achieved most fully by societies that conferred most completely and securely the flow of production surplus to maintenance from slaves to those who had acquired the slaves. Ancient Mediterranean societies, in a word, prospered in accordance with their readiness to create property in their members' slaves. "Of property, the first, the most necessary kind, the best and most manageable, is man."[26] More slaves were likely to be acquired and worked efficiently in those societies which recognized most clearly their members' property in their slaves. Those societies, together with their values and institutions, became dominant.

Property, which was essential for the survival and well-being of society in the individualist, slave-based economy of the ancient Mediterranean, was secured by law. Law, a more or less explicit corpus, determines relations between individuals and society. It incorporates the views of citizens as to what those relations should be; and it is amendable from time to time in an orderly fashion. Law frees man from the tyrannies of anarchy, despotism, and unchanging custom.

The rule of law in the ancient Mediterranean was an expression of the unique politico-economic relationship that existed between the individual and society in circumstances where land did not limit production and where the individual's production sustained himself and simultaneously enhanced the productivity and security of his fellows. Under these conditions, society was entirely dependent on individuals who were able to cultivate the unlimited available arable land. Individuals, for the most part, were not dependent on society, of which there were many nucleated ones, competing for the productive presence of the property-owning individual.

The principal concern of law has ever been the protection of the property that has been the economic basis of law-governed societies. Ancient Mediterranean civilization depended on the surplus that the slave produced over and above his necessary maintenance. To procure that surplus it was essential that the slave owner should have secure and exclusive property in the slave's output. All the power of society was directed towards that purpose, which was correctly deemed to be essential for society's survival. When rulers infringed the property of individual citizens, those infringements were perceived as aberrations and their perpetrators as tyrants rather than rulers; they were a threat to society. For infringements on property threatened its existence and acquisition and therefore threatened the existence of society itself, which depended on property.

The Dynamics of Individualist Slavery

The elevation of the enslavers and the degradation of the enslaved gave an awful urgency to the evolution of individualist slavery. People, in the ancient Mediterranean, for the first time acquired value. They were citizens, valued as contributors to the security and economic well-being of their society; and, with their slaves, they were welcome in neighboring societies, to which they could contribute security and economic well-being. Men became gods and created gods in their own image.

But the elevation of the enslaving citizen was secured by the degradation of the enslaved. People never before, and rarely after, had value. Land alone had value outside individualist Europe. A people's land might be coveted and appropriated; but, in land-limited economies, the land's occupants were valueless and were either exterminated or driven out by others who were more powerful. Land, except in specially favored locations like close to the citadel, was valueless in the ancient Mediterranean. But people had value, either as slave owners or as slaves. Conquest and its avoidance therefore acquired a new, urgent motivation, which gave direction and purpose to the development of individualist slavery.

The external and scale economies that accrue when increase in population is constrained by neither land nor capital gave impetus to individualist slavery.

Those of the numerous disparate groups which best adapted and best realized the potential of slavery under ancient Mediterranean conditions expanded, and, in doing so, grew disproportionately wealthy and powerful militarily. Those groups which adapted less successfully risked enslavement, or at best becoming the clients of the successful ones.

Success among the many contending groups in the ancient Mediterranean depended, in the first instance, on locational advantages. Access to fertile land and to the sea, control of important trade routes, and good natural defenses were helpful. But beyond that, success depended on the group's ability to adopt appropriate institutions and practices. That meant pre-eminently maximizing the benefits for individuals of acquiring and exploiting slaves and, by corollary, maximizing also the cost of failing to do so. That, in turn, implied conferring on individuals the exclusive enjoyment of the surplus over maintenance produced by slaves. It meant, in a word, establishing and securing the individual's property in his/her slaves.

Driven by the need to enslave and to resist enslavement, the meteoric rise of individualist slavery in the ancient Mediterranean was made possible by mobilizing, through slavery, the surplus labor produced by the pastoral steppe. As shown above, neither the enslaved labor nor the labor of the slave-owner was adequate to secure the laborer's reproduction. Reproduction was secured for the slave-owner by appropriating all the slave's produce above his maintenance needs. That was the production/reproduction relationship that existed from the beginning and that made individualist slavery uniquely possible in the ancient Mediterranean. That relationship persisted throughout the entire history of the ancient Mediterranean, for the culture's innumerable brilliant achievements did not include raising the cultivator's productivity to a level sufficient for reproduction. The lack of progress in raising the productivity of labor in the ancient Mediterranean was remarkable.[27]

However, the failure to raise the productivity of labor, though remarkable, is in fact quite understandable. The individual played many roles in ancient Mediterranean society. He was, in the first instance, a producer, though unable to secure sufficient for his reproduction from his product. He was therefore also, perforce if he was to reproduce himself, a slave owner. To be a slave owner, and not a slave, he had also to be a warrior. Finally, as a member of a society to the security and well-being of which he contributed by his presence as individuals nowhere outside Europe did, the individual in the ancient Mediterranean was also a citizen. He was, in that capacity, involved in the politics, or affairs of the polis, as members of no other society were. The least important, the least beneficial to the individual or society of all these activities was that of producer. Slaves could produce; but only citizens could fight and participate in political life. Production was servile and appropriate for slaves. War and politics were appropriate for citizens. "What we call 'production' was stigmatized by Greco-Roman society as a lower-class activity, possibly associated with slaves, necessary but dirty."[28] People understandably sought and secured advancement through military and political activities and left mere production to slaves and to those unfitted for war or politics. None of the latter had the competence or incentive to advance technologically. Progress was, therefore, confined to military and naval technology, to architecture, the arts, humanities, and philosophy. There was little increase in labor's productivity, especially in agriculture where almost all of it was engaged. Labor could not reproduce itself in the ancient Mediterranean at the end of the era of individualist slavery any more than at the commencement of that era, 1500 years earlier.

The initial and continuing inability of labor in the ancient Mediterranean to reproduce itself had two particularly important consequences. One was a tendency towards the concentration of economic and political power within society; and the other was a simultaneous tendency towards the geographic expansion of ancient Mediterranean influences. Returns to labor in a slave-based economy tended towards the level needed to maintain slaves, which was below the level at which citizens could reproduce themselves. From a basically equal starting position,[29] the fortunes of war and peace would have caused some citizens to lose their slaves. Slaveless citizens could not reproduce themselves, except by borrowing from slave owners. These conditions of production caused, within cities, an unavoidable polarization between slaveless and slave-owning citizens.

Simultaneously, the drive for slaves required successful polities or cities to extend their imperium. The conquerors, after the initial conquest, continued to draw taxes and tribute from those under their sway. While these might have sufficed to enable the capital's citizens to reproduce, their extraction left the rest of the dominion still less capable of reproducing its population without replenishment of its labor force. The need to acquire slaves to replenish a wasting labor force implied an unceasing need for conquest and expansion. Athens and Sparta dominated Greece, but in time both fell under Rome's sway, which eventually extended over the whole Mediterranean basin and beyond.

The Persian plateau on the east, the Sahara desert on the south, and the Atlantic ocean on the west forced Rome to expand northwards to secure the labor replenishments on which ancient Mediterranean society depended. The further northwards the empire spread, the less favorable growth conditions became and the lower yields fell. As observed above, the returns net of seed to crop-growing in Egypt, Rome and France were in the proportions of 9:3:1. If the Roman cultivator could produce in excess of maintenance but insufficient for reproduction, the excess being the slaveowner's profit, with a similar technology the cultivator in France produced less than was sufficient to maintain a slave.

Once the Roman *limes* extended to Hadrian's Wall in Britain and to the line of the Rhine and Danube on mainland Europe, where, at the state of the art, the cultivator's yield was insufficient for maintenance, existing conquests could be held only at a loss to the core, which would be increased by further conquests that extended the empire into territory even less favorable for crop-growing. The limits of ancient Mediterranean expansion had been reached; and with expansion ended so also ended the replenishment with captives of the ancient Mediterranean's wasting labor supply.

Slavery in Other Societies

The role of slaves in nonindividualist, land-limiting economies, where labor normally had low or zero marginal productivity, must have been peripheral. Occasionally they may have been used to make good losses of indigenous populations caused by war, disease, or famine resulting from a succession of crop failures. But normally enslaved captives would have provided only household or concubinage services. For example:

> Turkish slavery did not in the least resemble the slavery Europeans were simultaneously imposing upon plantation workers in the New World. ... The comparatively mild character of Turkish slavery was due to the fact that slaves were not valued primarily for the economic usefulness of their labor. Slaves were used instead to satisfy the desire of the upstart Ottoman notables (often slaves themselves) to accumulate a large household of attendants, thus attesting their own personal greatness.[30]

Again in India, "the number of slaves, who were mainly domestic and women, may have added to the personal comforts of the nobles and priests, but it did not affect agricultural production."[31]

Thus, though slavery has been ubiquitous, there have been in all only three economies that can be said to have been slave-based in the sense that slave labor was critical to their functioning. One of these was the ancient Mediterranean. The other two occurred in modern times, as adjuncts to the individualist capitalist system. They were the Caribbean plantations of the seventeenth and eighteenth centuries, producing tropical produce for European markets; and in North America prior to the Civil War, when slave labor grew cotton and tobacco, also for Europe at the height of its Industrial Revolution. Particular circumstances, to be dealt with later, made slavery profitable in the Caribbean and in the antebellum South. Particular circumstances also made it profitable earlier, and for a longer time, in the ancient Mediterranean. In this case, it was the combination of lactose tolerance and limitless arable land which, at the state of the art, yielded cultivators more than a maintenance but less than reproduction needs, that made slavery profitable.

Neither of the two later slave-based economies referred to secured its slaves by conquest. Seventeenth and eighteenth century Caribbean slaveryacquired its slaves, which were kidnapped in Africa, by purchase. The purchases were initially made in Africa for trinkets, but the delivered slaves cost substantially more following their transport across the Atlantic with its attendant costs, including particularly the mortalities incurred during the notorious journey. The imported slaves were bred, but not to an extent that allowed of their full reproduction or an increase in their number. A total of 849,000 slaves were imported into Barbados and Jamaica before the trade was prohibited. At prohibition, the slave population of the islands was 389,000; it declined further, to 320,000, at emancipation in 1834.[32] It was, in a word, cheaper to buy than to breed and rear replacement slaves.

The records of a Jamaican sugar plantation, which continues to exist, tell part, at least, of the story. The birthrate of the plantation's slave population was 19.2 per 1000 in the period 1783–1792. The death rate in the same period was 32.4.[33] But it was a question of economics and not, as Max Weber asserted, biology: "Human beings thrive only in the circle of the family. The slave barracks were unable to reproduce themselves; they depended for their recruitment on the continuous purchase of slaves. . . . The slave estates devoured human beings as the modern blast furnace devours coal."[34] The experience of the antebellum South in the United States, following the ending of the slave trade in 1807, makes this clear. The South's slave population increased by a phenomenal 2 percent annually between then and the abolition of slavery in the U.S. Civil War.[35]

The Limits of Individualist Slavery: The Decline of the Roman Empire

Responding to the basic precept, enslave or be enslaved, ancient Mediterranean society was built on conquest, at which it was supremely efficient. But the conquerors, regarding the use of the fruits of conquest as servile, used them inefficiently. As a result, when the need arose, when further conquest was no longer feasible, the ancient Mediterranean economy was unable to buy sufficient slaves, as the Caribbean plantation agriculture did; or to breed them, as the antebellum South did. The economic challenge of securing sufficient slaves other than by conquest came too at a time of great political turmoil, which exacerbated and in turn was exacerbated by the economic problem.

The limits of territorial expansion were reached almost at the same time as the ultimate concentration of political power within the empire. The last years of the Roman Republic were marked by acute instability as a tiny oligarchy struggled for power, steeping the empire in ruinous civil wars.[36] Rome and the ancient Mediterranean were rescued from unceasing civil war only by concentrating all power into the hands of the Divine Augustus and his successors. Thus, contemporaneously with the cutting off of the supply of slave labor on which the ancient Mediterranean depended economically, the rule of law was replaced by a despotism no different from that of riverine crop-growing or pastoral societies.

Individualism ended in the ancient Mediterranean once the whole of it fell under Rome's despotism. The individual could no longer, by his presence with his slaves, add to the well-being of a society, or detract from it by removing to a different one; for all cities paid taxes to Rome. While the concentration of the stock of wealth continued for some time, the total size of that stock diminished, because the wasting slave population ceased to be replenished through further conquests. The nature of the wealth also changed; for under divine emperors the rule of law ceased, and without it, property became mere privilege, granted or withdrawn at the tyrant's whim. Gibbon, of course, put it more eloquently: "But the empire of the Romans filled the world, and when that empire fell into the hands of a single person, the world became a safe and dreary prison for his ene-

mies. . . . To resist was fatal and it was impossible to fly."[37] The empire nevertheless survived for a few more centuries, sustained by the momentum of its
ancient vigor, until finally, drained demographically, economically, militarily,
and politically, it lay defenseless and exposed to the northern barbarians when
these crossed the frozen Rhine on the last night of the year 406 AD.

Individualist Capitalism

The early lactose tolerant pastoralists in central western Europe, associated particularly with the archaeological sites of Halstatt in Austria and La Tene in
Switzerland, were, even more so than those on the Mediterranean littoral, free
from major indigenous or external influences. They were free to adapt to the
new circumstance of having limitlessly available arable land. But two conditions, in particular, distinguished the opportunities and challenges encountered
in central western Europe from those on the Mediterranean littoral. These were,
as noted, first that the grazing in the region was suitable for cattle, not sheep;
and second, that, at the hoe-cultivator's state of the art, cropgrowing yielded less
than a maintenance for the grower.

Cattle grazing in central western Europe provided a challenge that was unknown to the pastoralists on the Mediterranean or, indeed, to lactose tolerant
pastoralists anywhere else in the world. The gestation period for sheep is five
months and the lactating period is three months. Thus a full cycle, from conception to weaning, can be completed within a growing season. The weaned lamb
and the barren, non-lactating ewe then have a good prospect of surviving the
dormant season.

Because calves cannot survive without milk for the first four or five months
of life, and because cows cannot lactate without adequate feed, they must normally calve early in a seven to eight month growing season. That implies, in
turn, that, since a cow's gestation period is nine months, they must be heavily in
calf for several dormant season months. Gestating a calf during the dormant
season places an almost impossible strain on both dam and fetus. That strain has
traditionally been relieved by pastoralists in two ways. One was to allow the
animals to draw on the fat stored during the growing season's abundance. The
other, more general way, and the only feasible way in harsher, northerly lands, is
by transhumance or nomadism, which is the seasonal movement of stock and
herders from summer to winter grazing areas.

Neither of these traditional means of dealing with dormant season dearth
was generally available to the pastoralists in the forest of central western
Europe. The winters were too long and severe to allow animals, especially heavily pregnant ones, to survive by drawing on fat stored during the growing season. The denseness of the forest—the underlying productivity of which was
what differentiated central western Europe from the steppe—precluded transhumance as a general solution to the problem of winter dearth. The substantial
numbers of cattle required by lactose tolerant pastoralists could only be kept in

the forests of central western Europe by feeding them supplementary fodder in the dormant season. The immigrating Indo-European pastoralists, in central western Europe, had no option but to adopt an innovation that was, and still is, peculiar to them among all the lactose tolerant peoples of the world: that is, to provide supplementary dormant season fodder for their stock.

Though some fodder may have been secured by harvesting the green leaves of trees, the only effective way of securing adequate winter fodder in central western Europe has been from the by-products of crops, supplemented with hay. But while crops were thus essential for the pastoralists in the forest, growing them in central western Europe was, and is, more difficult than anywhere else where crops are extensively grown. Because cropgrowing at the state of the art did not give the cultivator a maintenance, slavery was ruled out. People were free, but free only to starve, if they could not grow crops in the most challenging environment for cropgrowing in the world. The pastoralists' answer was to use their cattle intensively for cropgrowing. In a location where the net return for the seed planted was only one-third as much as on the Mediterranean littoral and only one-ninth as much as in Egypt, the only way to grow the crops that were essential for the survival of cattle was to use large numbers of cattle, to cultivate extensive areas of cleared land, to grow sufficient low-yielding crops, to fodder the cattle through the winter, and to feed the cropgrowers through most of the year.

In order to secure a given amount of grain, it was necessary to sow nine times as much seed in central western Europe as in Egypt, or three times as much as on the Mediterranean littoral. It was also necessary to plough, till, plant, weed, and harvest nine times as much land for the reception of that seed in central western Europe as in Egypt and three times as much as on the Mediterranean littoral. To secure a given crop output then, vastly more seed, more cultivating livestock, and more fodder to support those livestock in winter were needed. The same applied for implements to cultivate and weed the land, carts to gather the sparse harvest, and larger, sturdier barns to shelter the bigger volume of straw but equal volume of grain, against the longer, more severe central European winters.

The Indo-European pastoralists, in the forest of central western Europe, did not use any resource that had not been used before to do anything that had not been done before. But they were forced by circumstances—circumstances that also made these things possible for them—to use these resources in ways and in combinations that had not been used before. It was a question of proportions. The pastoralists who entered the central western European forest some 3,000–4,000 years ago, in order to secure a given output, had to use vastly more resources that had been saved from consumption than other producers. That is to say, they had to use far more capital. This greatly increased capital/output ratio was capitalist production.

It was also individualist capitalist production. Rulers, particularly in riverine economies, frequently used savings to sustain people who labored on hydraulic works to extend or improve the cultivated area. Those savings used in that way were also capital formation. But that capital formation differed in two critical ways from what occurred in central western Europe. First, the hydraulic works in riverine societies were undertaken by rulers; they were the results of decisions by rulers to save and to invest; they were social capitalism. The decisions to rear a calf, to make hay, and to clear and cultivate a patch of arable land were taken by myriads of individuals in central western Europe. They were not taken by rulers. The process was individualist capitalism.

Capital formation in central in central western Europe differed from that in riverine economies and from anything similar in other economies in a second important respect. The amount of capital formation possible in riverine societies was limited, in the final analysis, by the extent of land under command for irrigation. Irrigation canals could not carry water uphill. Thus Egypt for millennia has remained a fifty mile wide strip centered on the Nile River. Land, not capital, continued to restrict output. It was likewise with pastoralists whose output and numbers were limited by the natural carrying capacity of the communally grazed pastures in the dormant season, and not by the number of stock that the pastoralists wished to carry on that pasture. The labor of slaves determined the extent of cultivation, the amount produced, and the number of citizens supported in the ancient Mediterranean. It was different in central western Europe where there was effectively limitless land to which myriads of individuals could apply the capital that they acquired by saving what they had previously produced. Production was limited solely by the stock and productivity of that capital; and in that sense too it was capitalist production.

Individualist capitalism commenced virtually as soon as the lactose tolerant pastoralists left the steppe and entered the forest of central western Europe. For without the fodder produced and saved by the pastoralists—which was capital— the livestock could not have survived the first winter in the forest; and without the livestock, the pastoralists themselves could not have survived to reach a second winter in the forest. Individualist capitalism originated autochthonously in the forest of central western Europe long before there were markets there or production other than for subsistence and before there was money, other than the livestock that have always played the role of money for primitive pastoralists, or bankers, or any of the other paraphernalia commonly associated with capitalism. Once individualist capitalism was created by the conjunction of lactose tolerant pastoralism with the poorly penetrable forest and with abundant arable land of low producing quality, in an environment where individuals could adjust, free from external intervention, the rest depended on the willingness and ability of the mass of the people to save and to invest, with a view, first to securing, and thereafter improving, their condition. If the underlying social law for individualist slavery was enslave or be enslaved, the law for individualist capitalism was save or starve. The operation of that law was a new social force that in time determined not only Europe's, but the world's, future.

Slavery and Capitalism: The Parallels

There were underlying similarities in the responses evoked by the conjunction of lactose tolerance and limitless arable land under Europe's unique circumstances. Those circumstances were isolation from other major food producers and the requirement that the immigrating pastoralists settle in numerous, disparate groups. The similarity of the response was the realization of the potential inherent in the conjunction of lactose tolerance and available arable land. That potential was the much greater surplus of lactose tolerant pastoralists than lactose malabsorbent persons, which enabled them to extend the area cultivated. That extension of cultivation in turn made possible larger populations and scale and external economies. The realization of the potential inherent in the combination of lactose tolerant pastoralists and limitless arable land freed humanity from dependence on the extent and fertility of the land available and the state of the art. It made society dependent instead on the efforts and ingenuity of individuals in extending the cultivated area. That transformation of circumstances, which made people no longer absolutely dependent on socially controlled natural resources, but made society instead dependent on the efforts of individuals to mobilize limitless natural resources, was the emergence of individualism.

The immigrants mobilized the pastoralist surplus in two ways: by slavery and capital. The well-being of society and its members no longer depended on the quantity and quality of natural resources controlled but on the number of slaves, in the one case, and on the amount of capital, in the other. Immigrant pastoralists who successfully adjusted to the different circumstances that existed in Europe survived. Those who failed to do so became extinct. Extinction in the one case was probably hastened by enslavement by better adjusted individuals and, in the other, by submergence in a sea of forest or by absorption into other, better adjusted and expanding islands of population.

Extinction or survival depended in both cases on the acquisition by individuals of assets: slaves in the one case, capital in the other. That, in turn, depended on maximizing both the incentive to individuals to acquire assets and the deterrence for failing to do so. Property was the key institution which made this possible. Property is the recognition by society of society's interest in conferring on individuals exclusive rights to assets and society's willingness and ability to uphold those rights. Property's ultimate sanction was that those European societies which favored its acquisition survived; those which did not disappeared.

Property was a uniquely European, individualist institution, which made possible and evolved in economies that were not natural resource based. Property was significant only because of the elasticity of supply of the assets owned. Societies that enforced property rights encouraged their members to acquire slaves or capital and to operate them efficiently. These societies attracted slave/capital owners from other societies which failed to enforce property rights, or did so less effectively. Societies that enforced property rights also put pressure on individuals to acquire slaves or capital; for without these, which determined output, individuals could at best survive without reproducing themselves in the ancient Mediterranean and could not even survive in the forest of central western Europe.

Property in slaves or capital, while entitling owners to the exclusive use and enjoyment of the property and its produce, was, in a different sense, non-exclusive. It was non-exclusive in the sense that it did not preclude others from acquiring other slaves or capital, which, critically, were in elastic supply. Indeed, the more secure and exclusive were individuals' titles to slaves or capital, the more effective the society was likely to be; and therefore the better circumstanced were other individuals in the society to acquire similar assets.

Property was an uniquely European institution. It did not, and could not, obtain in the nonindividualist, land-based societies of the non-European world. That was because the only scarce resource in that world, to which property could therefore apply, was land and other natural resources. Property in natural resources was, and is, inherently contradictory.

Property, as perceived here, is the recognition by society, in society's superior interest, of the exclusive enjoyment by individuals of particular assets in order to secure an increase in the supply of the assets in question. Property in land cannot increase its supply, if that supply is fixed. Exclusive title to land in a land-based society is in inherent conflict with society's interest. It cannot benefit society. It can be exercised only in spite of, and not with the consent of, society. It is, in that sense, the antithesis of property. An exclusive title to land in a land-based society, established by force or otherwise, disrupts society.

Title to land, except in a particular, limited and non-exclusive sense, cannot contribute to output in a land-based economy where neither labor nor capital limit production. Rather, it is likely to reduce output. The limited, non-exclusive title to land, which is necessary and exists, in all societies, is the prior title of the cultivator or of the pastoralist to that portion of the product necessary for survival. Without such title, land could not be cultivated or livestock tended. But, in the case of cultivators, title applied only to a growth cycle, lasting normally a year or less. The land thereafter reverted to a common pool from which society's members drew such land as they could operate as efficiently as others, to produce as large a social surplus as others. Where the crop cycle lasted longer than a year, as in the case of bananas in Africa or tree crops in Malaya, the planters had title to the fruit while the trees bore; thereafter, the land reverted to the common pool, where it was available to other members of the society for planting.[38]

Pastoralists' titles to livestock have traditionally been vague, diffused, and complex. An individual's title was exclusive only to such part of the produce as was essential for subsistence. It was inconceivable that some could have more, while others in the group had less, than this.[39]

The forms of husbandry and the requirements of society in the non-European world required no more title than this. When, following colonization by European powers, European concepts of property were imposed on much of the non-European world, the results have been invariably socially harmful. The smallholders' rubber trees in Kampong Pasir Salak, in Perak State, Malaya, which were planted at the beginning of this century, have long since ceased to yield and the land has reverted to jungle. But this land, which is among the most fertile in Malaya, is not now available, as it was a century ago, to whoever in the village would plant it. The land now belongs to the heirs and assignees of the original planters, to whom title was given by the colonial power. These are either unable or unwilling to replant the land; but they could be expected to claim both the land and all on it at some time during the forty years after planting when a rubber tree is worth claiming.[40]

Virtually everyone in pre-colonial, tsetse-fly free Africa had a claim to cattle which was nebulous and ill-defined by European standards. For that and other reasons, cattle stocks did not become excessive on the communally grazed pastures. Africa's grazing lands remained productive, supporting cattle which, on good grazing, were also productive, and which in turn maintained a dependent human population in at least relative abundance. One manifestation of that abundance is that Sub-Saharan Africans did not, like Eurasians and North Africans, breed their goats to produce milk, presumably because they got enough of that from their cattle. The result today is that, though Africa has one-third of the world's goat population, those in Sub-Saharan Africa are incapable of yielding milk and are used exclusively for meat. That is so although Africa's much larger present population is now much less well nourished.

Following Western intervention, now typically in African societies that were traditionally cattle keeping and cattle-dependent, 10 percent of the population own 50 percent of the cattle, 40 percent own the other 50 percent, and 50 percent of the population own none and have no title to cattle or their produce.[41] Those with cattle now have the resources and incentives to increase their livestock holdings on land that continues to be grazed communally. For this, among other reasons, the land is overgrazed; the pasture has deteriorated; the cattle are unproductive; the land is frequently eroded; and the desert encroaches. Africa is threatened with mega-famine within a century of Western intervention.

Because, under non-European forms of production, titles to land, which was the only scarce resource, were neither necessary nor desirable, they were established in spite of, and not by, society. They were the antithesis of property. They represented a fragmentation, not a development, of society. That was the character of the title recorded in a fifteenth century ode to O'Reilly of Cavan, in Ireland: "The broadspear in the hand, the weapon from Vulcan's smithy, the sword, that is our charter."[42]

When the surplus was large relative to the area that produced it, society's power was great, as preeminently in the riverine societies of Egypt, China, and South America's Altiplano. Fragmentation was rare and individuals exercised power at the will of rulers who personified society. When cultivation was more extensive and the surplus relative to the area occupied was less, as in India, society's power was also less, fragmentation was common and subordinates could establish claims to land similar to that of O'Reilly. A similar condition obtained in Japan where an archipelagaic topography impeded the exercise of central authority. Numerous daimyos, as a result, had a title to local patches of productive land, which they defended against the encroachments of neighboring lords.

Titles to land, which was the only production-limiting resource in the non-European world, were fundamentally different from European titles of property in slaves or capital. Non-European property titles were established in spite of, and not with the sanction of, society. They represented a fragmentation of society. They were exclusive in that they denied access to land, except on the title-holder's terms. Titles to land, being neither necessary nor desirable for production, were held by potentates, who were great, like the rajahs of India and the daimyos of Japan, or less, like O'Reilly, a clan chief in pre-Tudor Ireland. Land titles were not held by producers in the non-European world. Property in slaves and capital in Europe, on the other hand, was established and sustained by society as a condition of its existence and well-being. Its owners operated that property.

Land in the forum in the ancient Mediterranean, or close to protecting castles in central western Europe, which was scarce and therefore valued, was also owned; it was individuals' property. But most of Europe's land was free for those with the slaves or capital to operate it. As indicated above, only a tenth of the territory was cultivated at the height of the Roman empire. Most of central western Europe's land was waste until the nineteenth century.[43] A foremost objective of the EEC's Common Agricultural Policy (CAP) now is the "extensification" of land use and the removal of land from production—"set-aside"—in order to reduce unwanted food surpluses.

Humanity progressed by natural selection. Groups that adopted and adapted appropriate technology and institutions survived and expanded. Others which failed to do so contracted and disappeared from history. The innovation of using food to produce future food, rather than for immediate consumption, was one of a number of critical steps in humanity's evolutionary course. Food production, by making it possible for many more to survive, accelerated the pace of innovation and adaptation, and so of human progress.

All of that progress was societal. It was societal in the sense that society had created the conditions where the next critical step was taken. Even if that step were taken by a single individual, as in the case of the first seed sown and the first feral female sheep or goat deliberately mated, it cannot have been taken with a view to the exclusive enjoyment of the fruits of successful innovation. If the seed was reproduced manifold, all the gatherers could gather the crop; if the feral sheep or goat had offspring, the bred animal and its progeny were hunted/husbanded by the group. Individual innovation was even less relevant in the evolution through natural selection of lactose tolerant races or in the adoption of caste and the apotheosis of the cow in India.

These nonindividualist, land-based societies progressed slowly, in Toynbeesque cycles. Conditions hardly changed perceptibly between similar points on successive cycles, even though these may have been separated by centuries or millennia. A phase of poor game would be followed by one of more abundant game when the hunter-gatherers would eat better, have lower mortality rates, and increase in numbers. Their added numbers would contribute to a fall in game stocks, with poorer hunting, lower nutrition, higher mortality, and declining population. After innumerable similar cycles, the Stone Age hunter-gatherers of Papua New Guinea now lead a life that is not perceptibly different from that suggested by the archaeological remains of other hunter-gathering societies that existed tens of thousands of years ago. Likewise Egypt, China, and the civilizations of pre-Columbian America had their rises and declines, but up to modern times remained unchanged in all essential respects from what they had been millennia earlier.

Individualism, as it emerged in Europe following the interaction of lactose tolerance and available arable land, generated new forces and new motivations in human affairs which enormously accelerated the evolutionary process. The conditions that gave rise to individualism freed humanity from its dependence on its natural resource base. The conditions in question made human well-being dependent instead on labor, in the case of individualist slavery, and on the saved produce of labor in the case of individualist capitalism. Individualism, in addition to mobilizing in humanity's service two new resources—labor and capital— also created new motivations for the use of those resources. These were the hopes and fears of individuals whose well-being depended on their possession and effective use of these resources. The institution of property, which was the core of individualism, differentiated the individual's fate from society's. The individual might perish though the society of which he was a member prospered. Equally, the individual could prosper though society suffered. Indeed, because the individual owner of slaves or capital could shift with his property to another, welcoming society, he might prosper though the abandoned society failed.

Individualism liberated humanity from its gregariousness and gave scope to its rationality. It made it possible for truth to be "acquired in a planned orderly way, by an individual, not slowly gathered up by a herd."[44] It made the individual, and not the herd, a potential innovator; and it intensified manifold the pressures for innovation. Individualism caused the replacement of natural selection by purposeful selection. The condition of individualist Europe became dependent on the efforts of myriads of individuals pursuing their individual interests, instead of society evolving acephalously in response to conditions as they arose. That was the great, original fountain spring of individualist dynamics. Tapping the fountain spring caused a change in tempo and a major acceleration in the rate of change of the human condition.

Slavery and Capitalism: The Contrasts

There were, as well as fundamental similarities in the response of migrating, lactose tolerant pastoralists to the availability of limitless arable land in Europe, important dissimilarities in the manner of response to the very different circumstances encountered in southern and in central western Europe. These dissimilarities cast additional light on the nature of individualism.

Southern Europe was a more favorable environment for migratory pastoralists than central western Europe. The pastoralists who reached the Mediterranean littoral, responding to the changing character of the grazing over which they passed, would have changed the composition of their livestock en route. They would not therefore have encountered at their destination any major problem in sustaining their sheep flocks over dormant winter seasons. The problem of keeping substantial numbers of cattle alive in the forest through long, hard, northern winters was, on the other hand, an immediate, major, and unprecedented one for the westward moving pastoralists.

Crop returns, at the state of the art, on the Mediterranean littoral were at the critical level of yielding insufficient for the cultivator's reproduction. If yields had been sufficient, all the arable land would have been cultivated, as in Egypt or China, and none would have been available for the immigrants. Yet the returns were more than sufficient for the cultivator's maintenance, which made slavery profitable. Yields at the higher, central western European latitudes were below the critical level of maintaining the cultivator at the state of the art. Slavery was therefore not an option. Capital formation was the only alternative means of extensively cultivating land, which was essential for wintering the cattle on which the immigrating pastoralists depended.

The immigrating pastoralists mingled on the Mediterranean littoral with an indigenous Phoenician people who were seagoing traders. The result was a synthesis comparable to that between the Aryans and Dravidians in India. The blended people, under the distinctive Mediterranean conditions, were able to profit from enslaving later waves of immigrating pastoralists. They were then able to extend the area of cultivated land without limit other than the supply of enslaved pastoralists. No commingling occurred in central western Europe between the indigenous, swidden farmers, whose circumstances must have been extremely bleak, and the incoming pastoralists. Or if it did, it left no permanent record as did that between the Phoenicians and pastoralists on the Mediterranean. The immigrating pastoralists had to adapt, on their own, in an essentially organic manner, to the entirely new conditions of Europe's forests. Adaptation occurred in central western Europe in the absence of the acute pressures to enslave or be enslaved that were the rule of life on the Mediterranean. But the pressure to adapt was equally acute, equally real. Those who failed to adapt successfully, by saving and investing, though not enslaved, starved.

The pastoralists who moved southwards to the Mediterranean and commingled with the indigenous Phoenicians, as well as changing the composition of their livestock en route, also changed directly from nomadic pastoralists to urban dwellers. It took millennia of individualist capitalist development in central western Europe before the majority of the population there were also urbanized. Meanwhile, the vast majority of central western Europe's population remained as rural as their pastoral ancestors on the steppe.

The central feature of the slow, organic adaptation in the forest was saving and capital formation, without which life in the forest would have been impossible for the pastoralists. The amount that the pastoralists could have saved must have been minuscule and their development correspondingly painfully slow. That contrasted with the meteoric development of the pastoralist/Phoenician synthesis on the Mediterranean littoral, which was governed only by the ability to enslave later waves of pastoralists from the steppes of Eurasia.

The pastoralist on the Mediterranean acquired new, or expanded old, roles. He became the absolute owner of property, which he had not been on the steppe. He needed to become more of a warrior, first to resist enslavement and second to capture the slaves necessary for his reproduction. (This was not unlike the situation in Sub-Sahelian Africa where the male population were necessarily primarily warriors, defending their own and raiding their neighbors' cattle.) It followed from his status as property-owner and warrior that the Mediterranean individual was also a citizen of the polis or civis. His relationship to society was governed by law, which is a more or less explicit corpus that determines relations between individuals and society.

The immigrant pastoralists in the central western European forest shed, rather than acquired, roles. Unlike his ancestors among the Golden Hordes of the steppe, who were required to help defend scarce, dormant season, grazing rights against other encroaching hordes, the pastoralist in central western Europe depended primarily on the forest for protection. Residual defense needs were met by a specialist warrior class while the bulk of the population perforce concentrated on the unremitting toil that was necessary for survival in the forest. This relationship was expressed subsequently by the medieval aphorism: "the priest prays, the knight defends, and the peasant works."

The immigrant pastoralist of necessity became a proprietor in the central western European forest as in the Mediterranean littoral. But the process was less dramatic and more organic. Central western European society was never dichotomized into property-owners and property-less as was Mediterranean society. The recognized title which all pastoralists had to a prior claim to their stock's produce was strengthened in the forest to exclude others' claim to share that produce. New titles were recognized in new products as the condition of their production. No one made hay unless he/she could retain it to fodder his/her cattle in the winter; and if people were unable to make hay, they perished or moved to where they could.

The need for winter fodder made property essential for pastoralist society in the forest, while the absence of that need makes property disastrous for pastoralist society outside the forest. Exclusive title to the produce of livestock on the communally grazed land of Africa and Asia, introduced under western colonialism, provides the incentive and means to those who, for one reason or another have stock, to acquire more, and to do so without limit other than the destruction through overstocking of the pasture and ultimately of the society that depends on it.[45]

Formal, explicit, written law came much later in central western Europe than in the precocious ancient Mediterranean. But because property in what people produced, saved, and used for further production was as essential in central western Europe as was property in captive slaves in the ancient Mediterranean, the one form of property existed as certainly as the other, and both from the beginning of pastoralist immigration to Europe. Only formal recognition of property rights, which were always essential for society's existence in Europe, came slowly and organically in central western Europe, while it necessarily came early in the ancient Mediterranean, if the individual were to be a slave owner rather than a slave.

Conquest was the condition of survival and success in the ancient Mediterranean. The conqueror enslaved the conquered. Individuals who, by military prowess, rhetoric, or philosophy, contributed to an organization of society that made conquest possible and that secured the results of conquest for the conquerors were esteemed and elevated by society. Those were the qualities which brought success to individuals in the ancient Mediterranean.

Frugality, which yielded savings, the prudent investment of savings (such as the choice of the right calf to rear, or the right piece of land to clear and cultivate in the right manner), and the assiduous attendance to the invested savings by labor, which would have been regarded as servile in the ancient Mediterranean, were the qualities needed, not merely for success, but for survival, in central western Europe. They were qualities conducive to the advance in tandem of capital accumulation and technological progress in the use of that capital for production. The qualities needed for survival and success in central western Europe evolved organically, through magic, mystery, and alchemy, towards science.

The brilliant attainments of the ancient Mediterranean were made possible by working to death the enslaved products of Eurasian pastoralism. Ancient Mediterranean society, notwithstanding its magnificent achievements in law, politics, philosophy, the humanities, and military prowess, at no time escaped from its parasitic dependence on the captive, unrequited labor of others.

While the pool of ancient Mediterranean slaves could be maintained and expanded only by conquest, the stock of capital could be increased only by saving. Individuals might increase their stock by appropriation; but that appropriation did not add to the total stock. Rather, by discouraging saving, it probably reduced it. Individualist capitalism was, therefore, self-reliant in the sense that the maintenance of the capital stock, on which society's existence depended, or the expansion of the stock, on which society's progress depended, were possible only by the savings of the proprietors of capital.

The inherently parasitic nature of individualist slavery and the inherently self-reliant nature of individualist capitalism gave a different dynamic to Europe's two forms of individualism. Individualist slavery required conquest and expansion to maintain its wasting labor supply. Expansion took it away from the Mediterranean littoral and the conditions which made individualist slavery necessary and possible. As institutions and technologies that evolved in one environment were extended to another, different one, they became less effective and less productive. Inherently parasitic individualist slavery was, in this sense, also inherently subject to diminishing long term returns.

Individualist capitalism depended on saving and technological progress. The greater the stock of capital and the pool of technological knowledge, the greater the amount of saving and of further technological progress that was possible. These in turn made possible further scale and external economies. Individualist capitalism was, in this sense, of an inherently accelerating character. These aspects of individualist capitalism are the subject of the next chapter.

Chapter 4

The Growth of Individualist Capitalism

The Economics of Individualist Capitalism

An Inhospitable Environment

Central western Europe was the last part of the Old World to be populated densely. It remains the furthest part of the earth from the equator that is densely populated. It was, in several respects, an inhospitable environment for those Indo-European pastoralists who strayed into it from the open Eurasian steppe. Tacitus described it 2,000 years ago as "a land that is thankless to till and dismal to behold for anyone who was not born and bred there. . . . It is covered either by bristling forests or by foul swamps."[1] As Professor Koebner put it: "We must think of some four-fifths of the land covered with forest and swamp."[2] The inhospitality accounts for the slow development of the individualism that emerged there, in contrast to the meteoric rise of a precocious individualism in the ancient Mediterranean.

The Indo-European pastoralists who moved into the forests of central western Europe, of all migrating pastoralists, found no numerous, indigenous people whose wealth they might plunder or genius they might share. The Mongols tapped the wealth of China; the Aryans the wealth of Dravidian India; the Scythians the cities of Mesopotamia; the Nilo-Hamites the Bantu cropgrowers; the Arabs the wealth of the oases and of the Nile valley; while the cousins of the Indo-Europeans who migrated toward the Mediterranean encountered and profited from the Phoenicians. The only indigenes of the cold, forbidding northern forest were swidden farmers, little removed from sparse hunting-gathering.

Though the great plain of central western Europe was more arable than any other area of similar extent, it was arable of the poorest quality. That is, with the prevailing hoe-type cultivation, it yielded insufficient return for the cultivator's maintenance, much less his reproduction. Its gross return of two grains per grain sown was only a fifth that of contemporary Egypt. The return net of seed was only one-ninth. Cropgrowing in primeval central western Europe must have been comparable to cereal-growing in Botswana in southern Africa now. The yield there is around 300 kg./hectare, compared to around four times as much for Africa as a whole, and eight times as much for the world as a whole.[3] The Botswana yield is about twice the amount needed to sow the land, as it was in primeval central western Europe also. But whereas Botswana now can engage in a small amount of cropgrowing because of its great wealth from diamond mining, the Indo-European pastoralists had no way of supplementing the meager and uncertain yield of crops on which their own existence and that of their livestock depended absolutely.

Enslaving later arrivals from the steppe was not an easy source of wealth, as it was on the ancient Mediterranean littoral. That was because the enslaved pastoralists would not, in central western Europe at the state of the art, have yielded a profit over their unavoidable maintenance cost.

The immigrating pastoralists could cope only by using the surplus they secured from their cattle, which had been dissipated on the steppe, to conserve winter fodder. Their own numbers, like all pastoralists, were determined by their stock numbers. But uniquely, in central western Europe, the number of livestock, and hence the number of pastoralists, was determined by the amount of winter fodder preserved. That depended on the amount of hay made and crops grown, which in turn depended on the existing stock of cattle, on seed to sow the land, and so forth. All these things, on which production depended critically in central western Europe, were things that had already been produced but not consumed. They were savings that were used for further production. They were capital, on which the extensive but cold, unproductive arable land of central western Europe was more dependent than any other land used for food production.

The only way to secure the capital on which the pastoralists' existence depended in central western Europe, in the absence of wealthy indigenes to plunder or slaves to produce it, was by saving. If one individual or group added to their capital by taking from others, the total capital stock was not increased, merely redistributed. Moreover, because the act of taking or confiscation increased risk and uncertainty, it also probably reduced saving and investment, and therefore the total capital stock. Saving for people newly arrived from the steppe and forced to adjust to a new and, in many ways, inhospitable environment and living at subsistence levels, must have been enormously difficult and painfully slow. The process was the antithesis of the meteoric rise of the ancient Mediterranean, propelled as that was by the synthesis of Indo-European shepherds and Phoenician cropgrowing-seafaring-traders, and then fuelled by a virtually inexhaustible supply of slaves produced by the Eurasian steppe.

The complex interrelationships involved are misunderstood by Brenner, among others, when he writes pertaining to early central European agriculture: "the inability to invest in animals for plowing and as a source of manure led to deterioration of soil, which in turn led to the extension of cultivation to land formerly reserved for the support of animals."[4] Without more cattle, there could be no more land tilled. Without more tillage to provide winter fodder, there could be no more cattle. With saving, and only with saving, cattle and tillage could be extended without limit into the surrounding forest with its underlying arable land.

But if the physical conditions in central western Europe were less inviting than in any other region of major human population in the world, there was latent potential there too. That potential was to be realized by the arrival of lactose tolerant pastoralists, who could derive far more nutrition from their cattle than the wretched, lactose malabsorbent, swidden farmers who preceded them. That additional nutrition, used to cultivate the limitless arable land, produced the wealth which, when saved, became the capital that transformed first Europe and then the world.

The deciduous forest of central western Europe, which had forced out the tundra, the reindeer, and the hunter-gatherers and which made pastoralism so difficult also, did provide conditions that were favorable to innovation to cope with those difficulties. The forest, though cold and naturally unproductive, did not shelter the trypanosomiasis-bearing tsetse fly which was endemic in most of the tropical forest of the Old World and was fatal to cattle. Although the warm soil under Africa's forest was sufficiently productive to maintain and even reproduce the hoe cultivators of yams and plantains, the forest also harbored the tsetse fly, so cattle had to be excluded until the land was first cleared by cropgrowers. Europe's tsetse-free forests, on the other hand, could be entered and occupied by pastoralists without first being cleared by cropgrowers.

The pastoralists who broke from the steppe horde to venture into the forest changed their character *ab initio*. They necessarily formed the small bands which could percolate with their cattle through the forest. Many such bands probably entered, but dependent substantially as they must have been on the sparse returns from hunting gathering and forest grazing, their early settlements must have been small and scattered, "islands of settlement embedded in the mighty forests."[5] That had two important consequences, each of which was conducive to the emergence of a new way of life.

First, as with the shepherds on the Mediterranean littoral, the fact that there were numerous, disparate settlements increased the probability of some of them successfully adapting to the new conditions. Second was the protection which the forest afforded. The forest, by precluding general transhumance, created the critical challenge of providing for winter dearth; but it also reduced mobility by hostile elements and left the settlers substantially free to cope with the difficult problems of adjusting to a new and naturally difficult environment. That contrasted with the situation in Sub-Sahelian Africa where, because of the tsetse fly, cattle had to be held in the open, forcing the male cattle keepers to be primarily warriors, defending their own and raiding their neighbors' exposed cattle. Additionally the pastoralists themselves, unlike those on the Mediterranean littoral, were valueless as slaves and had no need therefore to resist enslavement.

Finally, the Indo-European pastoralists were much better equipped to cope with central western Europe's forest than the swidden farmers who preceded them. They were, for one thing, expert in metallurgy, which they had learned about on the steppe. Demand for metals first emerged in the cities of Mesopotamia and Egypt. Ironically, the deep alluvium on which these cities and their civilization rested buried the bedrock in which metals lay.[6] Of necessity, they imported their metals. Most of these came from the north and the barbarians, in supplying the metal demand of the ancient civilizations, became skilled metallurgists:

"Copper and tin shaped the penetration of Europe . . . because these commodities were needed and were only available in [the advanced civilizations of] the near east in small quantities. Europe was the major primary producer of the ancient metallurgical world and also a major manufacturer . . . [the European peoples'] importance in history was to be that they would provide the stocks which would receive the impress of civilization later. At least in their metallurgy, the ancient Europeans serviced other civilizations' needs."[7]

First they worked copper ores. Then they added tin to the copper to make the much stronger bronze. But this required ores from usually distant deposits to be brought together. The breakthrough that made the Indo-European pastoralists invincible was the discovery of iron smelting, apparently "south of the Caucasus by the legendary tribe of Chalybes in the fifteenth century B.C."[8]

Their ability to smelt iron, which was an abundant and relatively low cost metal, was especially important for clearing the forest and for cultivating extensively the hard underlying soils. Possession of iron was one of the key factors that also enabled the Bantus, somewhat later, to colonize most of Sub-Sahelian Africa in a very short time. But skill in metallurgy would have been insufficient to bring the forest into production without lactose tolerance, which enabled the pastoralists to derive much more nutrition from their cattle than their lactose malabsorbent, swidden farmer forerunners.

A small minority of genetically deviant swidden farmers would also have been lactose tolerant mutants. But that mutation would have been no advantage in the forest, unlike on the steppe. Insofar as it encouraged mutants to attempt to divert the tightly limited, fixed supply of winter fodder derived from grazing to supporting milk production rather than draught cattle, it would have reduced total food production. Because the lactose tolerant mutant swidden farmers were a small minority, they could not have altered social practices, including especially making the provision of winter fodder the priority it must have been for the totally lactose tolerant, highly cattle-dependent, Indo-Europeans. The deviant lactose tolerant, swidden farmer of central western Europe who attempted to make hay as winter fodder for his milch cows would have received little sympathy from his normal, lactose malabsorbent fellows who had no desire or need for milk, or for hay to keep more cattle alive during the winter.

Winter Fodder

The compelling need of the Indo-European pastoralists in central western

Europe to provide winter fodder had a catalytic effect that changed utterly their way of life. First, meeting that need required a decisive break from the communalism of the steppe to a forest individualism. The naturally fittest stock survived the dormant season on the communally grazed steppe. Individual effort by stock keepers had little or no effect on which, or how many, animals survived. Every surviving animal reduced the survival chances of the others. The surviving stock, like the land they grazed communally, was therefore also primarily a communal or social asset in which individuals had sufficient title to foster sufficient husbandry for tending the grazing animals, but no more. Beyond that, the stock's produce, in meat, milk, or hides, was, like the land and the stock itself, largely communal. Individuals may have had a prior claim to the produce, but not an exclusive one.

Stock survival in the winter in the forest depended on fodder and shelter, which, unlike the steppe's communal grazing, were provided by the efforts of individual stockowners. Archaeological excavations at Parleberg in eastern Germany have revealed "substantial timber structures housing stock, fodder and food supplies" dating from c. 1000 BC. Similar structures at Elp "are of great interest for they were to become the norm in northern European settlements from the late Bronze Age down to the Middle Ages and beyond."[9]

While the livestock of each individual owner competed for that owner's limited fodder and shelter, the stock of different owners did not compete for these. If more of one owner's stock survived because he had more fodder, that did not reduce the survival chances of others' stock, as it would have done on the steppe. Likewise if more of an individual's stock perished in the winter, that did not enhance the survival prospects for the stock of others, which depended exclusively on the amount of fodder and shelter provided by those others. Indeed in the forest, so far from others gaining/losing, they tended rather to lose/gain by the death/survival of the stock of others That was because of the scale and external economies achieved by capital—including livestock—when land was effectively limitless. The more livestock belonging to the members of a community that survived the winter, the more productive was the community and the individuals comprising it. Greater productivity made it possible for each individual, *inter alia*, to harvest more fodder for the next winter. Land, including summer grazing and meadowing, being effectively limitless, the limit to the amount of fodder preserved was the labor and equipment required to produce the fodder. With limitless land, the crops grown or the hay saved by one individual, so far from curtailing, enhanced the capacity of others in the group to grow more crops and to save more hay.

These altered circumstances changed also fundamental social relations. The well-being of the group and its members ceased to depend on the extent and fertility of the grazing land that was controlled. It depended instead on the crops grown, on the fodder saved and on the shelter provided by individuals to sustain and protect themselves and their livestock in the long, hard winters. The critically important thing for society on the steppe was to maintain numbers, who would defend the group's territory and secure its limited winter grazing. That was best achieved by ensuring that none had insufficient food to survive while others had an abundance. The critically important thing for society in the forest was to enable individuals to conserve as much food and fodder as possible to cope with winter dearth and to provide shelter for man and beast against the winter weather. That could most effectively be achieved by maximizing the incentive to grow crops, conserve fodder, and build shelter, as well as the penalty for failing to do so. That implied recognizing and defending the exclusive title to the crops grown, the fodder saved, and the shelter built by those responsible. It implied, more fundamentally, recognition of the exclusive title to, or property in, the capital which was the sine qua non of cropgrowing and livestock husbandry in central western Europe. Individuals ceased to have even the significance that they had as defenders of the group's grazing on the steppe. They acquired significance instead as the possessors of capital—and only as the possessors of capital—which, through external and scale economies, could expand total production disproportionately and so enhance the group's well-being and security.

Groups or societies that effectively secured for individuals property, which was the capital that determined output, tended to be successful. Their own members' saving, capital formation, and production were facilitated; and they attracted others with capital who, by their presence and through scale and external economies, increased output disproportionately. Savings were less or nonexistent when conditions were less favorable; capital may have been consumed instead of increased; and some of those with capital may have decamped, to create new settlements in the limitless forest, or to join existing settlements more favorably disposed to capital formation where, with their capital, they would have been welcome. In an environment where the margin between progress and retrogression normally was slight, it was easy either to kill the goose that laid the golden eggs, or to cause it to fly to another, welcoming, less hostile location.

The unique need for the Indo-European pastoralists to provide fodder in the forests of central western Europe gave rise to a unique and uniquely productive cattle husbandry. The cattle of all lactose tolerant pastoralists, other than Europeans, are of *Bos indicus* type, which lactate only in the presence of their live calves. The unique and critical need for winter fodder for cattle in the forest impacted importantly on this genetic characteristic of the cattle entering the forest. The inherent scarcity of winter fodder necessitated choice in its allocation. Cattle/fodder owners were forced to decide every autumn to which of their cattle they should allocate the limited fodder, which was insufficient to carry through the winter all the cattle that survived easily during the growing season. Inevitably they chose to retain the animals that produced the most draught power, milk or meat, and they slaughtered and consumed the balance. In doing this they introduced an element of selection that no other pastoral people exercised. Livestock on communal pastures elsewhere survived on the residual grazing left in the dormant season; and the criterion of their survival was their natural fitness and not their productivity. Purposeful selection of the animals retained to share the scarce winter fodder led, over time, to the evolution in central western Europe of cattle that worked, milked, and fattened better than any other cattle.

As cattle were selected for their milking and other qualities rather than naturally selected by their ability to survive, the dominant *Bos indicus* characteristic of refusing to let down milk in the absence of the cow's live calf regressed and was replaced by the *Bos taurus* characteristic of lactating with or without the dam's live calf at foot. This made possible the selection at birth of the calves required to maintain or expand the milking and working herds, and the slaughter of the balance. That in turn avoided the sort of waste that occurs in India now, where 20 million calves are reared annually as a necessary condition of inducing their *Bos indicus* dams to milk, and in the process consume a substantial proportion of the little milk produced by cows selected by the survival of the fittest. In the second year of their lives, when cattle are most valuable in the West but when the young Indian cattle are no longer needed to induce their *Bos indicus* dams to lactate, the ten million of them which are surplus to replacement requirements of necessity are allowed to perish.[10]

The emergence of the *Bos taurus* characteristic in European cattle also heightened the capitalist character of production there. Rearing calves was a condition of lactation for the *Bos indicus* cows of other pastoralists. No choice, no saving, and therefore no capital formation was involved for them in forgoing milk consumption in order to rear calves. But saving and choice were involved in rearing *Bos taurus* calves. Given that the cows lactated in the absence of their live calves, each calf reared was at the expense of milk that might otherwise have been consumed by the cow owner or his family.

The danger that the immigrating, lactose tolerant Aryans would use their pastoral resources to produce milk at the expense of draught services, which would have reduced the total amount of food produced, has been discussed above in relation to India. That danger was avoided in India by the apotheosis of the cow which, while yielding abundant draught animals, has done so at great cost. Part of that cost has been a chronic tendency towards overstocking, and another part has been the loss of a valuable source of animal protein because of the taboo on beef eating. A similar danger never existed in Europe because of the need there for winter fodder, which did not obtain in India. The immediate, inescapable need for winter fodder implied that a choice had to be made at all times between consuming more milk now or forgoing draught services to sustain future milk production. More milk for present and future consumption could have been got by omitting to rear male calves for draught. Livestock owners who failed to rear replacement males for the draught herd quickly failed also to grow sufficient crops to feed themselves and to fodder their cattle. Europe could not, therefore, have become a land of milk and meat but of few crops and few people, like Africa. There was no need in Europe for the effective but costly apotheosis of the cow, which prevented India from becoming another Africa.

To summarize then, conditions that were in large part the result of keeping cattle in the forest of central western Europe gave rise to external economies that enabled the Indo-European pastoralists there to use their cattle more effectively than any other cattle keepers. These were:

i) because the forest sheltered themselves and their cattle, they were able to use these for draught, unlike Africans;

ii) because winter fodder was essential, there was no need to
    apotheosize cows, so they could eat their cattle, unlike South
    Asians;

iii) because their cattle were of *Bos taurus* type, they needed to rear
    only the most productive calves for herd replacement, unlike all
    other lactose tolerant pastoralists; and

iv) because they were lactose tolerant, they milked their cattle, unlike
    east and southeast Asians and Egyptians.

Moreover, unlike the inhabitants of the pre-Colombian New World, Europeans, like other Old World people, did have cattle—but cattle which they alone of all the human race milked, worked, and ate.

One further major advantage followed indirectly from the need to provide winter fodder for cattle in central western Europe. Even when cattle were foddered in the dormant season, milk production slumped. That was a serious concern for pastoralists whose diet consisted largely of milk and its derivatives. There were various ways of preserving milk so that its food value could be conserved after the liquid would have soured and decayed. The most common means of doing this was to turn milk into butter in temperate climates, or into butter's equivalent, gee, in warm climates. But butter or gee only preserved the fat content, which is only about a third of the total solids in milk. The solids-non-fat, comprising the nutritionally valuable protein and minerals, were not preserved. Various cheese-making processes, which depend on simple fermentation and which are ubiquitous among pastoralists, do preserve some of the solids-non-fat. But these cheeses are soft and short-lived. Much the most effective means of conserving the nutrients from the abundant but highly perishable milk produced during the growing season for consumption in the dormant season is by converting the milk into hard cheese. But this requires a complex chemical process for which the enzyme rennet is essential. While there are many sources of rennet, much the most effective one comes from the fourth stomach, or vell, of suckling calves. But killing a calf to get its stomach causes *Bos indicus* cows to cease to lactate, leaving the pastoralist with the means of preserving milk, but without milk to preserve. Only European pastoralists, with their *Bos taurus* cows, which continue to lactate when their calves are killed, have therefore traditionally been able to make the hard cheeses which most efficiently conserve milk nutrients.

Other External Economies

The changes in the lives of the immigrating pastoralists required and made possible by the forest opened an Aladdin's cave of external and scale economies. Some of these, which were associated particularly with the compelling need to provide winter fodder for their livestock, have been mentioned. But there were other important ones also.

Technology

Technological progress was particularly favored by the individualist capitalism of central western Europe. The capital, on which production depended to an altogether exceptional extent, had constantly to be renewed and, if possible, increased by myriads of individuals. Each of these had a compelling reason to seek new, more productive forms of capital into which to direct his or her savings, and new ways of using that constantly renewed capital. The most obvious, and possibly most important, instance of this technological progress was breeding from the most productive cattle, which was possible only for Europe's pastoralists with their *Bos taurus* cows. But every individual capitalist producer in central western Europe had an incentive and opportunity, which did not exist in the non-European, collectivist, land-based economies, to seek technological improvement across the whole range of investment decisions and production activities. "Progress was attained by thousands of forgotten tinkers and craftsmen, often replicating each other, many of them wasting their creative energy in the fruitless pursuit of alchemy and other dead ends. . . . It was carried out by peasants, wheelwrights, masons, silversmiths, miners and monks."[11]

Neither did those incentives or opportunities for technological progress in production exist in the ancient Mediterranean. Production there was undertaken by slaves and by persons who failed to progress from servile production into more rewarding military or political activities. These producers had neither the incentive nor the capacity to improve production methods. Thus, while southern Europe progressed in the arts, rhetoric, and military skills, central western Europe progressed in production technology, based on the interested practice and observation of the producers, which lead on, through craftsmanship, to science.

Not all technology originated in central western Europe. China, for example, contributed such major items as paper, gunpowder, and silk. Islam pioneered power and chemical technologies, as well, of course, as Arabic numbers.[12] But central western Europe, far more readily and more widely than elsewhere, adopted innovation from whatever source. Technological innovation fed on technological innovation. The more there was, the greater the productivity of capital, the more saving/capital formation that was possible; and the more capital formation and economic growth, the more opportunity there was for profitable innovation.

Political conditions too were uniquely favorable to technological innovation in individualist capitalist central western Europe. Those polities thrived, expanded, and dominated where capital was most abundant and productive. The polity that was non-receptive to innovation risked succumbing to others which, because they were more innovative, could generate more capital and more productive capital.

Nevertheless, life was as precarious in central western Europe as elsewhere. Capital too was liable to destruction in the hegemonic struggles that were to be an integral part of the individualist, capitalist, central western European scene for millennia. But technological progress could not be undone. When war, famine, or disease had wrought their havoc, people did not have to commence again from the beginning. Former skills, knowledge, and understanding survived. Individualist capitalist Europe, through the centuries, recovered repeatedly from frightful destruction. Never was the destruction as complete or the subsequent recovery as dramatic as during and after the Second World War.

Demography

Possession of capital was the condition of life in central western Europe, as was the possession of slaves in the ancient Mediterranean, and as was access to land in the non-European world. Labor on its own had no value and quickly perished. Whether by patrimony, matrimony, or parsimony, acquiring the capital without which life was impossible in central western Europe took time, and marriage and procreation were necessarily delayed until it was achieved. No such impediment to marriage and procreation existed in non-European, land-based societies, where young individuals, as members of the group, had access to land. In the ancient Mediterranean, the enslavement of a barbarian immigrant made marriage and reproduction possible for the enslaver. The well known west European phenomenon of delayed marriages and a higher incidence of people who never married caused lower birthrates and correspondingly lower death rates.[13] With fewer births and deaths, people lived longer and therefore more productive lives, with a smaller share of the total product being pre-empted to support fewer unproductive pregnant, parturating, suckling, and young people.

Nevertheless, population grew half as rapidly again in central western Europe as elsewhere (see table 4.1). Although births were fewer, deaths were fewer still. Although the natural environment was difficult, enriched with capital, the region, though containing less than 2 percent of the world's land area, supported a higher proportion of its population from an early time.

Table 4.1. Population 1 AD and 1600 AD
(millions)

	World	Total Europe	C.W. Europe
1 AD	170	31	10
1600 AD	545	100	48
Increase	3.21 times	3.23 times	4.80 times

Source: C. McEvedy and R. Jones, *Atlas of World Population History* (London: Penguin. 1978).

Population growth everywhere, by allowing greater division of labor, facilitated technological improvement, which in turn made possible further population growth. That growth, outside Europe, was always contained in the first instance by the fixed quantity and quality of land and, in the second instance, by the slow, societal improvement in technology, even among large populations.

Neither of these constraints obtained in central western Europe. The critical constraint there, which was capital, was relaxed by saving; and population growth implied that there were more individuals endeavoring more effectively—because of greater division of labor—to raise capital's productivity.

There was another advantage which accrued solely to central western Europe. Growth in the stock of capital, which allowed population growth in central western Europe, enabled that capital to be used more productively through the scale economies that exist when land is non-limiting. Thus ten oxen yoked to a single massive plough did more than ten times as much work as one ox pulling a small plough; and they did it better, because they ploughed deeper, bringing up fresher soil and burying weeds and trash deeper. The produce of two ten-oxen teams in a district was more than twice as valuable as that of a single ten-oxen team; because only a slightly longer, broader, higher barn was needed to shelter the produce of both teams; and only a slightly larger mill, but the same miller, would have been required to mill it. The total cost of roads, bridges, and canals was only slightly affected by the amount of traffic they carried, so the more traffic, the lower the unit cost.

The margin between production and the requirements for subsistence must have been pathetically narrow for the pastoralists as they moved from the Asian steppe into central western Europe. Those who secured that margin survived and possibly prospered; those who did not secure the margin disappeared. But like the slave-based production of the ancient Mediterranean, capital-based production in central western Europe had its own distinctive dynamic, which was very different from the cycles of hunting-gathering, riverine crop-growing, and pastoral economies which resulted in long term stasis. Capital, in a situation where land and people were effectively limitless, was subject to increasing returns. That is, in any particular situation, the more capital there was, the more productive that capital tended to be. This gave an inherently accelerating character to individualist capitalist growth.

There were, in addition to these scale economies, other, external economies associated with capital formation. The more capital that was accumulated, the more people who could be supported. The more like-minded, capital-using people there were, the more secure they were against the marauders who could still penetrate the forest. And, apart from being better able to share the services of specialists like millers, wheelwrights, and blacksmiths, because man is a social animal and because *proximus hominis primus homo*, people gained solace, comfort, and culture as well as productivity and security from the larger communities that saving and capital formation made possible.

Although capital was made more productive by technological improvement and scale, the living standards of the people who depended on that capital for the most part remained at, or below, subsistence levels. Real wages in England did not rise above the fifteenth century level until the nineteenth century.[14] One authority suggests that incomes in Elizabethan England and contemporary India were on a par.[15] French peasants in the seventeenth century could not have subsisted on less. Population growth was always able to outstrip the painfully slow accumulation of capital and the equally slow improvements in its productivity. These simply made it possible for more people to live in central western Europe; but for most of them, not to live better there. Average European incomes differed little from non-European incomes until recent centuries; and such difference as did exist was largely necessitated by Europe's more difficult environment, which required higher levels of consumption for survival.

Large sections of central western Europe's population did not reproduce themselves. These included especially those who failed to acquire capital. Even though population grew more rapidly in the region than elsewhere, that growth, which averaged 0.1 percent annually, was slight, especially in relation to an annual birthrate of around 4 percent, and a death rate therefore of 3.9 percent. If it is supposed that the wealthiest, best nourished, best housed and clothed 20 percent of the population had a crude death rate of 2.5 percent, the remaining 80 percent must have had a crude death rate of 4.25 percent, to bring the overall average up to 3.9 percent. With a death rate of 4.25 percent and a birthrate of 4 percent (and possibly lower because of fewer marriages), the poorer 80 percent of the population would not have reproduced itself.

The overriding importance of capital in this way caused, over the centuries, selection out for survival of those individuals and groups which, in one way or another, were best adapted to individualist capitalism. Individuals who were less well adapted died out; and less well adapted groups were absorbed by better adapted ones. Individualist capitalism was an irresistible force for change and development. But the elements composing it, both individuals and groups—the "small islands of population" in "a sea of forest"—were poor, weak, and vulnerable. Only the most fitted survived, in a manner analogous to the emergence of *Bos indicus* type cattle among nonindividualist pastoralists. Over time, values and institutions favorable to production, saving, and careful innovation became dominant in the surviving peoples and surviving societies of central western Europe; that too caused growth to quicken.

The Politics of Individualist Capitalism

A Different Environment

Politics is the relation between individuals and the society which they comprise and the relations between disparate societies. The circumstances resulting from the immigration of lactose tolerant pastoralists from the steppe into Europe gave a particular character to the continent's politics. There was no large riverine surplus to enforce individual compliance; nor a pastoral surplus that was easily exercisable, as on the open steppe, to enforce compliance. Society's relative poverty and lack of a large surplus were critical to making possible European individualism.

The relative weakness of society and the strength of the individual were manifested in the ancient Mediterranean by the rule of law, which asserts the rights of individuals in the face of society. But the distinctive dynamic of individualist slavery, which derived from the compulsion to enslave or be enslaved, in time undermined the rule of law. The geographical spread of conquest and the simultaneous concentration of power, which were inherent in individualist slavery, culminated in the Divine Augustus and the destruction of individualism.

The surplus between output and the reproduction needs of producers was even smaller in the colder north; and the coercive powers of society were correspondingly weaker. That coercive power, to have been effective, would have had to be applied virtually throughout central western Europe, where there was arable land available that could yield a reproduction to persons with capital, who were mobile. The central western European social surplus, which could be used to coerce individuals, as well as being smaller and having to be applied over an extensive area, had also to be applied in conditions where people had the shelter of the forest, where they could escape from coercion. The result was a society fragmented into many parts, in each of which there was little surplus, either to coerce its members or to impose on neighbors. McNeill, in a happy phrase, describes the position precisely and elegantly: "Multiplicities, autonomies, immunities, privileges pullulated everywhere."[16]

Hegemonic struggle existed between the islands of population in central western Europe's sea of forest, as it did between the cities of the ancient Mediterranean and between Africa's tribes. But that struggle was restrained in central western Europe as it was not elsewhere. First, unlike Africa, where livestock had to be held in the open to avoid trypanosomiasis, Europe's cattle were hidden in the forest, which hampered attack and strengthened defense. Second, capital was the only worthwhile objective of conquest: unlike the ancient Mediterranean, captive people were valueless as slaves; and because land did not limit output, as it did in non-European society, it also was valueless. Finally and most critically, hegemonic struggle, like everything else in central western Europe, depended on capital. If struggle depleted capital or hindered its formation, then, however militarily successful, the territory in question was weakened. Its capacity for further struggle was diminished as was also its capacity to defend itself against other, encroaching powers that had not depleted their capital, at least to the same extent. In the final analysis, those societies expanded and became dominant where, for one reason or another, most saving and most capital formation occurred and where capital was used most productively. Hegemonic struggle, which in Africa kept people poor and backward and which in the ancient Mediterranean culminated in the destruction of individualism, was, in this way in central western Europe, a factor contributing to the spread and success of influences and forms of organization that were conducive to the formation and effective use of capital.

Individualist capitalism was initiated by groups of like-minded pastoralists who had broken from the golden horde of the steppe and found shelter in the forest of central western Europe. Their security and ability to acquire essential capital depended primarily on the acceptance of the need for this in small, homogenous groups. But even at the beginning, a modicum of social power was essential to secure for people property in the hay they made, the calves they reared, the clearances they made in the forest, the cultivations on those clearances, and so on. Those rights, however socially desirable and non-exclusive in the sense of not encroaching on the possibility of others acquiring similar rights, were subject from the beginning to attack from within by deviant, unsociable individuals who exist even in the most homogenous groups. They became more subject to attack from within as the groups, with capital formation, expanded and became more heterogeneous. They also became more vulnerable to external attack as the islands of population expanded and the extent of the sheltering forest contracted. Feudalism was the distinctive means by which that modicum of security, without which saving and capital formation would have been impossible, was attained in central western Europe.

Feudalism was a form of governance that reflected central western Europe's natural poverty and its economy's dependence on the willingness and ability of individuals to save and invest. The lactose tolerant pastoralists' surplus had to be used in the forest for productive activities from which savings and capital formation were possible. Poor societies could afford to have only a small minority engaged in the socially necessary occupation of securing law and order. That small minority provided a limited protection against external attack, against which, in any case, the principal defense was the forest. A more secure defense, as in the walled cities of the ancient Mediterranean, was both unnecessary and impossible. It was unnecessary because the principal purpose of attack there, which was to enslave people, was irrelevant in central western Europe. It was impossible because of the more spatially diffused nature of central western Europe's capitalist economy, which would have entailed gathering within town walls both people and their livestock, and the food for both people and for the livestock without which people could not have survived. The logistics of such an operation were beyond the resources of central western Europe.

Apart from the forest, deterrence was the principal form of defense against external attack under feudalism. A military elite, occupying a strong point capable of withstanding siege, could counter-raid and recover stolen assets and/or inflict reprisary damage in the territory of the attacker. A feudalism that was defensive rather than offensive was also relatively inexpensive, at least in its earlier days and as befitted a society that was naturally poorly endowed.

Feudalism dichotomized society into the armed elites within castle walls and the mass of peasant producers outside. It was a dichotomy that did not exist on the steppe, where all the pastoralist group was required to defend scarce dormant-season grazing. Nor did it exist among African pastoralists, of whom all the males were required to defend their own and to raid their neighbors' cattle. Neither did such a dichotomy exist in the ancient Mediterranean, at least at the early stages when all citizens were required to share the business of capturing new slaves and of resisting enslavement.

It was inherent in the capitalist character of central western European production that the dichotomy should become more pronounced over time. Increased capital formation led to greater scale of production and to more specialization, especially specialization in providing the protection necessary for property even under the most favorable conditions. From strongpoint to moat, to castle, to palace, and ultimately to the golden cage at Versailles, the progressive divergence between the producer-saver-investor in the cabin and the protector in the castle widened with the centuries and millennia. It was a progression inherent in the character of individualist capitalism, conceived, so to speak, when the sperm of the pastoral steppe entered the ovum of the forest of central western Europe.

The precise form the subsequent development of capitalism took depended on the infinite variety of environmental circumstances that were encountered and that comprise the history of central western Europe and the world. The impact of the other form of European individualism, the individualist slavery of the ancient Mediterranean, ranked high among those circumstances which shaped the course of individualist capitalism's evolution. But notwithstanding the cogent arguments and massive documentation of Anderson, it is not possible to accept that "the feudal mode of production in Europe . . . was the result of a fusion of two modes of production . . . the slave mode . . . and the primitive communal mode . . . of the tribal populations. The slow Romano-Germanic synthesis during the Dark Ages eventually produced the new civilization of European feudalism."[17] Powerful indeed as was the influence of the ashes of the burnt out meteor of the ancient Mediterranean culture on the evolution of individualist capitalism, it was of a different order of significance to the creative necessity of providing fodder and shelter for the pastoralists' livestock during their first winter in the forest of central western Europe.

Though feudal society was remarkably dichotomized into elites and peasants, into castle-dwellers and cabin-dwellers, both elements of society were no less remarkably interdependent. The cabin-dwelling owners of capital depended on the castle-dwelling elites for their lives and for the secure possession of their capital, without which life would have been impossible. But the castle-dwellers were no less dependent on the cabin-dwellers who, with their capital, produced whatever was available to sustain cabin and castle-dwellers alike. Without the cabin-dwellers and their capital, the castle-dwellers perished and the forest encroached. "The peasant economy was recognized as early as the eleventh century by the bishop of Laon as that without which 'no free (i.e., noble) man could live.'"[18]

While the power of the castle over the cabin may have been absolute in the short run, in the longer run it was tightly circumscribed. First, given central western Europe's narrow margin between output and the producers' subsistence needs, excessive exactions quickly undermined production and created a desert around the castle in which it too perished. Thereafter, given the great extent of central western Europe's "sea of forest," it was always possible, in the final analysis, for the capitalist producers to shift, to escape the depredations of local tyrants as they had escaped those of the pastoral hordes and the riverine despots by moving from the steppes into the forest. As Georges Duby put it: "No man could exploit the workers excessively without seeing their productivity fall, or forcing them to take flight in a world where there was plenty of room for emi-grants."[19]

There existed therefore in central western Europe a unique division, of po-litical-military power located in the castle and of economic power located in the cabin. No such division of power existed anywhere else. It did not occur in riverine cropgrowing society or in pastoral society, where the total product accrued to society and where the individual, therefore, was totally dependent on society for his existence. Nor did any similar division of power exist in ancient Mediterranean society, at least prior to its regressing; citizens shared alike in the economy, defense, and politics of their cities. That unique division of power between castle and cabin which occurred in central western Europe is referred to as feudalism. The term correctly implies mutually dependent relationships.

Feudalism, Real and False

The term "feudal" is frequently, though very incorrectly, applied to social condi-tions that are backward and unjust, but that lack the interdependence that was the essential feature of relationships between cabin and castle in central western Europe. One authority has likened feudalism to "aristocracy" or "dictatorship," to describe "a general method of political organization rather than one unique constitution. And there is no reason why this method might not have been de-veloped by several peoples widely scattered in space and time."[20] The Irish land reformer Michael Davitt titled his book about the campaign which he led in the late nineteenth century as "The Fall of Feudalism in Ireland."[21] Feudalism is said to have existed in Tibet, at least until its invasion by China, and in Bolivia until the MNR revolution there in 1952.[22] But feudalism as practiced in central west-ern Europe up to the French Revolution was a unique constitution. Its unique-ness stemmed from the mutual dependence of ruler and ruled, of castle and cabin. The mutual dependence in turn derived from the unique combination of ecological and historical circumstances which obtained in central western Europe for a couple of millennia prior to the French Revolution and which gave rise to individualist capitalism.

"Feudal" is misapplied especially to Japan in the thousand years or so prior to the Tokugawan Shogunate, which commenced in the sixteenth century.[23] There were indeed striking parallels between the situation in feudal Europe and in contemporary Japan. Both societies, located respectively at the western and eastern extremities of the Eurasian landmass, were fragmented into innumerable tiny polities. Within these, the peoples were dichotomized into a mass of peas-ants and a castle-dwelling military elite. The military elite, in both cases, drew their support from the peasants' produce and provided a measure of defense, of a mainly deterrent nature, for the peasant producers. That, however, is the extent of the parallel. The differences were fundamental, making the term "feudal" in the Japanese context incorrect and misleading.

Use of "feudal" to describe the sixteenth century Japanese situation fails to distinguish between the essentially mutual interdependence of cabin and castle in individualist capitalist central western Europe and the absolute dependence of the individual on society, as represented by the daimyos or lords, in riverine cropgrowing Japan. Japan's narrow valleys and plains, with their alluvial or volcanic soils well watered by the summer monsoon, supported many more people than were needed to cultivate the soil. Labor's marginal product was zero: all the output accrued to land, sufficient only being left with the cultivators for their maintenance and reproduction. If one lord's or daimyo's peasants failed for any reason to reproduce themselves, there was an abundance of population to flow in from surrounding, overpopulated territories.

The existence in central western Europe and in Japan of a multiplicity of frequently warring statelets had different geographical causes as well as different social consequences. The fragmentation of political power in Europe was, as already argued, due principally to natural poverty. The fragmentation of political power in Japan was due to its archipelagaic topography. This, first, protected Japan from conquest by the neighboring continental powers. Second, it divided the country into four principal islands, none of which could easily dominate the others. Finally, the islands in turn were fragmented by mountains into numerous small, isolated valleys and plains. None of these was sufficiently extensive to generate the wealth that would have been necessary to establish effective, enduring rule over the whole country, fragmented as that was into numerous petty polities, each of which drew power from its own large, local surplus. In central western Europe the fragmentation of political power increased the dependence of the castle on the cabin and reinforced the network of tensions that sustained the transformation of pastoralism into capitalism. In Japan it led to a thousand years of bloody civil war which held the country in long term stasis and which ended only as a result of western intervention. The Portuguese introduced cannons which, in Japan, as previously in central western Europe, were used to demolish castles and to establish the centralizing power of the Tokugawan Shogunate.[24]

Change: Economic and Political

Political relations are determined in the first instance by conditions of production. The political relations of the pastoralists who left the steppe to enter the forest of central western Europe of necessity were transformed by the new conditions of production in the forest. These both necessitated and made possible saving and capital formation and the technological progress that accompanied that. The islands of population expanded and coalesced, and the forest retreated. Societies that were less favorable to the acquisition and effective use of capital were replaced or absorbed by others that were more favorable. Motivated by the aspirations and fears of myriads of individuals, who sought to realize their aspirations or to guard against their fears by saving and investing, and by operating their capital as effectively as possible, the only constant feature of central western European society was continuing, accelerating change. That change originated from the mass of the people, as indeed had all earlier change, like learning to control fire, improving primitive tools, sowing the first seeds, mating the first feral sheep or goat, and breaking from the hordes to infiltrate Europe's forests. But new force and purpose was given by individualist capitalism to those social forces of change which resided in the mass of people.

Change in individualist, capitalist, central western Europe was irresistible. The Horsemen of the Apocalypse—war, pestilence, and famine—might, and frequently did, devastate Europe's population. But the capital was largely untouched by pestilence or famine; and even if many of the people and much of the capital were destroyed by war, the technology was not. When devastation passed, the survivors, with the same individualist capitalist aspirations and fears, proceeded to save and to invest, and to reconstruct the devastated territories, but in new, better ways learnt since the original construction. The reconstruction, like the original construction, was probably long and painful in most cases. It took Germany centuries to recover from the Thirty Years War. Occasionally it was amazingly swift, as was "the German economic miracle" after 1945. The forces of individualist capitalism, released by the conjunction of lactose tolerant pastoralists with limitlessly available arable in the forest of central western Europe, while pitiably weak in the case of the individual or small group, in the mass were irresistible.

The stock of capital and the knowledge to use it effectively advanced at inherently accelerating rates. Islands of population expanded if conditions for capital formation, including security and taxation, were favorable in them. The expanding islands absorbed others where conditions had been less favorable. Leaders of the more successful migrating pastoral bands became in time lords. Some of those lords in turn became greater lords, whose power grew with the accumulation of capital and the advance of technology within their domains. As political power increased and became more concentrated, it also grew more distant from the producers, savers, and investors in their cabins. But however remote political power in castle or palace became, its dependence on the economic power which originated in the cabin never lessened. Rather it heightened. As economies grew, they became more specialized and market dependent. Nowhere was this more true than in the business of European rulers, which business was above all, as Machiavelli pointed out, making war: "A prince should have no other thought or aim than war, nor acquire mastery in anything except war, its organisation and discipline; for war is the only art expected of a ruler."[25] Michael Mann provides estimates of the cost to English kings of their warlike activities.[26] For rulers who were able to acquire on the market the increasingly specialist men and materials of war, it "meant the possibility of eliminating first the tumultuous and anarchic feudal levies, which were also ineffectual, as the French defeats at Crecy, Agincourt and Poitiers show so clearly."[27] The magnate who did so most successfully became *primus inter pares*—a king.

Kings, who were the forerunners of the modern state, became eventually a critical element in the network of tensions that sustained central western Europe as the tribal pastoralism of the steppes metamorphosed into a capital-based, crop-growing agriculture. Kings had interests that were different from those of the castle and the cabin. They had a common interest with the lords in maintaining the political supremacy of a military, aristocratic elite that protected property and, in return, took from the property owners a privileged share of the product. But they shared with the property owners a common interest in maximizing output and in minimizing the share of that output sequestered by the lords; for the less the lords took, the more there was available for the monarchs; and the less the lords got, the less able were they to compete in military and political power with the monarch—the fewer "over-mighty subjects" there were.

Monarchic power in central western Europe also contained its own internal balance. "States began to emerge about 900 AD; supposedly there were still one thousand polities in the fourteenth century . . . by 1900 there were twenty-five."[28] A king might be *primus inter pares* and, in time, with the progress of capitalism and the concentration of power, become an absolute monarch. But in Europe, there were never fewer than twenty-five countries, each with its ruler. Feudal Europe, unlike other polities, was never united under a single ruler, who must then become an Inca, pharaoh, or a divine Augustus and the antithesis of individualism. The economic surplus was always insufficient and the terrain was always too difficult to extend conquest. The fruits of conquest were always too meager: captives were valueless as was land itself. The most that could be won was an extension of hegemony and the uncertain prospect that offered of levying more taxes or services on more recalcitrant, mobile penny capitalists. Moreover, the whole business of conquest and defense was so dependent on saving and investment and on the efficient use of capital that no single center of economic and political activity was ever able to dominate all the others in central western Europe. As a consequence political power remained decentralized, with many centers of power and the power held at any center modest.

Absolute monarchs, no less than petty rulers, depended on the owners of capital to secure in the market the means to defend or extend their territory in unceasing hegemonic struggle. As Louis XIV of France, who was knowledgeable in these matters, observed: "after all, it is the last louis d'or which must win."[29] If too many resources were appropriated, the stock of capital declined, either by non-replenishment or by flight to the territory of a less predatory but competing ruler. Taxing capital threatened to drive out the footloose capital that was the basis of European wealth or to precipitate revolt by Europe's individualist property owners:

> If one leaves aside religious movements, it is striking that most of the rebellions in European states from the fourteenth to the seventeenth, and even eighteenth century, were tax revolts . . . the importance of fiscal rebellions has not been understood, and this despite the impressive number of tax revolts, several hundred in France under the single ministry of Richelieu.[30]

Many devices were used by feudal rulers to secure from the owners of capital the revenues that were essential for government, without simultaneously depleting or driving out the capital stock. The favorite was borrowing, an expedient that allowed immediate needs to be met at the cost of creating greater future needs. Europe's potentates were chronically indebted and repeatedly defaulted on their debts. Philip II of Spain, though indubitably the wealthiest among the contemporary European monarchs, thanks to the wealth plundered from the New World and to dynastic marriages that united the crowns of Austria, Spain, and the Netherlands, repudiated his debts on four separate occasions.[31] The situation in France was similar. "Most Bourbon kings had survived debt and bankruptcy; the financial difficulties in the later years of Louis XIII, Louis XIV and Louis XV were probably as bad as those on the eve of the French revolution."[32]

When the rulers' ability to borrow further ended, confrontation occurred between absolute monarchs and the possessors of the capital on which everything in central western Europe depended. Earlier Bourbon kings survived those crises. But the configuration of power in central western Europe had altered very materially by the time of Louis XVI's reign. Centuries of concentration of political power into the persons of the absolute monarchs and the simultaneous stripping of power from increasingly obsolete feudal lords had transformed the three-way division of power between producers, lords, and monarch into a two-way one, between producer and monarch—between a vastly developed economic power and a political power which remained as dependent as ever on the underlying economic, but which by then was no longer supported by a vibrant feudal lordship. Further, three centuries after the Reformation, in the Age of Reason, the Church was no longer the bulwark of stability and sustainer of a hierarchic ordering of society that it had been formerly.

> The first spark [in the French Revolution] was the government's declaration of bankruptcy following the American War . . . it would be useless to resort to the old, time-worn expedients: short term loans already amounted to 400 million *livres*; the *taille* . . . was already high enough to provoke peasant discontent; and it seemed unwise to increase the taxes on consumer goods at a time of recession and of falling industrial profits.[33]

Repudiating the king's debts had ceased to be politically feasible. It was deemed necessary instead to convene the Estates General to deal with the financial crisis. The rest is history.

The French Revolution was a particularly remarkable unleashing of forces for change which had outstripped the adaptability of old political forms. The origin of those forces was the unceasing striving of myriads of individuals to improve their lot by saving, investing, and improving the productivity of their capital and labor. The revolution and its aftermath succeeded largely though not entirely in obliterating the divergence between political and economic power, between those who governed and those who saved and invested, which had been such a distinctive and critically important characteristic of feudal Europe.

A somewhat similar process had occurred in England nearly 150 years earlier. How and why political and economic power converged earlier in England than elsewhere are considered in the next chapter.

The divergence between political power residing in the castle and economic power residing in the cabin was a distinctive and critically important feature of individualist capitalism in feudal central western Europe. But while it is important to recognize the fundamental importance and uniqueness to central western Europe of this divergence between political and economic power, it is scarcely less important to realize that the divergence was rarely if ever absolute and, like everything else in individualist capitalist Europe, was subject to unceasing change. The castle frequently engaged in activities that might more appropriately be deemed to lie within the provenance of the cabin. Less frequently, the cabin exercised direct political power.

The castle, from the beginning, sought to provide for its denizens from the produce of its own demesne lands, though relying for this purpose largely on the labor and capital of the people under its control to operate the demesne land. Feudal lords frequently owned mills, ironworks, and wineries. As capital formation and industrialization progressed, some of them at least played important parts in establishing and operating new industries.[34] In the opposite direction, the nobles of the robe in France were just one manifestation among many of the phenomenon of persons of cabin origin rising through economic success into positions of political power.[35]

The Influence of Rome

The Indo-Europeans who migrated from the steppe into Europe were the inheritors of humanity's evolutionary progress. They had acquired livestock husbandry and a knowledge of cropgrowing from the cradle of civilization in Mesopotamia. The pastoralists acquired skills in metallurgy in part in response to the demands of wealthy Mesopotamia and Egypt, where the mineral-bearing bedrock was buried under deep alluvium.

The knowledge and skills that the Indo-Europeans brought with them into Europe were supplemented by others acquired there. Those who moved southwards gained much from the indigenous Phoenicians. The precariously existing swidden farmers of central western Europe had little to contribute to the westward migrating pastoralists. But in time, these latter became heirs to the ashes of the meteoric rise and eclipse of the ancient Mediterranean civilization.

The great prestige among northern barbarians of Rome, which had been built on the forced labor of captive pastoralists, persisted after its economic and military collapse. Rome's literacy and monotheism, which in turn it owed in large measure to the great riverine civilizations of the Middle East, were readily absorbed by the northern barbarians and became part of their intellectual baggage.

Another inheritance was the concept of empire, which was the logical consequence of individualist slavery. That concept persisted into the era of individualist capitalism, although a monolithic European empire was incompatible with individualist capitalism, especially in its early, feudal phase. But like so much of central western Europe's intellectual inheritance, the concept of empire was given a distinctive feudal format. Society was organized in a hierarchic form that commenced with peasant producers at the lowest level and proceeded upwards through petty lords, great lords, and kings. The last ruled under a Holy Roman Emperor, who derived his authority ultimately from God, mediated by His Vicar on earth, who was the Pope.

The Church of Rome inherited much of the ancient Mediterranean's preoccupation with law, its humanism, its concern for the individual, and much of the universalism of Rome, capital of a polyglot empire. But the Church's law was the law of *civitatis Dei*. It was both canon law and natural law, which latter was the will of God for man's conduct on earth as interpreted by the Church. Conformity with canon and natural law would secure eternal salvation in heaven, while breach of it would result in eternal damnation. The Medieval Church's concern for law, which had been the cornerstone of individualist slavery in the ancient Mediterranean, helped central western Europe in its chrysalis-like escape from the tyranny of custom which had prevailed on the steppe. The Church's concern for the individual was as a creature of God possessing an eternal soul, which it was the Church's mission to guide towards eternal, heavenly bliss. The Church, like the authority of imperial Rome, overrode local interests in fulfilling a paramount mission. That mission was to secure the *pax Romana* in imperial times; and it was to establish God's order under the Church in post-Roman Europe. The Church recognized no superior authority as intervening between it and its followers, for whom it had the responsibility of preaching and demonstrating the path to salvation.

The Church contributed to securing a balance between the political power of the castle and the economic power of the cabin. It did so by emphasizing the hierarchic character of society, with each layer subordinate and owing allegiance to the one above it. The peasant was subordinate to the lord, the lord to the king, the king to the emperor, and the emperor to God, the origin of all power and authority. This emphasis on hierarchy implied the exercise of authority in conformity with the will of God, the source of authority. The Church claimed to be the arbiter of God's will and it enforced that claim by excommunicating those who were deemed to have acted contrary to the will of God, as interpreted by the Church. The very real and cogent restraint that was thus imposed on temporal powers by the medieval Church may be gauged from incidents like the Penitence of Canossa in 1077 AD, when the Holy Roman Emperor, Henry IV, did public penance and yielded politically to Pope Gregory VII in order to be readmitted to membership of the Church; or the public penance of King Henry II of England in 1174 AD at the tomb of Thomas à Beckett in atonement for the archbishop's murder by the king's knights because of his defense of the Church's position against the crown's encroachments. It was not until the sixteenth century that west European monarchs found it safe to defy the collateral power of the Church of Rome. Henry VIII was the first English king to succeed in defying openly the claims of Rome to be able to make and to unmake kings and emperors.

The Church, while tempering the power of lords and kings, simultaneously preached the obligation of subjects to submit to an authority that derived from God, even when that authority was harsh. By curbing lords' power and by enjoining obedience on subjects, the Church contributed to a more orderly and less violent society. It was a society in which the power of rulers, already curbed by economic and topographical considerations, was further restrained by religious sanctions; and in which religious sanctions also enjoined the ruled to submit without the use of force. The Church thus helped to prevent Europe from slipping into the unceasing, ubiquitous, internecine conflict that characterized pastoralist Africa.

The insistence on hierarchic order created conditions favorable to the rule of law and therefore favorable to property. The Church, more directly, favored property by preaching that, as property is essential for human well-being, it must have been ordained by God and is therefore divinely sanctioned.[36] Infringements on "the sacred rights of property," either by lords and kings through excessive taxes or other exactions, or by subjects by robbery or theft, were therefore equally immoral. Moreover the Church of Rome, long before the emergence of a "Protestant ethic," preached the virtues of abstinence, of restricting current consumption in order to store up blessings for the future. There was a close consonance between what the medieval Church taught as the will of God and what the peasants strove for: to defer gratification now in order to save assets that would make possible greater future output. The conviction that in saving one was storing up blessings, not only in this but also in a future life, must have increased the incentive to desperately poor people to save in order to alleviate their poverty in the future, on earth as in heaven.

The Church too must have powerfully influenced central western Europe's distinctive demographic practice of lower marriage rates and consequently lower birth and death rates. These lower marriage, birth, and death rates were important for Europe's economic progress. The Church played an important part in imposing and sustaining the institutional constraints that brought about these lower demographic rates.

People's virility, productivity, and fertility have normally been closely correlated. This was, and is, clearly so in hunting-gathering societies. Pastoral societies have traditionally made provision for members, on approaching adulthood, to acquire some of the clan's or sept's livestock so that they might have the means essential for a more-or-less independent social subsistence.[37] Young people, with a hoe and a bucket of seed in riverine crop-growing societies, could pay as much or more tax as older people and so could acquire land, forcing out older people whose productive powers had waned. Access to capital was the condition of production in post-Roman western Europe. The individual without capital was less productive there than anywhere else.

Young people in medieval central western Europe, where society was structured and deeply concerned to protect property rights, did not have customary rights to a portion of the family stock, as young people had in less structured, pastoral societies elsewhere. Crop yields were so low that the cultivator without capital got less than maintenance. Growth of population had reduced the product per person secured from hunting and gathering in central western Europe to a precarious supplement to a diet procured overwhelmingly from crop growing,[38] with hunting and fishing being increasingly reserved as a sport for the aristocracy. Young people in central western Europe, to acquire even the rudimentary independent economic existence that made marriage possible, were absolutely dependent on capital, which could be acquired only by parsimony, patrimony, or matrimony. The first implied prior access to the capital that was essential for the production from which parsimony made savings possible. The second and third sources were mere transfers of existing capital; they did not involve creating additional capital. Absolute dependence on capital implied that people could not marry until they acquired capital by saving, gift, or inheritance or until a prospective employer had done so. The result was the well known west European phenomenon of delayed marriages and a higher incidence of people who never married, which caused birthrates to be lower. Lower birthrates were matched by lower death rates. This meant that people on average lived longer, that there was a smaller proportion of dependent people, and that society was therefore more productive.

The medieval Church, by its anathema for extramarital sex, reinforced by religious sanctions the sexual mores of an increasingly property-oriented society. The Church, as well as buttressing the powerful economic constraints on the birthrate, reduced the anguish caused by those constraints. It did so by making a virtue of necessity and by preaching the blessings in a future life of a continence that was in any case hardly avoidable in this one; and it offered, in its monasteries and nunneries, an honorable and secure life for that large section of the population who, while still virile, were unable to secure the economic basis for a married life of the style to which they were accustomed.

The Church in the Dark Ages thus, in a variety of ways, eased the transition from tribal pastoralism to feudal, capital-based crop-growing. The principal contribution is seen as curbing the power of an encastled military elite who might otherwise have exercised a more arbitrary and retarding power over the productive population in their defenseless cabins. The Church simultaneously enjoined obedience on the people and in that way made it possible for society to operate with minimal use of force, the arbitrary exercise of which is incompatible with the formation of the capital on which the central western European crop-growing economy was increasingly dependent. The Church, by preaching abstinence, encouraged saving; and by preaching continence, encouraged a lower birthrate, hence a lower death rate and a more productive population structure. In these ways, it contributed importantly to the unique, organic transformation of Indo-European pastoralism into central western European, individualist capitalist crop-growing.

The medieval Church was part of that network of tensions which, in the first instance, made possible individualist capitalism in central western Europe. The Church of Rome impinged in many critical ways on the organic growth of that individualist capitalism, which in turn impacted indelibly on the Church.

Summary and Conclusion

The combination in central western Europe, several millennia ago, of lactose tolerant pastoralists and effectively limitless arable land of a naturally unproductive quality, under a unique set of circumstances, gave rise there uniquely to individualist capitalism. This was a totally new form of society in which it was both necessary and possible for individuals, if they were to survive and reproduce, constantly to save, invest, and enhance the productivity of their capital. Commencing from a low base and initially progressing imperceptibly slowly, individualist capitalist development had an inherent tendency to accelerate, bringing economic, technological, political, and intellectual change at an ever more rapid rate. Those individuals who accumulated capital and used it productively survived and reproduced; the rest failed to reproduce themselves in a society where living standards for most people were never far from the subsistence level. Those groupings of individuals or polities in which most capital was accumulated and used effectively tended to dominate and to absorb others. None, however, acquired a monopoly of military/political power in central western Europe, where individuals with capital, as a last resort, could move from less to more congenial political environments.

Though initiated by the encounter of lactose tolerant pastoralists with the naturally unproductive arable land of central western Europe, individualist capitalism was subject and responsive to external influences. Foremost of these was Rome, which encapsulated the forces of the other form of individualism which emerged in Europe, individualist slavery. Other external influences were trade with the northern, hunting-gathering Lapps, and, as individualist capitalism developed, conflict with Muslim forces in the Balkans and Iberia. The adoption and adaptation of outside inventions by an individualist capitalist society, which was bound by its nature to innovate, also influenced the course of development. Foremost of these adoptions were paper, gunpowder, and the compass, acquired from China.

Notwithstanding these external influences, it is a grave misconception to perceive individualist capitalism, as it evolved in central western Europe, as just one of many cultures which have occupied the stage of history but no longer do so. It is totally different in kind from the score of land based economies/civilizations, the courses of which Arnold Toynbee has charted.[39] Nor was it the inevitable product of a Hegelian/Marxist dialectical transformation of primitive communism into an "Asiatic mode of production," and thence into slavery, feudalism, and capitalism. To view it in such ways is grievously to misunderstand both the character of individualist capitalism itself and its impact on societies outside its central western European homeland.

There was nothing at all inevitable about the emergence of individualist capitalism in central western Europe. Had any key element of that unique combination of circumstances that led to its establishment there three to four thousand years ago been absent, it is unlikely that this form of production would have emerged in Europe, or anywhere else, at that time or since. Had, for example, the forest been less dense, or regenerated less vigorously, the need for winter fodder, and therefore for capital, would have been less pressing; and an entirely different society, with an entirely different economy, would probably have prevailed throughout continental Europe. It did in an offshore island, as is described in the next chapter.

Chapter 5

Europe of the Regions

Europe, though only slightly larger than Oceania, half the size of North or South America, and about one-third the size of Africa or Asia, has been from an early date culturally the most diverse of the continents. This has been so at both the macro and micro levels.

Five major cultural forms coexisted in Europe. Three of these were natural resource based and two were individualist. The pastoralist Golden Hordes dominated the eastern steppe, beyond the forest, until nearly five hundred years ago. Northwards, Lapps continue to hunt reindeer, as their ancestors did in mainland Europe before the deciduous forest, after the last Ice Age, encroached and drove out the tundra and the reindeer. Westward of the steppe, there developed the only two autochthonous individualist, non-natural-resource based cultures that the world has seen: the slave-based individualism of the ancient Mediterranean and the capital-based individualism of central western Europe. A bastard pastoralism that included some cropgrowing, similar to that of Sub-Sahelian Africa, existed in the extreme west. Europe did not however, as noted in chapter 3, contain any riverine cropgrowing.

Europe, which displayed the greatest cultural diversity at the macro level, also had a wide diversity of cultures at the micro level. Each island of population within the sea of deciduous central western European forest evolved in relative isolation. Its insularity was preserved first by the surrounding forest, and second by the soil's poverty which generated no large surpluses to sustain powerful, centralizing rulers. Those individuals and their characteristics persisted who most successfully acquired and used productively the capital which was the basis of production in central western Europe. Those societies dominated where more individuals were able to acquire and to use capital productively.

The Heartland

A region emerged within central western Europe which, a millennium or more ago, had acquired an ascendancy of sorts. This was the region identified by Marc Bloch as being from early on most clearly associated with Europe's distinctive, capital-based production. North of the river Loire and the Burgundian plain "was the classical area of the *seigneurie*, the one in which it was oldest and most solidly established."[1] This region is central western Europe and is perceived as having been the heartland of Western, individualist capitalism.

The ascendancy of this region may have owed something to the closeness of its contact with the Roman empire. However, contact between the barbarian north and the ancient Mediterranean was of longer standing and greater intimacy on the Danube than on the Rhine or Rhone. Yet it was in the basins of the last two rather than in the basin of the Danube that individualist capitalist production developed most rapidly. Clearly there were other factors more powerful than Rome's influence.

The deciduous forest, which was central to the emergence and evolution of individualist capital-based production, became first established in Bloch's "classical area of the *signeurie*." For it was there that the ameliorating influence of the Atlantic's Gulf Stream came first and most forcefully into play with the ending of the Ice Age. The soil was warmest and the forest was thickest there. The warm soil gave a better return there to the capital invested in it than anywhere else in central western Europe. It does so still: crop yields decline from a Danish and Benelux maximum in the west to a Romanian minimum in the east.[2] The denser forest gave better protection than elsewhere to its producers. The region moreover was farthest from the steppe, with its pastoral hordes, elements of which laid siege to Vienna as recently as 1683. Higher and more secure returns thrust this region into the forefront of individualist capital based production. An individualist capitalism with an inherent tendency to expand at an accelerating rate had also an inherent tendency to spread its influence outside its sphere of occupation. The technological progress, which was an inseparable part of capitalist development, provided the military capacity to expand and to take by conquest whatever wealth less advanced regions had. More durably, capital formation in the core area changed its factor endowment and hence its relative values. The price, or value, of capital-intensive goods, particularly manufactured armaments, tended to decline relative to the value of land-intensive products, particularly those secured by hunting or gathering. As capital formation proceeded at an accelerating rate in central western Europe, these conquest and trade motivations for the expansion of regional influences strengthened.

The South

Italy, the remnant of the Western Roman Empire, lay southwards of the core area of individualist capitalism. Its warmer, more productive soils, afforded naturally higher returns than those of central western Europe to the capitalist production with which the invading barbarians replaced slavery on the Mediterranean littoral. The new capitalism which replaced slavery was sufficiently productive to maintain the south's denser population and to yield a surplus which for long made Italy the richest part of Europe.

But though the returns to capital in the south may have been greater, conditions there were less favorable than farther north for the long term evolution of institutions and technologies conducive to sustained saving, capital formation, and technological progress. It was sheep land, where the forest was less extensive and less dense. There was less need for capital as winter fodder, or as draught animals and implements to cultivate extensively, or as seed, and so on. More so than in the north, land rather than capital tended to be limiting. Economic and therefore political power resided to a greater extent with magnates who, with the military technology brought in by the invading barbarians, controlled the south's land. Because capital was less needed and less scarce, capital and its cabin-dwelling owners could be squeezed more. And because there was less forest, which was less dense, there was less opportunity for the owners of capital to shift from areas of more, to areas of less, severe exploitation. Thus, though capitalism, when it replaced slavery, gave larger, quicker returns in Italy than elsewhere, it did not find there conditions as congenial for saving, investment, and technological progress as in the core area, where crop yields were lower, but where the forest was most dense and most protective.

The population of central western Europe, the home of individualist capitalism, overtook that of the Mediterranean littoral, where an exotic capitalism had replaced slavery, by around 800AD.[3] Italy, for a thousand years thereafter, was to be a source of funds for the capital-hungry north. Those funds were obtained variously by borrowing and by conquest. They offset the southward flow secured by Italy's persistent intellectual dominance, which found expression particularly in the long enduring supremacy of the Papacy. What Rome drained from the north in "Peter's pence" contributions to the papacy, the north recovered through unpaid debts and plunder.

The North

Scandinavia lay northwards of the core area of individualist capitalism. Climatic conditions for crop-growing were much less favorable in the Scandinavian peninsula than in mainland central western Europe. They were probably too difficult ever to permit the autochthonous emergence of the sort of capital-based, crop-growing economy that emerged in central western Europe. But there were offsetting compensations. Further to the north of the Indo-European Scandinavians were the Lapps. These, under the influence of European pastoralism, had partly domesticated the reindeer, unlike their racial cousins, the Eskimos, across the Bering Straits, who continued to hunt the caribou. The partly pastoral, partly hunting Lapps offered no threat to the rear of the agricultural Scandinavians; but they did produce enough from their reindeer to be able to pay tribute to, and to trade beneficially with, the Scandinavians.[4] With a secure and lucrative rear, the Scandinavians were strategically well placed to tap, by plunder and trade, the wealth of Europe as it pulled itself together and progressed at a perceptibly more rapid pace following the shock and instability of the period marked by what are variously referred to as the barbarian invasions of the Roman empire or the *volkerwanderung* of the Germans. The Scandinavians, in exploiting the opportunities afforded by their location, circumnavigated Europe, along the great rivers of Russia, by the Atlantic Ocean and through the Mediterranean Sea.[5]

Slaves were part of the wealth secured abroad by the raiding/trading Scandinavians. Anderson, however, relying on Foote and Wilson, may have exaggerated their importance in the early Scandinavian economy.[6] Foote and Wilson state: "In Norway it was apparently thought that the labor of three slaves was necessary to run a farm stocking twelve cows and two horses."[7] At that staffing level, there could have been little, if anything, above the slaves' maintenance to yield a profit to the owner. The slave's role in Scandinavia, as in Ottoman Turkey and in India, was almost certainly ancillary, executing the most arduous and unpleasant tasks and tending the land while the owner was absent on raiding or trading expeditions. The latter yielded the wealth necessary to make good agriculture's shortfall in a most difficult climate.

The Scandinavians evolved their institutions in ways particularly favorable to individual endeavor. For example, Vikings, often thousands of miles from home and alternatively oarsmen at sea and swordsmen on land, could be led by accepted leaders but could not be driven by despots, as—by contrast—were the massed land armies of the great riverine states. "The Viking age was, in fact, very much the age of the individual," as Popperwell put it.[8] With wealth secured from outside and with institutions especially favorable to individual effort, the Scandinavians, in a most difficult climate and after a late and slow start, developed more rapidly than the rest of Europe, and now have Europe's and the world's highest living standards.

The Eastern Marches

The first of the Indo-European pastoralists from the steppe, the Celts, reached Ireland, Europe's western extremity, during the first millennium BC. The Atlantic, like a great dam, then prevented the further westward flow of individualist capitalism. Capital and technology accumulated in the core area. From there, like water in an estuary as the tide flows, the forces of individualist capitalism began a reflux eastwards towards their origin in the distant steppe.

The Teutonic knights were in the vanguard of this eastward reflux. With the military technology of the more advanced capitalist west, they subdued the peoples in the march lands between the forest and the steppe. Scandinavian brigand-traders penetrated further east and established Kievan Russia.

Conquest was easy by the eastward migrants, who possessed the West's superior military technology. But continued rule could only be achieved by regular replenishment with that technology. That involved trade between East and West. Land-intensive products from the East, like furs, fish, hides, and wild honey, were traded for the capital intensive products, especially the military technology, of the West.[9] A new form of capitalist production was established in eastern Europe on the basis of this trade.

The new form of production was capitalist in two senses. First, though the surplus it exchanged for Western technology was mainly hunted, gathered, or pastoral produce, the economy was primarily crop-based; and to grow those crops in the region, capital was required in greater quantity than elsewhere. This was because yields were lower than anywhere else in Europe; as recently as the nineteenth century, a grain of cereal sown in Russia yielded only 2.4 when harvested.[10] More capital was required in Eastern Europe than elsewhere to secure a given output.

Second, there was more land in eastern Europe than elsewhere to which to apply that capital. Capital, in that sense, was more limiting than elsewhere. Crop production in eastern Europe was thus more capital dependent in the double sense of more capital being required to secure a given output, and of there being even more limitlessly available arable land to absorb any available capital.

But the capitalism of eastern Europe was not individualist. It did not represent the response of individuals, through saving and investment, to their aspirations and fears. Saving and investment occurred, under pressure from an external source, in a particular environment. The external pressure was the possession by elites of superior, Western technology, especially of a military and repressive character. That repressive Western technology was applied in an environment where the land, as well as being naturally less productive, was also less densely forested and offered less shelter. Producers on this land were more dependent for military protection from the pastoral hordes who continued to threaten the region until recent times. They could also less easily escape from the protectors' exactions than their counterparts in the West, where the denser forest offered better shelter.

The availability to elites of a superior, Western technology, in an environment that was naturally less productive than that in which the technology had evolved, gave rise to a distinctive form of capitalist production. It may be termed "autocratic capitalism" to distinguish it from the individualist capitalism of which it was a product. Military elites, equipped with Western technology, coerced producers to grow crops on naturally less productive land, which also offered less opportunity to shift. The producers, to subsist, had to use a large part of their produce as working capital. Tied to the naturally low-yielding land from which they could not escape, peasants produced little above their reproductive needs. Part of that surplus was appropriated by the elites, leaving little for investment. That investment was usually undertaken collectively by the *mir*, or village, which, rather than the individual, was the level of interaction between cabin and castle under autocratic capitalism. The collective investment of meager savings in land that was naturally unproductive and that gave a low return to capital, ensured that output continued low and that growth was slow. There was, as a result, a chronic tendency for the East's autocratic capitalism to lag behind the West's individualist capitalism. That lag in turn secured for the Eastern elites a constant flow of Western technology that was always in advance of the East's. This continuing access to a superior, repressive, Western technology by Eastern autocrats was, so to speak, the coping stone of the East's enduring subordination to the West.

It also accounts for the survival of serfdom in the East, long after its disappearance in the West. Russia's serfs were not emancipated until 1861 and Poland's in 1862. The essence of central western European feudalism was the mutual dependence of cabin and castle, of serf and lord. If, for any reason and especially because of the lack of investment, the cabin's productivity faltered, the dependent castle also suffered, and became prey to the hegemonic ambitions of neighboring castles, where the cabin's productivity had not similarly faltered. In Eastern Europe, as long as the lords could extract sufficient surplus from their less mobile serfs to acquire Western repressive technology, they could maintain their position and compel their serfs to labor, to produce, and to save and invest sufficient to generate the surplus needed to acquire Western repressive technology. The political/military power of the castle in the West was endogenous; it depended on the state of the economy as determined by the cabin's willingness and ability to save/invest. The political/military power of the Eastern lords was exogenous; it depended on their ability to acquire Western technology.

An elite oligopoly, with access to Western technology, extended their influence eastwards. Teutonic, Latvian, Estonian, and Polish elites, in martial competition, penetrated far into territory that is now Russian. They eventually encountered a new power, centered on Moscow, where the remnants of Kievan Russia had found sanctuary from the devastations of the Mongols in the thirteenth and fourteenth centuries. While the pine forest of northern Russia provided better protection against the Mongol hordes, its soil was even less productive than that to the south and west. Moscow was, therefore, dependent on outside sources of supplementary food supplies, secured in trade for hunted and gathered produce, including furs, fish, and honey. That trade was conducted with the distant west along Russia's river system, which flowed northwards into the Baltic Sea or southwards into the Black Sea.[11] It was possible for the descendants of the Scandinavian founders of Kievan Russia to secure command of the trade by controlling the rivers through which it flowed. Moscow, with that control, had a monopoly in the region of advanced military technology secured from the distant west. It was able, from the fifteenth century onwards, to establish a monolithic power, based on a monopolistic control of trade in land-intensive local products for capital-intensive western technology.

Moscow's monolithic czars, using Western technology, were first able to free their territories from pastoral intrusions, and subsequently, in the seventeenth century, extended their rule to the distant Pacific Ocean. Closer to home, Moscow was confronted with the oligopolistic powers of Lithuanian and Polish magnates and with that of Sweden. The Polish and Lithuanian magnates, because of their closer contact with the West, were able to get its military technology. That allowed them to dominate their own people and fed a competitive militancy that was expressed in the drive to the east. Once, however, a monolithic Moscow power had been established, through its monopolistic control of trade with the West and became dominant in the region, territorial expansion eastwards by Polish or Lithuanian magnates, or by Sweden, was no longer possible. On the contrary, Moscow began then a counteroffensive which, eventually in 1945, brought it close to the heart of central western Europe.

Also in the east was the Byzantine remnant of ancient Mediterranean society. Strategically located on the Bosphorus, Constantinople, the second city of the empire, the "new Rome," survived for a millennium after the collapse of the western empire and the sacking of Rome. Its existence for long provided some defense for Europe's southeastern flank against those pastoral influences which advanced from the steppe southwards of the Black Sea, through the Persian and Anatolian plateaus. But well before the city itself fell to the Ottoman Turks in 1453, the latter had bypassed it and had crossed from Anatolia into the Balkans. "The Turks' situation in Europe enabled them to acquire knowledge of the use of firearms which, as we learned, served them well in the struggle against Persians and Mamelukes for supremacy in western Asia."[12] The Ottoman Turks, combining steppe pastoral mobility with Western military technology, were for long a major threat both to eastern and to central western Europe.[13]

The Ottomans extended the steppe's influence into the heart of Europe, as recently as 1673 laying siege to Vienna. But that was the limit of their incursions. Ottoman culture remained firmly rooted in the steppe. The Turks, not having experienced the transforming influence of life in central western Europe's forests, remained the pastoral hordes of the steppe, without individualism, law or property, as these had evolved into the bedrock of European culture. They continued to be predators, extracting from their subject peoples for immediate consumption all that was possible. The frontier Balkan lands, over which their sway extended, as a result remained poor, backward, and incapable of yielding much booty over the long run. Individualist capitalism, by contrast, with its inbuilt dynamic of inherently accelerating growth, developed apace in central western Europe. Its eastern surrogates also grew stronger. The Ottoman Turks were in time forced back out of Europe by the combined power of Austria, Poland, and Russia. The Turks finally, in the present century, have been confined to the Anatolian plateau, where they first settled following their much earlier migration from Mongolia, apart from a European toehold around Istanbul.[14]

Britain

The islands of Britain and Ireland, lying offshore continental Europe, offered particular challenges and opportunities for migrant, lactose tolerant people whose ancestors came from the distant Russian steppe. Britain, where summers are cooler and the rainfall heavier than on the continent, marked the limit of sustainable cropgrowing. The Romans acknowledged this when they built Hadrian's Wall between the Tyne and Solway to exclude Scotland, which was likely to cost them more in conquest and occupation than it would yield in slaves, and when they chose not to extend their empire to Ireland. Britain's marginality for cropgrowing was further demonstrated by the early withdrawal of the Roman legions in 407 AD.

But though marginal for cropgrowing, Britain had pastoral advantages, a competitive relationship that is expressed in the English aphorism "up horn, down corn." England's chalk downs were good sheep grazing, a phenomenon which continues to be reflected in English farming's continued emphasis on sheep. The United Kingdom of Britain and Northern Ireland in 1980 had 162 sheep per hundred cattle; the EEC as a whole had seventy. Only the Mediterranean members, Greece, Italy, Spain, and Portugal, shared Britain's predominance in sheep; collectively those countries had 261 sheep per hundred cattle.[15]

Wool, like all land-intensive, pastoral, hunted and gathered products, tended over the long term, with capital formation, to rise in price relative to capital-intensive products, including crops. However, on those occasions when population growth outstripped capital formation, with consequent income decline, poorer people were forced to use a larger part of their small incomes on food rather than cloth or wool. It was then a case of "up corn, down horn." A phase of this sort occurred in central western Europe during the thirteenth and early fourteenth centuries,[16] causing a long, slow decline in living standards and nutritional levels. That left the population of a region, which is climatically more difficult than any other that is densely populated, peculiarly exposed to disease. The Black Death, which struck Europe in the 1340s, then wiped out almost half the continent's population.

The destruction by disease of almost half of central western Europe's population transformed conditions. It virtually doubled the capital/labor ratio. Incomes and living standards of the surviving population rose sharply, which facilitated saving and capital formation. The tempo of development and change accelerated sharply, giving rise shortly afterwards to the Renaissance, the Great Discoveries, the Reformation, and eventually modern Europe.

The Black Death had a particular significance for England. The demographic and economic changes which it caused were reflected particularly in three price changes. By comparison with prices in 1350, the price of wheat was reduced by a quarter, the price of wool went up by half, and the cost of labor also went up by half by the end of the century.[17] As peoples' incomes increased (reflected in the rise in wages), their demand for clothes and wool rose (reflected in the rise in the wool price) relative to their demand for bread (reflected in the fall in the price of wheat). This price transformation created a particularly powerful incentive in England, which at best was marginal for crop-growing, to shift from labor-intensive crop-growing to the production of wool, which was now high priced and which required little labor.

Feudal titles were of particularly little value in post Black Death England. It was difficult to exact the services of serfs when labor had become scarce and dear, with enhanced opportunities to abscond and to evade feudal exactions. The crops produced by the feudal services of the serfs, which at the best of times were exceptionally difficult to grow in England, simultaneously lost much of their value after the Black Death. In particular, it required twice as much wheat to buy a given quantity of wool as formerly; and after food, wool and the cloth from it were what people spent their resources mostly on. The high cost of labor and the low price of grain were powerful motivations for reducing cropgrowing in England. The motivations for increasing sheep farming, for which England was always especially well suited, were equally cogent. It used very little of the labor which had become scarce and dear after the Black Death; and its value, in terms of grain, was twice as high as formerly. It was therefore, in post-Black Death England, very much a case of "up horn, down corn."

Considerations other than product and factor prices were also relevant. Even if ecological conditions had been favorable for sheep farming in central western Europe—which they were not—it would still have been difficult if not impossible to stock the land with them. This was because a sheep-walk in continental Europe would have been a standing invitation to invade to an aggressive feudal lord, commanding a numerous if unprofitable cropgrowing peasantry. The sheep would have offered no resistance. A numerous peasantry was to remain a vital factor, for both attack and defense, in continental Europe until the high technology armies of the late twentieth century. Only in extremis, during the First World War, did Britain resort to the conscription which, in one form or another, has been practiced throughout continental Europe for eons.

England, however, a century after the Black Death, with wool still profitable and cropgrowing unprofitable, had ceased to be a continental power. The Plantagenet and Lancastrian monarchs, in the course of the Hundred Years War with France, had been forced to abandon all their French territories except Calais. England's defenses then became the "wooden walls" of its navy. Paradoxically, sheep could man these wooden walls better than a numerous peasantry. An island Britain, stripped of its continental territories and with the profits from wool, was able to construct a navy, provision and crew it, giving it its "wooden walls." Sheep thus became militarily more important than people for England.

The loss of its French territories and the construction of a navy, paid for by wool exports, allowed England to pursue the profit possibilities of sheep farming created by the Black Death without serious threat of invasion by a continental power. But intervention by feudal lords within the island remained a possibility. The Earl of Essex might opt for more profitable sheep, but unless the Duke of Norfolk could be dissuaded from invading the sheep walks of Essex with his Norfolk cropgrowers, Essex had no prospect of realizing the profits of sheep. Only a powerful overlord, king, or sovereign, capable of restraining aggressive feudal lords, would make it possible for the feudal aristocracy to escape from the particular difficulties of cropgrowing and to realize the particular profits of sheep farming in fifteenth century England. The bloodletting of the Hundred Years War and the shorter but bloodier internal War of the Roses had, in any case, made England's feudal lords more than usually disposed to peace and to accepting the sovereignty of a monarch who would confirm and enforce titles. The price that England's feudal lords paid to be transformed from an obsolete and unprofitable feudal lordship into a profitable landed proprietorship was the creation of an absolute Tudor monarchy.

Squabbling over the succession had cost the lives of one-third of the monarchs and their immediate families in the Norman, Plantagenet, and Lancastrian dynasties. It killed four English kings in the fifteenth century alone, before the accession of the Tudors in 1485.[18] Yet, during 120 years of Tudor rule, a usurping king, a syphilitic king, a boy king, and two queens regnant—of whom one, Elizabeth, was of questionable legitimacy—reigned more effectively in England than any earlier dynasty had done; reigned more effectively than any rulers in contemporary Europe did; and they all died natural deaths.

England's Tudor monarchy anticipated by nearly two centuries the absolute monarchies of continental Europe. Its absolute power was necessary to transform England's feudal lords into a new class, previously unknown in the world: the class of landed proprietors. The Tudor monarchy, at the same time as it created a class of landed proprietors, deprived all others of the right that every people everywhere previously had—of access to land. Society, for the first time anywhere, was dichotomized, under the Tudors, into the landed and the landless.

If the right of some to exclude all others from access to land was to be absolute, then the power of the bestower of that right had to be absolute also. The security of the newly created property in English land could be ensured only if the sovereignty of "the king (or queen regnant) in parliament" was absolute. That sovereignty was not to be qualified by any higher authority on earth, including that of God's vicar, the pope in Rome. The property titles bestowed by the monarch would have been less absolute and might have been subject to papal approval without the English Reformation.

Profits from wool from English land provided further powerful motives for reformation of the Church in England. The security of novel, questionable, and questioned titles to the proprietorship of land, which yielded great profits but resulted in a situation where, as Sir Thomas Moore observed, "sheep do eat up men," demanded secure and certain succession to the throne. However, Henry VIII had only one child, a daughter by his wife, Catherine of Aragon. Henry desired to divorce Catherine and to remarry in order to produce a male heir and so secure the succession. The erstwhile feudal lords, transformed into landed proprietors, supported Henry in this move which promised to make more secure their novel and precarious titles to land. They were prepared to support Henry in his divorce even if that course meant a confrontation and a break with Rome.

A third important consideration singled out England, which had been a peripheral, European backwater, to lead the Protestant Reformation. Up to a third of English land was in the possession of the Church,[19] a fact which in itself was perhaps an indication of English backwardness. Yet nowhere else in sixteenth century Europe did land offer such prospects of profit as it did in England where, if not already in pasture, it could easily be put to grass to graze profitable sheep. The confiscated Church lands made possible immediate rewards of land grants to the supporters of Tudor absolutism; and they provided the means over the longer run for the absolute Tudor monarchs to "live off their own," as traditional feudal kings did, without encroaching by taxation on the property rights in land they had created, sustained, and legitimized.[20]

To summarize with regards to the Reformation: England's revolutionary and unique transformation of feudal lords into landed proprietors and the resulting simple dichotomy of society into landed and landless made it peculiarly important for its ruling class to break with Rome. That break ensured the "sovereignty of the king in Parliament" and the absoluteness of the property titles that he bestowed. The break made possible the king's divorce and the enhanced prospects that offered of a son to secure the peaceful and orderly succession to the throne, and therefore the security of land titles, which stemmed from the throne. Finally in England, where land was valuable centuries before elsewhere, the Church's extensive lands were a far richer loot than was available in continental European countries. These attractions of the Reformation for England's ruling class explain what Macauley found so puzzling:

> The History of the Reformation in England is full of strange problems. The most prominent and extraordinary phenomenon which it presents to us is the gigantic strength of the government compared with the feebleness of the religious parties. . . . There was nothing in England like the fierce and bloody opposition which, in France, each of the religious factions in turn offered to government. . . . Neither Protestant nor Catholic engaged in any great and well organized scheme of resistance.[21]

The Tudor dynasty created in England what, in effect, was a totally new form of property. Property was the core institution of European individualism. Property was both possible and essential because it applied to resources in elastic supply, slaves and capital. Incidentally and in a secondary manner, property also applied to particular parcels of land that were in limited supply. But that happened only in the context of an effectively limitless total land supply. Particular parcels of land were appropriated as property, but land continued to be effectively limitlessly available both in the ancient Mediterranean and in central western Europe. Blum has described the situation thus:

> The great stretches of untilled, or intermittently, tilled land, some of it among Europe's most fertile soils, reflected the underdevelopment. There had been no appreciable increase in the farm land of western and central Europe since the great clearings of the Middle Ages. Indeed, during the difficult times of the seventeenth century, much land had been abandoned. In some regions, the number of deserted villages reached almost incredible proportions, as in Schleswig-Holstein, where, in 1700, one-third, and in some especially hard-stricken districts, as many as one-half of all peasant holdings lay empty. . . . In France the amount of land in crops, fallow and forage increased by only 3.5 percent, from an estimated 23.1 million hectares in 1700–1710 to 23.9 million in 1781–1790. Those 23.9 million hectares took up 45 percent of France's land

area. . . . Until well into the nineteenth century, population density in the Danubian principalities was so low that most of the land there lay unbroken. As late as 1837 only an estimated 8 percent was planted.[22]

The superabundance of land and the scarcity of people with capital to operate it were even more pronounced in Scandinavia, eastern Europe and Russia.[23] Like slavery in the antebellum South of the United States, serfdom in Europe was a means of tying scarce capital-endowed labor to the superabundant land in order to exact a profit from that labor.

The incidental and secondary type of property in land that occurred in continental Europe retained the non-exclusive character of property in slaves or capital; the titles that some held to particular parcels of land, as to particular slaves or capital, so far from inhibiting, facilitated other members of society to operate other land, or to acquire slaves or capital. The situation created by the "Tudor revolution" was very different from this. The concept of property was extended to all land. By giving exclusive titles to land to some, it excluded others, who were the majority, from access, except on the minority's terms, to a resource that had always, everywhere else, been regarded as for the use of all society's members. Land henceforth in England was to be regarded as for the profit of its proprietors; and the people of England were dichotomized into the landed and landless, the role of the latter being to pay rent for the former's land.

The transformation of feudal titles, or the military/political power to levy exactions from land's occupants, into property in land could have occurred only at a particular phase of individualist capitalism's development and it could have occurred then only in England. It required high labor, high wool, and low grain prices to make it both necessary and profitable a switch from corn to horn in a country that was marginal for cropgrowing. It also required the existence of trade links to market the wool on a continent where ecological and political conditions precluded a similar response to changed post Black Death price relations. The supply of wool from the other main European source, the Spanish *mesta*, was inelastic and could not easily be expanded to meet the increased demand. This was because the *mesta* comprised collective flocks which practiced transhumance. They moved south and north through Spain, according to season, grazing land after harvesting and again prior to plowing and sowing, as the land became available. Neither the area grazed nor the stocking level on that area could be altered by the *mesta* shepherds.[24]

Had increased wool production been extensively feasible in continental Europe, it would have been economically pointless. An extensive shift from crops to pasture would have quickly re-established the old wool/grain price ratio, making it no longer profitable to replace people with sheep on the land. But because England was a small, offshore island which, by the fifteenth century, had ceased to have territorial claims in, but had trade links with, continental Europe, it was able to expand wool production manifold without depressing the price unduly.

An island location, a climate more suited to grass than grain, grazing suitable to sheep, a trade in wool, and high wool and low grain prices were, in summary, the conditions that caused England, alone of all the countries of the world, autochthonously to make land the primary form of property. But the value which English land had acquired depended absolutely on capital formation in continental Europe. It was that capital formation which made wool valuable. Without it, there would have been no demand for wool exports in the fifteenth and subsequent centuries any more than there had been in earlier times.

The social cost of dichotomizing England into landed and landless was great. Real wages were forced below their fifteenth century level and remained so until the nineteenth century.[25] Forced off the land to make way for sheep, English people were less well able to marry; and England's population growth, which had been higher than continental Europe's, dropped behind and remained there until the eighteenth century.[26] The appropriation of English land as private property caused the common people, for centuries, to be less well fed and to be less well bedded.

The power and majesty of an absolute Tudor dynasty were necessary to make land England's primary form of property. But 118 years of absolute Tudor rule made England's erstwhile feudal lords the wealthiest and most powerful property-owners in Europe. While a three-cornered contest continued in continental Europe for centuries more between the emerging power of the State (personified by the monarch), the waning power of the feudal lords, and the ascendant power of the property-owners, the issue had been reduced to one between the state and property in Tudor England. But even there, new concepts, relationships, and political institutions could not easily emerge. "The idea that property and income counted for more than rights of lordship was only finally established by the cataclysm of civil war in the seventeenth century, and the extinction of the castle as a form of local defense."[27] The English Civil War of the 1640s, followed by the Glorious Revolution of 1688, gave to England's property-owners the control of the state that their peers in continental Europe did not acquire until more than a century later. This English political precociousness, which stemmed from its insular location on the pastoral margin of cropgrowing Europe, thrust a backward country into the forefront of European political, military, commercial and economic development.

Many misconceptions exist, particularly among economic historians, about England's rise to a dominant world position in the seventeenth and later centuries. That rise to power is traceable to a single factor: land becoming scarce and valuable in England while, by contrast, it remained abundant, effectively limitless and free in continental Europe. Why this should have been the case becomes clearer from a comparison of continental French and of insular English farming. The French, in a different ecological and political environment, engaged in the enormously time-consuming (i.e., capital-consuming) enterprise of wine production. The resources it takes to clear, to plant, and to tend an acre of vines until they yield a vintage; the further time that elapses before that is consumable: these resources, over the same eight to ten years maturation period, would bring about 200 acres into sheep production.[28]

English agriculture is normally, though incorrectly, presented as capital intensive, whereas French and continental European agriculture is deemed to be labor intensive. Thus: "Wine was to French agriculture what wool was to English agriculture and society. . . . Viniculture . . . was what economists call a labor intensive variety of agriculture requiring large amounts of fairly skilled peasant labor and relatively small amounts of capital."[29] Wallerstein makes a similar point:

> To make a sensible comparison of development in English and French land tenure in this period, we must bear in mind that they each had two major modes of utilizing the land, but that they had only one in common—cereals. The second mode in England was animal husbandry, which lent itself more to economies of scale than did wine production, the second mode in France; and animal husbandry required more capital investment. This simple economic fact may explain more about the differences in land tenure development than is explained by laws, traditions, attitudes, prior class structure, or the presumed heritage of "feudal" rights.[30]

Many others make the same error about English agriculture being capital-intensive and central western European agriculture being labor-intensive. But, as suggested, approximately the same amount of capital is required to bring an acre of vines or 200 acres of sheep land into production. An acre of vines and 200 acres of sheep land produce about the same value of annual output, of mature wine in the case of the vines and of wool and meat in the case of the sheep land. Both enterprises have approximately the same current labor inputs. Thus, output per person or per unit of capital was not very different from French vines and English sheep grazing. The great difference was and is that, for a given output, 200 times more land was required for English sheep-farming as for French vine growing. The distinctive and critically important, but generally unrecognized, characteristic of English agriculture was its land intensiveness. This transformed the resource endowment situation. It caused land to be scarce and capital to be relatively abundant in England, while land continued to be abundant and capital continued to be critically scarce in continental Europe. This transformation of the resource input relationship conferred power and wealth in the modern era on the English successors of the feudal lords who acquired control of a resource that, uniquely in England, was scarce in Western society. This happened at the same time as their peers in central western Europe saw their power ebbing away to the ascendant property-owners, on the one hand, and to the emerging absolute monarchs on the other. This is the neglected key to understanding England's enormously important world role since the Tudors dichotomized the English into landed and landless.

Capital and not land, on the other hand, remained the limiting factor for the French and other continental European peoples. There was little regard for the wastelands, either of Europe or of the new territories made available as a result of the Great Discoveries. It was understandable then that, at the Peace of Paris in 1763, when the French were given the choice between Canada, with a billion hectares of land, and Guadaloupe, with 178,000 hectares, they should choose the tropical island with its possibilities for the slave-based production of sugar that could not then be produced in temperate central western Europe, even with its limitless land resources. Only the English, for whom land had become limiting long before other Europeans, were interested in those extensive and generally less productive areas of the non-European world that were still, in the eighteenth century, occupied by hunter-gatherers.

It was as though the Fates conspired to confuse mortal man in his efforts to understand the social forces that shape his destiny. An extraordinary and totally unique set of circumstances thrust England into the leading position in world affairs at an especially formative time. England, for over two centuries, led the world economically, militarily and, in important aspects, intellectually. Its influence in the new discipline of economics was understandably overwhelming. It operated through such luminaries as Hume, Smith, Ricardo, Mill, Jevons, Marshall, Pigou, and Keynes, and did not exclude Marx and Engels who, though not British born, did most of their research and writing there. Understandably English socioeconomic institutions became the norm, the ideal, the exemplar. Deviations from them have been regarded as such—as aberrations caused by local malfunctions. Nothing has been more fully incorporated into the panoply of the norm, the universal, the unquestioned than the quintessentially English institution of property in land which, precisely because of its uniqueness to Britain, made that country the leading power in the world for centuries. Few, if any, misconceptions in history have caused as much loss and suffering.

Ireland

The North Channel, between the Mull of Kintyre in Scotland and Antrim in Ireland, is narrower than the Straits of Dover between England and continental Europe. But Ireland was for long much more isolated from Britain than Britain was from the continent. For one thing, Ireland was cut off from the continental land mass much earlier than Britain, which remained part of it until after the last Ice Age. Ireland's earlier isolation is reflected in a narrower range of indigenous flora and fauna than Britain has, which in turn is narrower than the continent's.[31] While people inhabited Britain 50,000 years ago, Ireland was among the last parts of the globe to be inhabited, within the last 10,000 years. Its people were, as Francis Bacon put it, "the last *ex filiis Europae*"—the last of the children of Europe.[32]

Ireland's location, as a western, offshore island of a western, offshore island of a continent that was eastern oriented, isolated it. Its location also gave it a climate that is more maritime than anywhere else in Europe. Its winters are milder, its summers cooler, and its rainfall heavier. It is a climate conducive to the growth of grass, which covers two-thirds of the island, compared to one-fifth of the EEC's land surface. Much of Ireland's remaining land is barren mountain or peat bog where poor drainage inhibits grass growth.

Table 5.1. Land Use in the EEC, UK, and Ireland
(percentage of total land)

	EEC (12)	UK	Ireland
1. Under meadow & grass	20.1	46.5	67.7
2. Under crops	30.3	28.5	14.9
3. Under timber	24.3	9.5	4.8

Source: Commission of the European Communities, *The Agricultural Situation in the Community: 1990 Report* (Brussels: EEC, 1990).

Only 15 percent of the total land area is cropped, compared to 30 percent in the EEC as a whole. Of that part of the land used for agriculture, 18 percent is cropped in Ireland compared to 53 percent in the EEC as a whole. Less than 5 percent of Ireland's land is under timber compared to 24 percent of the EEC's. This is so although there have been several decades of state afforestation in Ireland, and in continental Europe there have been millennia of capital formation and encroachment by "islands of population" on "the sea of forest." When the primordial forest was felled by agriculturists in Ireland, grass grazed by livestock on well drained land and peat on poorly drained tended to take over. Comparative data are given in the table above for the UK, where land use is most similar to Ireland's.

Ireland's maritime climate, its relatively mild winters which are shortened by late autumns and early springs, its good grass growth which tends to suppress tree growth, all had a particular and important effect on its husbandry. Climatic conditions made Ireland the only distinctive geographical area in central western Europe, from the steppe to the Atlantic, where cattle could be wintered without fodder. Both the Venerable Bede[33] in the eighth century and Geraldus Cambrensis[34] in the twelfth century commented on the absence of any provision for foddering or housing cattle in Ireland in the winter. The cattle were able to survive without fodder partly because the winters were relatively mild and short, and partly because, from an early stage, the land was deforested, making transhumance, or *boolying* in Gaelic, easy and general. There may have been other parts of Europe, such as the Scottish lowlands, where similar climatic and flora conditions obtained; but none of these was isolated, as Ireland was. All of them were subject to the immediate influence of neighboring regions where winter fodder for cattle was essential.

Cattle in Ireland were naturally selected by their ability to survive winters without fodder rather than, as in continental Europe, systematically on the basis of their productivity and claim to scarce fodder. This gave rise to a totally different type of cattle husbandry from that of the rest of Europe west of the steppe. It is incorrect to assume, because the two islands were so close, that the information available in historical records pertaining to English cattle husbandry would apply also to contemporary practice in Ireland.[35]

First and most critically, the *Bos taurus* characteristic of lactating without the stimulus of being suckled by the animal's own live calf receded in Irish cattle and was replaced by the *Bos indicus* characteristic of lactating only in the presence of the dam's live calf. The *Bos taurus* characteristic evolved uniquely among Indo-European pastoralists in the manner and under the circumstances described above, in the forest of central western Europe. That characteristic was lost in Irish cattle, which presumably reverted to the normal, *Bos indicus* character of the cattle of all lactose tolerant pastoralists, other than those of central western Europe.

Irish cattle, because they were naturally selected by their ability to survive winters without fodder, must have been less productive of meat and milk than those of the rest of Europe, where only the most productive cattle were retained and allocated a share of invariably scarce winter fodder. Moreover, of the small output of milk of naturally selected Irish cattle, much was pre-empted for calf-rearing. As is the invariable practice with *Bos indicus* cattle, all Irish calves had to be kept alive to induce lactation.[36] Probably not much more than a quarter of the calves of the *Bos taurus* cows of central western Europe were kept alive, the rest being killed or allowed to die at birth. The *Bos indicus* Irish calves, having been kept alive throughout their dam's lactation to induce milk let-down, the bull calves in particular had little value. Most of them probably did not survive their first winter, as continues to be the case with half of the calves reared annually in India. A.T. Lucas's statement that "male animals were reared only in small numbers for breeding and draft"[37] is only partly true. It was as necessary to rear all male calves as female ones. But when the cows ceased to lactate, there was less incentive to keep the males alive than the females. The latter were almost certainly more valuable, as they are in Sub-Sahelian Africa now.[38]

The worthlessness of male calves reared to the weanling stage may have accounted for vellum being the normal material used in ancient Irish manuscripts while, in Britain and Europe generally, a coarser parchment from older animals was more common. The hides of calves killed, or allowed to die, at birth elsewhere in Europe would have been less suitable for vellum making than those of Irish calves killed at around six months old, while the limited number of British and continental *Bos taurus* calves reared would have been too valuable to slaughter simply for their hides. Their hides would not have become available until the end of the animal's useful life as a cow or draught ox, when they produced parchment of poorer quality than Irish vellum made from weanling calves.

Cattle-rearing involved saving and investment in central western Europe. There was no such requirement in Ireland. That was because there was no choice about rearing calves in Ireland; they had to be kept alive as part of the price of inducing their dams to lactate. Fodder was not fed to them in winter. They survived if there was sufficient natural herbage and if they were fit enough. That is to say, the product of Ireland's cattle husbandry was determined by the extent and natural fertility of the land available, mitigated only to some extent by the common state of the art.

Another, final point is noted about Ireland's indigenous cattle keeping which gives insights into the nature of ancient Irish society and which continues to influence Irish living patterns. This is that hard cheese was not made and was not part of the diet in ancient Ireland. As explained above, hard cheese production was a distinctive feature of central western Europe's cattle husbandry. Only continental Europeans could kill their *Bos taurus* calves to get from their stomachs the rennet essential for hard cheese production, without setting their cows dry. The Irish, with their *Bos indicus* cows, could not do so. Understandably then, "the archaeological record provides no evidence of (cheese) manufacture." This is so although "the documentary evidence shows that (cheese) formed an important part of the Early Christian diet." But the cheese in question was "buttermilk cheese (which) perishes very easily and is only suitable for very quick consumption."[39] It quickly becomes putrid, as described by Fynes Moryson.[40] The Earl of Ormonde, in the Pale, was therefore understandably concerned to introduce cheese-making on English lines.[41] Because hard cheese, which lasted through the winter, was unavailable in Ireland, it was necessary to import it for Queen Elizabeth's army.[42]

Soft cheeses could not contribute to spanning the nutritional gap in winter. That could only be done in Ireland with butter, which is a much less efficient means of conserving the dry matter content of milk. Cheese therefore, though possibly "an important part," must still have remained a minor item in the traditional Irish diet. It continues to be so even after several decades of local cheese making, using either rennet from the stomachs of Irish calves, which are all now of *Bos taurus* type, or from synthetic rennet (see table 5.2).

Table 5.2. Annual Consumption of Dairy Products, Ireland, and the EEC

	Ireland (kg/head)	E.E.C. (kg/head)
Milk	190	89
Butter	10	5
Cheese	3	12

Source: Commission of the European Communities, *The Agricultural Situation in the Community: 1988 Report* (Brussels: EEC, 1988), Table 163.

Ireland's Celtic immigrants could operate without capital because cattle could be wintered without fodder. Because straw for fodder was unnecessary, there was less need to grow cereals, which even now can be grown only with difficulty in an Irish climate that is very different from the arid climate of the Middle east where cereals originated. Capital was therefore unnecessary, either to grow cereals extensively or in the form of hay. Production, under the circumstances, was limited only by the amount of winter grazing available. Ireland was thus the only part of Europe, from the steppe to the Atlantic, where, following the Indo-European immigrations, food production was constrained by land and not by slave labor or capital. Moreover, because of Ireland's isolation, it was possible for its Celtic inhabitants to evolve, with minimal external intervention, a form of production and an organisation of society appropriate to its peculiar circumstances.

A nonindividualist, noncapitalist, land-based economy/society evolved in Celtic Ireland. Because the winter carrying capacity of communally grazed land determined output, the individual, by his work or the work of his slaves or capital, could not affect output. Reflecting the slight significance of the individual vis-à-vis a land-based society, law in Ireland was the customary law of the *breathamh*, a statement of accepted norms of conduct, but lacking the powerful sanction that the economic significance of the individual and of the individual's property gave to law in central western Europe. "There was no public authority in Ireland to execute the law, but the sureties as well as the kin, played an important part in securing a man's rights."[43]

Property, as the institution evolved in Europe, was unnecessary in Ireland. Indeed, as pointed out above and as is illustrated by the modern experience of property under communal grazing conditions in Africa, property would have been counter-productive. "Property" was based on the strength of the holder, rather than on a social recognition of, and willingness to defend, individual rights. The traditional view was: "The Gaelic Irish first won the land by conquest, and ever since have adhered to the principle of swordland as the basis of title."[44]

Transhumance, or *boolying*, rather than nomadism, as on the original steppe home of the Celts, was the means of coping with winter dearth in ancient Ireland. The probable reasons for this were: the climate's mildness; the less open character of the countryside where surviving wood and scrub impeded movement; and the practice of some, even if only a little, cropgrowing. These conditions would have made the ancient Celts in Ireland less mobile and more territorially specific than their ancestors had been, or than contemporary pastoralists were, on the steppe.

Living conditions in ancient Celtic Ireland were therefore probably more akin to those of contemporary Sub-Sahelian Africa than anywhere else. Both were nonindividualist, land-based societies. Both had a "bastard pastoralism" which included some cropgrowing in a predominantly livestock economy. Both were sedentary, unlike the pastoralists of the Eurasian steppe or African Sahel. Conditions in Ireland, as in Sub-Sahelian Africa, were conducive to the fragmentation of society into numerous clans or tribes. Cattle-raiding, or *creach*, was endemic in both societies, where the object of the raids was to seize the other tribe's/clan's cattle and women.

These warlike activities were probably less profitable, and therefore less ubiquitous, in Ireland than in Africa for two reasons. First, the cattle were less accessible, and second, the women were less valuable. Because of the prevalence of the trypanosomiasis-bearing tsetse fly in the African bush, cattle had to be held in the open, where they were more vulnerable than in Ireland, where cattle could be hidden away in bushland and the residual forest. African women were more valuable because, with Sub-Sahelian hoe-culture, they could grow on the warm soils sufficient roots and tubers to feed themselves and their children and contribute to the maintenance of their owner-husbands. Irish women were much less productive as cropgrowers in a cold, wet climate, where the only crops were unproductive cereals that may not always have yielded as much as the seed needed to sow the land.

Nevertheless, although women may have been less valuable in Ireland than in Sub-Sahelian Africa, brideprice, known as *coibhche* in Gaelic, was paid for them as for African women.[45] This contrasted with the dowries paid by women on marrying in the rest of central western Europe. Marriage and reproduction were conditional on the possession of savings/capital in individualist capitalist Europe. No such conditionality applied in Ireland where, as throughout the non-European world, society was nonindividualist and land alone determined output.

Consideration of the Irish situation delineates more precisely the limits of autochthonous evolution of individualist capitalism. Knowing where and when individualist capitalism evolved helps to understand better its nature. The failure of individualist capitalism to evolve autochthonously in Ireland—because capital was less necessary, was less productive, and was less easily amassed—contributes further to appreciating the uniqueness of the conditions that made possible the emergence and the organic growth of individualist capitalism in central western Europe and the character of that individualist capitalism itself.

Ireland's location was critical for the evolution of a very different society from the rest of Europe. Because it was an offshore island of an offshore island in the extreme west of Europe, its climate was importantly different: by a few inches of rainfall the year round, and by a few degrees of temperature more in winter and less in summer. Of equal, if not greater importance, its location isolated Ireland. The forces of individualist capitalism, by the fifteenth century, caused food production to be capital-based everywhere in Europe except Ireland. Had the lactose tolerant Celts in Ireland been subjected to those forces, probably some variant of capital based production would have emerged there too. But in a Europe which for long looked exclusively towards its origins in the east, Ireland's pastoralists were left free to evolve in response to local circumstances.

The situation in neighboring Scotland, though similar in many respects, was critically different in one. While ecological conditions in the Scottish highlands were very similar to those in Ireland, those in the lowlands were much like those of continental Europe. As a result of the interaction between the neighboring areas, the highland clans acquired much of the accoutrements of feudalism, while the feudal lowlands also acquired many of the characteristics of the clans.[46]

The Celts who settled in Ireland were a branch of the same Indo-European people who had acquired lactose tolerance on the Eurasian steppe, who created individualist slavery in the ancient Mediterranean and individualist capitalism in central western Europe, where they operated "the heavy wheeled plough drawn by several pairs of oxen."[47] Whatever further characteristics and experiences they acquired in the course of the their possibly two thousand year long migration through the forests of central western Europe, they proceeded in Ireland to evolve a very different way of life from anything else in Europe. Only in sub-Sahelian Africa was there a close parallel.

Chapter 6

Capitalist Colonialism

Breaking European Bounds

Central western Europe, some three to four thousand years ago, uniquely provided the conditions where it was both necessary and possible to save and to invest. Saving and capital formation have an inherent tendency to grow. The more of it that occurs, the easier it becomes to achieve more of it. Given that saving and capital formation were unique to central western Europe, it was virtually inevitable that European influences would eventually spread worldwide.

It may have been inevitable, but the process was neither automatic nor constant. Individualist capitalist growth, from the start, had an inherently cyclical character. A cycle may be perceived as commencing from a base of low population and high capital, from high incomes, and from high rates of saving, capital formation, and output growth. Because of high incomes and good nutritional levels, death rates fall below average and population growth rises above average. Population growth, always able to outstrip capital formation and growth of production, causes declines in incomes, savings, capital formation, rate of growth of production, and nutritional levels. Population grows to a point of collapse when an impoverished and malnourished people, living under climatically more difficult conditions than those experienced by any other major center of population, are decimated. Meanwhile, technological progress and the capital stock survived, in the one case totally and in the other largely unimpaired.

The Black Death of the 1340s is the best known and was perhaps the most severe of these calamities which marked the cyclical progress of capitalist growth. The evidence of the growth of population and the decline in incomes throughout central western Europe at this time is abundant and is frequently referred to as "the crisis of feudalism."[1] Titow documents for the Winchester estates in England the failing capital formation and the approaching crisis of the Black Death.[2]

The latter half of the fourteenth century and the fifteenth century were something of a golden age for the surviving people of central western Europe. The population having been almost halved by the Black Death, the stock of capital—principally in the form of cleared and manured land, draught and milch cattle, stocks of fodder and seed, ploughs and other implements, houses and barns—per survivor had almost doubled. This made possible also a virtual doubling of incomes.

This in turn gave rise to accelerated capital formation, growth, and change. The Reformation was one aspect of that accelerated change. Feudal potentates who had previously been too insecure now challenged Rome's suzerainty successfully. Accelerated growth triggered also the Renaissance flowering of the arts, sciences, and philosophy. The revival of ancient Greek speculation on the spherical character of the earth was part of that flowering. This raised the possibility of reaching by a different route the fabulous East, at a time when the incentive to do so had become much greater.

The inherently expansionary character of individualist capitalism has already been noted (chapter 4). Expansion in the fifteenth century was directed at securing two items in particular, spices and specie (i.e., gold and silver). Spices were needed to cope with central western Europe's perennial problem of long, severe winters. They were needed to help preserve through the winter the meat of animals surplus to the fodder to sustain them and which were slaughtered in the autumn. They were also needed to disguise the bad taste of meat that was often inadequately preserved because of the scarcity and cost of salt.

The precious metals were required to facilitate the operation of markets that expanded much more rapidly than the total economy. This was because, with capital formation and expanded output, opportunities for profitable specialization increased. Production, which had originally been almost entirely for subsistence, became increasingly oriented to the market. As markets grew in an age that predated instruments of credit, so also did the need for gold and silver. None had greater need for these metals and the access to markets which they conferred than the lords and kings, who were chronically short of cash.

Europe's heightened need for the spices of the East occurred at a time when access to these had become much more difficult. The capture of Constantinople by the Ottoman Turks in 1453 completed Islam's stranglehold on Europe's route to the East. The supply of spices and specie was thus reduced just when the demand for them was much increased by the accelerated economic growth that had been triggered by the Black Death a century earlier. The newly rediscovered concept of the earth as a sphere acquired particular relevance under these circumstances. It opened the possibility, for speculative peoples, of reaching the fabulous wealth of the East by traveling southwards or westwards, thus bypassing the Islamic block in the Middle East.

The Iberian powers, Spain and Portugal, for good reasons pioneered the speculative southwards and westwards drive to the East. The ancient Mediterranean for eons had been a formative influence on the evolution of central western European individualist capitalism. That influence strengthened rather than weakened after the collapse of the Roman empire in the West, when the Church of Rome took on the role of civilizing and ameliorating northern barbarism. Much of the emerging strength of central western Europe was directed, under the Church's influence, to eradicating heterodoxy, at home by the Inquisition and abroad by the Crusades. The Muslim Moors, who for eight centuries after the fall of Rome had occupied much of the Iberian peninsula, were a prime target for Christian orthodoxy. A dynamic, capital-based Christianity, in its full Renaissance vigor, succeeded finally in 1492 in expelling the Moors from Spain, leaving Ferdinand of Aragon and Isabella of Castile the joint rulers of that country and the most powerful monarchs of central western Europe.

They were moreover rulers of a commercially strategic country. Fifteenth century Spain has been described as "the street corner of Europe," where the ancient trade of the Mediterranean mingled with the growing trade of the Atlantic seaboard, which in turn at the time was being augmented by the burgeoning trade of the Baltic.

More powerful following the expulsion of the Moors than other European rulers and strategically located on "the street corner of Europe," Iberia's monarchs had more resources, and better opportunities, for the highly speculative investment of finding new routes to the fabulous wealth of the East. From the monarchs' viewpoint, that wealth, if successfully tapped, would set them free from dependence on their own property-owning subjects, who were a reluctant and uncertain source of revenue.

The first expeditions that sought access to the East by traveling south or west had much in common with that other epoch-making though humbler act of the original consigning of gathered seeds back to the earth in the hope that more might be recovered at a future date—or with the first breeding, instead of slaughtering, of an adult feral sheep or goat, which triggered food production. The time and locations were propitious in both cases: there was relative affluence; people had become better off and, freed from immediate pressures, they had acquired a speculative turn; and they had the resources to finance the speculation—a handful of seed or a feral female sheep or goat in the one case and, on a larger scale, three small ships in the case of Columbus's expedition. The initiatives taken were, in retrospect, obvious and elementary. Their replication was easy and changed the human condition for ever.

Europe and the Wider World—Peoples Encountered

Hunter-Gatherers

Europe's colonizers encountered three types of situation in the non-European world. First, most of the non-European world continued to be inhabited by its original settlers, who were hunter-gatherers. All of the Americas, with the exception of the narrow Andean plateau between the Tropics of Cancer and Capricorn, were inhabited by people who were primarily hunter-gatherers, though some of them did practice swidden farming. There was no cropgrowing in Oceania. The Khoikhoi inhabitants of southern Africa did not grow crops, though they had recently acquired cattle from their Bantu neighbors. Other extensive areas were also then the domain of hunter-gatherers, as these areas, though on a more circumscribed scale, continue to be today. This was the case of the equatorial rainforests of Africa, Malaya, and Indonesia and the territories of "the tribal people" of India.

As Europeans quickly learnt from their original encounter with the Carib hunter-gatherers, there was no profit to be made from these people; and, of course, for the people themselves, the encounter was disastrous. That knowledge and that result were to be expressed subsequently by the American aphorism "the only good Indian is a dead one" and by the extermination of the last of the indigenes of Tasmania, William Larne, in 1869. By and large, the hunter-gatherers and their territories were neglected.

> Until the end of the eighteenth century, European authorities regarded all these outposts in much the same bleak light. They entered them, if at all, with extreme reluctance and for the purpose of advancing their interests in quite different parts of the world.[3]

Spain did establish a colony at modern Buenos Aires and claimed sovereignty over the southern cone of South America, though that area was inhabited only by hunter-gatherers. But that exercise was for the strategic motive of controlling access to Spain's great wealth-producing empire in Meso-America. Likewise the Dutch colonized the Cape of Good Hope, but did so to facilitate and protect the Netherlands' access to its East Indies colonies.

Generally these territories of North America, Oceania, and South Africa inwards from the Cape were subsequently occupied by emigrants or settlers from Europe. These settlers moved away from Europe, into the New World, in much the same way and for much the same reason as their forebears had penetrated deeper into the forest of central western Europe. Dissenters, they went often to escape harsh government closer to home; and they went in great numbers from Britain especially, because land there had been appropriated by individuals, was grazed by sheep, and was no longer freely available to individuals, as land was elsewhere. The colonies that these people established were without prospect of profit for the metropolitan powers, which therefore practiced in relation to them "an easy and salutary neglect."[4] These may be referred to as *settler colonies*.

East Asian Crop Growers

A second category of society encountered by Europeans in the non-European world was the densely populated, rice-growing countries of east Asia: Japan, China, and their associated territories, Korea and Taiwan. A xenophobic Japan has the distinction of being the only considerable territory of the Old World, apart from the tropical rainforests, never to have fallen prey to the expansionary movements of the pastoral peoples. Understandably it reacted vigorously and purposefully against western penetration. Having acquired from Europeans the cannon and military techniques necessary to unite the country under the Tokugawa Shogunate, Japan proceeded quickly to expel the Portugese in 1638. Similarly the Americans and Europeans were quickly eased out after Commodore Parry's intrusion in 1853 and again after Japan's surrender to the Allied forces in 1945.

The response of nearby China to European penetration was as different from Japan's as was its experience with earlier intruders. China for millennia had experienced recurring invasion by northern pastoralists, but had nevertheless succeeded better than any other people in retaining its distinctive character. Like oil and water, the indigenous cropgrowing and the invading pastoral cultures never blended, and sooner or later the invaders either withdrew or were absorbed into the vast mass of China's peasant culture. Possibly that record of surviving largely unscathed from successive invasions inculcated a somewhat ambivalent attitude towards western intervention from the sixteenth century onwards. But that intervention has had scarcely more impact on China's masses than earlier ones. However deeply the West penetrated on a narrow front, China's ancient culture reasserted itself. The European powers never established sovereignty over China; nor did they over the nearby territories of Korea and Taiwan.

Other Food Producers

The third category of non-European society encountered by Europeans as they expanded overseas were food producers whom, unlike those of east Asia, they were able to conquer and whom, unlike the hunter-gatherers, they were able to colonize and exploit for metropolitan profit.[5] This is the process hereinafter referred to as *capitalist colonialism.*

Capitalist colonialism was a new and importantly different phase in the process, which is as old as life itself, whereby successive colonizing waves overtake, overpower, and absorb, or are absorbed by earlier ones. The critical difference between capitalist colonialism and all earlier forms of colonization was the link established and maintained between metropole and colony. The capitalist colonizers were not like the settler colonists or the migratory lactose tolerant pastoralists, who moved into the wilderness to seek a new, different, stand-alone life elsewhere. The capitalist colonizers were the agents of the European, capitalist metropoles which financed them and dispatched them overseas to locate, to conquer, and to squeeze existing societies for metropolitan profit.

The Latin tag, *natura non facit salta*—nature does not take jumps—has been used by historians and economists to encapsulate their perceptions of the key processes in their respective disciplines: gradual evolution in the case of history and slight changes at the margin in the case of economics. Neither the historical nor the economic process, according to this view, normally proceeds in large, discrete steps. *Natura non facit salta* might also be applied to most processes of colonization, even to the expansionary movements of the lactose tolerant pastoralists. Successive waves of these moved ever further into adjacent territories, which were then either incorporated into the territory of the parent society or became the territory of a new society.

Capitalist colonialism was different; it was saltatorial. First, the territory colonized was in no case contiguous with that of the colonizers; capitalist colonialism did involve a shipboard jump. Second, it was not undertaken by dissidents, seeking to escape from an existing situation; the colonizers acted, in all cases, as the agents of metropolitan principals for whom capitalist colonizing was another investment made to secure a profit. Finally, it is noted that capitalist colonization occurred in all cases under the aegis of the nation-states of central western Europe. The initial phase of capitalist colonization was undertaken by Spain, Portugal, France, the Netherlands, Britain, and Denmark, where nation-states emerged earliest. The newer nation-states, Germany, Italy, and Belgium, capitalist colonized during a later phase of capitalism which was characterized by factory production.

The Phases of Capitalist Colonialism

Mercantilist Capitalist Colonialism

Early European colonizing activities that were successful and survived of necessity afforded large returns for small inputs. Europe at that time had few savings to invest overseas, and if the returns were not high, the investment was a failure. That happened to several early attempts to colonize Africa and Asia, the participants in which disappeared without trace. The early notable successes were the conquest of Mexico and Peru by Spain, the monopolization of the East Indies spice trade by Portugal, and, somewhat later, the development of slave plantations in the Caribbean by the British, French, Dutch, and Danes.

The conquest of the Aztec and Inca empires was, in both cases, accomplished by a handful of ruthless Spanish buccaneers.[6] These were steeped in the violence of the Old World, which derived in large part from the age-old conflict there between pastoralist invaders and indigenous cropgrowers. That violence was accentuated by the unceasing, hegemonic struggles within individualist capitalist Europe. The indigenous American food producers, by contrast, had no previous experience with pastoralism. They had evolved formalized methods of warfare which coped adequately with the only previous competition for territory—the food producers and the hunter-gatherers who inhabited most of the hemisphere. The Spaniards fell upon these Meso-American food producers like wolves on the fold. They were the more easily able to do this because the Aztecs and Incas had evolved along highly specialized lines to grow crops, without the benefit of draught animals, at high altitudes in the tropics. The cropgrowers were immobile captives in their narrow Andean plateau homelands, where they were easily conscripted to tear from the mountains the gold and silver for which Europe's appetite was insatiable.

Next to gold and silver, Europe's expanding economy needed spices. Having mastered the sailing and navigational skills needed to turn the Cape of Good Hope and armed with the cannon and gunpowder which, for more than a century, had been a major arm in European military activity, the Portuguese were equipped to wrest control of the spice trade from the less skillful Muslim sailors. Central to their success was the establishment of a number of strategic naval bases. These, located principally at Hormuz in the west, at Goa on the Malabar coast, at Malacca in the straits of that name, and at Macao in south China, made possible the domination by Portugal of the great maritime trades of Africa and Asia with relatively few resources of men or material. In doing so, the Portuguese diverted to themselves the large profits which the Ottomans had previously drawn from this trade in spices between the East and Europe's expanding economy.

In addition to gold and silver to sustain its expanding market economy and spices to slow and then to camouflage the putrefaction of its seasonally produced meat, Europe desired tropical goods like sugar, cotton, tobacco, and dyes like fustic and indigo. With increased capital formation, the price that Europeans were prepared to pay for these exotic, tropical goods rose in terms of their own capital-intensive, temperate-zone goods and services. Simultaneously, Europe's growing maritime skills and power provided the means to meet this demand. Those means were to kidnap cropgrowers from West Africa and carry them to Caribbean island plantations where they were worked to death growing tropical produce for Europe. Thanks to its military and maritime skills, Europe was able to incarcerate up to ten negro slaves per European overseer or slave-driver.[7] The slaves, fed mainly on temperate foods, of which much came from Ireland,[8] produced during their working lives sufficient valuable tropical produce to make the whole enterprise of enslaving and plantation agriculture one of the major sources of European profit and wealth throughout the seventeenth and eighteenth centuries.[9]

It took central western Europe 250 years to ingest the new wealth acquired by crossing the Atlantic and by establishing and controlling a sea route to the East Indies. The new wealth flowing into Europe greatly accelerated its own wealth producing process. But its impact was uneven. The spectacular success, first of the Portuguese monarchs in tapping the eastern trade in spices and then of the Spanish *conquistadors* in plundering the silver and gold of Meso-America, has few if any parallels in history. The vast wealth brought into Iberia from both East and West conferred absolute power on the monarchs who controlled that wealth. It freed them from their economic dependence on their subjects. In the long run that wealth destroyed the Iberian peninsula's capacity to produce wealth.

Massive wealth from the colonies upset the nice balance, the constructive tension, and the interdependence between rulers and ruled, between castle and cabin, which characterized central western Europe's individualist capitalism. The Spanish crown claimed one-fifth of all gold and silver mined in the Americas. Much of the rest of the bullion also ended up in the state's exchequer as the result of sales of state bonds to the holders of bullion. This wealth conferred on rulers autocratic powers that freed them from dependence on their subjects and made them similar to non-European rulers and to those of eastern Europe and Russia. The power of the state, greatly augmented by colonial wealth and concerned to maintain the flow of that wealth, curtailed the scope of subjects to produce, to save, and to invest.

The silver of Mexico, Bolivia, and Peru, as well as unduly strengthening the monarchy, weakened the economy through inflation. Increasingly English and Dutch manufacturers supplied both the Spanish domestic market and that of its colonies.[10] The wealth of the colonies, in these ways, suppressed the sources of wealth and growth within the Iberian economy and transformed the peninsula from being the growth point into being, for three centuries, the economic laggard of central western Europe.

Edmund Burke envisaged a similar fate befalling Britain some centuries later, following the conquest of India. In his speech on the impeachment of Warren Hastings, Burke spoke of the letting loose of "all the corrupt wealth of India, acquired by the oppression of that country, for the corruption of all the liberties of this. . . . Today, the Commons of Great Britain prosecutes the delinquents of India—Tomorrow the delinquents of India may be the Commons of Great Britain."[11]

The wealth of the Orient and the Occident flowed into the castles of Iberia and flowed out from there into the cabins of the rest of central western Europe. The new wealth from the colonies reached the bankers, merchants, and manufacturers of the rest of western Europe. These, less fettered by poorer and less powerful states, were able to supply the goods and services which, under the rigorous control of all-powerful states and in an inflationary environment, Iberia's own producers could no longer supply. The total tonnage of trade between Spain and its American empire declined by 60 percent between the periods 1606–1610 and 1646–1650.[12] This was indicative of an economic decline that was matched by Spain's military defeat in the Thirty Years War, whereafter Spain was relegated to second rank status among European powers. The wealth of America and Asia, in this way, helped to transform the relative wealth and power of European countries. Those which had once led became the laggards; and the laggards became the new leading powers of Europe and the world.

Factory-Capitalist Colonialism

The new wealth of specie, spices, and tropical produce which flowed in from the capitalist colonies, in the hands of the bankers, merchants, and manufacturers of central western Europe, acted as both solvent and stimulant. It expedited the process of political/constitutional evolution in England and the Netherlands especially. England's "Glorious Revolution" of 1688, which established the first property-owners' state since the ancient Mediterranean, marked the culmination of the process of economic growth and concomitant political evolution which had commenced with the entry of Indo-European tribal pastoralists into the deciduous forests of central western Europe millennia earlier. Consistent with that entire process, competition meant that other parts of the central western European kaleidoscope either adjusted similarly to remain abreast or, like the Iberian powers, failed to adjust successfully and were relegated to positions of less importance. The adjustment process lagged in France and its property-owners' state did not emerge for a century after England's, and then only after France's much more violent revolution.

Technological progress went hand in hand with economic growth and political/constitutional evolution. The emergence of science and scientific method in the age of Copernicus, Galileo, Descartes, and Newton accelerated the process. Science in turn facilitated technological progress, particularly in navigation, transportation, and military matters.

The accumulation of wealth, political adaptation, and scientific and technological progress, all proceeding over a 250 year period of mercantile capitalism, created the pre-conditions for a new phase of human existence. In a manner reminiscent of the almost miraculous combination of circumstances that made possible the original emergence of capitalist production, there was, around the mid-eighteenth century, a concurrence of conditions that made it possible for Europe to progress on to a new, higher plane of productivity, which may be referred to as *"factory capitalism."* It is necessary here to note only the most important of those conditions.

Factory capitalism needed wealth on a scale previously unknown. Wealth was needed, first, to finance the larger scale and more capital-intensive methods of production involved. Second, and possibly more important, wealth was needed to create an effective demand for goods produced in greater profusion than ever before. Transport and lines of communication were needed to assemble in sufficient quantity the raw materials and fuel needed to sustain factory production and thereafter to distribute the products sufficiently widely to absorb a productive capacity that was on a vastly larger scale than that of the earlier cottage industry. Banking and credit facilities were needed to assemble many small savings to finance a few large production units and to finance the distribution and sale of the goods between factory and final consumer. Additionally, the accumulated skills of metallurgy, chemistry, and fabrication were needed to construct the machines which, in factories, replaced human hands.

As the sheltering forests of central western Europe were an essential condition for the saving and investment of myriads of "penny capitals" which marked the original emergence of individualist capitalism, so too the large capitals required for factory production could only have been forthcoming in a favorable political climate. A political milieu of that nature had emerged in England especially, following the "Glorious Revolution" of 1688 and the establishment of a property-owners' state there. The same political process was in train, if at a slower pace, in all those central western European countries where the wealth of the capitalist colonies reached the cabins, and not, as in Spain and Portugal, the castles.

When these and other preconditions were met 250 years after the Great Discoveries, individualist capitalism was able to surmount another threshold similar to that of breaking its European bounds. The financial, technological, and military resources were available to extend capitalist colonialism outside the forts and naval bases to which it had been confined in Asia and Africa during the first phase. Initially the Indian subcontinent, then southeast Asia, and finally the whole of Africa were brought under the sway of the nine capitalist colonial European powers. In these vastly extended territories, the metropoles secured much of the raw materials, some of the fuel, and more of the markets that were needed to allow the factories to operate efficiently at their capacity.

This second, factory-capitalist phase of capitalist colonialism differed greatly from the first, mercantile phase. During the first phase, when capital was still very scarce in Europe, when production was on a small, cottage-industry scale, and when profits were modest and precarious, the metropoles sought from their colonies first gold and silver to support markets which, due to growing specialization, were expanding much more rapidly than the European economy as a whole. Second, they sought goods that complemented their own capital-intensive temperate zone products; they sought especially spices and tropical produce. What they did not want was temperate produce, which would have competed with their own chronically surplus, capital-based agriculture, or manufactured goods that would have competed with their own crude and expensively made cottage-industry products.

The needs of the European metropoles from their colonies were different in the age of factory capitalism. First, in an age of increasingly sophisticated banking, where credit instruments accounted for most of the money supply, specie was no longer of overwhelming importance. Second, since scale was of the essence in factory capitalism, securing raw materials, fuels, and markets became of primary importance. Finally, because of the economies of scale achieved by factory production in metropolitan Europe, where alone the financial, market, political, technological, transport, and other conditions for factory capitalism existed, industry there no longer feared competition from the cottage industries of the colonies.

It was no longer necessary, in the era of factory capitalism, for the metropoles to appropriate crudely by plunder from the capitalist colonies, as they had done in Mexico, Peru, and the slave-worked plantations of the Caribbean. Changed circumstances permitted the extraction of wealth from the capitalist colonies to be achieved less brutally but more effectively through the market and trade. Those changed circumstances were essentially the West's ability to establish sovereignty over much of Asia and all of Africa and thereafter to determine the conditions of free trade under which colonial produce was exchanged for metropolitan produce. This imposition by the metropoles on the capitalist colonies of free trade in the raw materials of the colonies for the manufactured goods and services of the metropoles has commonly been referred to as the *pacte coloniale*. It was a pact imposed unilaterally by the metropoles when they had secured, through factory capitalism, the power to conquer the colonies and thereafter to compete successfully with the colonies' craft producers.

The European colonizing powers, as noted, added little to their territories for a quarter millennium after the original conquest of Latin America and the Caribbean. But during the 150 years from around 1750 to 1900, the colonization of the non-European world was completed. The original six capitalist colonizing powers, Spain, Portugal, Britain, the Netherlands, France, and Denmark, were joined, in this later factory capitalist phase, by the newly created nation-states of Germany, Italy, and Belgium. Capitalist colonialism thus maintained the distinct pattern set from the beginning, which was that the colonizing process was undertaken in all cases by sovereign states, which proceeded to exercise sovereignty over the colonized peoples.

The only parts of the non-European world that escaped either capitalist colonization or settler colonization by Europeans by the end of the nineteenth century were the east Asian countries already referred to (China, Japan, Korea, and Taiwan), the disintegrating Ottoman empire of the Middle East, and three individual countries. These were Persia (now Iran), Siam (now Thailand), and Abyssinia (now Ethiopia). Siam was suffered to retain a nominal independence as a buffer territory between British and French possessions in Indo-China. Abyssinia's inaccessibility, which made it the exception to almost all African generalizations, preserved it from European colonization, except briefly from 1936 to 1942. Persia, along with most of the former Ottoman empire, came under British or French rule, initially during the nineteenth century and finally after the defeat of Turkey in the Great War of 1914–1918.

The islands of Hong Kong and Singapore were *sui generis*. As entrepots, established by Britain in the nineteenth century to trade with the surrounding territories, they were sources of profit for metropolitan interests and therefore did not enjoy the "easy and salutary neglect" of the British settler colonies. But they did have in common with the settler colonies the fact that western culture was established there on a *tabula rasa*. There was even less interaction with the handful of indigenous islanders than was the case in North America or Oceania. There was close metropolitan control, but that control was not exercised, as it was in the capitalist colonies, to establish a garrison elite to govern an indigenous food producing population for metropolitan profit. The islands therefore were not capitalist colonized, the essence of which was "squeezing" established, food-producing societies for metropolitan profit.

The Anatomy of Capitalist Colonialism

Distinctive Features

Life, in a sense, is a colonizing process. Strains, varieties, or species that are better adapted migrate to new environments where, if already occupied, they eliminate, assimilate, or dominate existing populations. Man has been the most successful colonizer. He has succeeded, by his extraordinary adaptability, in occupying virtually all parts of the globe other than the Antarctic.

Races of people who were able to derive more sustenance from given natural resources in time replaced others. Thus, over the past twelve thousand years, food producers have extended their control over most of the world, which had previously been occupied by hunter-gatherers. These latter by now have been confined, by and large, to the most barren locations, as on the edge of the Kalahari desert in southwest Africa; or to the densest equatorial jungle of Brazil, Malaya, and Borneo; or to the hills of Assam. They are accorded legal status in North America on areas reserved for them by the food producers, who appropriated the remainder of the land for food production. The hunter-gatherers have, in general, been obliterated by the food producers, leaving little more than archaeological traces.

More productive food producers have in turn replaced less productive ones. The riverine Sumerian, Egyptian, Chinese, and Inca empires all expanded hegemonically into neighboring territories and brought under their sway their less productive societies. These were then also organized as riverine cropgrowing societies. There were other movements of a non-hegemonic nature by more productive food producers into the territories of less productive ones. These colonizers sought better land or more land. If they were more productive and therefore more numerous and stronger than the indigenous society, they could eliminate, assimilate, or dominate it. The most important and widespread case of this colonizing by food producers of lands already occupied by other food producers was the spread of lactose tolerant pastoralists from their original homelands in the Eurasian steppe and the arid lands of the Middle East, North Africa, and the Sahel.

The establishment of sovereignty over nonindividualist, natural-resource-based, food-producing societies by individualist capitalist European countries from the sixteenth century onwards was a fundamentally different form of colonization from any that had preceded it and from the settler colonization that was contemporaneous with it. It was different, first, in that the colonized territories were not contiguous with the metropoles. Colonies and metropoles were invariably separated by sea or ocean. Colonization was only made possible—or in Ireland's case, as discussed in chapter 8, made necessary—because of the emergence in central western Europe of the skills and resources that opened a new, maritime age. Those new skills made possible transportation over long distances on an unprecedented scale. This gave capitalist colonialism its second distinctive feature: it was concerned, from the beginning, with securing for the metropoles produce from the colonies. That produce was gold and silver from Latin America, spices from the East Indies, tropical produce from the West Indies, and cattle and sheep from Ireland.

The ability to transport produce obtained in the capitalist colonies to the metropoles by sea conferred on this form of colonialism a third distinctive feature: the continuing intervention of the metropoles in the colonies. The capitalist colonies were never stand-alone enterprises, the survival of which depended on the colonizers adapting to new, local conditions as, for example, the migrating, lactose tolerant pastoralists did in Europe and India. This new form of colonization depended instead on the willingness and ability of the metropoles to apply resources, particularly of a repressive, military/naval character, in order to retain control of the colonies.

The impoverishment of territories occupied by noncapitalist colonizers was usually to their detriment and usually brought its own rectification. That came either as their elimination or their replacement by others better able to use the territories on a sustained basis. Thus, while hegemonic expansion may have usually resulted in tribute or taxes being transferred from the periphery to the core, the exhaustion of the periphery by a rapacious core invited intervention by neighboring forces. If these could acquire control of a depleted periphery, they were likely ultimately to threaten the core itself. Thus, the pillaging of the Balkans by the Ottoman Turks made it easier for Austrian, Polish, and Russian expansion into this region and for the ultimate destruction of the Ottoman empire.[13]

It was much the same earlier, in the ancient Mediterranean. The enslavement of conquered peoples provided that culture's economic basis and made possible a flowering of civilization superior to anything that preceded it or followed it for a thousand years. But the wealth of manpower plundered from the barbarous periphery only sustained an inherently parasitic economy, incapable of surviving on its own. When the plundering had to stop, the culture that it sustained at the core crumbled; the plundered periphery lay exposed to hostile outsiders; and the whole edifice collapsed and disappeared more quickly than other, earlier civilizations.

The constraints which applied in all other forms of colonization did not apply to capitalist colonies. The more that was extracted from capitalist colonies, the less attractive those territories became for other, putative colonizers. The more that was extracted, the more wealth the metropoles had for investment, including investment in military/naval power to secure their colonial source of wealth. Conceptually, there was no limit to the degree to which metropoles could extract the wealth of capitalist colonies. When Spain had taken all the gold and silver possible, with existing technology, from the Andes mountains and had destroyed a large part of the population in the process, Latin America became a much less attractive territory for other colonizing powers, even without the Monroe Doctrine's discouragement of further European colonial adventures in the Western Hemisphere. The working to death of slaves in the Caribbean did not, as had been the case in the ancient Mediterranean, lead to the collapse of the individualist capitalist powers who controlled the plantations there. Instead, the wealth extracted from the slaves contributed to the development of central western European capitalism, which made possible the colonization of Asia and the tapping of its cheaper labor; this, in turn, made Caribbean slavery obsolete. The possibility of extracting profit for the metropoles was, therefore, the only effective constraint on "squeezing" capitalist colonies.

Finally, the extension of metropolitan European rule over the capitalist colonies was a very different matter from the extension by European potentates of their rule over adjoining European territory through the hegemonic struggles which were a dominant feature of the European scene for millennia. The most fundamental difference was that these hegemonic struggles did not involve any change in the socioeconomic order of the territories involved. When the king of France extended the territory he ruled from the core Isle de France to France's "natural borders," life in the appropriated territories continued as before. Saving and investment continued to determine output. The same tribute or taxes were paid, though possibly to different collectors. The same conscripted military service was rendered, though probably under a different flag. The same God was prayed to, although very late in the day, after the sixteenth century Reformation, He may have been prayed to in a different style. Capitalist colonialism, by contrast, involved the forcible imposition of the institutions and technology of individualist capitalism on economies which, in all cases, were land-based and nonindividualist. The superimposition involved fundamental change in the socioeconomic order of the colonies. The impact on the capitalist colonies of these imposed institutions and technologies was, in many ways, the exact opposite of their effect in the metropoles, where they had evolved and where they had the effect of making central western Europe the dominant influence in the world.

Property in the Capitalist Colonies

The metropoles squeezed their capitalist colonies in particular by imposing the quintessentially European institution of property on them. The agents or local collaborators of the metropoles were given proprietorial rights over the scarce resources of the colonies, which they then held subject only to executing metropolitan policy in the colony in an adaptation of European feudal usage, "in fee simple," or directly from the crown in the metropole. There was a clear, fundamental difference between capitalist colonial property and property in individualist Europe. As the institution had evolved in Europe, property was in resources that were in elastic supply: slaves and capital. It evolved autochthonously in response to society's absolute need for these elastically supplied resources: slaves in the ancient Mediterranean and capital in central western Europe. Property was created in the capitalist colonies by the metropoles as a means of squeezing the colonies and of doing so without the constraints implicit in all other forms of colonization. Property in the capitalist colonies did not have the ultimate sanction that it had in Europe: that it was in the interest of those societies. It was sufficient, in the capitalist colonies, that property served the interests of the metropoles; its impact on the colonized societies was immaterial.

Property was created in the limiting resource and conferred on the agents and collaborators of the metropoles in the capitalist colonies. During the first 250 years of capitalist colonialism, before the tapping of Asia's limitless labor, labor was the limiting resource in the Western Hemisphere. Property was created in labor though the Spanish *encomienda* system in Latin America and through simple slavery elsewhere. The *encomienda* system of compulsory labor services persisted in Bolivia until 1956.[14] Slavery was abolished in most of the Caribbean in 1832, but it survived in Brazil for another sixty years.

There were similarities between slavery in the western hemisphere, which was part of the individualist capitalist system, and the individualist slavery of the ancient Mediterranean, which was itself a distinct socioeconomic system. Land in both cases was non-limiting. The limiting resource was labor which, on the limitless land, could produce a surplus over maintenance needs, which was in both cases appropriated by the slave owners. The surplus over the cultivator's maintenance was insufficient, at the state of the art, for reproduction in the ancient Mediterranean. It was that fact which caused limitless arable land of second grade to be available and to make slavery feasible in the ancient Mediterranean. It also necessitated continuous conquest to replenish the labor pool; and it forced returns to non-servile labor below subsistence levels, leading to the concentration of wealth and power that was the corollary of outward expansion in the ancient Mediterranean.

The surplus over maintenance in the western hemisphere was determined by market forces rather than by the state of the art. It was determined, on the one hand, by the cost of the slave's maintenance and, on the other, by the value of the slave's produce in central western Europe. The surplus may or may not have been sufficient for the slave's reproduction; but reproduction depended on whether it was cheaper than to purchase slaves newly captured in Africa. Over nine million Africans were brought as slaves to the Western Hemisphere between 1500 and 1810, when the slave trade was outlawed, though not stopped. In 1800 the black population of the Western Hemisphere was less than five million.[15] Deaths exceeded births by half the number of people brought in as slaves, mainly in the eighteenth century. The excess of deaths was caused principally by overwork and underfeeding. It reflected the fact that it was normally more profitable to buy newly captured slaves than to reproduce those already held.

Sufficient slaves were brought to, or reproduced in, Barbados between its colonizing in 1625 and the outlawing of the slave trade in 1810 for the small island's labor needs. Barbados therefore supported the outlawing of the slave trade, which could then benefit only the more extensive and more recently colonized territories like Trinidad and Guyana, the tropical produce of which would compete in Barbados's markets.

Following the abolition of the slave trade, the black population of the United States increased prior to emancipation by 2 percent annually, which was far faster than contemporary population growth anywhere outside North America.[16] Large profits were made by enslaving and reproducing negro labor to grow, on the virtually limitless land of North America, tropical and semi-tropical produce for sale to central western Europe. The prospect of this profitable form of capitalist enterprise being extended westwards into the new territories of the United States, where slave labor would then be in competition with free labor from the northern states, was a major factor in precipitating the American Civil War.[17]

Slavery in the Western Hemisphere therefore did not require, as in the ancient Mediterranean, continuous conquest to replenish a dwindling labor supply. That labor could be replaced by raiding Africa for slaves or by reproducing them *in situ*. Further, so far from depressing the incomes of citizens in the metropoles, as it did in the ancient Mediterranean, slavery in the Western Hemisphere raised those incomes. It did so by providing the populations of the metropoles with tropical produce that complemented their own temperate products. More importantly, Western Hemisphere slavery enhanced central western European profits, from which came the investment that made possible the transition from mercantilism to factory capitalism. That transition, in turn, made it possible for the metropoles to secure political control of Asia's large labor pool. That effectively ended the scarcity of colonial labor and caused land thereafter to be normally the limiting factor of production in the capitalist colonies.[18] The metropoles conferred property in land on their agents and collaborators in the colonies, in the same way as England's Tudor monarchs had created property in English land when that replaced capital as the limiting factor on production.

The distinction between capitalist colonial property and European property extended to the settler colonies. Property was created and sustained in these colonies by the settlers themselves, as it had been in the forests of Europe. It was not created and sustained by an external metropolitan power as a means of advancing its own interests. Property in the settler colonies, as in metropolitan Europe, was, for the most part, in non-land resources that were in elastic supply, including both slaves and capital. Princely grants of land were made in colonial North America. But without an effective army of occupation, for which the settlers were unwilling and probably unable to pay, and from which England, the colonial power, could expect no commensurate return, the land grants were worth little more than the paper on which they were written. Effective occupation was the only generally recognized title to North American land, as it had been to land in central western Europe.[19]

In Western Australia there was the well known case of Thomas Peel, second cousin of Robert Peel, the English prime minister, who organized and financed settlement in the new colony of Swan River. The expectation was that, on arrival in Australia, the settlers would operate and pay rent for land that the entrepreneur had previously been granted. The rent would constitute a return on the cost of transporting the settlers from England. "He landed 300 settlers, and spent altogether fifty thousand pounds, but in a very little time his stock had wasted away, and most of his settlers had left him."[20] Subsequent efforts to colonize Australia by financing emigration through land sales, as advocated by Wakefield and the Colonization Society, were also undermined by the ease with which the need to purchase land was avoided by moving beyond the limits of officially settled locations.[21]

Without metropolitan intervention to create and to enforce property titles, land in the settler colonies remained, as in central western Europe, free or virtually free. That relatively easy access to, and abundance of, land in central western Europe and in the settler colonies persists and is manifested now by such phenomena as the U.S. "land bank" and the EEC policy of land retirement or "set aside."[22]

The effects of property in people in the Western Hemisphere during the first quarter millennium of capitalist colonialism were as disastrous as those effects had been for the enslaved peoples conquered by Rome.

> Within a century of Columbus reaching the Antilles, the population of the Americas (14 million people) had been reduced by a fifth. Allowing for the fact that considerable areas and populations remained (as yet) unaffected by the invasion—for example the million natives north of the Rio Grande—this translates into an average drop of about a quarter in the occupied zone, with some really catastrophic declines in particular places.[23]

The effects of property created in the land of the capitalist colonies have been less dramatic. But because this form of property has been more pervasive and enduring, its effects in total have been far more damaging than those of property in people. Why this should have been follows, in part, from the discussion on why property evolved primarily in people and capital and could not have done so in land.

It is true that property that was primarily in land did evolve autochthonously in England, but the circumstances there were quite exceptional. Those exceptional circumstances first made it possible for land to become the primary form of property in England and thereafter for that fact to cause England to be for centuries the foremost power in the world. The cost to the English people of that greatness was severe. Prosperity for the masses did not follow for four centuries, even though during that time all of the profits from English land were spent, and some were invested, in England. By contrast, the profits from capitalist colonial land have, for the most part, been consumed or invested in the metropoles.

The leading role that England occupied, in large part because of the unique establishment there of property in land at a particularly formative period in the evolution of economic thought, has given rise to widespread, serious misconceptions about the economic significance of the institution. Apart from the quite exceptional and thoroughly misleading case of England, property that has been primarily in land has ever only existed in capitalist colonies. There it was created as the principal mechanism of the metropoles for squeezing the colonized nations.

Creating property in the land of the capitalist colonies meant that land, which previously had been solely for the sustenance of people, became primarily a source of profit for the agents and collaborators of the metropoles. The colonized peoples thenceforward had access to that land, which was their sole sustenance, only insofar as that access was profitable to the metropoles' agents and collaborators. The people could use the land only if that was as profitable to its owners as using the land to produce for metropolitan markets under the *pacte colonial*. There were no offsetting economic advantages. Property in land, as well as being exclusive in this sense, is also powerless to affect the supply. It differs fundamentally, in these two respects, from property in slaves or capital, which were the primary forms of property in individualist Europe, where alone the institution of property evolved autochthonously. The consequences for the peoples of the capitalist colonies of making land the principal form of property, for the profit of the agents and collaborators of the metropoles, have been disastrous in a multiplicity of ways according to local circumstances.[24]

Capital in the Capitalist Colonies

Capital has been traditionally used in central western Europe to complement labor in order to expand output. Myriads of individuals, as the price of their existence and reproduction, saved part of their small, normally non-cash, incomes and invested those savings in such forms as winter fodder, calf-rearing, equipment, land-clearing, and land-fertilizing. That capital made it possible for family labor, which without capital could have produced virtually nothing and would have starved, to produce sufficient for a subsistence and, in some cases, sufficient for their reproduction. The savers/investors of traditional central western European individualist capitalism always had available the labor of family members, the support of whom was the entire purpose of producing, saving, and investing and who, without capital, would have been unproductive and would have perished. The opportunity cost of the family labor—or the cost that would have been saved by not using it—was virtually zero. Investment, under those circumstances, was made solely to complement family labor and to increase output. It was not undertaken to replace zero-opportunity-cost, family labor.Very much later in the evolution of individualist capitalism, especially during and following the Industrial Revolution of the eighteenth/nineteenth centuries, much of the labor ceased to be that of the investor's own family. It was hired labor which cost at least the wages paid. However poorly paid the hired workers were, they had an opportunity cost that traditional, pre-industrial family labor did not. The fact that hired labor had a cost gave investors an objective to save labor which traditional, pre-industrial, central western European investors did not have. As increasingly the labor employed was hired, investment acquired the dual objective: (a) of increasing output by complementing the existing stock of labor; and (b) of producing the same quantity of goods/services with fewer workers and so at lower cost by substituting capital for labor. Empirically the original, complementary role of capital has outweighed its new, substituting role in the metropolitan West. At least until very recent times, the amount of labor used in central western Europe has continued to increase with capital formation, as it had done for millennia. It has done so even though investors now have a powerful incentive to replace labor that, with rising incomes, has become very costly.

The original complementary role of capital with labor has continued, at least until recently, to outweigh capital's new, substituting role, in part because of a firm demand for output. That demand has made it profitable for investors to use capital to complement labor in order to expand output and to do so in sufficient numbers and on a sufficient scale to outweigh the simultaneous objective of using capital to substitute for increasingly costly labor. The complementary, labor-employing role of capital has outweighed the substituting role, in large part because of the Walrasian effect that the higher the level of incomes and cost of labor, the greater the demand for the products of labor and capital.[25]

But complementing labor with capital to produce more has also been profitable because of trade with non-metropolitan capitalist regions. An early form of that trade was with eastern Europe and Russia. Capitalist colonialism, following the Great Discoveries of the fifteenth and sixteenth centuries, greatly extended those trading opportunities. That has been especially so in the era of factory capitalism. Trade between the metropoles and colonies has supplied the metropoles with food and other primary products at low cost, which has contributed also to keeping metropolitan labor costs low. That has had two effects. First, it has reduced the incentive to replace labor with capital; and second, for any given level of labor costs, it has meant that more income has been available to buy the products of metropolitan secondary and tertiary industry. For example, the decline in the real cost of food in nineteenth century Britain, as well as contributing to holding down the cost of British labor, left sufficient income available to that labor to buy the manufactured goods and services of industrializing Britain. Investment of a labor complementing character was thus warranted on both accounts: because labor was cheap and because there was, nevertheless, a good demand for the products of investment. Trade with the colonies also, of course, added to the demand for the secondary and tertiary products of metropolitan investment, again warranting the use of capital to increase output, by complementing rather than replacing labor.

The role of capital has been very different in the capitalist colonies. Investment from the beginning was with a view to production for the market rather than for subsistence. It was undertaken principally by the agents/collaborators of the metropoles, who hired indigenous labor to produce for metropolitan markets. Though the labor was low cost, it was not family labor with zero opportunity cost. There was, therefore, from the beginning in the capitalist colonies an incentive to use capital to replace labor. Moreover, because incomes in the squeezed capitalist colonies were low and, for the reasons considered in the preceding section and in a following section on demography, tended to go lower, and were therefore incapable of generating a local demand, it was generally not profitable to produce for the domestic market. Further, such local demand as did exist in the capitalist colonies was, under the *pacte colonial*, being eroded by imports of low cost, factory-made products from the metropoles. As a result, south and southeast Asia ended the nineteenth century with smaller proportions of their workforces engaged in manufacturing and larger proportions in agriculture than at the beginning of the century. "The proportion of the Indian population engaged in agriculture rose and that engaged in industry and commerce fell."[26] The same was true of Latin America where, at this time, "exports were developed at the expense of subsistence economic activities."[27]

Capital could be used profitably in the capitalist colonies to produce for the metropolitan markets; it could not usually be used profitably to produce for the local market. Capital could also be used profitably to integrate more closely the metropolitan and capitalist colonial economies with assembly, communication, transport, and distribution facilities. Finally, capital could be used profitably in the colonies, not to expand production for that market, but to produce the same amount for it with less labor. Gandhi's spinning wheel was of symbolic significance only; it did not prevent modern mills replacing craft labor in producing Indian cloth for local use.

Capital formation was normally undertaken in the capitalist colonies by the agents/collaborators of the metropoles. There were, however, some cases, at the early stages of factory capitalism, where investment was undertaken by the colonized peoples themselves. Notable among these cases were smallholding cocoa in the Gold Coast, or modern Ghana, and smallholding rubber in Malaya. The indigenous populations of these countries, a hundred years ago, had as yet very little experience of the effects of capitalist colonial rule. However, they quickly perceived that a return could be got from planting these new tree crops, which matured after four years in the case of cocoa and after seven in the case of rubber. Smallholders in Malaya, at the beginning of the twentieth century, planted rubber extensively, despite official discouragement, which aimed to reserve this new crop for investment by metropolitan capital.[28] But the destabilizing effects of a few generations of capitalist colonial rule have now left the smallholders, who took a foremost part in establishing cocoa in Ghana and rubber in Malaya, no longer able effectively to participate in the production of these crops.

Low and declining incomes compel the inhabitants of the tropics to direct their resources towards activities that generate an immediate return in order to support their increasing numbers of surviving children. Because their resources have become more limited, including especially their ability, as increasingly malnourished people, to work, the indigenes of the tropics are forced to neglect the slower maturing, longer lasting tree crops that are most suitable for tropical agriculture and, if they cannot get day labor, to conserve their limited energy by remaining idle. Smallholder rubber production declines in southwest Perak, one of the most densely settled and fertile parts of Malaya.[29] Ghanaian cocoa production, a smallholder enterprise, declined from an average annual production of 454,000 tons in the period 1961–1962 to 1965–1966 to 245,000 tons in 1990, a period during which world cocoa production increased from 1,400,000 to 2,400,000 tons.[30] As the supply of family labor in the tropics increased and its value decreased, the stock of smallholder capital to employ that labor also decreased. The same Western influences that caused a rapid increase in the labor supply caused simultaneously a decrease in the effective demand on small farms for that labor, so that less of it is employed even at lower real wages. This point is developed later.

There was a fourth use for savings in the capitalist colonies apart from producing for export to the metropoles, for investing in the linkages between the metropoles and the colonies, and to substitute for labor in producing for local consumption. That was to deposit them with the metropolitan-type and metropolitan-controlled banking systems that were established in capitalist colonies in the era of factory capitalism. The banking systems were as much part of the linkage that bound the capitalist colonies to the metropoles as were the shipping lines, the railways, the go-downs/warehouses, and the telegraph services.

The banking systems, as well as channeling metropolitan finances to the capitalist colonies, through their branches in the colonies, collected the pence and shillings of the savers for transmission to the metropoles, where they added to the stock of savings available for investment. The banking systems of all capitalist colonies appear to have built up net credits in the metropoles; the banks normally held more assets and fewer liabilities in the metropoles, and they normally held fewer assets and more liabilities in the capitalist colonies.[31] Given the role of capital in the capitalist colonies, the question of whether, in thus acting as conduits for transferring savings from the capitalist colonies to the metropoles, the banks harmed or benefited the colonized peoples is a moot point.

On the one hand, removing savings from the colonies benefited the colonized peoples (a) by reducing the substitution of capital for labor and (b) by reducing the amount of natural resources incorporated with capital in production for the metropoles and so leaving more of those resources available for the indigenes. On the other hand, the transfer of savings by the banks to the metropoles harmed the capitalist colonized peoples (a) by increasing the supply and reducing the cost of capital in the metropoles and so increasing the competitive capacity of metropolitan secondary and tertiary industry vis-à-vis that of the colonies, and (b) by providing an additional outlet for the profits of the agents/collaborators of the metropoles and so enhancing the returns to them from operating the *pacte colonial.*

Although the return on savings on deposit with the banks was low, the savings were secure, and "money in the bank" conferred status in societies where incomes tended inexorably to fall to the ever lower limits that have obtained throughout the era of capitalist colonialism. But whatever ambiguities there may be about the net effect on the colonized peoples of the removal of their savings by the banking system, the banks themselves indubitably profited from their role in squeezing the colonized nations for metropolitan profit.

The Demographic Results of Capitalist Colonialism

Impacts on Western Populations

Populations expand to the limit of the resources available for their support. As with other species, that has been true of man until relatively recent times. The resources available increase slowly over the long term, so populations dependent on those resources can also increase only slowly over the long term. Because of the inability of populations to increase greatly over the long term, mortality rates must, over the long term, approximate closely to birthrates. Birthrates of all species, including man until recently, have been determined biologically. The biological human birthrate is about fifty per thousand per annum.

The world's estimated population was four million in 10,000 BC and 190 million in 500 AD.[32] That represented an average rate of population growth of 1.5 percent *per century,* which was not significantly or perceptibly different from zero. That is to say, over the long run, the human population has been stable, with virtually no difference between death rates and birthrates, which were for the most part determined biologically. Any protracted tendency for death rates to fall below birthrates caused population to increase beyond the increase in capacity to sustain it, with consequent lower nutritional levels, higher mortality rates, and a restoration of equilibrium.

The social forces released by individualism in Europe made possible an exceptional expansion in output there. That in turn made possible an exceptionally rapid growth of Europe's population, causing it to increase from 10 percent to 20 percent of the world's total during the last five millennia BC.[33] Within Europe, the precocious individualist slavery of the ancient Mediterranean made possible population growth there earlier than in central western Europe. But though commencing later and at a lower rate, population growth was better sustained by the individualist capitalism of central western Europe, with the result that its population surpassed that of the Mediterranean region around 800 AD.

But even within Europe, population growth was slow over the long term. It is estimated to have increased from thirty-one million at 1 AD to sixty million at 1400 AD. That was an average annual rate of about 0.47 per 1000; or about one-hundredth of the 50 per 1000 of biologically determined human birthrate and corresponding death rate. Again death rates were kept close to birthrates by nutritional levels which, for the bulk of the population, rarely, and never for long, rose above a level that allowed death rates to fall below the birthrate.

Death rates did seem to decline slightly in Europe between around 1000 AD and 1300 AD, causing population to grow by around 2 per 1000 per annum instead of the more normal, long term rate of 0.5. That exceptionally rapid population growth depressed living standards and left the population exceptionally vulnerable to the Black Death, or bubonic plague, which wiped out up to half the population of much of Europe in the 1340s.

The adaptations made by mankind, including those made by individualist Europe, enabled more of those born to live longer at nutritional levels which, for the mass of populations, rarely departed from a subsistence level: that is, the level at which a population can reproduce itself. Birthrates, in the case of *homo sapiens* in comparatively recent times, have been influenced by cultural factors. These have included an appreciation of virginity, which, in some societies particularly in the East and Middle East, has delayed sexual intercourse beyond puberty. Polygamy in Africa, which is an inchoate form of property, may also have lowered birthrates. The need for capital, and the dowry system to which that need gave rise, gave to central western Europe a distinctively low marriage rate and consequent lower birthrates.

Apart from these cultural influences, people did not generally attempt to regulate birthrates. Of course many societies, particularly of hunter-gatherers, have reduced their populations from time to time by abandoning infants and old people. But that was death, not birth, control. It was a matter of withholding from infants and the aged essential resources of food and shelter, which involved no cost to, but increased the amount available for, the survivors. Infanticide was very different from what Malthus was to term "moral restraint" in avoiding conception and birth.

Two sets of conditions explain the general absence of birth control. First, under the conditions which have obtained in most societies, at most times, of long term, virtually microscopic population growth, excess of population was not perceived to be a problem. When out of every 1000 population, some 50 were born and 49.5 or more died in most years, the excess of births over deaths—neither of which was registered—was imperceptible. Moreover, given the inequality of incomes that was normal, it is virtually certain that the bulk of the population in most societies normally failed to reproduce themselves. A privileged minority of better nourished, better housed persons probably had lower than average mortality rates, the majority having correspondingly higher than average mortality rates. Given that average mortality rates were very close to biological birthrates, the higher than average mortality rates of the masses were probably above their birthrates. This implied a process of peoples gradually sinking in the social scale, until their genes disappeared, to be replaced by those of better nourished individuals of higher social status.

While for most people at most times, family deaths probably exceeded family births, ancient society was inured to the catastrophes of famine, pestilence, and war which caused sudden, massive, and painfully obvious reductions in populations. Death was frequent and perceptible. It was dramatic population falls which, until little more than two centuries ago, informed people's outlook on demographic matters. The common view was that, for an individual, as well as for society, the most that could be expected was reproduction, and not increase of population.

The second condition that accounts for the absence of birth control in ancient societies is related to the first. It is that, until recent times in virtually all societies, the mass of people lived close to the subsistence level. People at that level are too preoccupied with the problems of the present to contemplate the future. To the extent that they did contemplate the future, an excess of children would rarely have ranked as a sufficiently serious pressing problem to warrant the type of "moral restraint" on conception to which Malthus referred.

The only society where a substantial section of population normally subsisted at levels where it was both possible and necessary for people to contemplate the future was that of central western Europe, though even there, average incomes, in the sixteenth century, are thought to have been no higher than those of India and to have been only one-and-a-half times as high in the eighteenth century.[34] Those Europeans whose immediate needs were not so pressing as to allow them to contemplate the future, saved and invested to provide for that future as no other society had ever done. Although central western Europeans contemplated the future, they did not generally practice birth control. This was because for them also an excess of population was rarely considered a problem. For the individual central western European couple, who married later than other peoples, the rare possibility of a large surviving family implied abundant free, or virtually free, family labor to operate the family property, yielding a good return to the parents until their deaths, when the property normally passed to their surviving sons and daughters.

Both of these conditions, which account for the absence of artificial birth control—i.e., the long term close identity between birth and death rates, and subsistence levels that were too low to allow contemplation of the future—were coming to an end in England at the end of the eighteenth century, or at the beginning of the era of factory capitalism. That too was when Malthus addressed the new problem of population growth in his *Principles of Population,* which was first published, anonymously, in 1798.

The population of England, the birthplace of the Industrial Revolution, had increased during the preceding half century from 6 to 9.25 million, which exceeded the population growth of the preceding five centuries.[35] This expanding population was also being concentrated into manufacturing centers, where its growing size could not be overlooked. Although periodic censuses had not yet been introduced to England, there was perceptible evidence to shatter the old presumption of long term population stability.

England's eighteenth century population growth apparently owed something to higher birthrates. This was because, with accelerated capital formation, the old, distinctively European constraint on marriage weakened. Many more capital-less individuals secured employment in mines, mills, and large construction works like canal building, and therefore had access to the minimum socioeconomic conditions for marriage and procreation. Age at marriage declined, and marriage and birthrates increased in England at this time. However, to an increasing extent over time, England's accelerating population growth was due to declining death rates. These were made possible in the first instance by higher incomes and better nutrition and, subsequently, as part of rapid technological progress, better public and private hygiene, and other forms of disease control.[36] This experience was repeated, with a lag, throughout central western Europe and in the settler colonies of North America and Oceania.

The nineteenth century, which witnessed the West's most rapid population growth, was also the first century of factory capitalism. During that century the area of mainly temperate and productive land available to the West more than doubled. A large extension of the farmed area was possible in Russia because of the earlier subjugation of the pastoral hordes by Russian forces using Western military technology: "At the outset of the nineteenth century, the sown area in New Russia was estimated to have been 800,000 desiations, and in four Volga provinces 1 million desiations. In the 1860s, these figures had risen to 6 million and 4.6 million desiations respectively."[37] In North America, in the pampas of Argentina, in South Africa, and in Australia and New Zealand the farmed area was extended simply by exterminating or driving out the indigenous hunter-gatherers.

Land in lower latitudes, warmer and therefore inherently more productive, was brought into production with minimal capital, by the application in these settler colonies of the livestock and draught animal agriculture that had evolved in central western Europe. The result was an explosion in food production. This occurred at a time when public hygiene and medical science were still rudimentary so that, notwithstanding improved nutritional levels, death rates were only slowly brought down from traditionally high levels.[38] The result was that the population of Europe (exclusive of Russia), North America, and Oceania increased by less than 1 percent annually during the nineteenth century, the period of its most rapid growth.[39] This was much less than the rate of expansion of the food supply available to it.

Table 6.1. World's Farming Area, in 1800 and Since

		Million Hectares
Total area of world's crops and pastures:		4,540
Of which in:		
	Americas (North and South)	1,169
	USSR	607
	Oceania	507
	South Africa	96
Sub Total:		2,379
(Being land brought into production mainly during the nineteenth century)		
Balance:		2,161
(Being land in production pre-1800)		

Source: FAO, *Production Yearbook* (Rome: FAO, 1981).

Economic growth, and especially the explosion of food production, enabled the masses of central western Europe and of the European settlements in the New World to secure what no masses anywhere had ever previously secured: living standards substantially above the subsistence level. The price of wheat in Britain declined by two-thirds while the general price level dropped by half between the opening and closing years of the nineteenth century. Average real incomes in Britain increased fourfold over the same period.[40] The masses of central western Europe and of European settlements in the New World were no longer exclusively preoccupied with the immediate problems of subsistence. The peoples of these areas were able to do what no proletariat mass had previously done: they could contemplate the future. In doing so they could perceive and consider the matter of a property-less proletariat having numerous children. In increasing numbers, for the first time ever, they opted to restrict, by one means or another, birthrates that had previously been determined biologically. These declined generally from the mid-nineteenth century onwards.[41] This, the most recent of the epoch-making changes in the human condition, like sowing seed, migrating into the European forest, and there saving/investing, was an achievement of the masses. With birthrates increasingly determined rationally rather than biologically, it has been possible for the peoples of central western Europe and of their overseas settlements to attain ever improving living standards and to aspire to a want-free status.

The Impact of Capitalist Colonialism on Colonial Populations

Capitalist colonialism's initial demographic impact on the colonies was similar to that of ancient Mediterranean individualist slavery. The surplus labor of the steppe, in the latter case, was enslaved to cultivate the limitless arable land of the Mediterranean littoral. In the era of capitalist colonialism, the indigenous food producers of the Western Hemisphere and captive African slave labor were likewise forcibly mobilized. The indigenous food producers were mobilized to tear mineral wealth from the Andes mountains; the Africans to cultivate the tropical land of the Caribbean, the indigenous hunter-gatherers of which had been exterminated. The effects of this forcible mobilization of labor in the Western Hemisphere were as disastrous for the populations affected as they had been for the slaves of the ancient Mediterranean.

Ancient Mediterranean slavery, to secure new, replacement labor, required continuous territorial expansion. This eventually took the Roman empire into the heart of central western Europe where, at the state of the art, labor could not secure even a maintenance and slavery was no longer profitable. Retaining control of these regions was a charge on the Mediterranean core. Parasitic individualist slavery could expand no further to conquer and enslave more people. It could no longer maintain its labor supply, and it declined. The *encomienda* system and slavery in the Western Hemisphere were integral parts of individualist capitalism and operated differently from ancient Mediterranean slavery. Some at least of the profits from the two former activities were invested in metropolitan central western Europe. These invested profits contributed importantly to effecting the transition from mercantile to factory capitalism.

Factory capitalism enabled the leading colonial powers of the eighteenth century, Britain and the Netherlands, to secure political control of India and Indonesia, with their large rice-fed populations. In these land-limiting and labor-surplus territories, control of land, not labor, was profitable. That control was secured by designating the agents/collaborators of the colonizing powers the proprietors of the land, subject to the payment of land taxes that financed the colonial administration. Cultivators, to secure access to land, had to produce a marketable surplus that was at least sufficient to pay the land tax. Competition for land in populations that, at the state of the art, exceeded the number required to operate it, forced cultivators to pay more than this, which surplus constituted the zamindars' or land-owners' profit. Taxes and rents could be earned, in the final analysis, only by producing for the metropoles.

There was no consumption of labor and depletion of populations in the Afro-Asian Old World, as there had been in the ancient Mediterranean and, during the era of mercantile capitalism, in the Western Hemisphere. Surplus Afro-Asian labor was "freed" from land by the land's appropriators and left free to reproduce, or fail to reproduce itself, according to circumstances. Those circumstances, for the most part, enabled colonized populations of the Old World more than to reproduce themselves. They, as well as the population of the Western Hemisphere, during the era of factory capitalism, expanded at accelerating rates, because of declining death rates.

Imposing the *pax coloniale* was one factor in reducing death rates in the capitalist colonies. Prior to colonization, more or less continuous internecine conflict, from clan level to countrywide level, was the condition of most non-European territories—as of course it was also of Europe. Capitalist colonization, which subordinated all other interests to the prime one of metropolitan profit, outlawed these local conflicts and to that extent reduced death rates. That allowed the populations of the colonies to reproduce themselves, or to expand, even though part of what they now produced was pre-empted as rent for the newly created proprietors of the colonies' land. Even if nutritional levels fell, mortality rates could still decline because of the simultaneous imposition of the *pax coloniale*.

The public hygiene and medical skills, both human and veterinary, which the West slowly acquired during the age of factory capitalism, followed the *pax coloniale*. Though introduced initially primarily to reduce mortality rates among expatriate western populations, these practices often dramatically impacted on mortality rates among the indigenes. Combined with the effects of the *pax coloniale*, public hygiene and elementary medical skills caused crude death rates to fall dramatically from a homeostatic, pre-colonial level of around 50 per 1000 per annum to around half that level by the mid-twentieth century.

Table 6.2. Global Demographic Conditions, 1950–1955
(Rates per 1000 per annum)

Region	Crude Birthrate	Crude Death Rate	Pop'n Growth Rate
World average	35.6	18.3	17.3
West	22.7	10.1	12.1
Africa	48.1	26.9	21.2
Middle East	47.9	25.3	22.6
Latin America	41.4	14.5	26.9
China	39.8	20.1	19.7
East Asia	36.6	30.0	6.6
South Asia	43.2	24.6	18.6

Source: M. P. Todaro, *Economics for a Developing World* (London: Longman, 1982), 167.

The reduction in death rates in the capitalist colonies, which resulted from exogenous factors (i.e., the metropolitan imposed *pax coloniale* and the metropolitan introduced, western originating, public hygiene and medical skills), occurred in the absence of any improvement in nutritional standards. On the contrary, the reduction in death rates occurred when, for a number of reasons, consumption levels in the colonies were declining. This was, first, because of the appropriation of the colonies' lands by the agents and collaborators of the metropoles; second, because of the *pacte coloniale*, which required the colonies to concentrate on primary agricultural and mineral production which are subject to diminishing returns; and third, because of the substitution of capital for labor.

Because consumption levels tended downwards from an initial subsistence level, crude birthrates continued at, or close to, their biological level. The result was a sharp increase in population growth rates as shown in table 6.2.

Rapid population growth in the capitalist colonies was both a cause and effect of low incomes. In Java, the principal capitalist colony of Southeast Asia, "the quality of peasant diet deteriorated, with an apparent decline in calorie intake. Per capita rice consumption in Java and Madura seems to have started its long decline shortly after 1850 and, if the figures are to be trusted, average annual consumption per head in the late 1930s was only four-fifths of that seven decades earlier." [42]

Jones[43] and others following him[44] emphasize the arbitrariness of precolonial government and the resulting frequency of famine in the non-European world. Yet this seems at variance with the facts, at least in the case of India, the most populous of the former capitalist colonies. There "the frequency of famine dramatically increased under the British Raj. There have probably been 90 famines in that country in the last 2000 years; but 66 percent occurred since 1701."[45] It was estimated that around 1918 India had available about 20 ounces of food grain per day per head of population. "By 1945 . . . the average daily quantity of food grain available per capita had fallen to about 15 ounces, and per capita food supply diminished substantially between 1945 and 1952."[46] Myrdal made the same point a little earlier: "The average standard of living of humanity as a whole is still below the level of 1900."[47]

Capitalist colonialism disrupted the normal feedback mechanism which maintained demographic homeostasis. Prior to capitalist colonialism, biological birthrates were balanced by death rates that were correspondingly high, partly as a result of internecine struggle and partly because of high natural mortality rates among vulnerable sections of the population, such as the very young, parturating mothers, the old, and those enfeebled by disease or injury. If, for any reason, population tended to outstrip the means of subsistence so that nutritional levels declined, all those influences tending to raise mortality rates were strengthened, and population was brought back into line with the means of subsistence. The *pax coloniale* and metropolitan-introduced, western-originating public hygiene and medical science disrupted this balance, so that although nutritional levels declined, mortality rates did also. Populations grew rapidly and generally at accelerating rates.

The process applied to livestock as well as to people. The Third World is relatively well endowed with grazing lands and domesticated ruminants. While it contains 76 percent of the world's total population, it has only 54 percent of its cropland and of its crop production, and only 17 percent of the world's annual GNP. But it has 62 percent of the world's grazing lands and 68 percent of its cattle, sheep, and goats.[48] Long term balance between the numbers of grazing stock and the carrying capacity of Afro-Asian pastures, which were normally grazed communally, was maintained by a feedback mechanism similar to that which applied to human populations. If individual proprietors of *Bos indicus* cattle, who always sought to increase without limit the number of stock they held on the communal pasturage, succeeded in doing so, and caused the stocking level to rise beyond the pasture's natural carrying capacity, two things happened. First, total output from the livestock on the now overgrazed pastures declined. Human nutritional levels fell as a result and levels of stress increased. This intensified internecine strife, including particularly cattle-raiding and the slaughter of captured stock. This contributed to restoring balance between stock numbers and the carrying capacity of the pastures. Second, as stock numbers increased, the nutritional level as well as the product of the stock declined. Lower nutritional levels left the stock more vulnerable to epizootic diseases which, from time to time, wiped out large numbers of livestock and restored balance between stock numbers and the natural carrying capacity of the pastures.[49]

Capitalist colonialism intervened in at least three critical ways in the balancing mechanism between livestock numbers and the carrying capacity of the communally grazed pastures, which had maintained homeostasis for millennia. First, the *pax coloniale* effectively terminated cattle-raiding, which was a traditional means both of reducing stock numbers and of consuming surplus stock, because raiders were more willing to slaughter and consume captured stock than their own. Second, western-originating veterinary skills introduced to the colonies in the first instance to make living there safer for the agents/collaborators of the metropoles, prevented livestock dying even when their nutritional levels declined because of overstocking.

Finally, the colonial powers, while generally retaining communal grazing in the Old World colonies, changed the character of property in livestock. This had been ill-defined and diffuse in precolonial times, but was given a more absolute, western form by the colonial powers. One effect of this change was greatly to concentrate ownership of livestock. Whereas in the cattle-keeping regions of precolonial Africa, there were few people without title to cattle, now most of the populations of these areas are without cattle, while small minorities own large herds.[50] Another effect of making more absolute property in livestock was that it increased the incentive and the resources of individual stockowners to expand their herds, a process that was simultaneously facilitated by the *pax coloniale*, which suppressed cattle-raiding, and by western veterinary medicine, which made possible the survival of stock at far lower nutritional levels than formerly.

European concepts of law and order, European concepts of property, and European veterinary medicine were introduced into Afro-Asian livestock systems that had evolved over millennia in response to conditions that were very different from those of Europe. Specifically, those non-European systems had not to cope with the acute problem of seasonal dearth that had been a major factor in shaping central western European cattle culture and its entire economy. Afro-Asian cattle are thus of *Bos indicus* type, the calves of which must be kept alive to induce their dams to lactate. Moreover, as part of the adjustment to local conditions, eating cattle was tabooed in south Asia and continues to be so; and cattle were, and continue to be, the favored form of money in most of Africa. Because these conditions have persisted into and through the colonial era, stockowners continue, as in precolonial days, to attempt to increase their stock numbers without limit. The social and biological limits of precolonial times having been largely eliminated by metropolitan intervention, stock numbers have increased far beyond the carrying capacity of the pastures. Overgrazing in turn has damaged the pastures and lowered their carrying capacity, causing further deterioration in a vicious circle that is frequently referred to as "the tragedy of the commons." It has all culminated in the capitalist colonies' extensive pastoral resources producing ever less milk, meat, and draught services for their expanding, but ever poorer populations. Cattle husbandry in these countries is now largely a matter of using crops that would be otherwise available to feed people, for feeding cattle to produce milk and beef for elites.

A Mirror Image Effect

Central western Europe's capitalist colonialism brought individualist capitalist institutions and technologies with it to the non-European world, which was neither individualist nor capitalist. It forcibly imposed, for metropolitan profit, on most of the non-European peoples those institutions and technologies which, in the course of some millennia, had brought central western Europe from being one of the most backward to being the most advanced region of the world. But the institutions and technology that had evolved autochthonously in central western Europe and that had opened for man the prospect, at least, of becoming master of his destiny, had an entirely different effect on the peoples of the capitalist colonies, on whom they were forcibly imposed.

Individualist Europe's core institution of property enabled it to mobilize the surplus labor of the pastoral steppe to create the glories of the ancient Mediterranean. Property, less spectacularly but more durably, enabled the wretched peasants of central western Europe to accumulate the capital that made civilization possible in an otherwise impossibly bleak environment. But property took an entirely different form in the capitalist colonies. Property in Europe served the societies that created and upheld it. Property in the capitalist colonies likewise served the societies that created and upheld it. But in the capitalist colonies, those property-creating societies were the metropolitan powers, which conferred on their agents/collaborators in the colonies title to the scarce resources in return for executing metropolitan policy. Whether it was in scarce manpower in the western hemisphere during the mercantilist era, or in scarce land in all the capitalist colonies during the era of factory capitalism, property in those colonies has been equally effective in facilitating the squeezing of the capitalist colonized peoples who, themselves or their land, were made the property of the metropoles' agents/collaborators.

Capital was created in central western Europe to complement labor and thereby to make human existence possible on that region's limitless arable, but cold, northern land. Capital became, in the capitalist colonies, a means of extracting profit for the metropoles at the expense of the indigenes. It did so either through incorporation with land, which would otherwise have been for indigenes' support, for production for the metropoles or by substituting for labor in operating that land.

Trade with the colonies, and especially with the settler colonies, lifted the masses in Europe, for the first time ever, above a total preoccupation with the needs of the moment and enabled them to contemplate the future as no masses had ever done previously. But that trade, which, through the *pacte coloniale* elevated the masses in the metropoles, condemned the peoples of the capitalist colonies to be forever the growers of crops to feed the metropoles and to be the producers of the raw materials for fashioning into manufactured goods and services in the metropoles.

The *pax coloniale,* which was imposed to allow the more effective pursuit of metropolitan profit in the capitalist colonies, removed, without substituting anything in its place, one of the means of balancing population with the means for its support. The resulting imbalance was much accentuated by the subsequent introduction of western originating medical science.

This mortality-reducing knowledge evolved in the West in part as a response to the dreadful mortality rates of the early industrial cities, which hampered the process of industrialization. It was also part of the corpus of technological knowledge, the acquisition of which was, throughout the history of individualist capitalism, an integral part of the process of capital formation. But that western originating, slowly acquired, medical knowledge never reduced mortality rates sufficiently to cause the growth of western populations to outstrip the growth of capital and technology necessary for their support. It was otherwise in the capitalist colonies. The introduction of medical science served metropolitan interests by enabling people to survive at ever lower levels of nutrition and therefore at lower cost and with greater profit to the metropoles. Because nutritional levels declined, the pressures of the moment intensified, and people became ever more the creatures of their environment and ever less capable of influencing it. Societies that had drained and irrigated land, with benefits that flowed for millennia, could no longer mobilize the energy to maintain, let alone extend, those constructions. Because the needs of the moment grew more pressing, effort was concentrated increasingly on securing quick returns—most quickly by day labor for the agents/collaborators of the metropoles; after that from quickly maturing annual or semi-annual crops; and least attractively for ever poorer people, from tree crops, which were often most productive and agronomically most suited but which yielded returns only slowly and over a long term that was of decreasing significance for peoples becoming poorer and ever more preoccupied with the present.

Veterinary science enhanced the productivity of the *Bos taurus* cattle of the West. Introduced to the capitalist colonies for metropolitan profit, veterinary science removed one of the two restraints that for millennia had maintained balance between the carrying capacity of pastures grazed communally by the *Bos indicus* cattle of milk-consuming peoples, who rationally must always seek to increase their livestock numbers without limit. Epizootic diseases could no longer play their critical control role. Nor, thanks to the *pax coloniale*, did cattle raiding. Hence "the tragedy of the commons," which largely destroyed one of the major resources of the colonized peoples.

The indigenes of southeast Asia and Latin America are lactose malabsorbent and do not drink milk. The increasing pressures of the moment among populations which, thanks to western originating medical science, survive at lower nutritional levels, cause them to slaughter their cattle and buffaloes for immediate consumption, rather than breed them for future benefit. Laws in every country in southeast Asia and Latin America prohibit the slaughter of female bovines; but because the folly of governments that think that people can be compelled to breed their livestock is matched by their incompetence, the laws everywhere fail to prevent a secular decline in bovine numbers.[51] Thus the want created by a century of capitalist colonialism in Malaya has reduced people below the level at which, twelve thousand years ago, the first shepherd opted to forgo the immediate consumption of a mature feral sheep or goat and to breed it in the hope of getting a future supply of young animals.[52]

The metropolitan West, in these various ways, has been elevated at the same time and by the same institutions and technology as the capitalist colonized peoples have been debased. The drive for profit, which achieved so very much in central western Europe, was, of course, at the root of capitalist colonialism. But it alone does not by any means account for the great harm done to the colonized peoples. Possibly of even greater import has been the failure to understand the consequences of transferring a set of institutions and technologies from one context, where they worked brilliantly, into a very different context. Had the transferred culture been required, as with all other colonizations, to adjust to the new circumstances, it might well have enriched the territories and peoples to which it was introduced. It did so very remarkably in Japan, where it was adopted eclectically. But unlike all earlier colonizations, capitalist colonialism did not stand alone. Its uniqueness and its unique destructiveness was that, in a maritime age, it was enforced on distant colonies and supported for the profit of distant metropoles. The colonized societies, and not the colonizing culture, were forced to adapt.

The Colonization of Ireland

This section provides a summary of part of the material treated more extensively in chapter 8. The aim is to introduce the key features of the Irish case to demonstrate its illuminative value in the general context.

The earliest waves of lactose tolerant pastoralists—the Celts—arrived in Ireland about 250 BC. Celtic Ireland remained more or less isolated from the developments in Europe which were described in chapter 5 until late in the eighth century. The Romans quite overlooked the island, and, apart from sporadic raiding forays and the efforts of early Christian missions, very little interaction took place between the Irish Celts and the emerging individualist capitalism of England and mainland Europe. In the intervening thousand years, however, the customs and institutions of the Irish Celts evolved and consolidated in the manner outlined in chapter 5, to produce a primitive, but reasonably stable set of relationships between the various tribal groups who occupied the country.

The first of the Viking raiders arrived in Ireland in about 795 AD. As in most other parts of maritime Europe, the Vikings' objectives were plunder and trade. They did not settle in Ireland in numbers and so their direct cultural legacy is slight. The principal results of their activities were a general destabilization of the existing tribal politics and the establishment of trading outposts at key estuarial locations, of which Dublin, Cork, Limerick, and others survive to this day.

The Anglo-Normans were a different matter. Invited in by a deposed tribal king, Diarmuid MacMurrough, to help in restoring him to power, they came in numbers at the direction of Henry II, under the leadership of Richard de Clare—Strongbow—and took all before them. They introduced individualist capitalism as it then existed in its feudal form with all of its legal ramifications. They also brought new technologies, the most important of which were their construction methods and military techniques. With the first of these they built castles and churches; with the second they eradicated all resistance to their domination of the island.

It was one thing, however, to control the country militarily; it was quite another to gain a living there. England was/is on the margin for capital-based crop growing; Ireland, because of its climate, was and remains beyond that margin. Only in the southeastern corner of the country are the rainfall low enough and the summers warm enough to sustain anything like continental methods of crop-growing. This corner of Ireland, known as the Pale, became the only part of the country in which Norman dominance persisted. And even here, over time, the Normans and their institutions were slowly transformed; they and the native Irish blended, until eventually the two peoples became indistinguishable, the newcomers becoming "more Irish than the Irish."

The relative indifference of the English state to affairs in Ireland was transformed by the circumstances surrounding the emergence of the absolute monarchy of the Tudors. It became imperative for this absolute rule to be extended to Ireland for two main reasons: initially, following Henry VIII's break with Rome to ensure the strategic defense of England's western flank and subsequently to extend the territory in which absolute ownership of land—for the individual owner's profit—could be exploited as it was in England, to reward the supporters of the crown. The various Plantations of Ireland, from Elizabeth through to William of Orange, served both of these objectives. Loyal English and Scots subjects, settled in Ireland, helped to secure the island militarily to the benefit of the English crown and in return were granted secure ownership of the land for their own profit. Between 1600 and 1700, the proportion of the population of Ireland that was British or of British descent increased from less than 2 percent to 27 percent.[53]

The consequences of the conquest of Ireland were momentous for both countries. For England, the enormous cost of the initial conquest and of maintaining a military presence there sufficient to suppress the various insurrections that occurred before the island was finally secured in the battle of Kinsale in 1601 virtually impoverished the Tudors, with results that led more or less directly to the Civil War and the establishment in England of the first modern property owners' state.

The consequences for Ireland, though equally significant, resulted in nothing so progressive for the native Irish. In the first place Ireland was now divided into two classes of people: the land-owning, enfranchised, protestant British; and the property-less, powerless, catholic indigenes (Gaelic and Anglo-Norman). Ownership of Irish land was securely vested in the first of these, in a group of people for whom profitable use of that land was the only objective; and profit from Irish land could be maximized only by responding to changing circumstances in the external world economy. From the early Stuarts onwards, through four main historical phases, the requirements of the indigenous people of Ireland had absolutely no bearing on the manner in which Irish land was used. The pursuit of personal profit by the British owners of Irish land rendered the indigenous Irish powerless to influence these processes. The four phases of Irish economic history and their effects on the people of Ireland are outlined below and are discussed in more detail in chapter 8.

1600–1660 Cheap land and favorable natural conditions made Irish livestock cheap, resulting in high demand in England. Cromwell and others found it convenient to ship troublesome Irish as forced labor to the Caribbean and to allow their place to be taken by cattle and sheep. Also revenues to Irish landowners were relatively easily taxed by the English crown, strengthening the crown's position, vis à vis the growing force of the English landowners.

1660–1760 The Cattle Acts—banning imports of Irish livestock—introduced by English landed interests threatened by Irish imports also helped to reduce the tax income and power of the Stuarts. The result was the development of a triangular provision trade by which Irish beef, pork, and butter were shipped to the West Indies to feed slaves who produced tropical produce much in demand in Europe. The consequences for Ireland included sustained but undramatic economic growth and population increase of about 0.3 percent annually.

1760–1820 The English Industrial Revolution brought about an increased demand for high energy foods to feed workers. In response, Irish grain, butter, and pig/bacon exports rose, and cattle/beef exports fell. Irish land use focused on tillage and dairying, with increased demand for labor which was fed on potatoes grown to rest and clean the soil for grain. Population rose from 3.2 million in 1754 to 6.8 million in 1821, greatly overshooting the sustainable level.

1820–1921 The end of the Napoleonic Wars, resulting in a general collapse in prices—particularly of grain—and increased prosperity in England during the Industrial Revolution, led to increased demand for better, high-protein foods like meat. The collapse in the price of grain destroyed the economic basis of potato-fed grain production in Ireland. The blight years in the 1840s resulted in the death of one million and the emigration of another million Irish. Thus began the modern era of cattle-for-people replacement on Irish land; half of every generation born in Ireland has emigrated since that time, each emigrant being replaced consistently and almost exactly by an increase of 1.2 in Irish cattle stocks.

This brief summary is intended to point up two key features of the English colonization of Ireland. First, as the Anglo-Normans presumably discovered, Ireland was no source of gold and silver nor of spices or anything else which might have been traded with the rest of Europe, so it provided no incentive for the earliest extractive forms of colonialism.

Secondly, the peoples encountered in Ireland, by both Normans and Tudors, were relatively numerous tribal pastoralists, not dispersed hunter-gatherers who might have been displaced or exterminated completely by settlers; and, given Irish climatic conditions, neither were they settled cultivators who might have been allowed to continue cultivating their crops while being squeezed by a small garrison force for metropolitan profit.

The Irish experience was an awkward combination of both of these forms of colonialism, one which in many ways reflected the worst aspects of the two. But whatever the result, it was essential to the Tudors that Ireland should be colonized. England's flank had to be secured and land had to be provided for the supporters of the crown. And, given the nature of the indigenous people, the English crown could hold the island only by placing a large population of loyal settlers there, living cheek by jowl amongst hostile natives, who like them were white-skinned, consequently distinguishable from them only by their religion.

Once the settlers were in place, with the knowledge that any security problems that they might experience would be resolved by the forces of the English crown, the long term dynamics of Irish economic history were established. Neither fully English, nor ever fully Irish, the landed gentry of Ireland lived in a middle world, responding only to external market conditions in their pursuit of whatever profit they might make from exploitation of "their" land. Through all the massive changes in external demand conditions outlined above, the needs, wishes, and ambitions of the native Irish counted for nothing; the Irish people were entirely incidental to the ambitions and programs of the land owners.

The point however is this. In the period from about 1830 to 1850 the natural resources of the island of Ireland supported a population of over seven million people. They may have been desperately poor people and external market conditions may have been very unusual, but the fact remains that in those years the volume of agricultural production in Ireland was sufficient to support a population level never previously, nor since, observed. Though usually clouded by memories of the famine which followed them, these years provide an indication of just how productive Ireland could be—given the right external conditions and given the right domestic policies. They offer a target of sorts against which the results of subsequent agricultural and economic policies might be measured. As will be seen, those policies, whether operated by the English or by their post-colonial successors, have never since achieved volumes of output as those reached in the pre-famine years.

Chapter 7

Political Independence

We have described the mechanisms whereby individualist capitalism, having created Europe as we know it, expanded outwards beyond the boundaries of Europe through two main types of colonizing process: settler colonialism, involving the elimination of the indigenous societies and the creation of new, individualist capitalist states on the *tabula rasa* that resulted; and capitalist colonialism, based on the exploitation of indigenous food producers by metropolitan garrison forces in collaboration with local elites, for the benefit of metropolitan interests.

The next phase, the latest stage, in the development of individualist capitalism came with the ending of colonial interests in these countries. The manner in which this came about in the two types of colonies was enormously important in shaping the present structures of those societies. Those processes are the subject matter of this chapter. The general nature of the process of de-colonization is discussed in the context of the severance of their metropolitan links by the American colonies; the similarities and contrasts of experience between settler and capitalist colony are outlined. The Irish experience is then introduced and discussed in some detail in order to illustrate the general process that applied in all of the capitalist colonies. The discussion here focuses on the Irish case largely because of the author's relative familiarity with the Irish material. The discussion of the Indian and African cases is taken far enough to indicate the generality of the Irish experience; it is left to students with greater knowledge in these other areas to complete the individual country by country analysis.

The Demise of Empires

There was no overseas European empire in 1500 AD. There will be none in the year 2000. At least in its transience, Europe's overseas empire has been no different from the other empires of history, since the commencement of food production and civil life ten thousand years ago. But in the manner of its passing, no less than in its distinctive character, Europe's overseas empire differed fundamentally from other empires.

Reference that was largely incidental has been made here to the passing of empires. The collapse of the empire of the ancient Mediterranean has been ascribed to internal failure: to the inability of its economy to reproduce its labor force and its consequent parasitical dependence on the captive labor of other economies. When the Roman empire had reached the limits of conquest and could no longer renew its wasting labor with fresh captives, its economy ceased to meet current needs. Old wealth was consumed, and when the barbarians approached, they entered through an empty shell in the West. Lord Macaulay put it more eloquently, though possibly less accurately: "The torpor was broken by two great revolutions, the one moral, the other political, the one from within, the other from without."[1]

Arnold Toynbee's voluminous *A Study of History* purports to describe the decline of some twenty-one separate empires.[2] All but two—the ancient Mediterranean and modern Europe—are non-European. Toynbee's thesis is that these empires were first weakened by failure to cope with internal challenges, which either caused the empires to disintegrate or left them weak and vulnerable to external attack. Mann emphasizes internal disintegration as the cause of empire collapse.[3] It has been suggested above (chapter 2) that the migrations of lactose tolerant pastoralists caused the disruption of many riverine, crop-based civilizations. These included the Indus-based civilization, which was overwhelmed by the Aryans, and Sumeria, which was desolated by Hittites, both sets of invaders from the Eurasian steppe.

A combination of internal and external causes is discernible in the most recent collapse of empire—Russia's. The First World War caused the collapse of tsarist Russia's autocratic capitalism; but the empire received a new lease on life when an allegedly scientific socialist autocracy replaced the old, allegedly divinely appointed autocracy. The revitalized empire survived a violent assault by Germany fifty years ago, but its command economy has failed to survive fifty years of economic competition with the market-led economy of the individualist capitalist West. Its inadequacies undermined trust in the autocracy and led to disintegration from within—a disintegration that did not occur fifty years earlier under military assault by Germany.

The demise of other empires was caused by internal weakness or external attack. That cannot be said of Europe's overseas empire, which was acquired and lost during the past five hundred years. There has been no European decline or disintegration, either absolutely or relatively. Europe's population, in no small measure because of the wealth it received from its overseas empire, increased at least as rapidly as the world's, up to the end of the nineteenth century.[4] While non-European population growth has since been more rapid, Europe's economic development, again in large measure because of the contribution from its overseas colonies, has been much more rapid. European incomes, which two hundred years ago were two or three times greater than Afro-

Asian and Latin American incomes, have since increased to an average of some thirty times greater.[5] The nine European colonizing powers—Spain, Portugal, Britain, France, the Netherlands, Denmark, Belgium, Germany, and Italy—now, with Greece, Luxembourg, and Ireland, comprise the European Community, which is the largest, wealthiest economic bloc in the world.

The passing of Europe's overseas empire cannot be attributed to external attack. There was no serious military challenge to colonial Europe until the rise of the world's superpowers, the United States and the USSR. But that did not occur until forty years ago, when most of Europe's colonies had already gone and the rest were about to go.

The winding up of Europe's overseas colonies differed from the ending of other empires in that it was not due either to internal weakness or external attack. The end of Europe's empire came, in all cases, because of the assertion of independence by the colonies. The attainment, or recovery, of local independence on the break-up of other empires occurred because of the failure of the core; but local independence in Europe's overseas colonies came from elements within the colonies. Those elements, moreover, had been implanted and nurtured in the colonies by the metropoles; they were not indigenous to the colonies. Other influences collaborated with these non-indigenous elements within the colonies in securing independence and the end of empire; but in all cases the primary impetus was provided by those non-indigenous elements that had been implanted and nurtured by the European metropoles.

The publication by William Molyneaux of *The Case of Ireland's being Bound by Acts of Parliament in England Stated* was an early example of an initiative towards independence by one of individualist capitalist Europe's overseas colonies. Published in 1698, only nine years after the battle of the Boyne, which secured the ascendancy of England's Protestant elite agents/collaborators, Molyneaux's pamphlet challenged the right of the Westminster parliament to legislate for Ireland. These attempts were illegitimate in the view of Molyneaux, who was a correspondent of John Locke and was imbued with Lockean concepts of a social contract. The Westminster parliament's attempt to legislate for Ireland were, in Molyneaux's view, a breach of a mythical social contract between the English crown and the Irish nation.

Molyneaux was a member of the one-fifth or so of the island's population that was of recent British origin, Protestant and individualist, and that, as a result of the conquest of the sixteenth century and the reconquest of the seventeenth century, had been superimposed on the indigenous, tribal, Catholic, Celtic majority. The Protestant minority proceeded to "squeeze" that majority through a system of Penal Laws. As Burke put it:

> Their [the Penal Laws] declared object was to reduce the Catholics of Ireland to a miserable populace, without property, without estimation, without education. . . . They divided the nation into two distinct bodies, without common interest, sympathy or connection, one of which bodies was to possess *all* the franchise, *all* the property, *all* the education. The others were to be drawers of water and

cutters of turf for them.[6]

Molyneaux may not have been the first, and was certainly not the last, member of a colonial elite, whose privileged position was created and maintained by the metropole, to claim to speak on behalf of a colonized, "squeezed" nation in opposition to aspects of metropolitan rule.

Molyneaux's tract was of little other than academic significance. The Protestant nation was far too outnumbered by the Catholic one, which long continued to seethe with the rebellion that had characterized seventeenth century Ireland, to be able to survive without the active support of metropolitan Britain. Nor was Britain itself disposed to concede independence under circumstances that were even more likely to result in Ireland's occupation by a hostile power than two hundred years earlier, when the Tudors conquered the island to preempt such occupation. But though of little practical significance, Molyneaux's tract was to be one of the sources of inspiration for the American independence movement a century later.

Independence in the Americas

Untrammeled by the baggage of millennia of evolution in the forests of central western Europe, but availing of the rich store of technology that was a product of that evolution, the settlers' progress in the American wilderness was rapid. An abundance of fertile land helped, as also did trade with Europe in the slave-grown sub-tropical produce of Virginia and the Carolinas. The settlers secured themselves against the indigenous hunter-gatherers, whose lands they appropriated, by exterminating them or expelling them from the settled areas. Their security against external attack by France or Spain was obtained by metropolitan Britain's defeat of those powers in the Seven Years War, which culminated in the Peace of Paris of 1763, when France willingly exchanged its titles to Canada for the small Caribbean island of Guadeloupe.

Political attitudes evolved no less rapidly than economic circumstances in the North American colonies. Conflict between the political power of the castle and the economic power of the cabin, which emerged slowly over the centuries and millennia in central western Europe, came to a head much more rapidly in the North American colonies. The old issue of the right of the castle to tax the cabin, which had been the source of so much dissent in Europe surfaced under a new guise in the colonies. It did so when the King of England attempted to recover through taxation on the colonies part of the cost of the Seven Years War, which had been fought, to some extent at least, in the colonies' defense against France and Spain.

Circumstances in North America in the 1770s were conducive to a confrontation between castle power and cabin power—between the rights of monarchs and the rights of property, such as had occurred in Britain in the 1640s, and as was to occur fifteen years later in France. William Molyneaux's tract was one small contribution to the body of enlightenment thought which made Europeans, in Europe and in the Americas, increasingly dissatisfied with political relationships that were rooted in the past and that became increasingly incongruous by the day with contemporary economic and technological conditions, which were changing ever more rapidly. The Americans were particularly influenced by the boost to the Whig position in Britain that was given by the final ending, at the battle of Culloden in 1746, of the Stuart challenge and the threat of a revanchist absolute monarchy, sanctioned by Divine Right. Criticism was emboldened, in Britain particularly by the Whig oligarchy, of the exercise of the royal prerogative independently of Parliament. The levying by the King's governor of new taxes on the North American colonies was a case in point. If the King today could tax his North American subjects without Parliament's consent, he might attempt tomorrow to do the same to his British subjects.

Opposition in the colonies to what was perceived as an unjust exercise of the royal prerogative to levy taxes was led by the elected representatives of the colonists in Congress. Those were men of substance. Their leaders included George Washington, one of the Colonies' wealthiest citizens, proprietor of an extensive Virginian estate stocked with negro slaves to operate it. Thomas Jefferson, author of the American Declaration of Independence, was also a planter and slave owner. Benjamin Franklin was a successful newspaper publisher, and John Adams a successful barrister. They were the elite of a colonial society, who had gained much from the establishment of individualist capitalism in the American wilderness.

The colonists' armed rebellion was facilitated not a little by Britain's ambivalent attitude towards a settler colony which, unlike a capitalist colony, was of questionable economic benefit to the metropole. Rebellion was encouraged by Whig support within Britain, enunciated most cogently and eloquently by Edmund Burke in parliament in his speech on the American Revolution. Parliamentary support for the rebellion was mobilized by Fox. Finally, the American rebels were aided and encouraged by the armed intervention, first of France and later of Spain, as well as by other European powers that were ready to avail of Britain's involvement in a colonial war to settle old scores.

The broad pattern of North America's successful rebellion against metropolitan rule was to be followed throughout the whole process of stripping Europe of its overseas colonies. First, a local elite achieved eminence in the colony through the process of individualist capitalism that was imposed by the metropole. That eminence was attributable in part to the wealth amassed by the elite, as in the case of George Washington's extensive plantation. It was achieved in part by debasing the indigenous masses, which was achieved in North America by the extermination or expulsion of the hunting-gathering indigenes. Had the indigenous population not been weakened by its contact with the settlers, it is doubtful if American independence would have been sought as early as it was.

The pattern was that, at a certain stage, when the metropolitan-created elites in the colony had secured a sufficient eminence, it challenged metropolitan rule. Meanwhile, because of the change inseparable from individualist capitalism, new political elements had emerged within the metropole, some of which, like the Whigs in Britain, favored independence for the colony. Finally, all successful movements of independence from European colonialism have had, as in the case of North America, the support of other metropolitan powers, ready to fish in the troubled waters of colonial rebellion.

The sequence of cause and effect distinguished the securing of independence by European colonies from the disintegration of other colonies. Other empires disintegrated because of internal weakness and/or external attack, which conferred independence on the outlying regions by default. Political independence came to the overseas colonies of individualist capitalist Europe, by contrast, because of initiatives taken by elites in the colonies. Those elites were themselves the products of individualist capitalism and challenged metropolitan rule on the grounds of its being incompatible with their individualist capitalist rights. Only after that challenge had been mounted by elements within the colony did support come from others within the metropole and from competing metropoles.

The process of European decolonization, which differed from the disintegration of other empires, had much in common with the denouement of the castle/cabin conflict that, for eons, was central to the politico-economic evolution of individualist capitalism in central western Europe. The tensions between the colonial elite and the metropole were similar to those between the cabin and the castle in feudal Europe. Whereas in central western Europe, the accumulation of economic power in the cabin resulted eventually in the property-owners' state, in the colonies, the accumulation of wealth by the elites culminated in independence. Change, in both cases, was an aspect of individualist capitalist development. The loss of empire was not, as in the case of other empires, a manifestation of disintegration. Europe lost its overseas colonies in the same way as it lost its feudal lords and absolute monarchs, in the process of individualist capitalist development.

The Central and South American colonies rebelled against their Spanish masters in a manner similar to that of the North American colonies. In the first phase of Spanish colonial rule in America, lasting for about a hundred and fifty years:

> The ruling class was composed of men directly connected with Spain, integrated in the apparatus of the State and in key positions of control of the productive system that yielded the surplus transferred to the mother country. In the second phase the landowning class, having little connection with the mother country and strictly local horizons of interest, became increasingly important.[7]

After three centuries of colonial rule these creole *haciendados,* the locally born descendants of the *conquistadores,* were confident enough of their ability to maintain, without metropolitan support, their privileged position against the local masses. It was "under the auspices of the creole elites in the more outlying regions" that the Spanish South American countries secured their independence.[8] Meanwhile and quite typically:

> The great mass of the colonial population, the *mestizos* and the Indians, paid little heed to the dramatic events transpiring across the seas and in their homelands. . . . The great majority of the creoles, less educated and far more provincial (than the leaders) were disinclined towards any move that might upset the social order. They sided with the independence leaders because Spain had been overrun and because of their class interest in displacing Spaniards who ruled in America.[9]

The success of the Latin American independence movement depended critically on the overthrow of the Bourbon monarchy in Spain by the invading armies of Napoleonic France and its replacement by a radical party that supported the rebellious colonists. Finally, Britain, the premier colonial power, then at war with France and occupied Europe, gave to the Latin American revolutionaries aid similar to that given by the French to their own North American rebel colonists fifty years earlier.

The Americas After Independence

The post-independence experience of the two continents, North America and South America, illustrates the different character of settler colonialism and capitalist colonialism. Settler colonialism was part of a process as old as life itself. It was, in particular, the continuation of the process that began almost from the beginning of food production and civil life, which was the appropriation of land by the more productive food producers from the less productive hunter-gatherers. The North American settlers were in the tradition of the individualist capitalists of central western Europe who moved into what was once a limitless wilderness, in search of better land, a more propitious environment, or to escape the exactions of feudal lords. The hegemony exercised by Britain over the settlers, which was characterized by Edmund Burke as "an easy and salutary neglect," had much of the character of the feudal hegemony that was integral to individualist capitalism in Europe. An age-old reflex commitment to hegemonic expansion caused English kings to attempt to impose a feudal rule over distant American colonies, in a time and place where feudalism had no relevance.

The Iberian colonization of Latin America was directed at securing for Iberia's rulers the gold and silver which would make them financially independent of their own reluctant and frequently unruly subjects. When through "squeezing," as considered in chapter 6 above, the indigenes had been reduced to impotence and when simultaneously the creole elite agents/collaborators of the metropolitan powers had gained a sufficient eminence, the elites rebelled against metropolitan sovereignty.

Washington, Jefferson, Adams, and the others who led the American war of independence were elites in a settler society that had transferred from central western Europe and had developed rapidly in North America where it was unen-cumbered by the impedimenta of history. A vibrant society, it was an extension of all those others which, throughout human existence, had generated change—from more to less primitive methods of hunting gathering; from hunting-gathering to food production; from steppe pastoralism to slave-based crop-growing in the ancient Mediterranean and to capital-based crop-growing in central western Europe. Change was of the nature of this human society, and never more so than in postcolonial North America, where it had at its disposal the technology and institutions of individualist capitalism as these had evolved over the eons and where there was a continent of fertile land to be had for the taking from hunter-gatherers.

The situation was very different in Latin America. There the agents/collaborators of the metropoles had been imposed forcibly on the indi-genes, to "squeeze" these for metropolitan profit. Only when the process had proceeded to the stage where the indigenous masses no longer represented a threat to the elite status of the agents/collaborators did the latter cast off metro-politan rule. At that stage, which was the final stage of capitalist colonial unde-velopment, the colonized, indigenous masses had been deprived, through the process analyzed in chapter 6, of the capacity to effect beneficial change. The masses could thereafter only continue to retrogress.

Elites, of their nature, never seek change in the social order that raised them to elitism, although they continuously vie for control of that order. Washington, Jefferson, and their kind, like Molyneaux in Ireland before them, objected to and sought to change the government of the North American colonies by rulers in distant Britain. But while they sought to change the rulers, they did not seek change in the manner in which the colonies were ruled and which had resulted in their being the proprietors of extensive plantations and numerous negro slaves. It was likewise with the elites of Latin America, who resented, and rebelled against, metropolitan control. They successfully cast off that control, which left them, like the elites of North America, masters of a continent.

There was a striving, individualist capitalist mass of settlers underlying the elites of North America. These generated, by their efforts, continuing change, similar to that which characterized central western Europe, from where the mass had emigrated, but at a much accelerated pace, in the more congenial environ-ment of the New World. Integral to that change was the expansion of homestead farming and manufacturing in the northern states and of slave-based plantation farming in the south. These two disparate socioeconomic systems coexisted un-easily within the United States for almost a century. But as both systems ex-panded into the western territories of the continent, conflict arose on whether, in the newly occupied territories of the West, the free labor of the North would have to compete with the slave labor of the South. On that, and on the associated issue of the South's right to secede from the Union, a civil war was fought that cost more lives than any previous war. The American Civil War was an exten-sion, on a heroic scale, of the unceasing political change that was made un-avoidable in central western Europe by the saving, investment, and technological advances made by myriads of "petty capitalists" whose survival depended on doing so. That political change, or adjustment, was normally, like the growth of capital and technological progress which necessitated it, slight and imperceptible; but occasionally, when it lagged behind the underlying socioeconomic change, the political change was cataclysmic. That happened in Britain in the seventeenth century and in France from 1789 onwards. The American Civil War was occasioned by a similar failure to adapt political relations sufficiently rapidly to keep abreast of the very rapid socioeconomic development of a settler, individualist capitalist society.

Conditions were very different in post-independence Latin America. The indigenous mass, beneath the creole elite, had been ruined by the forcible imposition of individualist capitalist institutions and technologies for metropolitan profit, as explained in chapter 6 above. Independence was secured only when that ruin of the masses had proceeded to the stage where they were no longer a challenge to the metropolitan created elites. Capitalist colonialism had destroyed within the mass the power, which exists in all noncapitalist-colonized masses, to generate beneficial socioeconomic change. Post-independence Latin American society was, therefore, a peculiarly inert one, deprived of the ability to generate change from within, but subject to forcibly imposed institutions, technology, and laws, as well as to continuing external influences like foreign investment which were free to profit at the expense of a society made impotent by capitalist colonialism.

Latin America's elites, like all elites, vied with one another, as they had with the metropolitan powers, for control of a socioeconomic system that had made them elites. But, again like all elites, they were concerned to preserve, not to change, the system that had made them elites. Because the masses whom they ruled had been ruined and were incapable of generating the socioeconomic change which has invariably emerged from the masses, change did not occur. The socioeconomic system that was imposed by the Iberian powers to squeeze Latin America for metropolitan profit persisted after, as before, independence. The benefits that a gravely malfunctioning system yielded now accrued to the creole elite rather than to the metropoles. Much of those benefits were squandered by the elites in squabbles to control, but not to change, the socioeconomic system that had made them elites.

The impotence of the indigenous, ruined masses to effect change in the socioeconomic system imposed on them by capitalist colonialism and the squabbling among elites were characteristics of post-independence Latin America that were to be repeated in all former capitalist countries. But two other characteristics emerged that were also to become distinctive features of countries that had experienced capitalist colonialism and that further illustrate the impotence of capitalist colonized masses.

First, the boundaries of the countries into which the region fragmented following independence were those that coincided with the administrative provinces of the former colony. They did not, as with the boundaries of countries that were not capitalist colonized, reflect differences in ethnic composition and the interaction over the ages of those differences. The single most important divide, that between the former Portuguese empire, Brazil, and the former Spanish empire, which comprised the rest of Latin America, was settled by the papal bull of Alexander VI, *Inter Caetera,* in 1493. The capitalist colonized masses have been unable to assert their identity over the territorial arrangements made for metropolitan convenience; territorial borders, like the institutions, technology, and fundamental laws imposed by the metropoles, have been retained in the former capitalist colonies. This pattern was to be repeated in all former capitalist colonies, including those of Africa, the territorial boundaries of which were largely settled by the major European powers in the remarkably short period from 1880 to 1914. It has obtained in Ireland too, where the partition imposed on the island by Britain in 1921 persists.

The second of these other distinctive characteristics of Latin America, as of all capitalist colonies that were subsequently made independent, is that the *lingua franca* in all of them, like the territorial boundaries, the institutions, and the fundamental laws, has remained that which was imposed on them by the metropolitan power. An indigenous language has never been restored as the *lingua franca* in any former capitalist colony.

The Ending of Colonialism in Ireland

The age-old conflict between cabin and castle first came to a head in England. It gave rise there to the Lockean concept that the proper exercise of political power was the protection of property, which was the economic basis of European individualist, capitalist society. The state, in this view, was the cabin's instrument for property's protection. While this was a realistic assessment of the situation in England at the end of the seventeenth century, the position of Irish property owners was far too precarious at that time for any such aspiration to be realistic there. Molyneaux's *The Case* was, to that extent, premature.

But a century of economic growth, the influence of the Enlightenment in Europe, and, above all, the American War of Independence altered matters. The property-owning ascendancy, the agents/collaborators of metropolitan Britain, were emboldened and grew impatient with the castle power of Westminster. There emerged, towards the end of the eighteenth century, a growing "patriotism," or consciousness of a distinction between Irish and British interests and a concern that those of Ireland should no longer be subordinated to those of Britain. Availing of the removal of Britain's large standing army from Ireland to fight in America, the Protestants of Ireland formed their own Volunteer militia.

The Dublin parliament, with the backing of the Volunteers, won concessions from a British administration under pressure because of the war in America. Poyning's Law, which invalidated all acts passed by the Dublin parliament unless endorsed by the King in Council at Westminster, and the Declaratory Act, which asserted the right of the Westminster parliament to legislate for Ireland, were both repealed in 1782. While appearing to concede a large measure of home rule, these changes were largely cosmetic: "ultimate authority for public expenditure lay, at the last resort, out of the hands of the Irish parliament. . . . Irish parliamentary management continued to enable Castle government to get its business done after 1782 as much as before."[10]

The concern of the Dublin parliament "patriots" for the rights of Irish people was selective, like the concern of the Founding Fathers of the American Revolution for the rights of man. In the one case, it was concern for the rights of the Irish Protestant ascendancy, who supported the conquest and included in their rights the right to squeeze the indigenous, Catholic majority. In the other case, it was concern for the rights of white men, including their right to enslave black men and all the progeny of black women and their offspring.

The constitutional relation between Ireland and Britain established in 1782 continued uneasily until the outbreak of the revolutionary wars with France. The war situation introduced another metropolitan power that was ready to assist those in Ireland who sought to break with Britain. But it also achieved a degree of unity in Britain that had scarcely existed since the Glorious Revolution of 1688. Whigs and Tories were united in defense of the constitutional status quo against French Jacobin influence, wherever that appeared—in Europe, Britain, or Ireland. French revolutionary influences also gave second thoughts to some in Ireland about the desirability of major constitutional change. Though excluded by the Penal Laws from acquiring landed property, many Irish Catholics had acquired wealth from the provision trade and other commercial and manufacturing activities during the eighteenth century. When confronted with the choice of a Catholic alliance with the island's mass of potato-dependent coolies or of cleaving to the other men of substance, though these were Protestants, class interest outweighed the religious interests of Ireland's Catholic property owners. The politically radical proved to be socially conservative. The secessionist movement collapsed, and Ireland, neighbor and colony, cleaved more closely than ever to Britain through the Act of Union, which was supported by both Protestant and Catholic churches and by most property owners of both denominations.

The nineteenth was a century of unprecedented change in Britain, which led the world technologically, economically, and militarily during this century of Industrial Revolution. Change in Britain, in its various aspects, sent corresponding waves of change over its neighbor and colony, Ireland. The effect of these waves of change, emanating from a transforming Britain, was to sweep away most of what had emerged in Ireland during the preceding two centuries, and in their ebbing they contrived to leave cattle and sheep scarcely less dominant than William Petty had envisaged over two hundred years earlier.

Technological and economic change in Britain resulted in unprecedentedly rapidly rising incomes for a rapidly expanding population there. As incomes rose, political power too was diffused ever more from the castle to the cabins, including the cabins of the new class of property less proletariat, which became numerically dominant by the close of the century. There was a parallel diffusion of power in Ireland, but it was of a quite different character.

Once revolution in Europe had been checked by Napoleon's defeat at Waterloo and rolled back at the Congress of Vienna, the elite among Ireland's Catholics once again sought to free themselves from the disabilities of the Penal Laws, through the Catholic Association. They sought Reform, which would place well-to-do Catholics on an even footing with Protestants. They mobilized popular support by linking the Reform issue with the issue of Repeal of the Union, which was held out to the masses as the key to redressing their desperate and worsening socioeconomic conditions. This was a tactic that was to be used repeatedly, not only in Ireland but throughout the Third World in the anticolonial struggle. The elites in the colonies, striving to remove the disabilities placed on them by colonialism, appealed for support to the populist nationalism of the masses, the deterioration of whose socioeconomic conditions was the obverse of the elites' elevation. Their appeal to the masses was that there was nothing inherently wrong with the socioeconomic order that created, on the one hand, an indigenous elite and, on the other hand, an impoverished mass—nothing that would not be rectified by removing the over-arching control of the metropole on the colony's affairs.

The Catholic elite secured the Reform that rid them of the disabilities of the Penal Laws. They succeeded in part because of their mobilization of the masses along the lines of the contemporary Chartist movement in England, and in part because of the diffusion of political power from the castle to the cabin, which was a pronounced feature of the nineteenth century scene in Britain. But, during the first half of the nineteenth century, Repeal of the Union was not a serious issue. The Protestant ascendancy needed the Union to protect their still privileged position against the ascendant Catholic elites; and both the Protestant ascendancy and the Catholic elites needed the Union to protect them from the still swelling mass of starving, potato-dependent landless rural population. Though Daniel O'Connell and his class were prepared to appeal to, and to mobilize, the starving mass of Irish people in support of Reform, they were loath to terminate a Union that protected their own privileged position against the members of that class. Much later, Kevin O'Higgins concluded at the end of the Anglo-Irish conflict of 1916–1921 that: "We were probably the most conservative-minded revolutionaries that ever put through a successful revolution." But O'Connell's biographer commented: "He should have excepted O'Connell, whose second cause of pride in the achievement of Emancipation was its shoring up of the existing social structures." His first cause of pride was that Emancipation allowed him to practice at the Bar as an equal with Irish Protestants.[11]

The Great Famine, which sounded the knell of the rural proletariat, transformed the class character of the Irish nation. The clearances effected by the Famine facilitated the expansion of sheep and cattle numbers. Cattle exports, which had remained unchanged between 1660 and 1820, increased from an annual average of 76,000 in 1821–1825 to 451,000 annually in 1866–1870. Exports of sheep, "the poor man's cattle," increased twice as rapidly, from 50,000 to 681,000 annually over the same period.[12] A new elite emerged in Ireland. These were the predominantly Catholic proprietors of the cattle and sheep that replaced the rural proletariat. The same agronomic conditions and the same socioeconomic institutions and basic laws that created the rural proletariat under one set of metropolitan market conditions destroyed that class and replaced them with graziers of substance under different market conditions.

The nineteenth century brought a remarkable inversion of circumstances in Ireland and of relations between the two islands. The Act of Union accorded to Ireland, which then had one-third of the United Kingdom's population, one-sixth of the seats at Westminster. That representation, coupled with direct rule from Britain, secured the socioeconomic position of the ascendancy against a seething, increasingly revolutionary Catholic mass, though at the cost of the pretensions to sovereign, political power that the ascendancy had entertained in the eighteenth century. A century later, Ireland continued to have slightly more than a hundred MPs at Westminster, or slightly less than one-sixth of the total complement, although its population had by then shrunk to one-tenth of the UK's total. Of Ireland's one hundred MPs, eighty belonged to the Irish nationalist party which, following the Parnell split, was reunited in 1900. That party, holding one-eighth of the seats in a House of Commons that was otherwise divided between Conservatives and Liberals, was securely under the control of a relatively small number of predominantly Catholic, Irish graziers of substance and their class allies in Ireland. Timothy Healy's entrenched "conservative Catholic nationalist order" thus exercised a quite disproportionate influence, not only on Irish affairs, but on those of Britain's thirty-five million population, and even on those of a British empire which, at the end of the nineteenth century, spanned a large part of the globe.

Notwithstanding the transformation of conditions in Ireland and of relations between the two islands, centrifugal forces continued, as they did a century earlier, to divide the islands politically. Though now the character of those centrifugal forces were very different from a century earlier.

The principal concern of the Anglo Irish Protestant elite in Ireland at the beginning of the nineteenth century had been to secure, through the Union, a bulwark against indigenous radicalism. A major concern of the indigenous Catholic grazier elites and their associated classes at the beginning of the twentieth century was that some of Britain's current radicalism would seep into "a conservative, Catholic nationalist" Ireland as a result of the Union. That concern surfaced especially over Lloyd George's "People's Budget" of 1909, which proposed, inter alia, a land tax to help finance the recently introduced old age pensions and unemployment insurance. The newly reunited Irish Nationalist party at Westminster opposed the Budget.

The reservation of an unduly high proportion of administrative and judicial positions for Protestants was a further irritant to the Catholic bourgeoisie (see table 7.1). Though of a second order of importance to the land and rent issue, it did tend to grow over time. A high proportion of Ireland's predominantly middle-class children received secondary education; and of those who did, a good proportion proceeded to take a university education at the Queen's Colleges in Cork and Galway, which were founded in 1845, or at the Catholic University in

Dublin, founded in 1882. Catholic students previously had not generally attended the Protestant University of Dublin. All three colleges in Cork, Galway, and Dublin were consolidated into the National University of Ireland (NUI) in 1908.[13] The protégés of the Catholic secondary schools and of the NUI, who were emerging from the turn of the century onwards in increasing numbers, found their career prospects in Ireland impeded by the pre-emption of a high proportion of the senior positions by the Anglo-Irish Protestant elite.

Table 7.1. Catholic Males as a Proportion of All Males and Professions

	Percent
All males	74
Civil servants	59
Local and county government officials	52
Army officers	14
Barristers	44
Physicians, surgeons	49
Civil engineers	36
Veterinary surgeons	49

Source: British Parliamentary Papers 1912–1913 CXVIII (Cd. 6663)

Revolutionary nationalism, fed for the most part by the Irish diaspora, continued to have a subliminal effect on the dwindling population of the non-landed. Its populist appeal was that socioeconomic conditions for the colonized masses would improve only when colonial British power was removed from the Irish scene. Reinforcing these secessionist tendencies in Ireland there was in British political circles also a desire for some loosening of political ties between the islands—a desire to get the Irish political monkey off Britain's back. It was accepted generally that, notwithstanding the defeat by the House of Lords of the 1886 and 1893 Home Rule Bills, Home Rule for Ireland was only a matter of time. Legislation was envisaged which would confer a measure of legislative and administrative decentralization on Ireland, while there would be a corresponding reduction in Ireland's disproportionately large representation at Westminster.

A number of centripetal forces operated to hold the islands together under the Union, countering the tendency for disruption. There was, first and foremost, Britain's concern for its defense and the strategic role Ireland played in that. This was as live an issue for Britain in the twentieth century as it had been in the fifteenth. Related to the issue of Britain's defense and the means of securing it in the past were the million or so Protestants in the north east of the island. These were the descendants of the settlers Britain had planted there in the seventeenth century to secure its control over the whole island. There was apprehension that a decentralization of power from Britain to Ireland would leave a Protestant, industrializing minority under a government controlled by the Catholic, grazier interests of the larger part of the island. There was too concern, in this, the heyday of European imperialism, that the secession of the oldest colony from the empire would initiate an unraveling process that would spread first to India and later offset the colonization of the rest of Asia and Africa, which was then in full spate.

Finally, demographic change that emerged in Ireland at the turn of the century probably on balance did more to unite than to separate the two islands politically. Emigration, which spurted in the 1880s, declined very much in the early decades of the twentieth century. That decline can be attributed mainly to two causes. First, Irish agriculture moved into a phase of long term equilibrium resulting from the relationship already emphasized between tillage, winter fodder, cow numbers, and cattle numbers. By the end of the nineteenth century, with seventy-five cattle reared per hundred cows, there was little possibility of increasing the stock of the former without also expanding the number of the latter. Cow numbers could only be increased by reversing the long term decline in tillage. But the tillage acreage could only be expanded by reducing cattle numbers! With agriculture held thus in an equilibrium that left little room for maneuver, cattle numbers ceased to expand and there was less pressure on people to leave.[14]

Second, by the turn of the century Ireland had become a substantial net beneficiary from the UK treasury. Ireland, in 1901–1902, contributed £9.8 million, or 6.6 percent of total revenue to the UK exchequer. Non-military expenditure in Ireland in the same year was £7.2 million, or 15.0 percent of total UK civilian expenditure that year. Ireland's contribution to Imperial Expenditure (i.e., the army and navy) was £2.6 million, or 2.5 percent of the total. By 1913–1914 these quantities had changed to an Irish revenue contribution of £11.1 million, which was 5.7 percent of the total; non-military expenditure in Ireland was £12.4 million, or 13.9 percent of the total, with Irish expenditure being subvented by a contribution of £1.3 millions from Imperial funds. Ireland had 12 percent and 10 percent of the total UK population in 1901 and 1913 respectively.[15]

The character of government expenditure in Ireland at the time was probably more important than its excess over taxes gathered. The expenditure, in line with Britain's increasing democratization, was directed largely toward the less well off in Britain and Ireland. It was directed towards the grassroots in Ireland: to primary and secondary school teachers; to dispensary doctors; to postmen and policemen; and, after 1906, to Ireland's disproportionately large number of old-age pensioners. Money was also spent by the Congested District Board in the poorer west, and there were programs of light railway construction to service those areas. These expenditures, which went directly from the UK treasury to the grassroots in peripheral Ireland, stabilized population more effectively there than far larger transfers in recent years from the EEC. Because these latter flow more to the elites than to the grassroots, they tend to exacerbate rather than ameliorate emigration. Much reduced emigration would have led in time to a more "normal" population where the grazier, middle class influence would have been less dominant. A larger population with fewer emigrants and receiving increasing benefits from the UK connection might have been less keen to break the

Union. Ireland might well have settled permanently for Home Rule along the lines of the 1914 Act.

The First World War reactivated Fenian/Irish Republican Brotherhood aspirations for forcibly breaking the link with a Britain now desperately involved in war with Germany. The resulting rebellion of Easter 1916 of itself commanded little popular support. But as Britain, sorely pressed for manpower, proceeded with arrangements to introduce military conscription to Ireland, the scene changed. Large numbers of the remnants of the Irish proletariat had been swept into the British army at the outbreak of the Great War in 1914 and during successive recruiting drives. A soldier's pay and maintenance, with allowance for wife and children, was, for many of Ireland's residual proletariat, more attractive than the conditions that they could secure at home. The Anglo-Irish ascendancy, their economic, social, and political position made as obsolete in Ireland by the Land Acts as cavalry had been made by the machine gun and barbed wire on the Western Front, also flocked to the colors in a final gesture of *noblesse oblige*.

The Great War brought unprecedented prosperity to the Irish bourgeoisie. The value of everything farmers sold, particularly cattle, rose rapidly and continuously. There was an unbroken rise in cattle prices from 1913 to 1920, the longest such rise that has ever been recorded.[16] Perhaps the best barometer of the self-confidence engendered by the continuously rising prices was the manifold increase in land values that occurred during these years. Farmers, many of whom themselves, and all of whose parents, had been rack-rented tenants before the passing of the Land Acts, found themselves, in the course of a few war years, proprietors of landed properties of very considerable value. The associated commercial and professional classes shared in the prosperity and self-confidence of the farmers.

The sons of Ireland's prospering bourgeoisie, in 1917, were the last surviving pool of well nourished, healthy manhood in the United Kingdom. They had not been caught up by the 1915 conscription legislation, which had only applied to Britain. They had not been driven by poverty, nor had they been drawn by *noblesse oblige*, to the mud and massacre of Flanders. As a police report of the time noted: "Young farmers, shop assistants, clerks, school teachers and others of that class . . . in this country rarely if ever join the army."[17] The imminent threat to the sons of the Irish bourgeoisie posed by the Irish Conscription Act mobilized the economically and politically dominant forces of the Irish bourgeoisie against English rule in Ireland. Overnight, those whose main concerns had been the maintenance of the established system of law and order, the value of property, and the generation of profits, were converted into rebels against those laws and that order which now sought to dragoon their sons to fight in a bloody war that, however profitable it had been, impinged on no vital Irish bourgeois interest. Farm, shop, office, and pulpit resisted conscription with all the force and determination that a century of rapid bourgeois development made possible.[18]

The threat of conscription and the resistance it generated burnt bourgeois boats and threw the overwhelmingly dominant class in the land, which for half a century had toyed desultorily with independence, irrevocably on the side of secession from the United Kingdom of Great Britain and Ireland. Once the powerful bourgeoisie were committed to independence, independence could not for long be withheld. It was quickly conceded by postwar Britain, despite reservations that were held about the possible effects of Irish secession on India and other restive parts of the empire.

Independence was secured by the new generation of political elites in Ireland, although independence now involved the partition of the island, with the predominantly Protestant northeast remaining within the UK. With the attention of southern politicians focused firmly on securing sovereignty, debate on the Anglo-Irish treaty, which broke the Union, centered on esoteric matters like the degree to which that sovereignty might be circumscribed by a requirement for Irish legislators to take an Oath of Allegiance to the British monarch and by Ireland's status within the Commonwealth. It was of secondary importance that the treaty left half a million fellow Irish Catholics within what was now a sectarian Protestant statelet concerned above all else to defend Protestant status and privileges against the island's hostile Catholic majority. "The Oath of Allegiance was a major issue in the (Dail) debate (on the Treaty); partition was not."[19]

Endorsement of the Anglo-Irish Treaty which allowed the secession of twenty-six Irish counties from the United Kingdom of Great Britain and Ireland and established an Irish Free State was given by a majority of voters in the General Election of 1922. The number of votes cast for pro-Treaty candidates was 486,000,[20] out of a total electorate of some four times greater. The total population of Ireland, including the Six Counties, at the time was 4,300,000. There were in the region of another four million Irish emigrants and their sons and daughters living abroad. That is, the elites had secured sovereign control of twenty-six of Ireland's thirty-two counties with the electoral support of about one-twentieth of the Irish nation.

Independence Movements Elsewhere

The Indian mutiny of 1857 had much in common with the Irish rebellions of the seventeenth century. It was, like them, a revanchist attempt by indigenous elements to undo the conquest and to turn back the clock to pre-conquest times. However, within a few decades of the suppression of the mutiny, a new India, created by capitalist colonialism and rapid economic growth, was stirring. Viceroy Dufferin, in 1886, complained to Lord Kimberley, the Secretary of State for India, that "all the arts of Irish agitation had come to India."[21] Conceding Home Rule to Ireland under these circumstances was indeed, as Joseph Chamberlain and others warned, likely to have repercussions that would extend far beyond Ireland.

India's colonial rulers held the commanding heights of politics, commerce, and banking in British hands. But virtually all the land and the vast bulk of the capital belonged to the new breed of Indian proprietors. Their titles were as secure as those of the English owners of property in England, in a manner that was quite alien to Indian culture. Where there had been no property, there now was, subject only to conforming to the law of the land, which was that of the colonial power. The wealth, power, and influence of these proprietors grew *pari passu* with the economy.

There was, in addition to the owners of real property, a large and rapidly growing body of civil servants, professionals, educators, and skilled and semi-skilled in the new industries, like the railways and post office, brought into existence by the economic growth of the capitalist colony. These men, their associates, and dependants "owed their changed status to British rule and had learnt the language and the political idiom of their rulers."[22] From amongst them came the founders of the early associations that sought to represent and to advance the distinctive interests of the new type of Indian. From their ranks came the men, mainly lawyers and graduates, who organized the first Indian National Congress at Bombay in 1885 and in other major cities in subsequent years. An awareness grew, along with the colonial economy, of an Indian identity which was distinct from the colonial power; that India had interests that were not only different from, but in important respects conflicted with, those of the Raj.

Indian nationalism emerged in the late nineteenth century when it had begun to make political sense for India's elites to claim, in their opposition to the government, that they represented the nation against the Raj. It was a tactic similar to O'Connell's appeal to the coolie Irish masses fifty years earlier for mass support for his reform program; and like that, it had inherent dangers. A careful path was necessary between mobilizing for political change desperate masses who had little to lose and the destruction by those mobilized masses of a socioeconomic order that had brought great wealth and power to the mobilizers. The Raj's critics and their program, for the present at least, "depended on the existence of the very imperialism of which they were both the inveterate castigators and the conspicuous beneficiaries."[23]

India's new elites did retain control of the new nationalism. They sought at Congress level from an early date to have Legislative Councils established, where Indians of substance would have a say. They hinted at a parliament for India in the future, although, as in contemporary Ireland, it was realized that home rule would bring to the surface divisions within the country that were muted under colonial rule—divisions between Catholics and Protestants in Ireland and between Hindus and Moslems in India. At the populist level of political agitation, "the Rowlett report of 1918 stated that extremist nationalism, which took the form of acts of terrorism, found its main basis of support among higher caste Indians of student age. . . . There were also cases of low caste Hindu groups cooperating with the Raj in a common opposition to high caste Brahmins with western education and nationalist sentiments."[24]

If "the radical change that allowed the development of a western type middle class in India came only with British rule,"[25] it is equally true that the great swelling of the masses who supported that middle class also came only with British rule. Capitalist colonialism, in India as elsewhere, "rested on four columns: stability, order, security of life and property, and a sound treasury."[26] These conditions made existence easier for the masses and made it possible for more of them to survive, just as they facilitated the acquisition of wealth by the middle class. The introduction additionally of the rudiments of medical science and public hygiene could reduce death rates, even at lower nutritional levels, sufficiently to boost population growth from an average of 0.2 percent annually before colonization to an average of 0.6 percent in the last century of colonialism. The population of the Indian subcontinent increased from 100 million to 160 million between 1500 and 1750, on the eve of colonization. It increased to 225 million in the following century. It then almost doubled, to 430 million, between 1850 and 1950.[27]

Population growth accelerated despite the more frequent famines that occurred under the British Raj. As the nutritional level required for survival declined and the margin between that level and starvation narrowed, famines occurred more frequently. "Legends and records mention more than ninety famines (in India) in the past 2500 years; 66 percent took place after 1701."[28]

As Cipolla points out, around 1918, "the average daily quantity of grain available for the Indian population was about twenty ounces per head. By 1945 . . . the average daily quantity of grain available per head had fallen to about fifteen ounces. After 1945 the situation worsened and per head food supply diminished substantially between 1945 and 1952."[29]

A larger Indian population, subsisting at lower nutritional levels, generated more profit for the proprietors of the land and capital on which the masses depended. Capitalist colonialism thus gave rise simultaneously to the impoverishment of the masses and to the wealth of the middle class.

India's middle class, by the mid-twentieth century, was sufficiently strong and the masses sufficiently debilitated to make the former confident of their ability to maintain their privileges vis-à-vis the latter without the support of the British Raj. The Raj, which had created the middle class, by then was no longer necessary and had become irksome. The middle class, in India as elsewhere, appealed to the masses for their support in ejecting the colonizers, offering the prospect that, with fellow Indians operating the socioeconomic system, conditions for the masses would be transformed.

Paralleling the support of the Whigs for North American independence, of the Spanish radicals for Latin American independence, and of the Liberal party for Irish independence, the British Labor party supported Indian independence. Following Lenin's interpretation, the Labor party perceived in imperialism "an undeniable connection between: (i) the existence of highly developed capitalist societies creating surpluses, which their distribution of income made it difficult for them to invest profitably at home; (ii) a high rate of foreign investment and (iii) the acquisition of much of the habitable globe by those societies as their colonies."[30]

Colonialism was an alternative to domestic income redistribution and to domestic investment. Decolonization was, therefore, a milestone on the road to a more equitable metropolitan society for which colonies would be unnecessary.

The foreign influence that was relevant in India's case and in the case of Asia generally was Japan and the United States:

> From the time of the first World War, the incipient nationalist movements in the non-European world profited substantially from the rivalries among the colonial powers, and the sudden collapse of the European empires after 1947 was to a large extent a consequence of external pressures and of the impact of world politics. In Asia, neither Britain nor France nor the Dutch ever recovered from the blows inflicted by Japan between 1941 and 1945, while in Africa and the Middle East they were checked and forced into retreat by pressure from the USA.[31]

Russia, in a manner that was reminiscent of the fourteenth century Mongolian penetration through China as far as the South China Sea, acted as the external influence in Indo-China. One consequence of Russo-Chinese intervention in Vietnam was the quite exceptional concern of that country's independence movement to change the social order as well as to secure political independence.

The termination of European colonialism adhered to the same pattern in Africa. Educational advantage rather than property was the material basis of African nationalism, which culminated in independence. Better educated Africans found their advancement to higher positions in the colonial administration blocked by the established network, which reserved senior positions for expatriate, white officials, possibly of inferior quality. The "new elites and strata—wealthy cash crop farmers, businessmen and managers, workers and intelligentsia—none of which had pre-colonial roots . . . formed political associations and parties and constituted the driving force . . . behind the movement for independence and national integration after independence."[32]

Virtually all parties in metropolitan Europe were, in the 1950s, disillusioned with colonialism. There was little opposition to African independence in a Europe that was, in any case, experiencing full employment and unprecedented prosperity. In some countries, like the Belgian Congo, there was precipitous haste to discard the responsibilities of colonialism, and chaos filled the resulting void. The principal foreign influence in the decolonization of Africa, along with the United States, was Russia. Russia, in Africa as in Vietnam, offered the possibility of a new social order to the independent colonies, as well as military and economic support to achieve independence. But the continental Russian power was less committed to securing change in the social order in Africa than it was in Indo-China, with which, through its quondam ally China, it had land contact.

Chapter 8

The Capitalist Colonization of Ireland

The Early Colonization of Ireland

The hegemonic expansion of individualist capitalism that happened throughout Europe occurred also in Ireland; but failed there. More successful polities extended their sway in central western Europe and, in doing so, initiated the process of reducing a multiplicity of petty lordships to the handful of states in Europe now. The expansionary, individualist capitalist influence of central western Europe led to the creation of a different, autocratic capitalism in the marchlands of eastern Europe and, beyond that, in Russia. The economies of all these polities in continental Europe were founded on crop-growing on effectively limitless, but naturally unproductive, arable land, with the use of vastly more capital than in the non-European world. In Europe, including Russia, capital limited production; elsewhere land did.

That capital-based crop-growing was marginal in England; and England's marginality for crop-growing, through the unique set of circumstances described in chapter 5, caused it to become in time, and for a number of centuries, the foremost world power. But Ireland lies beyond England, beyond the margin for capital-based crop-growing. The Celts, who settled in France and Britain and grew crops there to provide the fodder that was essential for their cattle's survival in winter, did not do so in Ireland. They did not do so, at least to anything like the same extent, because crop-growing was more difficult and less necessary in Ireland's maritime climate.

The hegemonically driven Normans could quickly penetrate to every distant part of Ireland and erect their moats and castles there. But it was one thing, with superior Norman military power, to wrench land from the pastoral, nonindividualist, noncapitalist, indigenous Irish; it was a very different matter to grow in Ireland the crops that were necessary to sustain the Norman and continental way of life. There is thought to have been a Gaelic revival in the thirteenth and fourteenth centuries.[1] If this was so, it probably owed less to a resurgence of Gaelic power and more to the year-round rain and cool summers that make crop-growing virtually impossible in most of Ireland. Ireland's weather and not its warriors confined the Normans within the Pale, or the southeastern corner of the island where the rainfall is less and the summers are warmer, and where, too, virtually all Ireland's crops are grown now. The nine most eastern counties of the province of Leinster (i.e., excluding Counties Longford, Offaly, and Westmeath), which the Normans controlled longest and most securely, now contain 27 percent of the island's total agricultural land area but have 62 percent of its cropped area; 20 percent of the land in these nine counties is cropped but only 5 percent in the rest of Ireland.[2]

Neither the Celts nor the Normans succeeded in establishing capital-based crop-growing in most of Ireland. It was the only part of food-producing Europe where that did not occur. Ireland was also the only part of Europe and indeed of the world where individualist capitalism came into direct contact with nonindividualist, noncapitalist tribalism. The march lands of eastern Europe and Russia intervened between the individualist capitalism of central western Europe and the pastoralism of the steppe. But the Pale marked the boundary where uniquely there came into direct contact the two utterly different cultures of central western Europe's individualist capitalism and the noncapitalist collectivism which persisted in most of Ireland as it did throughout the non-European world.

The Tudor and Stuart Conquests

Ireland was left to go its own pastoral, nonindividualist, noncapitalist way for as long as European eyes looked eastwards. But matters changed with the marked quickening of European life in the centuries following the Black Death. The Reformation and the Great Discoveries, in particular, transformed Ireland from a cul-de-sac into a location of great strategic importance in a Europe that had become maritime and looked increasingly westwards.

The Strategic Impulse

The Reformation saw Henry VIII, the quondam *defensor fidei*, in conflict with Rome. That conflict was part of the process of establishing the "sovereignty of the king in parliament" which was necessary to make England's land, which had always been for everyman's use, a source of profit for a small minority. The break with Rome created a new, external challenge to the crown of England, in addition to those originating internally and which had caused the violent deaths of one-third of the heirs to the throne in three dynasties. Ireland, which lay athwart Britain's western flank, thus became critical to the defense of the political status quo there in the new maritime age. As the Tudor quip put it: "he who would England win, let him in Ireland first begin." That consideration remained valid throughout the centuries, right up to modern times. It was essential too for England's magnates, if the metamorphosis from an unprofitable feudal lordship to a profitable landed proprietorship were to be accomplished successfully, that the sovereignty of the king in parliament be defended against attack from all quarters, including Ireland.

These considerations justified the protracted and costly Tudor struggle to establish, in fact as well as law, the title to the crown of Ireland which Henry VIII gave himself in 1541. But there was another consideration, which was the same as caused English people, through the following centuries, to lay claim to that large part of the non-European world that was occupied by hunter-gatherers and that was, for the most part, ignored by other Europeans. This was the fact that English land became valuable centuries earlier than land elsewhere in Europe; and if English land was profitable for sheep grazing, it was not unreasonable to expect that land in nearby Ireland, where the grass grew better, should also show a profit. These expectations were articulated by Francis Bacon, among others:

> This I will say confidently, that if God bless this kingdom with peace and justice, no usurer is so sure in seventeen years space to double his principal, and interest upon interest, as that kingdom is within the same time to double the stock both of wealth and people. . . . It is not easy, no not upon the continent, to find such confluence of commodities, if the hand of man did join with the hand of nature.[3]

Thus began the capitalist colonization of Ireland: the only part of food-producing Europe where, as in the non-European world, agriculture was not based on capital-intensive crop-growing; where land was the limiting factor on production; and where society was nonindividualist. England's neighbor, Ireland, thus became Europe's only, and the Old World's first, capitalist colony. Ireland remained a capitalist colony from, say, the coronation of Henry VIII as King of Ireland in 1541, until the Anglo-Irish Treaty of 1921, which gave political independence to twenty-six of Ireland's thirty-two counties. That was the longest period of capitalist colonial rule experienced by any country. The next longest was Barbados in the Caribbean, which was a colony from 1627 to 1966.

The difficult, early conquest of Ireland in the sixteenth century and, following two major rebellions in the seventeenth century, its reconquest twice, which were necessitated by strategic considerations, were extremely costly. The conquest and reconquest yielded neither spices nor species, nor yet again even exotic tropical produce. This profitless colonization had two particularly important consequences, one for England and the other for Ireland.

The Political Consequences

The result for England of colonizing Ireland was, in key ways, directly opposite to that experienced by the Iberian powers following their colonization of the Far East and Mezzo-America. The Iberian monarchs secured great wealth, in spices and species, at little cost from their easily won colonies. This easily won wealth made the Iberian monarchs the best endowed and most powerful in Europe. It swung the balance of power strongly away from the cabin towards the castle in Spain and Portugal and caused there the arrest for centuries of individualist capitalist development.

The Tudors, on the other hand, in conquering for strategic purposes the bogs and woods of Ireland, lost there all the wealth that they had secured from the confiscation of the Church's property in England, which wealth had been critical in giving them the absolute power to establish property in English land. "The cost of conquering Ireland was enormous; more than any other single factor, the cost of Elizabeth's Irish campaigns set parliament and crown on the course which culminated in civil war in the 1640s."[4] That dissipation of wealth left the crown of England exceptionally impoverished under the succeeding Stuart monarchy, at a time when the cabin power of property had become far more powerful in England than elsewhere in Europe. That was because, a century and more after the first post-Black Death enclosures, the English people had come to accept as normal what an absolute Tudor monarchy had been required to establish initially: that the land of England was for the profit of its proprietors rather than for the use of its inhabitants. In a mirror-image of the Iberian situation, there was in England, under the Stuarts, a tremendous shift in the balance of power away from the castle, towards the property-owning cabin. Accordingly the forces of individualist capitalism advanced there more rapidly than elsewhere, in no small measure because of the strategically necessary, but for the crown, financially unrewarding, conquest of Ireland.

Ireland's proximity to Britain, the necessity which that created to capitalist colonize it two centuries before any other part of the Old World, the difficulties implicit in that task, and the prospects for British people of making a profit from land—especially land close by in Ireland—all conduced to creating in Ireland another phenomenon which, though not unique, was rare in the annals of capitalist colonialism.

The General Nature of Settler Colonialism

The settler colonists, of mainly British origin, in the New World lands occupied by hunter-gatherers, followed the normal practice of food producers coming into contact with hunter-gatherers: they exterminated them or otherwise cleared them from the land. The settlers in North America and Oceania, like food producers throughout the ages, then proceeded to operate the land appropriated from the hunter-gatherers. The colonizers in the capitalist colonies which were occupied by food producers operated differently. They were normally content to leave the indigenes in possession of the land, either drawing rent from the occupants, as in the case of the creoles in Latin America, or, more usually, merely controlling the pinnacles of economic power as in the Indian subcontinent. When land was appropriated for capital-intensive, plantation agriculture, the amount involved was usually relatively small. In Malaya where land was appropriated to a greater extent than elsewhere for rubber production, only about one-fifth of the total area had been appropriated by the 1970s, and most of that had gone to local, or Chinese, planters, and not to metropolitan planters.[5]

There were some exceptions to this policy of leaving the land of the capitalist colonies in the possession of the indigenous food producers, operating it for the profit of the agents and collaborators of the metropoles. Those exceptions were mainly in Africa, where they occurred principally as part of the great carving up of Africa among the European metropolitan powers that occurred between 1880 and the First World War. But the first of these cases, where African food producers were replaced on the land by farmers of metropolitan origin, was in the eastern parts of the Cape Province of South Africa: in Natal and the Transvaal where the Boer farmers, following the Great Trek through the savannahs occupied by the mainly hunter-gathering Khoikhoi, appropriated land that had been farmed by Bantu peoples. The second occurred in Algeria, following the conquest of that territory in the 1830s, when French colons appropriated and operated the land of the indigenous Arabs and Berbers. A third was Rhodesia/Zimbabwe, seized by the British South African Company in the 1890s. The White Highlands of Kenya was another case, which occurred mainly between 1903 and 1911, and again in the years immediately after the First World War.

Settler Colonization in Ireland

Special circumstances accounted for all of these cases of appropriating land from indigenous food producers and settling it with farmers of metropolitan origin, which were rare in the annals of capitalist colonialism and were confined to Africa. But another case had occurred much earlier in Ireland. The motive was strategic: to secure, as was the case with the Portuguese colonies in Africa 300 years later after the Berlin Conference, "effective occupation" of the colony at minimal cost to the metropolitan power.[6] That was done by planting it with "loving subjects of good behavior and account, none of the mere Irish to be maintained in any family."[7]

The first systematic attempt to do this was the Plantation of Munster under Queen Elizabeth. Others followed; but the most important, most successfully accomplished, and most enduring was the Plantation of Ulster under James I. The influx of English and Scots settlers to Ulster raised the proportion of the island's population that was of metropolitan, British origin from less than 2 percent in 1600 to 27 percent a century later.[8] These settlers were relatively more numerous than persons of metropolitan origin in any other capitalist colony; and they were settled in Ireland centuries before others were similarly settled on land appropriated from indigenous food producers in Africa.

The plantations, and especially that of Ulster, established two different classes in Ireland. The one was an armed garrison class, concerned to maintain the conquest and the privileges conquest conferred on the conquerors. The other was the disarmed but fractious indigenes, a lesser breed without rights, whose disabilities were the corollary of the garrison's privileges and who had nothing to gain, but all to lose, from the colonial connection between the two neighboring islands.

Race distinguished the European garrison from the non-European garrisoned in the non-European capitalist colonies. White Europeans could be relied upon, especially in crises, to support and defend a capitalist colonial regime which the black or brown majority could be expected to undermine, oppose, or assault. Ireland diverged from this otherwise universal pattern of racial distinction in the capitalist colonies. Colonizers and colonized in Ireland were distinguished instead by their religions. The former were Protestant; the latter were Catholic. These fine theological distinctions have proved more durable than the sharpest racial contrasts. The inevitable miscegenation between white colonizers and black or brown colonized produced sub-classes of mestizos, mulattos, and Eurasians who occupied the middle ground and eroded in time the sharp distinctions between black/brown and white. But successive generations born in Ireland, whether of mixed parentage or not, were Catholics or Protestants, with no diminution over the centuries of the religious distinctions between them.

Converts from Catholicism, whose motives might be suspect, were not immediately accepted into the privileged garrison class. Converts were regarded as potential enemies within the camp at a time of crisis. Only the children or grandchildren of the converts could aspire to the privileges of the garrison. Meanwhile, "such as conform and go to the state church are derided and oppressed by the multitude."[9] The prospect of being rejected by the class aspired to and anathematized by the class from which escape was sought, was an investment on behalf of children or grandchildren which impoverished people could not contemplate. It was a measure only to be contemplated by persons of substance, for whom the adoption of Protestantism helped to secure their property, which property in turn insulated them against Protestant suspicion and Catholic hostility. Understandably, therefore, "the eighteenth century had seen a steady stream of defections to the Established Church from the ranks of the Catholic gentry and middle class. But among other sections of the population, in the absence of any serious missionary effort from a lax, worldly Church of Ireland, the number of losses through conformity had been negligible."[10] The majority of the Irish, *faute de mieux*, adhered to the old religion.

There are not many parallels in history for the incompatibility between the religions of the rulers and of the ruled which obtained in colonial Ireland.[11] The normal role of religion has been to sustain the temporal power, which frequently has been perceived as the terrestrial manifestation of society's spirit world. It may please the Irish to attribute their stubborn adherence to the Roman Church to their religious constancy, which caused Ireland to be the only part of western Europe where, after the Peace of Augsburg in 1555, the pragmatic principle *cuius regio eius religio* did not apply. A more plausible explanation is the fact that Ireland was the only country in Europe within which a new social order— that of individualist capitalism—had been superimposed on, and ruled uneasily over, an older order of tribal pastoralism. In the resistance of the indigenous culture to the superimposed culture, Catholicism has been to Irish nationalism what race has been to nationalism in other capitalist colonies.

There is no parallel in capitalist colonialism for the differentiation along religious lines between colonizers and colonized, of substantially similar racial type which occurred in Ireland. Parallels do, however, exist in other, noncapitalist colonial situations, where, as in Ireland, colonizers sought to retain and to "squeeze" indigenous agriculturists who were of similar racial type to themselves. One such case was the pastoral Aryan invaders of India. These were able to have a wide range of relationships, including sexual ones, with the indigenous crop-growers, without being swamped by the much larger indigenous population (as the erstwhile ruling whites of the West Indies have been, in large measure, by the more numerous blacks). This was because the progeny of alliances between persons of different castes never attained the caste of the upper caste parent.[12] A similar caste-like arrangement existed between the Nilo-Hamitic pastoralists and the crop-growing Bantus of interlacustrine Africa. It obtained especially between the Tutsi pastoralists and the Hutu crop-growers of Rwanda.[13]

Indeed, had the Reformation and the subsequent division of western Christianity into Catholic and Protestant not occurred, it is difficult to see how the capitalist colonization of Ireland could have been sustained much beyond the sixteenth century and the Tudor dynasty. It would have been difficult if not impossible, without religion, to distinguish the garrison from the garrisoned. Language was an impermanent barrier. The imposition of caste-based arrangements, as in India and interlacustrine Africa, would have been totally at variance with the character of individualist capitalism, central to which were change and adaptation. Only adherence to the old Catholicism, which offered the indigenous Irish a point of resistance to the conquest, identified them also as opponents of the new regime, and therefore to be treated accordingly for centuries.

The Use of Land as a Source of Individual Profit

Ireland was the first capitalist colony where land was appropriated and used for profit. (The encomienda system of Latin America was designed to secure the services of its inhabitants rather than the use of the land, which remained for long non-limiting.) It was the first society where land was appropriated and used for profit regardless of the consequences for its inhabitants. England's land had been appropriated a century and more earlier than Ireland's; but notwithstanding the absolute Tudor monarchy, it was not, and could not be, used regardless of the consequences for the land's inhabitants. The Tudor State was administratively weak and perpetually concerned about the maintenance of a fragile internal peace:

> Tudor policy was quite tender to vested interests. . . . The idea that a whole industry should be wiped out because the same goods could be produced elsewhere made no sense to the Tudors; and if their economics were crude, their knowledge of the cost of suppressing the riots and rebellions of men thrown out

of work, being founded on experience, was most precise. The vast mass of Tudor legislation on economic activities rests solidly on three principles—privilege, regulation and supervision. The purpose was to prevent the unchecked greed and ambition of any group—middle class or other—from dislocating social order.[14]

It was otherwise in Ireland. "Did insurrection break forth in Ireland? The aristocracy of the country never stirred; it was English artillery that subdued the insurgents; and when everything was restored to order, the aristocracy continued to receive the revenue of its land as before."[15]

Land in Ireland, for longer than anywhere else other than England, has been used for profit, in a manner more unrestrained by consideration of the consequences for its inhabitants than anywhere else. Possibly the best measure of the success with which profit from Irish land has been pursued over the centuries and through the changing pattern of metropolitan demand is the increase in the value of that land. The English parliament sold Irish land at one old penny an acre in the 1650s to pay Cromwell's soldiers in the reconquest of Ireland after rebellion.[16] Now that land, especially if it has an European Economic Community milk quota, is worth up to £4,000 an acre. (It is worth far more if it is in, or near, a town or city.) This represents an average annual 4 percent appreciation in land values over the centuries. Of course, much of the appreciation in land value merely represents a decline in the value of money, which represents no increase in real value. But Cromwell's soldiers received a penny a day for their work, or the price at the time of an acre of farmland. The modern Irish soldier's pay is about £20 a day. At that rate, it now requires 200 days soldiering to earn the price of an acre of land, compared to one day 340 years ago.

The Exploitation of Irish Land

For four centuries, since the battle of Kinsale in 1601, which marked the completion of the Tudor conquest of Ireland, Irish land has been used for profit, in diverse ways according to the opportunities presented by changing external conditions and regardless of the impact on Irish society. Society has, at all times, been forced to adjust drastically to the superior requirement of making a profit from Irish land. There were, during those centuries, four distinct sets of external demand circumstances or phases, each of which required a particular pattern of Irish land use to make a profit, and each of which in turn shaped the response of Irish society.

The first of these phases was characterized by a demand in England for Irish livestock, which lasted through the early Stuart reigns of James I and Charles I. That was followed by a century, from the restoration of Charles II in 1660 to the coronation of George III in 1760, which was dominated by the Cattle Acts. The third phase corresponded with the sixty year reign of George III, from 1760 to 1820, which witnessed also England's Industrial Revolution. The final, fourth phase, which corresponded with the era of advanced factory capitalism, lasted from the death of George III up to, and beyond, Irish independence in 1921. These phases are discussed successively in the sections which follow.

Phase 1—A Seventeenth Century Livestock Trade

If the financial and political cost to the English crown of Ireland's conquest was great, the magnates who favored that conquest with a view to profit from Irish land were not misguided. A remarkable livestock trade from Ireland to Britain developed under the early Stuarts. Starting from scratch at the beginning of the century, the trade was shipping annually by 1640 some 45,000 cattle and a similar number of sheep.[17] Given that England's population and their real income per head were both about one-tenth their present level,[18] the development of this trade was a remarkable testimony to the efficacy of capitalist colonialism in mobilizing a colony's resources for profit.

A similar trade could not have been developed anywhere else in Europe west of the steppe. The cattle and sheep were the natural products of Irish land, with few inputs of either labor or capital. By appropriating the land by conquest, the appropriators also acquired the land's produce of cattle and sheep. The realization from the sale of these animals was virtually pure profit, or rent, for the new proprietors of what had formerly been Irish clan land. Later Sir William Petty, with the perspicacity of "one of the most original social engineers who ever lived" [19] and who had himself nefariously acquired the extensive Irish lands on which the House of Landsdowne was founded, drew the logical conclusion from the fact of ownership of Irish land by metropolitan interests. Petty, in *A Treatise of Ireland*, written in 1687, recommended that most of the disaffected Irish be removed to England, to work there as laborers and tradespeople; that the country be converted into a cattle walk, supporting six million cattle; that these cattle to be tended by 200,000 people left in Ireland; and that the cattle's produce to be shipped to England.[20] He argued that the island, by the removal thus of most of the disaffected population, could be most easily secured by England against foreign enemies and could in this way also be made to yield the greatest profit to its new proprietors. Had Petty's recommendations been implemented, there would have been no "Irish question" any more than there has been a North American, New Zealand, or Australian "question."

One part of Petty's proposal had been put in train by Cromwell as part of his Western Venture to develop colonies in the Caribbean. As well as being sent "to Hell or Connaught," many Irish were shipped for forced labor on the plantations of the Barbados and other British colonies in the Caribbean. However, the export of Irish people as slaves to the West Indies and of Irish cattle and sheep to Britain both failed, the one for racist and the other for politico-economic reasons.

As noted already one of the largest and most profitable trades of the time was in slaves from West Africa to the Caribbean. Removing to the same place for the same purpose the rebellious Irish, who were not needed to produce store cattle or sheep, could have been expected to be profitable in itself and to have made the island more secure for England. That was how it seemed to Oliver Cromwell, who had to suppress rebellion in Ireland and who had a "western policy" for the development of English plantation interests in the Caribbean. The development of the trade was stymied by the fact of the Irish being, unlike all other capitalist colonized peoples, of the same Caucasian racial origins as the colonizers.

Profits from Caribbean slavery depended critically on a high slave/supervisor ratio—which was up to ten to one. That was far higher than in the other major slave-based societies, those of the ancient Mediterranean and the Antebellum South in the United States. In both of these cases, the slave populations roughly equaled the free. Race was the key which enabled a small number of European supervisors to control and exploit a much larger number of producers in the Caribbean, as it was to remain throughout the whole course of capitalist colonialism, except in Ireland, where both colonizers and colonized were of the same Caucasian race. There religion distinguished the one from the other. Elsewhere, blacks or browns were the colonized peoples who opposed the established order; the whites were the colonizers, who profited from, and supported the capitalist colonial order.

The transported Irish did not fit into this arrangement on the Caribbean plantations. When hostile shipping approached, the Caucasian and Catholic Irish greeted them as liberators, especially if they were ships from Catholic France or Spain. For blacks it was different, for they realized that all Europeans treated them similarly, as slaves. Thus it was, as early as 1644, well before the influx of Irish transported on the instruction of Cromwell began, "an act was passed (by the Council of the Barbados) 'for the prohibition of landing Irish persons . . . and such others as are of the Romish religion.'"[21] Irish and other transported white laborers regarded as liberators hostile European forces when these attacked the island colonies. The white convict laborers made common cause with the invaders in assaulting the garrison. Understandably, therefore, the Council of Barbados in 1690 decreed: "We desire no Irish Rebels may be sent us, for we want no laborers of that Color to work for us; but men in whom we may confide to strengthen us."[22]

The shipment of people from Ireland to the West Indies failed for racial reasons. The shipment of livestock from Ireland to Britain failed for politico-economic reasons. It fell foul of the interests of the ascendant English landed oligarchy. The trade's rapid growth affected adversely the English oligarchy in three ways. First, the crown, by customary right, levied duties on imports of cattle and sheep from Ireland. This crown revenue was independent of parliament, which was using its control of the purse to extract constitutional concessions from the crown. The Stuart dynasty was vulnerable to these pressures in large measure because of the costly Tudor conquest of Ireland, which left it, notwithstanding the wealth appropriated by the earlier Tudors from England's monasteries, as impecunious as most feudal monarchs were.

Second, profits from Irish land depended on the maintenance of metropolitan imposed law and order. Ireland's landed proprietors had secured their titles to the land a century or more later than their British counterparts and those titles were correspondingly fragile and vulnerable to assault. A strong executive was needed in a frontier, rebellious Ireland if the livestock trade and its profits were to continue to flow. Understandably then, the Dublin parliament, representative of Ireland's new landed proprietors, was more amenable than the Westminster parliament to voting taxes for the executive. A vigorous Lord Lieutenant, Sir Thomas Wentworth, was able to exploit this situation to acquire, on behalf of his master, the king, resources for the support of the crown in its increasingly sharp conflict with parliament. Those resources included an army that was financed by taxes levied by the Dublin parliament on Irish land and paid for ultimately by the livestock trade from Ireland to Britain.[23]

The third way in which the import into Britain of livestock from the neighboring island adversely affected Britain's landed interest was through the trade's impact on the domestic British price for pastoral produce. This point was put, with only a little hyperbole, by a speaker in the Westminster House of Lords: "The infinite number of Foreign Cattle that were daily imported did glut our markets and bring down the price of both our home-bred cattle and our land."[24]

England's landed oligarchy were ascendant in Westminster's Restoration parliament, following the Civil War, which itself had been largely precipitated by events in Ireland. The parliament lost no time in passing a series of Cattle Acts which had the effect of excluding all Irish agricultural produce from Britain other than raw wool. The acts ended the livestock trade from Ireland to Britain which had developed so rapidly under the early Stuarts.

Phase 2—A Three Way Provisions Trade with the Indies

The effect of the Cattle Acts on Irish pastoral produce prices was dramatic. The price of cattle, over forty shillings in 1663, fell to ten or twelve in 1667.[25] Irish land became virtually valueless, although with metropolitan law and order more firmly established, it was now more securely held for the profit of the metropole's agents and collaborators.

Two factors, each related to Ireland now being a colony in a wider colonial system, allowed Irish land to continue to yield a profit or rent, notwithstanding the exclusion of its pastoral produce from Britain. One was the potato, which had recently been introduced to Ireland from Britain's North American colonies; and the other was the demand for provisions to feed the slaves on the Caribbean plantations.

The potato, which originated in the Altiplano of South America, had a transforming influence on Irish society. A tuber that grows well in Ireland's cool, damp climate, it yields, from a given area, over five times as much food as cereals.[26] It produced sufficient nutrition from a small area that could be cultivated with a spade for the maintenance and reproduction of the cultivator. The potato made it possible for Irish people to maintain and reproduce themselves by cultivating land with virtually no capital, like the peasants, or coolies, in tropical and semi-tropical riverine valleys. It reduced the cost of Irish labor virtually to zero.

Irish labor was "free" in a number of ways that did not apply to contemporary continental European labor, or even to Protestant settler labor in Ireland. It was "free" firstly in that, with the potato, it could be produced and reproduced without capital. Secondly, it was "free," or without employment, because cattle and sheep for the livestock trade were pastoral products that required hardly any labor for their production. Thirdly, Irish labor was "free" in a Marxian sense: it was not tied to the land as European serf labor was; nor could it be shipped as slave labor to the West Indies; and, finally, as a conquered, colonized people, it was "free" of any prescriptive rights.

Irish land, other than that which was planted, was also "free" in a particular sense. It had been freed by conquest of any primordial, prescriptive rights on the part of the indigenes to it. These henceforth acquired rights to land only by contract, involving rents or other payments to the expropriators, their heirs and assignees. Land in post-Restoration and post-Cattle Acts Irish land was also free in that it could no longer be used to produce livestock for Britain.

The Irish colony, in the later seventeenth century, thus, uniquely, had two free resources: labor and land. Market forces combined these resources to meet, with profit to land, the distant West Indian demand for provisions to feed the slaves. The free labor made hay, which had not been made previously in Ireland; and cattle could be over wintered, to mature and fatten on pasture. They were then slaughtered, salted, and barreled for the provision trade. So also were pigs fattened on potatoes surplus to human needs and on skim milk left when the cream was removed for butter. The butter itself, from the cows that bred the cattle, was also shipped. During the century between the Restoration of Charles II and the coronation of George III in 1760, which year is generally taken as marking the beginning of England's Industrial Revolution, Irish agricultural exports changed as in table 8.1.

In the words of a contemporary writer, quoted by O'Donovan:

> After some years (of the Cattle Acts) Ireland found a way of salting, barreling and exporting beef. So that in lieu of exporting 70,000 head of live cattle to England at 40s. a head, which cost England but £140,000 and which they manufactured afterwards and had all the hides and tallow into the bargain, Ireland now exports that beef to the value of £20,000 and butter worth £200,000 more; and about 3,000 raw hides to England, 70,000 raw hides to France and Spain, and about £70,000 worth of tallow.[27]

Table 8.1. Irish Agricultural Exports 1665, 1758

Year	Oxen (Nos)	Beef (Cattle Equiv.)	Butter (Cwts)	Pigs (Nos)	Bacon & Pork (Pig Equiv.)	Sheep (Nos)
1665	57,545	14,632	26,413	1,446	3,134	99,564
1758	22	81,724	197,552	-	60,004	-

Source: R. D. Crotty, *Irish Agricultural Production* (Cork: Cork University Press, 1966), 16.

Notes   1758 Figures, average of five years ending March 25, 1758.

One carcass or two barrels taken as one cattle equivalent; and one-half barrel of pork, one cwt. of ham, or two flitches of bacon taken as one pig-equivalent.

These exports were achieved at a time of chronic surplus in Europe of temperate food produce and of general prohibition on imports along the lines of the English Cattle Acts.[28] They were achieved by getting production costs sufficiently low to make it profitable to engage in a long distance, triangular trade. The temperate provisions, which were unwanted in Europe, were needed in the West Indies to feed the plantation slaves. In turn, the tropical produce grown by the slaves, which was procured in the West Indies in exchange for temperate provisions, was welcome and valuable when brought to Europe. Only England's North American colonies supplied more provisions than Ireland to the West Indies plantations.[29] The North American colonies had the advantages of being much closer to the West Indies and of having much more land which, being located at a lower latitude, was also generally more productive.

The growth of the Irish economy during the century between the Restoration of Charles II and the coronation of George III was slow and steady rather than spectacular. The century, especially by comparison with earlier and later times, was the closest Ireland attained to a golden age in its doleful history. The key to that relative prosperity was its economic isolation from the metropolis in this mercantile age. Its trade relationship with metropolitan Britain was indirect, via the triangular trade with the West Indies. Isolation gave rise to a moderate demand for labor, which did not exist during the preceding phase of the livestock trade, and for a much more moderate demand for capital than obtained in that phase. Population growth, at around 0.3 percent annually,[30] was rapid by comparison with the long term past and contrasted sharply with the contemporary depopulation of the other capitalist colonies in Latin America and the Caribbean. But it was modest by comparison with the rate of population growth reached in the following, early factory capitalist phase of Irish colonialism. Irish economic and population growth between 1660 and 1760 was governed by the tempo of moderate growth of metropolitan Europe which prevailed during the quarter millennium of mercantile capitalism, between the Great Discoveries and the beginning of factory capitalism. That growth affected Ireland indirectly, through the demand for tropical produce, to which Ireland responded via the triangular provision trade.

Ireland's contribution to the growth of mercantile capitalism was substantial. Its free land and labor enabled its temperate produce, which Europe did not want, to be used to feed the West Indian slaves producing the tropical produce, which Europe did want. The Irish colony thus helped to reduce the cost of that produce in the metropoles; additionally, some at least of the profits from the trade contributed to metropolitan growth through the rents of absentee Irish landowners.

Phase 3—Feeding the Industrial Revolution

Ireland's economic growth accelerated after around 1760. It did so in response to a shift in metropolitan demand for Irish produce, which was associated with the beginning of England's Industrial Revolution. As population growth in England accelerated from around 0.3 percent annually to around 0.7 percent annually and as the number of English people engaged in the heavy manual work of the early industrial age expanded much more rapidly, there was an increased demand for high energy foods—bread, butter, and bacon—to feed these people. The Cattle Acts, which had excluded Ireland's pastoral produce, were repealed in response to the changed demand situation.

There was too, more or less at the same time, an increase in the supply of tropical produce. This occurred because, in the age of factory capitalism, European colonialism spread eastwards and brought under its control the rice-fed masses of south and southeast Asia. These were able to grow tropical produce more cheaply than West Indian slaves fed on temperate provisions brought from Europe and North America. The price of temperate foodstuffs rose relative to those of the tropics. This caused a decline in West Indian plantation profits, which was later followed by the abolition of slavery and, over the long run, a shift of tropical crop production from the Caribbean to Asia, with its abundant, low cost, rice-fed labor.

Agriculture in Ireland, where the pursuit of profit from property rights was unimpeded by any consideration of prescriptive rights on the part of the indigenous, Catholic population, responded quickly to the changed demand. The most dramatic change was in cereals. England had been a grain exporter in most years prior to 1760. Under the Corn Laws, subsidies were paid on exports in years of good crop so as to keep up the price of grain and to ensure the payment of remunerative rents to the country's landed oligarchy. Much of England's surplus grain had been exported to the Irish colony, which was a "captive" market for the dumped grain. This made Ireland a net importer of grain up to around 1760, a factor which greatly modified the demand on its agriculture. But after 1760, England became a grain importer first in most years and then every year. Responding to that changed demand, Ireland moved from being a net grain importer in the 1760s to having annual net grain exports in excess of a third of a million tons, or over half of total British imports, in the early 1840s.[31] Over the same period, annual butter exports increased from around 250,000 tons to over 800,000, and pig/bacon exports from the equivalent of 100,000 to 500,000 animals. Significantly, cattle/beef exports meanwhile declined from around 100,000 to the equivalent of 80,000 beasts annually.[32]

The shift in demand from provisions for West Indian slaves to bread, butter, and bacon for English industrial workers effectively translated into a demand for potato-dependent, coolie labor in Ireland. The primary demand was for grain for human consumption in England. Almost as important in Ireland was the straw by-product, which was essential winter fodder if more milch cows were to be kept to meet England's demand for butter. The price of straw in Kilkenny in the early nineteenth century was half that of grain.[33] But extensive cultivation of cereals, which originated as wild grasses in the semi-arid Middle East, in a cool, wet Ireland, was a defiance of nature; it was "unnatural." Grain could be grown in Ireland only on land that was frequently manured, rested, and cleaned by a root crop—e.g., by a potato crop. Virtually limitless land that needed rehabilitation with potatoes in order to grow on it a profitable grain crop was, therefore, available. Capital-less young Irish people could grow on that land enough potatoes to maintain and reproduce themselves and still have enough left most years to fatten a pig for sale. There is an almost perfect correlation between population and pig exports in Ireland between 1712 and 1831. For every additional pig exported there was an associated increase in population of 6.88 persons.[34] The pig paid for those family requirements not supplied by potatoes. Young people then did in Ireland what the young of all species have always done when the opportunity was available: they mated and reproduced. Only now, with abundant potatoes to feed them, more of their offspring survived.

The sixty-year reign of George III, which coincided in Britain with the first phase of factory capitalism, witnessed in Ireland the expansion of a coolie class, which had hardly existed at the commencement of the reign, into the largest class in the land. Potatoes made it possible to grow on most parts of Ireland's cold, wet land as much food as coolies could grow on selected land in the tropics, and to do so with no more resources than the coolies of the tropics—a bucket of seed and a hoe. Ireland was not, of course, the only country in Europe where people maintained and reproduced themselves by cultivating land, with no more capital than a spade and bucket of seed. But it was the only country in the world's temperate zone where such a coolie class became the largest social class.

A unique combination of circumstances, analogous to that which caused the emergence of individualism in Europe or of individualist capitalism in central western Europe, caused the emergence of the potato-dependent coolies as Ireland's largest social class during the reign of George III. It was a combination of agronomic, market, and institutional circumstances. The agronomic circumstances were the key role of potatoes in Ireland in expanding the output of cereals, milk, and pigs. The market circumstances were rising and exceptionally high relative prices for the high energy foods, cereals, butter, and bacon. A unit weight of beef in Kilkenny in 1810 was worth only two units of wheat and only one-third of the same unit weight of butter.[35] A hundred and fifty years later, a unit weight of beef was worth ten of wheat and one of butter.[36]

The institutional circumstances were the acceptance that the sole function of land was to yield a profit for those who had become its proprietors through capitalist colonial conquest and their heirs and assignees and, by corollary, the denial of any prescriptive rights in land to the three quarters of the population who were indigenous, Irish and Catholic. The only rights these latter had were those paid for by competitive rents on a land market that was uninhibited by consideration of prescriptive rights.

One of these conditions, the particular institutional arrangements which obtained in most of Ireland, did not do so in northern Ireland. The British, Protestant, settler farmers of that part, being members of the garrison ascendancy class, were of necessity armed. The relationship between these armed, Protestant, settler farmers and the proprietors of the land that they farmed was very different from the relationship between the unarmed, Catholic, Irish peasants and the Anglo-Irish proprietors of the land that the Catholics farmed. The relationship was enshrined in the "Ulster Custom," a body of practices that, as in England, implicitly recognized certain prescriptive rights of tenants in the land they farmed. These included security of tenure, subject to the payment of rents that were required to be "fair," and compensation on the termination of the tenancy for improvements effected. The capital-less young could not acquire land so readily in northern Ireland, where Protestant tenants were under less pressure to maximize incomes by subletting land and where, if sub-tenants got possession of land, they could not be so readily evicted as in the rest of Ireland, where the Ulster Custom did not apply.

Because this one of the elements of the combination of circumstances which, uniquely outside the tropics, made the coolies the largest social class, did not exist there, northern Ireland did not experience that emergence to dominance of the coolie class which occurred especially in Leinster and east Munster. The Irish census returns of 1821, 1831, 1841, and 1851 provide abundant evidence of the different rates of growth of the proletariat in different parts of Ireland at the time. The central western European, capital-dominant structure of production was better preserved in northern Ireland.

Ireland's population increased from 3.2 million in 1754 to 6.8 million in 1821.[37] It did so with virtually no increase in the capital stock or in the land available. It occurred as a result of technological change. Ireland's population growth in this period was, to that extent, similar to the growth of population in the Third World, which was also initiated by metropolitan intervention but which did not occur until a century later. Third World population growth was caused principally by the introduction of medical science, while Ireland's resulted from the introduction of the potato into a particular agronomic and institutional context. Both of these technological changes made it possible for labor to be maintained and reproduced at lower cost, and so at greater profit for the agents and collaborators of the metropole.

Population in both cases increased through a reduction in death rates, as more people survived at lower incomes, and with less land and capital per head. Population growth in the metropoles and settler colonies, by contrast, was made possible by increased capital formation, accompanied by continued technological progress and by access to more land. Living standards and incomes there were at least maintained, without the reduction in subsistence needs and incomes which, through the potato in Ireland and medical science in the Third World, made possible the expansion of their capital-less, self-employed, coolie populations. Further, population growth in the metropoles and settler colonies was an endogenous phenomenon, caused by capital formation and the extension of the cultivated area; but it was the result of exogenous influences in Ireland and the Third World: the introduction of the potato in the one case and of medical science in the other. In both, population growth was a response to economic change in the metropoles.

Phase 4—Reversion to Livestock

A second, more advanced phase of factory capitalism began in Britain around 1820, the year in which George III died. By then the economy had adjusted from a wartime to a peacetime footing and had commenced a period of long term growth. For almost a century Britain led the world, economically and politically. While the population grew rapidly, incomes also improved. Reflecting the sustained rise in British incomes and of critical importance to Ireland, prices in the metropole of beef and sheep meat, both superior, high-protein foods, rose relative to prices of the high-energy foods, bread, butter, and bacon. The effect of this changed metropolitan demand on the Irish colony was magnified by the much improved transport system, especially the introduction of railways and steam shipping, which facilitated the export alive of cattle and sheep to Britain, instead of produce that was salted and barreled and sent to the Caribbean. The changed metropolitan demand and the improved transport together caused farm produce prices in Ireland to change as shown in table 8.2.

Table 8.2. Irish Agricultural Prices, 1816–1820 and 1911–1915

(1911–1915 Prices as a Percent of 1816–1820 Prices)

Wheat	66
Butter	125
Bacon	129
Cattle	320
Sheep	137

Source: *Crotty Irish Agricultural Production*, 283, 356

Irish cattle and sheep numbers expanded rapidly to meet changed metropolitan demand. Cattle exports, which had remained virtually unchanged between 1660 and 1820, increased sixfold over the following forty years, and doubled again before the end of the century. Sheep exports increased even more rapidly, rising from an annual average of 50,000 in 1821–1825 to 681,000 in 1866–1870.[38]

The general price collapse which followed the conclusion of the Napoleonic wars and which was coupled with a greater buoyancy in cattle and sheep prices, placed Ireland's coolie population under an impossible strain. That population's expansion had already carried it up to, and beyond, the limits of reasonable cultivation margins, even for potato-based crop-growing in Ireland. Its access to land had been dependent, in part, on rising prices, which made it possible to pay otherwise unwarrantable rents.[39] When prices fell, the coolies could not pay their competitive, one-year, conacre rents and so lost their right of access to land. They became squatters, growing potatoes wherever and under whatever circumstances possible. The coolies, whose rents had built Georgian Dublin and made it the second city of the British empire, could no longer contribute to land's profit. An awareness of this was expressed by a contemporary in 1825: "The landlords of Ireland are at length deeply convinced that, though a stock of cattle or sheep will afford profit, a stock of mere human creatures, unemployed, will afford none."[40]

But the demographic momentum created by the earlier rapid population growth persisted and population continued to expand while, simultaneously, numbers of cattle and sheep commenced to increase rapidly and to appropriate land that had formerly been tilled by the coolies. More and more of the population became more totally dependent on potatoes that were grown under ever worsening agronomic conditions. It was a disaster waiting to occur. It duly did, with a succession of wet years in the 1840s and the rapid spread of blight to an exotic potato crop, which was unknown in Ireland three centuries earlier and which was now grown under the worst possible husbandry conditions. In a crisis comparable in severity, if not scale, to that which struck Europe precisely half a millennium earlier in the Black Death of the 1340s, one million people, or one-eight of Ireland's population, starved to death, and another million fled the country between 1845 and 1850.

Ireland's coolie population by 1820 had probably reached the agronomic limit at which it could have been sustained, just as the coolies in the tropics and subtropics were confined to riverine alluvial valleys. Even if metropolitan demand conditions had remained unchanged, there would have been a demographic crisis in Ireland in the second quarter of the nineteenth century as the momentum of earlier years was halted and population stabilized. But changed demand conditions after 1820 destroyed the economic basis of the coolies. If profits from Ireland's land were to be maintained or increased, Ireland's human population should not merely be stabilized, but should be replaced by cattle and sheep. As table 8.3 shows, there was a virtually perfect negative correlation between numbers of cattle and people in Ireland (twenty-six counties) during the sixty years following the Great Famine.

The replacement of people with cattle and sheep in Ireland after the Great Famine was facilitated by emigration. The Industrial Revolution, which was well under way by the mid-nineteenth century, created a demand for labor in central western Europe and in the settler colonies which, as noted in chapter 6, caused a sustained rise in incomes there. Ireland's Caucasian and generally English-speaking population was well placed to meet that demand, which has been a dominant influence on Irish life ever since. Almost every second person born there and surviving childhood has emigrated from Ireland. This linking of the Irish labor supply to the West's labor market determines Irish incomes independently of government in Ireland. The latter, since the 1840s, has merely determined the proportion of the Irish who can obtain in Ireland incomes that are exogenously determined. That proportion, over the long term, has been slightly more than half. The emigration of half the Irish in the nineteenth and twentieth centuries has left the land clear for cattle and sheep, just as their removal to Connaught and the West Indies did in the seventeenth century.

Table 8.3. Cattle and Human Population, Ireland (26 Counties), 1851–1901

	Cattle (000s)	People (000s)
1851	2,967	6,552
1861	3,472	5,799
1871	3,976	5,412
1881	3,957	5,175
1891	4,449	4,705
1901	4,673	4,459
1911	4,689	4,390

Source: Crotty, *Irish Agricultural Production*, 354–55.

It is unlikely that any society has ever been so dominated by market forces as Ireland's was through the two centuries, from 1712 to 1911. For the first 120 years of this period, the population increased precisely in line with pig exports: every additional 100 pigs exported led to an increase of 664 in the human population, through the mechanism explained above. Between 1851 and 1911, under different external market demand conditions but unchanged institutional and agronomic circumstances, population in the twenty-six counties declined precisely in line with increasing cattle stocks; every increase of 1,000 in cattle stocks lead to a decrease of 1,215 in the human population. The expansion first, and then the contraction, in the Irish population in response to external market demand that changed over time, perhaps more clearly than any other phenomenon, reflects the unparalleled thoroughness of the capitalist colonization of the neighbor, Ireland, by the foremost capitalist colonizing power, Britain. It is almost inconceivable that any society could have been more thoroughly subordinated to market forces over such a protracted time.

The Age of Factory Capitalism and the *Pacte Coloniale*

The genius of William Petty perceived in 1687, 150 years earlier than others,

that the appropriate relationship of Ireland as a pastoral, offshore colonized island of Britain's was to be an extensive cattle and sheep walk, sparsely populated with herders and shepherds who would ship the produce to Britain as payment of the rents due to the British-resident proprietors of Irish land. An arrangement along these lines would have both maximized the profit from Irish
land and the security of the island against occupancy by a hostile maritime
power, possibly in collusion with a rebellious local population.

Other, superior, British politico-economic considerations, however, intervened and prevented Ireland, during a 160 year aberration, lasting from around
1660 to 1820, from fulfilling what Petty had perceived as its appropriate role.
During the first hundred years of this period, a mercantilist concern to protect
domestic profits overrode any consideration of securing profit from competing
colonial produce. The final sixty years, which marked the beginning of England's Industrial Revolution and the move to free trade, was also a period of
almost continuous warfare, which created in Ireland an exceptional demand
from Britain for the high-energy foods, bread, butter, and bacon. But the conditions that Petty had postulated as a premise—that is, a colonial, pastoral appendage with an unimpeded link to the metropole—were restored around 1820, with
the progress of Britain's Industrial Revolution, the emergence of free trade, and
the *pacte coloniale*.

The new conditions required a reversal of the economic and demographic
trends that had become established in Ireland during the 1660–1820 aberration.
Ireland, from being a major exporter, became a major importer of grain. Instead
of rapidly expanding butter and bacon production, at a time when other countries produced little of these, Irish production of these commodities went into
long term stagnation from around 1840 to 1970, a time when other western
countries were rapidly expanding production. Cattle and sheep exports which,
live or dead, had not changed between 1660 and 1820, thereafter, alive, became
the country's dominant export. Around 1800, the value of cattle (live and dead)
and sheep exports was about a third of the combined value of cereal, pig, and
butter exports. A century and a half later, in 1962, the value of live cattle and
sheep exports was over twice the combined values of pig, pig meat, and butter
exports, while Ireland meanwhile had become a major cereal importer.[41]

Changed British demand, from high energy bread, butter, and bacon to high
protein beef and mutton, required cattle and sheep to replace coolie Irish labor.
Conceivably labor no longer wanted in agriculture could have been used in industry, producing manufactured goods for home and export. Sir Robert Kane
argued that, with Irish labor at only half the cost of contemporary British labor,
Irish industry could compete with British industry, notwithstanding the scarcity
of coal and iron ore in Ireland.[42] But that, or anything like it, did not happen.

Possibly even more remarkable, though less remarked, than nineteenth century Irish rural depopulation, was the failure of Ireland's urban population to
grow during a century when worldwide urban populations increased manifold.
The combined populations of the 100 largest towns in the twenty-six counties
which now comprise the Republic, exclusive of Dublin and Dunlaoghaire, de-

clined, between 1841 and 1926, from 694,000 to 525,000. The only Irish (Republic) towns to register population growth during this period were Dublin and its environs, some British army garrison towns, and some small seaside resorts.[43] The population of Dublin and its environs expanded because, as relations between the colony and the metropole grew ever closer, Dublin was the crucial Irish link through which, in accordance with the *pacte coloniale*, the colony exported primary produce and its labor, and imported manufactured goods and services. It was also the locus of powerful metropolitan rule over the colony.

The expectations of Kane and others that low cost Irish labor would offset the colony's other competitive disadvantages vis-à-vis its metropolitan neighbor omitted the demand factor. The lower the cost of labor, the smaller the local purchasing power and the greater the dependence on exports to achieve a given scale and efficiency of production. At the limit, when labor costs were reduced to starvation levels, all production had to be exported. An approximation of this occurred during the Great Famine, when manufacturing employment declined almost as rapidly as agricultural.

Local demand for manufactured products failed with the ending of demand for the products of coolie labor and therefore of demand for the coolies themselves. The cattle and sheep, on which agriculture increasingly concentrated, required little labor and no other inputs for their production on farms and none but a handful of drovers to drive them on to the trains and ships for export alive. The provision trade, which had slaughtered and processed cattle and pigs for export, went into decline as the livestock trade took over. Increasingly Irish agricultural income was concentrated into the hands of two classes, the bourgeois graziers and the landowners.

Much of the share of agricultural income that went to the landowners was transmitted to England where, following the Act of Union and the closing of Dublin's parliament, an increasing proportion of the owners of Irish land resided. Another part of landlords' incomes went to London to service mortgages taken out during the earlier phase of rising prices and coolie-based agricultural expansion.

Little of that part of Irish agricultural income that went to farmers was spent in Ireland. The new demand situation in Britain placed enormous pressure on Irish farmers to save. Possession of savings became the condition of survival to a far greater extent even than the possession of savings/capital had been critical for survival in ancient central western Europe (chapter 3). The person with savings, or with the cattle and sheep which savings could buy (and which could quickly and easily be reconverted into cash savings), was king or a queen who could be sure of avoiding the spinsterhood that was the inescapable fate of the nineteenth century dowerless Irish woman.

It will be recalled that while dowries were an important and distinctive feature of life in pre-industrial, individualist capitalist Europe, brideprice was the practice in tribal, pastoral, pre-conquest Ireland. During the era of the coolies, 1760–1820, when young Irish people had ready access to land for potato growing, neither brideprice nor dowry was required for marriage. But after 1820, in the age of factory capitalism and the *pacte coloniale*, dowries became a more brutally dominant feature of Irish life probably than it had ever been elsewhere in central western Europe.

At least twenty-four witnesses before the Devon Commission (which took evidence into socioeconomic conditions in rural Ireland on the eve of the Great Famine) referred to the extent to which farmers encumbered with debt the sons who succeeded to the farms to pay fortunes or dowries to those sons and daughters who left the farms. A typical such witness was John Carroll, farmer and middle-man from County Kilkenny, who stated that none of his tenants, on farms from thirty to forty acres, "have ever given or received less than £100 fortunes with their children."[44] The person without savings was nothing: hopelessly competing for land, on which to produce what the market no longer required, against cattle and sheep, which the market did want.

Rarely can an impoverished economy have saved so much as nineteenth century Ireland's . Most of those savings were held in the mushrooming banking system or invested in expanding cattle and sheep stocks, which were highly profitable and made possible more saving/investment. But none of this added to the demand for non-agricultural goods and services.

The returns to capital were understandably good in an agriculture where, for 160 years, there had been little capital formation and where, under new metropolitan market demand conditions, a capital-intensive, pastoral agriculture was now required. The best measure of the rate of return to capital in Ireland's cattle-dominated economy was the margin between the value of forward stores, which are cattle ready for shipment to Britain for final fattening, and the price of young cattle. An indication of that margin is given by the stock book covering the years 1813–1840 of Mountainstown Farm in County Meath. The cattle, which were bought in annually, increased in value over the year in which they were held by an average of 38 percent over their purchase price throughout the period.[45] For a comparable period a century later, between 1916 (during the world war) and 1931 (before the outbreak of the "economic war"), the corresponding margin was 19 percent on their cost. [46]

The graziers' margin was so good in the post-Waterloo years partly because of the ready availability of calves. Up to then and for many subsequent decades, most calves were slaughtered at birth. Grazing margins narrowed when, with capital accumulation and the increase in cattle numbers, effectively all calves born were reared.[47] Unsurprisingly under the market dispensation of the post-Waterloo years, cattle and sheep numbers were increased as rapidly as a poor population could make the necessary savings and as a still expanding population could be cleared from the land to make way for the grazing animals.

Savings other than those invested in cattle and sheep were deposited in banks and fostered one of the few successes of the nineteenth century Irish economy. Modern banking commenced in Ireland in the post-Napoleonic war years, as metropolitan demand shifted from the produce of coolie labor towards cattle and sheep. "The twelve years from 1825 to 1836 formed a period of important development in joint stock banking. Most of the banks which are operating to-ing today in Ireland were founded about this period."[48] The role of the banks was, through a network of branches that in time extended into every corner of the country, to gather up the proceeds of "rack renting slum landlords . . . (of) grinding exploitation of workers, (of) petty swindling of customers, (of) learning how to 'fumble in a greasy till and add the halfpence to the pence and prayer to shivering prayer.'"[49]

The number of bank branches in the island increased from 174 in 1850 to 859 in 1910. Growth continued and in the twenty-six counties of the Irish Free State alone there were 1,018 offices in 1934 serving a population of 2,970,000, or 34.3 branches per 100,000 people.[50] No other country seems to have been as well served with bank branches. The UK in 1930 had 17 and the United States 14 per 100,000 population. A list of the hundred oldest, and therefore by definition most successful, banks in the world in 1962 showed that the United States had the most, with thirty-five; Britain was next with fifteen; and Ireland came third with six banks, including the banks now incorporated into the Bank of Ireland group and the Allied Irish Bank.[51]

There was a symbiotic union between the country's banking system and its livestock trade. The trade's establishment brought about also the establishment of the banking system. By fostering saving and facilitating the transmission of money as well as livestock between Ireland and Britain, the banks contributed to the profitability of cattle and sheep. Because, apart from cattle and sheep and ancillary activity, there were few opportunities for profitable investment in Ireland, much of the savings were passed on to the London money market where they helped to finance Britain's expanding factory industry, which was competing with Ireland's declining cottage industry. The banks, in this way, acted as "a conduit pipe for the bringing of money out of the country for employment outside it," as the first Minister for Finance in the Irish Free State, Ernest Blythe, observed in Dail Eireann.[52] How much they took out is reflected in the consolidated balance sheets of the IFS banks for 1931, as shown in table 8.4 below.

Table 8.4. Balance Sheets—Banks of the Irish Free State

	Liabilities £ (000s)	Assets £ (000s)
Within IFS	139,774	62,623
Elsewhere	51,392	128,543
Total	191,166	191,166

Source: *Report of the Commission On Banking, Currency and Credit* (Dublin: Government Stationery Office, 1938).

Over half of the Irish banks' total deposits were on loan to the London money market. The *pax coloniale* and the *pacte coloniale* made Irish branch banking in the nineteenth century a virtually foolproof source of profit. Tight police and military control, coupled increasingly with the emigration of virtually every element of dissent, minimized political risks to banking. With tremendous pressure to acquire savings as the condition of access to land and marriage, and with few local investment outlets other than cattle and sheep, Irish savings had to be transmitted for investment in Britain. The process, as with any collection and delivery service operating overseas, was of an inherently oligopolistic character, yielding correspondingly high profits. The Bank of Ireland estimated in 1864 that it made a net profit of fifteen thousand pounds on every million pounds it held on deposit from its Irish customers.

The failure of domestic Irish demand occurred when the colony's and the metropole's economies were being drawn much closer by the nineteenth century's major improvements in transport and communications, including banking. These improvements, of course, operated both ways: as well as bringing in British products, they opened up the British market for Irish products in compensation for the failure of domestic demand. But in practice, the trade was very much one way. Irish producers, with a poor local demand, would have had to export a much larger proportion of their output to achieve a given scale of production than their British competitors, whose main market was on their doorstep and who had only to export a fraction of output, at marginal cost, to the Irish market. The closer links between the metropole and colony thus operated to flood every corner of Ireland with British factory produce, while simultaneously facilitating marketing in Britain the cattle and sheep that were driving people off the land. The railways and ships brought in manufactured goods and took out live cattle and sheep and the emigrants whom the cattle, sheep, and imported manufactures had replaced.

The rapid rise in Irish incomes after the Great Famine, as a result of emigration, meant of course an increase in local purchasing power. But what was gained in increased local demand was more than lost in increased local costs as Irish incomes and wages moved more closely into line with those in Britain. An already gravely defective, colonial Irish economy became saddled with the further handicap of incomes and labor costs that were determined exogenously, by those obtainable in the successful metropolitan and settler economies to which the Irish emigrated, and without reference to the ability of the Irish economy to absorb the supply of labor at those exogenously determined costs.

Aspects of Irish Colonialism

The Role of Capital in the Irish Colony

Capital hardly featured, and certainly did not limit output, in pre-conquest, Gaelic Ireland, as was also the case throughout the pre-Colombian, non-European world. Cattle, which were the principal means of subsistence, were, almost like the land, a natural resource. The calves of the *Bos indicus* cows had to be reared to induce their dams to lactate. Only the strongest, best adapted calves survived their first winter, without hay or other fodder, on the communally grazed pastures. There was little to exchange the reared cattle for. "Celtic Ireland had a simple, agrarian economy. No coins were used and the unit of currency was the cow."[53] Blood drawn from the male cattle was an important item of diet, and the male cattle were not normally killed except for a celebration. Otherwise they were normally consumed immediately preceding, or following, a natural death.[54] The female cattle either produced, or had the prospect of producing, milk, which was the principal item of diet, and a stream of calves. Society's members had an incentive to maintain and to increase without limit their cattle stocks. There was no sacrifice involved in their doing so. The effective limit to cattle stocks therefore was the natural carrying capacity of the pastures in the winter.

The Tudor conquest and confiscations changed the economic nature and role of cattle (and of sheep which also now became important). Both were transformed from a natural, land like resource into capital. The grazing of land in severalty meant that individual graziers could supply winter fodder, or could conserve pasture as foggage, for their stock, knowing that only their stock would benefit. The resulting autumnal selection of the most productive stock to retain for feeding on the limited winter fodder commenced the same process which, millennia earlier, had resulted in the emergence of *Bos taurus* cattle uniquely among lactose tolerant pastoralists in central western Europe (chapter 4). The emergence of *Bos taurus* characteristics was probably expedited by the use of bulls of *Bos taurus* type, which were readily available from Britain and were probably already in use within the Pale. With *Bos taurus* cows, which milked in the absence of their live calves, with winter fodder and grazing in severalty, and with a market for cattle and sheep in Britain, cattle (and sheep) ceased to be a natural product, as in traditional pastoral societies, but were transformed into capital, the product of saving. Saving was involved in forgoing milk consumption in order to rear *Bos taurus* calves. Making hay to keep cattle alive during winter was saving/investment. Above all however, in an economy that had become market-oriented, retaining marketable livestock as they matured was saving/investment.

The capital into which the Tudor conquest transformed Irish cattle and sheep was different from the capital that was employed in the central western European heartland of individualist capitalism. The latter was created from the savings of the masses in their cabins and used to complement their labor in order to expand output, for consumption in the first instance and thereafter for saving and further capital formation. Capital, in the form of cattle and sheep in early Stuart Ireland, was created by an elite. It forced people from land and generated profits for the agents and collaborators of the metropole. William Petty most clearly perceived the role of capital in the economy of the Irish colony when he proposed converting the country into a giant, depopulated, cattle and sheep walk.

The formation of capital, in the form of cattle and sheep in early Stuart Ireland, was designed primarily to generate profit rather than output. The appropriation of land and its stocking with cattle and sheep were more likely to have reduced than to have increased output, as the disinherited were forced by cattle and sheep from the land, on which they could no longer grow a smattering of crops for their subsistence. The pastoral produce that had previously been available for the people's subsistence was thereafter mobilized for the appropriators' profit.

Capital was thrust into the background in Irish agriculture between 1660 and 1820, during which period almost all the increased output was attributable to potato-supported labor. The Cattle Acts reduced the value of cattle to a quarter of their former value[55] and so also the value of the capital they represented. With cattle at a quarter of their former value, less capital was employed, even if the cattle were held for twice as long, to be fattened, salted, and barreled for export. Sheep, which were a major item of farm capital in early Stuart Ireland, then ceased to feature until post-Waterloo, because their flesh could not be salted for export to the Caribbean. Increased butter exports during this period would have been largely due to increased milk yields secured by feeding a largely unchanged number of cows with more labor-intensive fodder or by lower domestic consumption as diets became increasingly potato-dependent. The pigs, pig meat, and grain, which accounted for most of the increased agricultural exports, were intensive-intensive and capital-extensive.

Capital was reinstated with a vengeance in the Irish economy after the 160 year aberration from 1660 to 1820. In the form of cattle and sheep, it contended for possession of Irish land with the coolie population. Capital's role in Ireland, as in the capitalist colonies generally (chapter 6), was to substitute for labor, not to complement it.

O'Grada has estimated values of Irish agricultural output in post-famine years as shown in table 8.5.

Table 8.5. Values of Irish Agricultural Output (£ millions in current prices)

1854	1876	1908	1929
47.4	46.7	45.6	72.6

Sources: (1854, 1876, 1908) C. O'Grada, *Ireland Before and After the Famine* (Manchester: Manchester University Press, 1988), 68,129.

(1929) *Commission of Enquiry into Banking, Currency and Credit* (Dublin: Government Stationery Office, 1938), 434.

Prices of Irish agricultural produce, especially that three-quarters of it accounted for by livestock and livestock produce, were buoyant during these years.[56] When allowance is made for that buoyancy, it is clear that the value of Irish agricultural output at constant prices, or the volume of output, declined between 1854 and 1908. Moreover, O'Grada's figures are for gross agricultural output, which differs from net agricultural output, or the value added to GNP by agriculture. To arrive at the latter figure, which is the economically more significant one, it is necessary to deduct the cost of materials like feedstuffs and fertilizers bought by farmers to assist their output. While negligible in the earlier years, the cost of these items was substantial later and was an estimated £9.3 million in 1929, leaving the net output, or value added of Irish agriculture in that year, as £54.5 million.[57] These findings reinforce the point made by the present writer in 1966: "between the Great Famine and the First World War . . . the volume of total agricultural output increased little if anything."[58] This was a period in which cattle numbers increased by half and sheep numbers doubled.

The volume, as distinct from the value, of agricultural output may have increased slightly between 1908 and 1929. This was a period when, because of complex, interlinking agronomic relationships, there was no increase in livestock numbers, i.e., there was no capital formation.[59] If production did expand, it did so because there was no capital formation.

The incremental capital output ratio (ICOR) measures the relationship in metropolitan and settler economies between increased capital formation and the higher output which results. The normal value of ICOR in modern economies is around three or four. That is: for every three or four pounds increase in the capital stock, annual output or Gross National Product increases by around one pound. ICOR, in the case of Irish agriculture in the nineteenth century at least, appears to have been a negative value: the more capital formation, the less output.

The other principal forms of capital formation in the twenty-six counties of southern Ireland, apart from cattle and sheep, was Guinness's brewery and the railways. Much of the Guinness expansion was at the expense of the 220 small breweries that existed at the commencement of the nineteenth century, but that had been reduced to a handful at the end, in a process of concentration that went far beyond the contemporaneous consolidation of breweries in Britain. The expansion of Guinness's brewery in nineteenth century Ireland, like the replacement of Gandhi's spinning wheel by cotton mills in India, was mainly a matter of producing the same amount with less labor and more capital.

Railway investment was part of the worldwide process of tying capitalist colonies more closely to their metropoles during the age of factory capitalism, which facilitated the drawing of primary produce from the colonies in exchange for the secondary and tertiary products of the metropoles.

Capital, which was the basis of central western Europe's individualist, capitalist economy and society, was an alien element in Ireland's, nonindividualist, tribal, pastoral economy. There was no foothold for it there without external support, either under the Celts or the Normans. The former abandoned the heavy wheel plough and other forms of capitalist production practiced by their cousins in Gaul; and the latter were compelled by the weather to become "more Irish than the Irish themselves," which included especially the adoption of tribal pastoralism.

Ireland thus differed from eastern Europe and Russia, where capital was also an exotic element, but where, once capital formation had been initiated by western-originating adventurers and traders, the process took root in the form of autocratic capitalism. Autocratic capitalism acquired an independent existence in eastern Europe and Russia. The surplus which it produced from capitalist crop-growing was adequate, on the one hand, to resist further penetration from the west and, on the other hand, to beat back and eventually to overwhelm the pastoral hordes of the steppe. No similar, independent purchase was available for capital in pastoral, pre-Tudor-conquest Ireland.

Capital formation in Ireland, under capitalist colonialism, was profit-driven, whereas in the rest of Europe and in the settler colonies, it was output driven. Profit followed from capital formation in Ireland because of the character of the capital, which channeled the product of the colony's natural pastoral resources exclusively through the metropole's agents/collaborators. That process occurred within a global capitalist colonial context.

Capital formation has throughout been of a different character in Ireland and in the other capitalist colonies from the same process in central western Europe. In Ireland and the other capitalist colonies, because of imposed socioeconomic institutions—especially property in land—capital formation has generally been a malign influence, replacing, rather than complementing, labor for the profit of the metropoles and of their agents and collaborators in the colonies. This has been due neither to the inherent nature of capital itself nor to the character of the capitalist colonized peoples. It is because capital formation in the capitalist colonies took place within institutional frameworks imposed on the colonies for metropolitan profit, regardless of their effect on the colonized societies.

The Demographic Aspects of Irish Capitalist Colonization

Ireland's population probably grew less rapidly than that of the rest of Europe prior to the Tudor conquest. That was because of the land-based character of its nonindividualist economy, with few if any slaves being brought in or capital formation occurring, which might have sustained more people. Ireland's preconquest demographic trends, like its socioeconomic structures, probably had more in common with those of Sub-Sahelian Africa than with those of the rest of Europe.

The initial effect of the conquest, apart from the loss of life caused by warfare itself, must have been to reduce population. This was because the rapid expansion of the livestock trade under the early Stuarts meant that there was less livestock produce available to sustain an indigenous population that no longer had prescriptive rights of access to land or to share in land's pastoral produce. Ireland's demographic experience during this, first phase of capitalist colonialism was therefore probably in line with that of the Spanish colonies in Latin America and of the slave plantations of the Caribbean.

Ireland's population, throughout the eighteenth and nineteenth centuries was, as has been seen, totally dominated by external market forces. Its demographic experience probably came most closely into step with that of the rest of central western Europe during the century between the restoration of Charles II in 1660 and the coronation of George III in 1760. Capital formation and economic growth in central western Europe impacted on Ireland at a remove, through a demand for provisions to feed the Caribbean slaves. That demand was met in Ireland by a slow growth of population, sustained increasingly on a low cost potato diet, as well as by some capital formation.

Irish demographic experience, having moved in line with that of the rest of central western Europe between 1660 and 1760, continued to do so over the following sixty years. The accelerated capital formation associated with the Industrial Revolution in Britain and central western Europe resulted in a demand for intensive-intensive agricultural products in Ireland. With readier access to land on which to grow potatoes and therefore, having more food and experiencing lower death rates, Ireland's landless population expanded during these years, but unaccompanied by any or much capital formation in Ireland. This anticipated by a century or more the similar expansion of population, without a concomitant increase in capital, that occurred in the Third World. Population growth in Ireland and the Third World was triggered by developments in the metropoles. In Ireland's case it was made possible by more abundant potatoes; in the Third World it was due to the more widespread application of medical science. Both of these developments owed their origin to capital formation and economic growth in the metropoles.

Ireland was uniquely placed, as a neighbor, to meet metropolitan demand for fresh meat once incomes had risen above the level where people were virtually solely concerned with securing sufficient energy. Cattle and sheep came into direct competition for land with its coolie population in a unique manner. That competition resulted, in Ireland 170 years ago, in the sort of generalized famine conditions that are now commonplace in the Third World.

Being Europe's only capitalist colony, as well as causing Ireland's demographic crisis of the second quarter of the nineteenth century, also brought about a unique resolution to that crisis. Britain's demand for cattle and sheep restricted access to Irish land to those with the capital to stock land with cattle and sheep. Even if young people were prepared, as in pre-famine decades, to subsist on a potato diet, with land being rapidly set down to pasture and the grain acreage contracting by 2 percent annually, there was simply no land available for cultivation by coolies. Emigration or celibacy were the only choices open to the capital-less young.

Celibacy was imposed on the Irish by market forces to a degree that has probably been unequalled in human history. Almost every second girl born in Ireland since 1820 has failed to reproduce in Ireland. Those who married in Ireland did so late in life, when they had acquired the necessary savings; and then, as all couples traditionally did, including central western Europe's property-owners, they proceeded to have biological families. But unlike other biologically determined families, those in Ireland after the famine experienced rapidly rising incomes and those other conditions in contemporary central western Europe which were reducing death rates there. Nevertheless, Ireland's property-owning married couples in the nineteenth century did not, like the contemporary proletariat of Britain, continental Europe, and the settler colonies, practice artificial birth control. The net result of an exceptionally low marriage rate, biological marital fertility, and declining death rates was a continuing natural increase in population of around 0.5 percent per annum, which was about half the pre-famine rate but not much less than the contemporaneous growth of Europe's population.[60]

Notwithstanding a natural increase at all times except during the Great Famine, Ireland's population halved between 1840 and 1920. That was due to yet another Irish phenomenon that has been unparalleled elsewhere: its emigration level. With livelihood opportunities more tightly circumscribed in Ireland than anywhere else as cattle and sheep forced people off land, the latter responded to the demand for labor that was of Caucasian race, in Britain and the settler colonies, which expanded rapidly with the progress of factory capitalism in the nineteenth century. Emigration had been of demographic significance since the late eighteenth century.[61] There was a strong flow of emigration from Ireland between the battle of Waterloo and the outbreak of the Great Famine in 1845, as the coolie population came under pressure from falling grain prices and increasing cattle and sheep numbers. "Between Waterloo and the Famine over 1.5 million people left Ireland for good."[62] The flow turned into a flood during the famine years, when another million people left. Thereafter, with the channels of emigration broadened, deepened, and smoothed by usage, the outward flow has continued and, over the long term, has removed almost every second person born in Ireland and surviving childhood.

This level of emigration has been a function of Ireland's dual role of neighbor and colony. It has been the dominant feature of the socioeconomic history of Ireland since the Great Famine. It has facilitated the de-stocking of land with people and their replacement with more profitable cattle and sheep. Ireland's unique neighbor role among capitalist colonies has facilitated the assimilation of the island's surplus, Caucasian population into the workforces of Britain and the settler colonies. One consequence of the emigration of almost every second person born there has been to link Irish incomes ever closer to the countries to which the Irish emigrate, rendering those incomes quite independent of the Irish economy's performance. As a result, incomes have risen more rapidly in Ireland since the Great Famine than in most other countries, while contemporaneously they have declined in the other, the non-European, capitalist colonies, which comprise the Third World. In the Third World countries populations have doubled at the same time that Ireland's, because of a low marriage and high emigration rate, has halved.

The Successes of the Nineteenth Century

There emerged out of the socioeconomic decay of nineteenth century Ireland four outstanding "successes" which tower dramatically above the socioeconomic decay upon which they flourished. Consideration of their successful growth in the context of the otherwise moribund socioeconomic system throws light on their role in the process of social decay and on that process itself. Reference has already been made to one of these "successes," the Irish branch-banking system. The others were Guinness's brewery in Dublin, which emerged as the largest brewery in the world in 1900; Harland and Wolfe's shipyard in Belfast, which again was the largest in the world in 1900; and the Catholic Church.

Guinness's Brewery

Contrary to Lynch and Vaizey's sycophantic theme,[63] Guinness's success owed little to any exceptional ability of the Guinness family. According to them, Guinness's success was due to the family's ability which, had it been more common in Ireland, could have saved the country much of the disaster it experienced in the nineteenth century. Guinness, in fact, owed its success in the first instance to being brewers at a time when a ruined people sought oblivion in alcohol, which was thus one of the very few commodities for which demand was growing in nineteenth century Ireland. Even then, Guinness could not have survived in competition with English brewers had it not, like other Irish brewers, swindled the excise of malt taxes.[64] Thereafter it was mainly a matter of retaining the position acquired by Arthur Guinness when, in 1759 with a gift from the Protestant archbishop of Cashel, he bought Dublin's largest brewery. As Catholic, Gaelic Ireland retrogressed, Dublin, the navel that joined the colony to the metropolis, became exceptionally predominant. Dublin brewed 53 percent of Ireland's beer while London brewed only 22 percent of Britain's beer in the 1850s.[65]

Guinness, like the other Irish brewers, gained enormously from the consolidation of the Irish and British spirit duties between 1852 and 1862, which doubled the cost of whiskey in Ireland.[66] That consolidation of the duties only became possible when the colonial administration had acquired sufficiently firm control to suppress illicit distilling and the associated shebeens which were regarded as hotbeds of sedition.

Being a brewer in a country that sought solace in alcohol, having survived by swindling the excise, being the largest brewer in a Dublin that dominated a ruined hinterland, and experiencing an upsurge in sales when a sharply increased duty on spirits doubled the price of whiskey, Guinness was ideally placed to benefit from the next twist of fortune. This was the introduction, in 1869, of legislation to curb drinking by Britain's working class. The legislation, which applied throughout the United Kingdom, tightened the issuing of licenses to premises for the sale of intoxicating liquor. Getting these licenses had, up to then, been a formality; thereafter, new licenses became virtually unobtainable.[67] Local British brewers availed of the new legislation to buy up licensed premises in their localities and to "tie" these to their own beer, excluding the national brewers' products. The latter, in order to expand nationally, had to divert the bulk of their resources away from brewing, into real estate, by buying the now limited and therefore costly houses licensed to sell alcohol.

The legislation had a different effect in Ireland. There, because of the halving of the population in the preceding decades and its continuing decline, there was a chronic surplus of licensed public houses. Irish local brewers could not use the defensive tactic that saved their counterparts in Britain. While the British national brewers were stymied by having to divert their resources from brewing and marketing beer into real estate acquisition, Guinness, free from such hindrances, was able to continue its expansion in Ireland and, on the basis of its exceptional dominance of the Irish market, to win an increasing share of the British market.

Harland and Wolfe

The success of the Harland and Wolfe shipyard, like the industrial growth of Belfast as a whole, rested on a far firmer foundation than the racist one suggested by Black: "(The reason) Ulster had so much industrial growth when the rest of Ireland had so little . . . it seems to me that in most instances personal initiatives overcame the comparative lack of natural advantage."[68] Ulster's industrialization rested solidly on, and grew out of, the privileged garrison status of the Protestants of Ulster.

A perfectly freely working land market that was uninhibited by any rights of Catholic Irish tenants made it possible, under appropriate price conditions, for young capital-less people to acquire land and to make, in the course of George III's reign, the cottier-coolies the largest social class in Ireland. The capital-less young could not acquire land so readily in Ulster. Because young people could not, under the Ulster Custom, get access to land so easily, they were forced to remain dependent on their parents, who thus had exclusive tenancy of the land, the capital to finance its operation, and the cheap family labor to operate it.[69]

There was, during the early phase of England's Industrial Revolution, an increased demand for cloth for the more rapidly expanding industrial population, which paralleled the increased demand for high-energy food. The coolie-dominated agriculture of southern Ireland could better meet the demand for high-energy food, while the more capital-endowed agriculture of Ulster could better meet the demand for cloth. Potatoes, planted in March, can be marketed in the form of a fat pig by the following March. Flax sown at the same time cannot be marketed as yarn until September of the following year, at the earliest. Irrespective of the difference in returns, starving, rack-rented coolies had no option but to grow potatoes, which enabled them to meet their rental obligations at the earliest moment and so gave them a chance of renting another patch of land for another year.

Neither could Leinster and Munster's more substantial farmers grow flax profitably. These, though they had the capital to grow grain crops and to stock land with cattle, did not have the high quality, low-economic-cost family labor that was needed to grow flax and process it into linen cloth. Their sons and daughters on a freely working land market could, and did, rent a plot of land, grow potatoes, and thereby attain sufficient economic independence to become separate social units. In this way, outside Ulster, labor and capital became separated and gravitated into different production units or firms.

Ulster's farmers, protected by the Ulster Custom, had the capital and the cheap family labor to grow flax and to undertake the time-consuming (i.e., capital-consuming) work of processing it into linen cloth. Moreover, because of the spreading proletarianization of the rest of Ireland and the consequent difficulty there of processing yarn into cloth, such yarn as was produced in the "flax counties" of the south was drawn to the north for processing. The south's decline thus furthered the growth of the linen industry in the north.[70]

The rest followed. An indigenous linen industry was solidly rooted in agronomic conditions of production; in institutional arrangements that recognized the prescriptive rights of armed, Protestant, garrison tenants in the land they worked, while denying similar rights to disarmed, garrisoned, Catholic tenants; and in the prevailing market conditions. It grew and adapted to changing circumstances. Part of that adaptation was the transition from cottage to factory production and the growth of Belfast. The factory production of linen cloth required different machines from those used in the British textile industry. It was necessary, in order to transform Ulster's cottage linen industry into a factory industry, to design and then to build machines suitable for processing flax into cloth. Hence the development of Belfast's engineering industry.

Abundant, deep-water dock space within rapidly growing Belfast, a labor force already accustomed to the discipline of factory production, and engineering skills acquired in the linen-machinery manufacturing industry; these were substantial attractions for the newly emerging industry of iron-shipbuilding. Traditional wooden-ship building yards, including Dublin's, could not easily adapt to the new technology. The old yards, in the old cities and towns, were hedged in by urban growth and, accustomed to building ships weighing at most hundreds of tons, they had neither the space nor the access to deep water necessary for handling ships ten or a hundred times larger, which the new age required. At least as serious as these problems was the fact that the old centers of the shipbuilding industry had become riddled with restrictive labor practices which had become embedded in the craft of building wooden ships. The new city of Belfast, uncluttered with the accretions either of urban sprawl or of craft regulation and tradition, offered both the space and the freedom to apply newly acquired, local engineering skills to the highly innovative business of building iron ships in the nineteenth century.

Ireland's major industrial weakness of an inadequate domestic demand hardly affected shipbuilding. Relative to the volume of business transacted, little personal contact was required between vendor and buyer. The goods, which incorporated a tremendous amount of local value added to the crude, imported raw materials, could be sailed, under their own steam, to wherever the buyer wished to take delivery.

Belfast had a further major and unique attraction. This was the close identity of interests between the Protestant owners/managers and the Protestant craftsmen in the shipyards. Nineteenth century iron shipbuilding was, above all, an innovative industry. Innovation and flexibility were of the essence. Even in new, non-traditional British yards, these qualities were constrained by the basic class conflict between owners/managers and workers. Any such conflict that may have existed in Harland and Wolfe's Belfast yard was quite overshadowed by the common interests of a Protestant, settler, garrison minority in the face of the implacable hostility of the garrisoned Catholic masses of Ireland. Disunity, or weakness of Protestant resolve, threatened to drown all—Protestant owners, managers, and craftsmen alike—in the morass of poverty, social disintegration, and famine that had engulfed Catholic Ireland.

Fear of the Catholic enemy outside the shipyard, which had fallen upon the Protestant minority at every opportunity—in 1641, 1688, and again in 1798— was a tremendously powerful unifying factor that facilitated flexibility and adaptation in an industry and at a time when these qualities were particularly important. A similar identity of interests and absence of class conflict was to be observed throughout the capitalist colonies among expatriate Europeans (including Irish) in the face of the overwhelming mass of hostile black or brown indigenes of Latin America, the Caribbean, Africa, and Asia.

Flexibility and adaptiveness were the easier to achieve inasmuch as their cost fell mainly on the Catholic helots (as on the black or brown indigenes of the other capitalist colonies). When trade declined cyclically, or when innovation caused lay-offs, the marginalized Catholic workers could be fired, and the status and security of the established Protestant workers were preserved.

Harland and Wolfe is a monument to Protestant/Catholic antipathy in Ireland. That antipathy deepened as the value of Protestant privilege and the cost of Catholic disability grew in a Victorian Ireland that saw the Irish Catholic coolies wiped out. The intensity of the antipathy was the strength of Harland and Wolfe.

The Catholic Church

The Catholic Church was the fourth of the nineteenth century Irish successes which, by any standard, were remarkable, but which, in contrast to the decay of the society from which they sprang, were startlingly so. The success of the Church was remarkable in terms of the growth in the numbers of male and female clergy,[71] the building of churches and of schools and hospitals operated by Catholic clergy,[72] and the world-wide spread of Irish missionaries and teachers. All of this occurred during the reign of Victoria, which also witnessed the obliteration of Ireland's largest social class, the potato-growing coolies. It is possible to identify a number of factors which, while helping to account for the Church's remarkable growth, also throw light on the pathology of nineteenth century Irish society.

The most remarkable demographic characteristic of Irish society since the death of George III has been a very low marriage rate. Rather less than half those who were born in Ireland and who survived childhood acquired the basic socioeconomic independence necessary for marriage. Never was sexual continence forced so rigorously on so large a proportion of any people. Celibacy is, for many, the greatest sacrifice required by the life of a Catholic cleric, male or female. But as celibacy was in any case unavoidable for very many Irish people, little additional sacrifice was involved in becoming a cleric. Only as marriage opportunities increased in Ireland in the 1960s and 1970s did becoming a Catholic cleric involve the sacrifice of celibacy, and since then the number of persons becoming clerics has dropped sharply.[73]

The Victorian reign marked the transformation of the market for Irish produce and thereby the destruction of the potato-based coolies and their replacement by the cattle-grazing bourgeoisie. The rise of the Irish bourgeoisie meant also an upsurge of Irish nationalism or an awareness of differences, particularly differences of economic interest, between the colonized and the colonizing. The unique, critical role of religion in Irish capitalist colonialism has already been noted. It was understandable, therefore, that as cattle prices rose fivefold relative to wheat and threefold relative to milk, and that as the coolies were destroyed and replaced by the bourgeois cattle-graziers, there should also have been a great upsurge of Irish Catholicism.

The Irish bourgeoisie invested in cattle and sheep, or placed their savings in bank deposits, to secure their position in the harsh existing world; they invested in churches and convents to secure their position in the next. They favored also Church-operated schools, where those of their children for whom there was no scope on the cattle-grazed land could get, at little cost, an education that would equip them better for a struggle for life that, in Ireland, was quite desperate.

Catholicism, for all its spirituality, supported and sustained property, particularly the property of its bourgeois members. It had contributed importantly to the growth of capitalism in central western Europe, in part by helping to enforce the celibacy that was necessary for capitalism's growth, and in part by preaching the divine origins of property and by imposing sanctions on those who infringed property rights. The restraint that the Catholic Church preached to the property-less had clear attractions for a bourgeois society struggling to curb the sexual license of the reign of George III, which had culminated in the Great Famine. The preaching of the Church was often a better bulwark to property than even the well organized Royal Irish Constabulary, at a time when the only defense the starving, potato-dependent coolies had against encroaching cattle was to hough or kill them. Moreover, Catholic teaching on property rights was sufficiently flexible and discerning to distinguish between Catholic and Protestant property. It allowed leading Church members to play a major role in the eventual confrontation between the Catholic owners of property in the form of livestock, and the predominantly Protestant owners of land, over the sharing of the agricultural product of Irish property.

Religion, finally, was one of a number of escapes from, or sources of solace for, the grinding poverty and the unparalleled sexual deprivation that marked Irish society. Other escapes were alcoholism and lunacy, of which, together with celibacy and numbers of clerics, Ireland had the highest incidence in the world.[74] There was of course also emigration, which almost half the population chose.

It is, however, a misconception and a serious misrepresentation of the role of the Catholic Church to suggest that its preeminence was the cause of Irish socioeconomic decline in the nineteenth century. Rather, the Church's role was like the success of the banks, of Guinness and of Harland and Wolfe; it was like the destruction of the coolies; it was like Irish socioeconomic disintegration in the nineteenth century. These were all consequences of Ireland's capitalist colonization. It was the capitalist colonization of Ireland, uniquely among European countries, that gave to religion in Ireland the role that race played in the other capitalist colonies. That role was to distinguish easily the colonized from the colonizer, and to be a focus of anti-colonial sentiment. It was the capitalist colonial concept of land as a source of profit that first created the Irish coolie. It was that concept of land for profit, combined with the fivefold rise of cattle prices relative to wheat prices, that spelt the ruin of the Irish coolies, the rise of the Irish bourgeoisie, and the Irish, bourgeois Catholic Church. It is interesting that, in the 1841 census, per 1,000 population, England had 1.29 and "priest-ridden" Ireland had 0.88 clergy. But by 1901, per 1,000 population, England's 1.84 were dwarfed by Ireland's 4.33 clergy.[75]

Political Aspects of Irish Colonialism

The determination of political relations by the economic conditions of production has been a central theme of this work. It was introduced in chapter 2, the first substantive chapter. It was developed mainly in chapter 4, in the context of the accelerating economic change associated with individualist capitalism in central western Europe, which compelled political adaptation. Clearly, given the enormous transformations caused by capitalist colonialism, political change occurred also in the colonies. Nowhere was this more so than in Ireland, the neighbor and colony which was so dominated by economic forces emanating from the metropole that, over two centuries, its population first expanded and then contracted precisely in response to those forces.

Indeed, the very continuance of society in Ireland and of political relations within that society was largely a fortuitous consequence of events in the metropole. Petty's proposal to convert Ireland into a pastoral appendage of Britain, if implemented, would have removed the Irish nation from the stage of history as effectively as the aborigines of the settler colonies have been. But superior metropolitan interests precluded that outcome and the result was a 160-year-long aberration during which a coolie-dominant population grew in Ireland to be, by 1820, half as large as Britain's population. That coolie-dominant population, which existed in Ireland twenty-five degrees of latitude farther from the equator than any other coolie race, was transformed during the following century, through the unimpeded operation of market forces, into what was probably the most bourgeoisie-dominated society that has ever existed. Market forces caused the coolies to be replaced by cattle and sheep and by the bourgeois proprietors of these, who, for the most part, were Irish and Catholic, like the coolies they replaced. The unique dominance of the bourgeoisie in Ireland stemmed from the fact that, unlike the middle classes in other societies, which developed *paripassu* with the proletariat, Ireland's middle class grew, so to speak, by consuming the proletariat.

The emergence of a numerous Irish Catholic middle class from the ashes of the proletariat commenced during the second quarter of the nineteenth century in a cauldron of socioeconomic pressures, which culminated in the Great Famine.

When the famine passed, the middle class Irish grazier had arrived and the coolie was in hasty retreat. Marking its arrival as a major force, the grazier class founded, in 1850, the Irish Tenant League, which was concerned to have extended to the whole country the practices of the Ulster Custom. While the case for doing so had no greater moral, legal, or economic claim than a similar claim on behalf of the coolies, the grazier could back his claim with organized political action while the coolie could only attempt to enforce his through blind, self-defeating, agrarian outrage.

However, for thirty years after the Great Famine, the newly arrived middle class graziers were content to expand their flocks and herds with minimal political action, and the Tenant League became moribund. But in the late 1870s a crisis developed in Ireland's pastoral farming that precipitated major political initiatives. The course of that crisis gives insights into the character of the new society created in the Irish colony by the progress of factory capitalism in Britain.

Cow numbers declined by 9 percent in Ireland in the 1870s. It was the first such recorded decline, and was probably the first decline since the introduction of the Cattle Acts, over two centuries earlier in the 1660s.[76] Its cause was almost certainly the massive drop in tillage—again after centuries of expansion. The area tilled contracted by 15 percent between 1850 and 1870. It fell by a further 18 percent in the 1870s.[77] This was part of Irish agriculture's response to the shift in British demand from high energy to high protein foods. This adjustment encountered serious agronomic bottlenecks in the 1870s. The tillage decline reduced the supply of tillage by-products for winter fodder. It did so when fodder requirements were increased by the larger number of cattle that grazed the land set down to pasture. The increasingly severe fodder shortage affected cows most because, as already explained, these can endure dormant season dearth less well than drystock. Hence the 9 percent drop in cow numbers in the 1870s.

Drystock numbers continued to increase in the 1870s. But because of the decline in cow numbers, overall cattle numbers, in the twenty-six counties, increased by only 2 percent in the 1870s, compared to 14 percent in the 1860s and 20 percent in the 1850s. There was a corresponding smaller reduction of 4.5 percent in the 1870s in the human population, compared to reductions of 8 percent and 14 percent in the preceding decades (table 8.3).

The continued increase in dry cattle numbers, while cow numbers remained stable and then dropped in the 1870s, created another bottleneck, in addition to the fodder shortage already mentioned. That was in the supply of calves and young cattle. It meant that more calves had to be reared from a declining number of cows. There were in the twenty-six counties in 1861, 33.6 cattle under one year per 100 cows. That proportion rose to 53.2 in 1871 and to 63.5 in 1881.[78] This almost doubling of the number of calves reared per 100 cows was technically relatively easy; but to achieve it, the price of young cattle had to rise, not only absolutely, but relative to mature cattle prices. That not only increased returns to rearing young cattle, but simultaneously reduced returns to the alternative enterprise of maturing these young cattle.

The price of one to two year old cattle rose by 50 percent between 1845 and 1870, while the price of cattle over two years increased almost twice as rapidly. The supply of immatures was not a constraint in those years and their price lagged behind that of matures, for which there was a firm British demand. But the situation changed dramatically in the 1870s when, following the continued and accelerated contraction in tillage and the unprecedented contraction in cow numbers, the price of one to two year old cattle increased by 54 percent while the price of two to three year old animals rose by only 33 percent.[79] Rearing immature cattle suddenly became more profitable because of their higher price. Simultaneously grazing matures became less profitable, partly because of the smaller increase in their price and partly because the cost of immatures to convert into matures had risen more.

The twin, associated bottlenecks of declining fodder supplies and scarcity of young cattle enforced a period of economic deceleration, consolidation, and reorganization in the 1870s. The focus of activity shifted during that hiatus towards political adjustment.

Three externally initiated events were particularly important in shaping the course of Irish politics in the post-famine decades. These, in chronological order, were: reform of the UK franchise in 1850, the establishment of the Fenians/ Irish Republican Brotherhood in 1858, and the introduction of the secret ballot in 1872.

The UK franchise reform of 1850, which regularized and broadened the franchise, resulted in the general election of 1852 returning forty Irish MPs who were committed to "independent opposition" to both major British parties in the House of Commons, while supporting claims for tenant right for Irish farmers. Lacking direction, this initiative in constitutional politics achieved little other than a precedent for Irish MPs being more responsible to the Irish electorate and articulating, if not actually implementing, a policy of independence from the major British parties at Westminster.

The political initiative passed to the remnants of the Young Ireland movement of 1848 which, like the contemporary Young Italy, was a manifestation of the Europe-wide revolutionary spirit of that time. Living in exile after the abortive rebellion of 1848, these remnants of Young Ireland found support among Irish emigrants in America and Britain for action that promised independence for Ireland. The establishment of the Fenian movement in 1858 was a result. Fenianism was dedicated to establishing an Irish republic by armed insurrection. Drawing impetus and financial support from the Irish diaspora, Fenianism gained support also in Ireland. That support came principally from the urban artisan class, from small farmers and from the younger sons of other farmers. But, "though it throve on social discontent (in Ireland), Fenianism had no program of reform—it would be time enough to think of that when national independence had been achieved."[80]

Though never of any military consequence, Fenianism strongly influenced political events in Ireland for decades. Immediately, it awakened opinion in Britain to the continuing antipathy in Ireland to the Union. That, in turn, led to the Land Act of 1870 and to other concessions by the Gladstone government to Fenianism. The concessions, though of little practical importance, caused a conservative reaction in Ireland. The Home Government Association (HGA), founded in 1870, was one manifestation of that reaction.

The HGA advanced the concept of delegating more regional autonomy to Ireland, where it would be exercised by the existing ascendancy elite for reform of a conservative character. British neglect and ignorance of the established order, according to the HGA, were the source of Ireland's woes. A larger measure of local control would allow the better operation of the existing order, and that was preferable to its overthrow, which was threatened by ill-informed British intervention.

Control of the HGA, in the event, passed from Irish conservatives to Irish liberals, who had become disenchanted by the performance of Gladstone's Liberal government with respect to Irish affairs. The HGA was dissolved and reconstituted as the Home Rule League (HRL) in 1874, shortly after the Secret Ballot Act of 1872. The HRL had fifty-nine MPs elected in the general elections of 1874. This marked the emergence of a constitutional party dedicated to securing constitutionally change in the relations between Britain and Ireland. It was, however, heavily dependent on the nationalism that had been engendered by Fenianism. The fifty-nine HRL MPs were elected to a House of Commons with a large Conservative majority. Their impact on proceedings was minimal and they were effectively ignored. That was so until Joseph Biggar, a Belfast Presbyterian elected for Cavan, initiated the practice of obstructing the House's business: if the House would not legislate for Ireland, then it would not legislate at all.

Charles Stewart Parnell, a Protestant Wicklow landlord, elected in 1875 under HRL auspices, joined Biggar in obstructing the House and attracted a growing number of Home Rule MPs to support the process. Quickly the young, aristocratic Parnell, fired with an antipathy to Britain similar to that of his grandfather and great-grandfather, who were prominent in the eighteenth century in asserting the right of the Protestant elite to rule Ireland free of British control, rose to a commanding position in the Home Rule organization.

A juncture was effected at that point between three disparate strands of Irish nationalist politics. One of those strands was the Irish parliamentary party, in which Parnell had quickly achieved prominence and which was dedicated to achieving Home Rule by constitutional means. A second was the demand for land tenure reform in the shape of the three "Fs"—fixity of tenure, fair rent, and free sale of tenant right. This was pressed by the grazier class, which had greatly consolidated its economic position since the famine. Michael Davitt set about mobilizing and articulating this agrarian discontent which had previously been desultory and ineffective in character. Davitt, the son of a Mayo smallholder who had emigrated in 1851, was jailed for his Fenian activities in 1870 and was freed under an amnesty in 1877. This background qualified Davitt to act both as an agrarian agitator and as a mediator between constitutional nationalism, led by Parnell, and the third main strand in Irish politics in the 1870s, which was

Fenianism, or insurrectional nationalism. The Fenian movement was prepared to collaborate with the agrarian and constitutional movements, provided collaboration offered a prospect of rapid progress towards independence. Its involvement was important particularly in securing financial support from American emigrants for this "New Departure" in Irish politics: the collaboration of parliamentary, agrarian and revolutionary nationalism.

The three elements, of very different character and temperament, were conjoined in uneasy alliance for a little over a decade in extracting concessions from the British government. Their collaboration had much of the character of the draught teams comprising a horse, an ox, and a donkey which William Tighe records as common in south Kilkenny in the early nineteenth century and used for endlessly plowing and harrowing the land in a desperate effort to drag the last morsel of crop from the exhausted soil.[81] Parnell had the political skill to handle this unlikely team and to use it in a manner that resulted in major concessions pertaining to the land tenure system during the 1880s.

The circumstances in which the agrarian element was activated and brought into conjunction with the parliamentary and Fenian elements for concerted action at the end of the 1870s are revealing. A public meeting, in April 1879, in Irishtown, Co. Mayo, which is the dead center of the province of Connacht, initiated a local movement, which became the National Land League in the following August. Endorsed by Parnell, now prominent in the parliamentary party, the Mayo organization quickly acquired a countrywide dimension. Widespread agrarian agitation between 1879 and 1882 appeared to threaten anarchy and quickly led to legislative reforms that set the country firmly on the course to owner-occupancy of the land.

Much emphasis has been placed on the bad weather, poor crops, and simultaneous low farm product prices of the late 1870s for precipitating agrarian agitation, especially in the west of Ireland.[82] Indubitably it was a period of exceptional hardship for the landless and near landless of the west, who were still nearly as dependent as in the 1840s on their potato crop, which yielded especially poorly in these abnormally wet seasons. But that is a partial and misleading view of the situation. Contemporaneously with the impoverishment of the landless and near landless masses, there was, in the west of Ireland in the late 1870s, an elevation of the grazier class similar to that which occurred in the east in the 1840s and which there, at that time, also aggravated the suffering due to the failure of the potato crop.

The fact and the significance of the rise of the grazier class in the west is lost sight of in large part because of the erroneous way in which the value of farm output in the years in question has been calculated by commentators. Output according to these calculations comprises on-farm consumption plus off-farm sales. But this omits stock changes, which were critically important at a time of rapid change in cattle numbers. A decline in farm output, as measured by on-farm consumption and off-farm sales,[83] is as likely, under the circumstances, to reflect grazier prosperity as agrarian distress. Average annual cattle exports, the barometer of grazier prosperity, increased by 22 percent between the first and second halves of the 1870s. But expansion was not steady. Exports dropped from 729,000 in 1878 to 641,000 in 1879, rose again in 1880, slumped in 1881, recovered in 1882, and so on. Graziers played the market, selling many animals when prices seemed good, and selling few when there was a prospect of a better price in the future. Reduced sales, under the circumstances, so far from reflecting agricultural depression, were a manifestation of confidence and a willingness to save and invest in livestock. A 23 percent increase in Irish bank deposits between 1870 and 1880, when the Sauerbeck general price index fell by 9 percent, supports that view.[84]

The year 1879, the farming year prior to the foundation of the Land League at Irishtown in April, had been a moderately successful one. The value of crop production, at £5.7 million, was only slightly down on the average for the decade of £5.8 million. Cattle exports reached a new record, and sheep exports were also buoyant.

Connacht lost a higher proportion of its population in the blizzard of the Great Famine; its population declined in the 1840s by 29 percent compared to 18 percent for the rest of Ireland. Its more homogenously poor and potato-dependent population suffered more widely from the loss of the potato crop than the more socially differentiated population of the rest of Ireland, where the worst effects of the famine were confined to the cottier/laborer class. By contrast, Connacht retained its surviving population better in the three post-famine decades. While population declined in the twenty-six counties as a whole by 15 percent, 8 percent, and 5 percent successively in the 1850s, 1860s, and 1870s, it declined by 10 percent, 7 percent, and 3 percent in Connacht. The proximate cause of this slower population decline in Connacht was a less rapid growth in the province's cattle stocks.[85]

There was especially a slower growth of cattle other than milch cows (i.e., dry cattle), and especially up to 1870. Milch cows were not distinguished from other cattle-over-two-years in the early agricultural censuses, but they were so distinguished from 1855 onwards. Between 1855 and 1870, the number of dry cattle increased in the rest of Ireland by 15 percent but only by 5 percent in Connacht. With dry cattle encroaching less and population holding better, it is unsurprising that tillage, between 1850 and 1870, declined less rapidly in Connacht, by 2.3 percent, than in the rest of Ireland, where it contracted by 17 percent. In a word, Connacht's smallholder, more subsistence-oriented agricultural economy survived better during the 1850s and 1860s than that of the more market-oriented agriculture of the rest of Ireland.

The principal reason for the better survival in the immediate post-famine decades of Connacht's more subsistence oriented agriculture was that it was less exposed to competition from dry cattle than that of the rest of Ireland. Only younger, lighter store cattle could be grazed profitably on Connacht's generally poorer land. As noted, the price of these lagged behind the price of matures during the immediate post-famine decades, when there was no shortage of calves. The price of one to two year old cattle rose by 50 percent between 1845 and 1866–1870, while that of two to three year olds increased by 86 percent. On the other hand, the price of butter, which the cow-keeping smallholders of Connacht sold to pay the rent, rose by 45 percent and the price of oats, their principal cash crop, by 19 percent.[86] Connacht's smallholder, more subsistence oriented, farming was under less pressure from encroaching cattle than similar farming on the better land in the east and south, where mature cattle, the price of which was rising rapidly, could be successfully grazed.

That situation was transformed during the following decade as the bottlenecks of winter feed and the supply of calves became more critical. The price of one to two year olds increased by 54 percent and of two to three year olds by 33 percent, while the price of butter declined by 3 percent and of oats by 9 percent.[87]

Socioeconomic change, which had been slower in Connacht than elsewhere prior to the 1870s, now accelerated there and continued more rapidly there than elsewhere beyond the 1870s. The tillage area dropped by 21 percent in Connacht in the 1870s, compared to 17 percent in the rest of Ireland. The number of cows, which produced calves for rearing, butter for sale, and skim milk for human consumption, dropped by 25 percent in Connacht compared to 6 percent in the rest of Ireland. By contrast, the dry cattle population, which had increased less rapidly in Connacht than elsewhere up to the 1870s, in that decade increased by 17 percent compared to the very modest increase of 4 percent elsewhere. Dry cattle numbers continued subsequently to increase, and tillage and the human population to decline, more rapidly in Connacht than elsewhere.

One other change is worth noting. As dry cattle numbers increased without a corresponding increase in cow numbers, the number of calves reared per cow increased. That number, or the proportion between cattle numbers less than one-year and cows, was virtually the same in Connacht, forty-five, as in the rest of Ireland from the commencement of the recorded statistics in 1854. It increased slightly to fifty between then and 1870 throughout Ireland. During the 1870s, however, it increased to sixty-nine in Connacht and, more slowly, to fifty-nine in the rest of Ireland.

Oddly however, Connacht's human population continued to decline more slowly than the rest of Ireland's in the 1870s, as had been the case since 1851. The close link between human population and cattle stocks persisted in the 1870s in Connacht and the country at large. Although dry cattle numbers increased rapidly in Connacht, cow numbers declined there in the 1870s. The overall result was a slight decline, of less than 1 percent, in Connacht's total cattle population between 1870 and 1880 and hence presumably the continued slow decline of the human population.

The full impact of the shift in British demand from high energy to high protein foods and the consequent ascent of pastoralism in Ireland only reached the poorer land of Connacht in the 1870s. There was therefore in Connacht in the late 1870s a particularly sharp conflict between expanding dry cattle production and the province's smallholder agriculture based on oats and butter for sale and potatoes for subsistence. Thanks to the increase in young cattle prices, the Connacht grazier was pressing hard on the tillage and milk-based smallholder and on a population that had been slower than elsewhere to adjust downwards. The situation in this respect was similar to that of the rest of Ireland on the eve of the Great Famine, with people also under pressure from expanding numbers of dry cattle. Like then also, a succession of wet seasons devastated the potato crop on which the smallholders of Connacht were still heavily dependent for their subsistence. Nor was the food situation helped by the diversion of a larger proportion of the reduced supply of skimmed milk from feeding people to rearing the province's larger number of young cattle. There was, therefore, severe distress in Connacht in the later 1870s. But apart from the weather, that distress was the obverse of the prosperity and growth of dry cattle production, which was stimulated by the growing demand for young cattle. The land of Connacht could produce these almost as well as the rest of Ireland.

Irishtown, the dead center of Connacht, was thus a most appropriate place, and 1879 was a most appropriate time to initiate a movement for agrarian change. There existed there then, as was the case in the rest of Ireland prior to the Great Famine, a mass of desperately poor people, threatened with the loss of their land by encroaching graziers and, with nothing to lose, prepared to engage in violent lawlessness. But there also existed in Connacht then, and throughout Ireland, a large body of substantial grazier farmers, who had been brought into existence mainly since the famine and who, by the late 1870s, were ready to challenge a tenure system that was perceived, with increasing clarity, to have little to commend it in terms of equity, efficiency, or legitimacy.

Organization, direction, and financial support were given to these forces of agrarian protest by Irish emigrants who were themselves the victims of the tenure system against which protest was made and who sought redress for Ireland through the Fenian movement. The revolutionary activities of the Fenians having come to nothing, by the late 1870s elements of the movement were prepared to give conditional support to agrarian protest as a means of heightening opposition to British rule in Ireland.

Simultaneously the Home Rule MPs, following the obstructionist example of Biggar and Parnell, were adopting a more aggressively anti-establishment stance in Westminster. The popularity of that stance was endorsed by Parnell's election to the presidency of the Home Rule Confederation of Great Britain in 1878. His consent to accept the presidency of the Land League in the following year was instrumental in securing his election as leader of the parliamentary Home Rule party following the General Election of 1880. The New Departure was on its way.

Fenian support for the New Departure was forthcoming largely because it was believed that the demand for owner occupancy, which it advanced, was more than any UK government could conceivably concede. The Fenian leadership believed that failure to secure owner occupancy under British rule would help mobilize opinion in Ireland in favor of a break with Britain, which was the Fenian objective. However, concessions on the land tenure issue came more quickly and completely than was anticipated. The Land Acts of 1881 and 1887 and the Ashbourne Land Purchase Act of 1885 effectively transferred ownership of most Irish land to its occupiers and opened the certain prospect of ownership to the remaining occupiers. By the end of the 1880s, the land tenure issue had been resolved in favor of the occupiers and had ceased to be a critical political issue.

A major part of its work accomplished, the troika of Fenianism, parliamentary struggle, and agrarian agitation quickly disintegrated. Michael Davitt, the founder of the Land League, held, like his American mentor, Henry George, and his Irish predecessor, James Fintan Lalor, that the rents which had gone to the landlords should continue to be paid, but into a central exchequer, where they would be used for public purposes, benefiting all society. But the grazier occupiers, having effectively secured ownership of the land, had no intention of allowing the benefits of that appropriation be taken from them for public purposes. Their resistance to any such development was made easier by an upsurge in the emigration of the country's disinherited in the 1880s and 1890s. Both Davitt and Fenianism were isolated.

A similar fate befell the Protestant, aristocratic Parnell. With proprietorship of the land secured to its occupiers, Parnell who with Davitt had been largely instrumental in securing that proprietorship was expendable. Following the O'Shea divorce case in which he was cited as correspondent, Parnell came into conflict with Gladstone in Britain and with the Catholic church in Ireland. The support of his party and of Ireland melted away in the ensuing split. He was ousted from leadership of the parliamentary party by Timothy Healy and his other lieutenants. "Firmly astride the pig's back of nationalist historical inevitability, he [Healy] was the first nationalist leader to grasp that an irreversible shift in social power through the unfolding evolution of land purchase had reshaped the terrain of Irish politics. While Healy looked to the entrenchment of a conservative Catholic nationalist order, Parnell . . . sought to contain precisely those tendencies which Healy sought to exploit."[88]

Chapter 9

The Aftermath of Capitalist Colonialism— Ireland as a Case Study

Countries/societies that have been capitalist colonized retrogress; others progress. In seeking to understand why, the nature of individualism in general and of individualist capitalism in particular has been considered. The motives of, and the manner in which, nine individualist capitalist, European countries capitalist colonized most of the non-European world have been considered, as well as how that capitalist colonization damaged the colonized societies, so far irreparably. Finally, it has been argued that the ending of capitalist colonization comes when the capitalist colonized masses have been permanently debilitated and the local elites, who have been the agents/collaborators of the colonial powers, are in unchallenged ascendancy and no longer require the support of the metropoles to sustain them.

This chapter is concerned with the manner in which socioeconomic retrogression persists in the postcolonial era. It uses a case-study approach, the case being the twenty-six counties of Ireland which now comprise the Irish Republic and which have been independent for over seventy years. The chapter reviews as briefly as possible the course of socioeconomic events in Ireland (twenty-six counties) during those years, using insights from the general theory of perpetual capitalist colonial undevelopment to secure a better understanding of those events and, with that better understanding, using the Irish case to illuminate the general process of perpetual capitalist colonial undevelopment.

It would be difficult, if not impossible, to identify any one of the 140 or so countries that have been capitalist colonized as being typical or representative. And, superficially, Irelandwould appear to be the least so. It is the only European capitalist colony and the only country that is both a neighbor and a colony of a capitalist colonial power, which conditions have profoundly influenced both its colonial and postcolonial experience. That reduces its relevance to the general phenomenon of capitalist colonialism. Yet, in another sense, Ireland's non-representative-ness gives it a special value in understanding the phenomenon studied. Largely because of its dual neighbor/colony status, Ireland has experienced the conditions that are most commonly deemed to be requisite to securing development.

Ireland, when it became independent in 1922, had average incomes that were the tenth highest in Europe and that were exceeded outside Europe only by the United States, Canada, Australia, and New Zealand.[1] It had had a system of national education since the 1830s and free, compulsory primary education since 1882. So far from experiencing the pressure of population that is commonly regarded as a major handicap for undeveloped countries, Ireland had experienced, by 1922 and subsequently, a population implosion. At its nadir in 1961, Ireland's population was less than half what it had been 120 years earlier. It had an extensive rail and road system and other infrastructure facilities, which have since been regularly updated. Ireland had immediate, ready access for its agricultural produce to the British market, which, in 1922, was generally accepted as the world's best. Subsequently as a member of the EEC, the country secured an even more lucrative outlet for its agricultural exports.

Ireland was one of the few European countries that remained neutral during the Second World war (and has not experienced major warfare on its territory in 300 years). It has a competent and trustworthy public administration. It has a written, liberal constitution, which is scrupulously adhered to. There have been twenty-four general elections to the Dail, or parliament, since 1922, all of them conducted legally. Government changed in only thirteen of these elections, allowing each government on average seven years in office, followed by the orderly transfer of power to its successor. Ireland, in a word, proves, or tests, all the conventional rules, or generalizations, pertaining to the development of former capitalist colonies. In doing so, it invalidates most of them and confirms the single generalization that countries that have been capitalist colonized retrogress unceasingly, while those that have not been capitalist colonized progress.

But how can a country circumstanced as Ireland was in 1922, and more so seventy years later, be reasonably described as retrogressing? Obviously not if the criterion is average income per head of population. After some 140 years during which real incomes increased by 1.6 percent annually on average,[2] Irish real incomes are now some eleven times greater than they were. But to repeat, the same institutions, basic laws, and technology that first created, and then, 140 years ago, destroyed the Irish landless peasant class continue to operate. Irish society continues to exist at the whim of external market forces, as it did throughout the eighteenth and nineteenth centuries, when first its population was determined by pig exports and later by expanding cattle stocks.

Irish society continues to adjust to those imposed institutions, basic laws, and technology. It does not do as, for example, Japan, Korea, and Taiwan have done, which is to adapt their institutions and basic laws to new technologies of individualist capitalist origin, which they have adopted eclectically. Irish society's adjustment, for over 140 years, to the imposed institutions, basic laws, and technology has been for almost every second person born there to emigrate permanently. That adjustment by society, rather than adaptation of the imposed institutions, basic laws, and technology, raised Irish living standards for those who remained as well as for those who emigrated, but at the cost of every second person born in Ireland having to emigrate and of an ever declining number of people securing a livelihood there.

The number of people at work in Ireland fell from 1,307,662 at independence to 1,125,000 in 1992.[3] Over the same period, the numbers at work in the UK increased from 19 million to 25 million;[4] in the OECD countries from 187 million to 373 million;[5] and in the world at large from 668 million to 2,443 million in 1992.[6] Ireland fails now to provide a livelihood for its people, as it did 140 years ago, and as all the other countries that have been capitalist colonized fail to provide livelihoods for their peoples. In those cases, as in Ireland 150 years ago, that failure is manifested by a widening, deepening morass of poverty. Failure in Ireland's case for the past 150 years, is manifested by emigration and by the declining number able to secure a livelihood.

The period since Irish independence falls conveniently into two chronologically equal parts of thirty-five years each, from 1922 to 1957 and from 1957 to 1992. Each of these two periods is dealt with here in successive Parts 1 and 2. A final Part 3 evaluates the effects of seventy years of postcolonial rule in the light of the proposition that societies that have been capitalist colonized retrogress permanently and offers a prognosis for the undevelopment of Ireland, neighbor and colony.

Part 1:   The First Thirty Years

The first thirty years of Ireland's independence saw groping, unsuccessful attempts by a succession of essentially populist governments to employ the three classical approaches to economic policy: the *laissez faire*, free market approach; protectionism; and Keynesianism. Each lasted for about ten years; each was as unsuccessful as its predecessor.

A Decade of Laissez Faire

The United States of America, shortly after securing independence, moved the seat of government from New York, where the British king's representative had resided and governed, to Washington D.C. The move implied more than a symbolic change in the purpose and methods of government. Seventy years after the foundation of the Irish state, all the major offices of state are still located in, or within a mile radius of, Dublin Castle, the seat of foreign rule in Ireland for centuries, even before the Tudor conquest. The locational immobility of the state's offices reflect the continuity of purpose and method of government. That continuity was elevated to a guiding principle by the state's first government, that headed by W. T. Cosgrave's *Cumann na nGael* party, which lasted from 1922 to 1932.

One of the first acts of the new government was to establish in 1922 a Commission on Agriculture which was required to inquire into and report on "the causes of the present depression in agriculture and to recommend such remedies as will secure for agriculture, and for industries subsidiary to it, an assured basis for future expansion and prosperity."[7] The Commission, in the introduction to its report, quoted from Edmund Burke: "It is in the power of government to do much evil, and it can do very little positive good." Those sentiments informed the Commission's work and recommendations. More importantly, they informed the policy of the first Irish government. Its *laissez faire* policy was concerned to maintain the existing system of law and order, following the transfer of control of that system from the British occupiers to the elected representatives of those members of the Irish nation living in the twenty-six counties. The incongruity of *laissez faire* government for a newly independent people whose numbers had been precisely determined by external market demand for the two preceding centuries was overlooked.

The policy of minimalist government rested on two beliefs. The first was the nationalist expectation, common to and fostered by colonial independence movements everywhere, that insofar as socioeconomic conditions were unsatisfactory, the cause was colonial rule; once that rule ended, satisfactory socioeconomic conditions would follow.

More immediately, the new governing elite was concerned to avoid causing wealthy persons to move with their wealth to Britain, as some did. That concern focused particularly on holding income tax at, or below, the British rate. This was done by reducing the Irish rate from five to three shillings in the pound in 1928. This was achieved by allowing total state expenditure to increase by a mere £2M, from £28 million in 1924 to £30 million in 1929. It was the equivalent of 18.6 percent of national income in the latter year.[8]

Yet independence resulted in three particular losses to Ireland, neighbor and former colony. One of these was the transfers from the UK treasury which had become relatively substantial prior to independence, and were directed to grassroots level where they achieved the greatest good.

The second substantive loss caused to Ireland by independence was the political influence of the less contented half of its population which emigrated. These emigrants in Britain, and in the United States and elsewhere also, had had a major influence on the governing of Ireland for fifty or so years prior to independence. That influence was exercised by pressing the UK government to reform its Irish policy, and by encouraging and supporting resistance in Ireland to metropolitan rule. These influences for change, generated by the Irish diaspora, effectively ended with independence. Emigrants generally have been supportive and uncritical of the new state.

The third particular loss associated with independence was partition and the consequent isolation of government in the twenty-six counties from Northern Ireland and from the Protestant, industrial culture of the region. The south relapsed into a pastoral quietude, undisturbed by dissidents north of the border or by those born within its own borders but who removed themselves in a fresh, post-independence upsurge of emigration.

The changes that occurred after 1922 were cosmetic. They affected such things as the emblems, flag, and anthem of government. The pillar boxes, which had been red, were painted green. A couple of hundred new men moved into the higher echelons of the public service,[9] which was otherwise unchanged and operated the same imposed institutions and basic laws that had caused undevelopment under colonial rule.

A sovereignty that was, therefore, not without cost but that was exercised by new people in command, with some cosmetic changes, merely to uphold the existing socioeconomic system, could hardly have failed to injure the national mass. There were two indicators in particular of that deterioration. The first was a cut in the old-age pension from the ten shillings a week rate bequeathed by the British to nine shillings, in order to balance the budget at a lower income-tax rate. The other was the rise in the Irish cost of living vis-à-vis Britain's, as the cost of government, no longer supported by subventions from Britain, was directed increasingly towards indirect taxes. The cost of living index in the Irish Free State, which was already in 1923, 6.3 percent higher than Britain's (on a common 1914 base), rose to 10 percent above the British rate by the end of the Cosgrave era in 1932.[10]

Little enthusiasm was evinced for the government of the newly independent State. Annual emigration, which fell from 12 per 1000 in the 1890s, to 8 per 1000 in the 1900s, rose again in the 1920s to 10 per 1000. At 29,000 annually, emigration was almost half the birthrate. It caused a population drop of 170,000 between 1921 and 1930.[11] As well as voting against the government of the day with their feet, by emigrating, the people increasingly in successive general elections cast their ballots for the populist *Fianna Fail* party, which promised more interventionist policies than those to which the *Cumann na nGael* government party was committed.

Dissatisfaction with the government increased sharply in the early 1930s as a result of changed external conditions. The worldwide slump reduced Irish emigration from 29,000 annually to 4,000. The country's population, which had fallen in every year since the Great Famine, commenced to increase and rose by 44,000 between 1930 and 1934.[12] Unemployment increased from 26,000 in 1930 to 96,000 in 1933.[13] Although GNP was falling, increased expenditure was forced on a reluctant *Cumann na nGael* government, and state expenditure as a proportion of national income rose from 15.5 percent in 1929 to 17.9 percent in 1932.[14] The deteriorating economic conditions added to popular disillusion with the conservative *Cumann na nGaedheal* government of the 1920s. Support moved more strongly to the *Fianna Fail* opposition party, which was elected to government in 1932 in the depths of world depression.

The demographic changes brought about in Ireland by the worldwide depression of the 1930s had major political and economic consequences. The pressures for change, which are the normal consequences of capital accumulation and associated technological change, were, during those years in Ireland, no longer dissipated through emigration. Instead, as in contemporary Germany or the United States, they forced the country towards radically new policies.

A Decade of Protectionism—The Revolution That Never Was

Coincidental with the reversal in the decline in population and the election of a new *Fianna Fail* government, the number of people at work, which had declined every year since the Great Famine, commenced also to increase. The number at work in manufacturing industry increased from 120,000 to 141,000, and in construction from 38,000 to 58,000 between 1926 and 1936. These and other employment gains in the service industries more than offset a reduced outflow of workers from agriculture so that the total at work increased, for the first time since the 1840s, from 1,220,000 in 1926 to 1,235,000 in 1936. All of the increase occurred after 1932.[15]

The reversal in the long term decline in the number at work, and the reversal of other long established trends noted below, was the result of a *volte face* in state policy brought about by the new *Fianna Fail* government. The quantitative import restrictions and tariffs introduced by the new government afforded one of the highest level of protection to any manufacturing industry anywhere.[16] Additionally, incentives were given by the government to individuals and local authorities to build houses. The number of houses built with state aid increased from 2,000 in 1932 to 17,000 in 1938. This was the first spate of house-building in Ireland since the eighteenth century. The urbanization, that was such a marked characteristic of all other western countries in the nineteenth century, had missed southern Ireland, where the populations of virtually all the towns of significance, apart from Dublin and its environs, had declined from 1841 onwards.[17]

The long term rise in the cattle/wheat price ratio was reversed during the 1930s.[18] This was partly because of government action to support the price of wheat and partly because of retaliatory action by the UK government to initiatives undertaken by the *Fianna Fail* government.

First, the new government abolished the Oath of Allegiance to the king of England, which the 1921 Treaty required newly elected members of Dail Eireann to take. Second, they introduced intensive industrial protection at a time of worldwide slump. And third, the *Fianna Fail* government decided to retain to itself the annual payments made by farmers under land purchase arrangements, which had previously been paid to the UK government. These payments were made to the Land Commission, which was established by Act of the Westminster parliament in 1881 and was charged with managing the financing of the transfer of ownership of Irish farmland from landlords to tenants under successive Land Acts. In the hands of the Irish government, the payments were used to contribute to increased public expenditure on housing and other items.

The UK government reacted to these moves by imposing quotas and tariffs on cattle imported from Ireland. These restrictions caused the price of two to three year old cattle to fall from an average of £15-12-9 in 1930 to £6-16-6 in 1934.[19] With an output of about a million cattle annually, this represented a reduction of some £9 million annually in the incomes of grazier farmers, the one interest that had been ascendant in Ireland since the price changes that were ushered in by the end of the Napoleonic wars in 1815. The grazier farmers now suffered because of industrial protection, which provided new jobs for the landless at the cost of higher priced consumer goods for the landed, and because of the retention by the state of the Land Commission annuities, which led to the halving of the price of cattle, their principal product.

While the UK imposed import restrictions that caused cattle prices to collapse, the Irish government reduced the amount of annuities payable by farmers from £4.1 million in 1932 to £2.4 million in 1934.[20] This was some offset to the drastic fall in cattle prices. Additionally government guaranteed the price of wheat and expanded the protected market for sugar beet. The halving of the annuities and the higher, guaranteed prices for tillage crops and for milk, which were principally produced by small farmers, largely compensated the latter for the losses from lower cattle prices. The cost of government policy thus fell mainly on the larger grazier farmers, whose interests, to repeat, had hitherto been paramount for a century.

Agricultural production adjusted to the new dispensation, and major trends, which had been established at least since the Great Famine, were reversed. The tillage acreage expanded every year from 1932 to 1936, the only peacetime occasion it did so since the 1840s. The number of cattle reared declined from 1,016,000 in 1932 to 999,000 in 1937, having previously increased almost every year, from 406,000 in 1861. While the number at work in agriculture continued the decline commenced in the 1840s—the first such decline recorded anywhere in modern times—that decline in the intercensal period 1926–1936, at 6 percent, was smaller, proportionately and absolutely, than in any earlier or later decade.[21]

Although protection for industry and tillage was the principal instrument of policy, government also, despite a continuing emphasis on frugality, increased its expenditure, both absolutely and relative to GNP.[22] The increased expenditure was financed in part by higher tax revenues, especially from income-tax. The new government relaxed the aim of holding the Irish rate below the contemporary British rate and raised the rate from three to five shillings in the £ in 1933. To a small extent also the increased expenditure was financed by borrowing, a procedure that caused the 1936 Banking Commission much concern over the growth of "dead weight debt." In 1937 it amounted to about £37 million, or 25 percent of GNP.[23]

The changes wrought by Ireland's near revolution of the early 1930s were modest by comparison with such paroxysms as the French or Russian revolution or the changes occurring in contemporary Germany under Hitler. Nevertheless, in terms of breaking with distinctively Irish trends that had been established for so long, the changes that took place between 1932 and 1936 were remarkable. They were remarkable also by comparison with events in contemporary Britain. For over a century Ireland had lagged badly behind Britain in most material respects and in two in particular. First, the number of people at work declined in Ireland while it increased in Britain; and second, though income per head of

Ireland's declining population rose more rapidly, total Irish incomes, or GNP, had grown much less rapidly.[24] Now, during these few years, Ireland performed better in both respects. While employment in UK manufacturing declined from 8.6 million in 1929 to 8.5 million in 1935, Ireland's increased by 20 percent. While the UK's real GDP fell by 8.7 percent between 1929 and 1933, Ireland's rose by 4 percent.[25]

However the changes in Ireland were only transient—a blip in established long-term trends. UK unemployment peaked at 2.8 million in 1932. In 1934 it was down to 2.2 million and continued to decline to 1.5 million in 1937. Irish emigration quickly responded and between 1935 and 1938 averaged 26,000 annually, again about half the current number of births. Population declined by 34,000 in these years.[26]

Protected industries had replaced most manufactured imports by 1936 and there were few more jobs to be created by import substitution.[27] Likewise house-building had peaked and employment there had leveled off.[28] In farming, following a coal/cattle pact with the UK in 1934, cattle prices commenced once more to rise relative to crop prices. Tillage reverted to its normal peacetime decline, more young cattle were reared to stock the expanding pasture acreage, and the numbers employed in agriculture commenced once more to decline rapidly.[29]

State expenditure continued to rise slightly, but less rapidly than prices. It maintained the same, higher proportion relative to GNP reached by the new *Fianna Fail* government in 1933. But GNP itself commenced to contract and by 1938 was back to the 1929 level.[30]

Persons at work in protected industries and in the public sector did not fare badly during the later 1930s. Their wages rose at least as rapidly as prices which, after 1935, commenced to move upwards. Farmers also fared well. The Land Commission annuities, which had initially been loosely related to competitive rents, having been halved in 1934, thereafter sank into insignificance as prices commenced their long term upward movement.

Conditions outside the privileged circle were less favorable. Once more, expanding cattle and sheep numbers reduced the demand for the labor, which was all that the landless majority of agriculturists had to offer. A contracting economy further reduced the demand for labor. Simultaneously prices rose more rapidly than in the UK.

While the cost of living rose by 16 percent during the 1930s, wages of the largest single class of employees, farm laborers, rose by only 15 percent. Workers in unprotected industries and in non-government services, as well as the unemployed, suffered also from the declining quality of the goods produced by the heavily protected industries.

**Table 9.1. Cost of Living, Ireland and the UK
(Base 1914 = 100)**

	Ireland	UK
1931	165	146
1936	166	151
1939	192	169

Source: Department of Trade and Commerce, *Irish Trade Journal and Statistical Bulletin*
(Dublin: CSO, December 1939), 208.

As is usually the case with governments in power, the reality of *Fianna Fail*
government proved less attractive than the promise. Support for it fell sharply
between the 1933 and 1937 general elections. That was reflected partly in a
smaller turnout and partly in a smaller share of the votes cast. But in another
election in the following year, after the completion of a trade agreement with
Britain and the recovery of control of the naval ports retained by Britain under
the 1921 Treaty, the government's position was much restored. However, if the
178,000 who, in emigrating between 1935 and 1938 voted with their feet against
the conduct of affairs, had instead remained in Ireland and voted against the
government, it would have been forced from office. In the event, given renewed,
large scale emigration, reversion to conservatism was the politically expedient
course.

Industrial protection in Ireland was justified on the standard infant industry
argument associated particularly with the German economist Friedrich List: that
industries needing protection to get established would, in time, become competitive and able to operate, without tariff protection, on home and export markets.[31]
It was, however, a peculiarly specious argument when applied to Ireland. First,
the small size of the Irish economy precluded the attainment of the scale economies that enabled the initially protected industrial complexes of Germany, the
United States and Japan, to become in time competitive and major exporters.
Second, Irish incomes have been determined, since the Great Famine, by income
levels in the countries to which the Irish emigrated, and by their willingness and
ability to emigrate. Protection implied a reduction in real living standards for
those in non-protected industries, and therefore a greater propensity to emigrate.
Emigration from a small, protected, and therefore costly and inefficient economy ensured that the economy remained small, costly, and inefficient and that
its people, once afforded the opportunity, would emigrate more rapidly.

A Decade of Keynesianism—Public Sector Deficit Financing

During the 1940s Ireland experienced the usual wartime increase in marriages
and births. That plus its neutrality, the country's escape from the death and destruction of the Second World War, and some easing of emigration caused
population to rise by 50,000, or about one-and-a half percent, between 1939 and

1948.[32] In the latter year, *Fianna Fail* lost office for the first time since 1932, being replaced by a coalition government. This was headed by *Fine Gael*, the successor party to the *Cumann na nGaedheal* party which governed in the 1920s. Mr. J. A. Costello was *taoiseach*, or prime minister. *Fine Gael* was joined in office by the Labor Party and by two new parties, *Clann na Pobhlactha* and *Clann na Talmhan*, the one party representing more extreme republican and anti-British views, and the other a more radical, small-farmer view.

The coalition government responded to changed conditions at home and abroad. In Britain a socialist government was committed to maintaining full employment, if necessary by incurring public sector deficits, the economic expediency of which was argued by the large, influential, Keynesian school of economists which emerged during the post-Second World War years. Keynesian policies strengthened demand in Britain for Irish labor which, for the first peacetime occasion, could now be sure of immediate employment on going to Britain. Emigration increased and population declined in every one of the following thirteen years. It reached a nadir in 1961, at 2.818 million, or 43 percent of its 1841 level.

Keynesianism made its mark in Ireland also. Notwithstanding the strictures of the 1936 Banking Commission on what it called "dead weight debt," deficit financing did now appear to have merit. After all, the British and American allies had just financed a successful world war in large part by government borrowing. It was argued that if it was in order for governments to borrow to fight wars, it was surely even more so to borrow to create jobs and to build a nation's economy. Strong intellectual support for that view was given by the new insights and concepts provided by Keynesian economics. Moreover, because of wartime restrictions on imports, the Irish banking system was now, even more than previously, well endowed with foreign currency—its sterling assets. Finally, the political array that emerged in 1948 was less conservative. The *Fine Gael* party, a bastion of Irish conservatism, though heading the government, had secured its smallest ever share of votes. It was bound, therefore, to heed the views of its more radical coalition partners, who, between them, had secured twice as many votes in the 1948 election. Considerable retrospective intellectual endorsement of deficit financing was given by the quasi-independent, Ford Foundation-financed Economic Research Institute in an influential paper, *Public Debt and Economic Development* (1962).

The Irish state, among post-capitalist-colonial states, had an extraordinary ability to borrow. This was based on a century and a quarter of extreme financial rectitude on the part of the Irish administration, which had been maintained regardless of the social cost—first by state coercion, then by the emigration of the less contented half of each generation. It was manifested especially in the extraordinary success of the Irish banking system which, as Ernest Blythe observed, "acted as a conduit to remove savings to create jobs outside."[33] After 125 years of this, Ireland had in 1948 what was probably the largest inward flow of net factor income in the world relative to national income. In 1938 these factor payments inwards added 7.6 percent to gross domestic product. Britain in the same year added only 3.7 percent to its gross domestic product from the over-seas wealth it had accumulated during the centuries it had been the world's lead-ing colonial power.[34] By 1948, while Ireland's receipts from abroad continued at 7.4 percent of national income, Britain's, as part of the cost of financing the war, had fallen to 2.2 percent of GNP.[35]

The Irish state thus enjoyed an unparalleled public confidence in its fi-nances, secured at great national cost. It also had a population which, even more than in the nineteenth century, had relatively high incomes, a relatively high propensity to save, and few opportunities to invest in Ireland. That population was more than willing to lend its savings to the state for a small premium over the alternative of a very small interest on bank deposits.

Fuelled by government deficits equivalent to over 4 percent of current GNP, the economy grew by around 2 percent annually, which was much more rapid than in the inter-war years, as was the case generally in the West.[36] There was a substantial increase in employment in construction, where there was much state capital expenditure and where, because of its nature, there was little competition from imports. Employment in highly protected manufacturing industry also in-creased somewhat as imported raw materials and fuels became more readily available. But beyond the initial postwar expansion, there was no indication or prospect of further jobs in manufacturing. Meanwhile, whatever jobs had been gained there and in construction were more than offset by an accelerated decline in the agricultural workforce. Thus, the number at work, having recovered in the early 1930s to reach a peak in 1936, continued to decline in the early 1950s, notwithstanding the incurring of public sector deficits and the somewhat accel-erated GNP growth.[37] Imports grew *pari passu* with GNP between 1948 and the mid-1950s. Although exports expanded more rapidly, they did so from a smaller base and the import excess remained high, at nearly 20 percent of GNP in 1955.[38] There were persistent balance of payments deficits and between 1950 and 1955 the external assets of the banking system were reduced from £245.4 m. to £192.4m, or from the equivalent of 153 percent of current annual imports to 94 percent.[39] In those pre-Eurodollar and pre-OPEC oil-dollar days, those for-eign assets could not be replenished so readily as subsequently. T. K. Whitaker, who was then Permanent Secretary of the Department of Finance, later wrote feelingly: "I have unpleasant recollections of the difficulty of raising even a few million pounds on a short term basis in London in 1956."[40]

The loss by the banks of 22 percent of their external assets in 1955 alone caused them to squeeze credit.[41] While they had increased their assets within the state by 26 percent between 1953 and 1955, between then and 1959 they added only another 11 percent, though prices meanwhile had risen by 14 percent.[42] The credit squeeze forced on the banks by their loss of external reserves impacted first on GNP growth. That fell from 8.7 percent in 1953 to 0.7 percent in 1954; and in 1956 GNP declined for the first time since the 1930s.[43] For the first time since the state's foundation, the number at work in the non-agricultural sectors fell, from 711,000 in 1954 to 661,000 in 1958, while agricultural employment continued its long run decline.[44] Emigration rose during the 1950s to an annual

rate of 41,000, which was two-thirds of the birthrate. Population fell by 5 percent between the 1951 and 1961 censuses.[45] With the country's people and external reserves both hemorrhaging, it was time to cry "halt." As the head of the
Civil Service wrote: "After 35 years of native government, people are asking
whether we can achieve an acceptable degree of economic progress."[46]

Part 2:   The Mid-Fifties To The Early Nineties

The longest-sustained and apparently most successful set of economic policies
employed by native Irish governments is the one which was introduced in the
mid-1950s and which is still largely in place today. These policies focus on the
provision of public support to exporting industries. The concept, the flaws in its
application to the Irish case, and its impacts on the economy are discussed in the
following sections.

Borrowing for Exports—The Concept and Its Operation

Personalities and factional interests alone divided the major Irish political parties
by the 1950s. Thus it was that the initiative for dealing with the crisis of the
mid-1950s came from the bureaucracy. More specifically, it came from T. K.
Whitaker, the person who, as head of the civil service, had shared an ignominy
familiar to many lesser mortals, of sweating in a banker's office while importun-
ing for ready cash, though in his case it was for "a few million pounds."

Shortly after his appointment as Secretary of the Department of Finance,
Whitaker published his assessment of the situation in a paper, *Capital Formation, Savings and Economic Progress*, read in 1956. This emphasized the high
proportion of Irish capital formation that was accounted for by the state and, of
that, the high proportion that was in the form of houses, hospitals, and schools.
No attempt was made to assess the social benefits from this investment. It was
sufficient that the financial returns, in terms of foreign exchange earnings, were
inadequate relative to the foreign exchange costs incurred, in part at least as a
result of the public sector deficit financing. The subsequent *Economic Development* prepared by the same author in 1958 set the course of Irish economic policy for the following decades. Economic development was informed by the then
popular Rostovian doctrine of "an economic take-off."[47] Whitaker writes: "it is
doubtful whether investment in public utilities and facilities in countries that
lack other essentials of development will allow them to "take off." The usual
sequence of events is that a step forward is made in one sector of the economy
and that this makes it easier for the rest of the economy to advance."[48]

The essence of the new economic policy was, first, the abandonment of protection and a move to free trade, first with Britain under an Anglo-Irish Free
Trade Agreement, and later with the EEC, which Ireland joined in 1973. The
second main plank of economic policy was the encouragement of exports by:

a) the provision of state grants to exporting industries, including tourism and other traded service industries;

b) allowing tax exemption on those profits of manufacturing industry that could be ascribed to exports;

c) the provision of low cost capital to manufacturing exporters, by exempting banks from tax on that part of their profits which could be ascribed to lending to exporters;

d) the removal of restrictions on foreign manufacturing firms establishing in Ireland and on the repatriation of their profits.

The third plank of economic policy was the financing of export promotion by shifting state capital expenditure from houses, hospitals, and schools to factories, hotels, and offices: i.e., "that capital development of a productive character should be stimulated."[49]

There were two other major elements in the new economic policy which became explicit over time. One of these was a relaxed monetary policy. The other was the attraction to Ireland of foreign transnational firms. The combination of tax holidays on profits attributable to exports and double taxation agreements with the companies' host governments enabled these companies, by administering their prices, to avoid taxation on profits made not only in Ireland, but also on upstream and downstream operations outside Ireland.

This initiative, implemented in 1958, was a break with the 1920s' *laissez faire*, with the 1930s' protectionism, and with protectionism supplemented by deficit financing as practiced from 1948 to 1955. All three of these earlier policies were inherently inappropriate to Irish circumstances. The *laissez faire* of the 1920s, as well as ignoring the unsatisfactory socioeconomic conditions that were the result of centuries of capitalist colonialism, also ignored the material deterioration that followed independence. This included especially the cessation of transfer payments from Britain, which could only be offset by a vigorous exercise of sovereignty. The protectionism of the 1930s and 1940s was inappropriate because of the small size of the Irish market and the propensity of the Irish to emigrate. Emigration would keep the market small and production inefficient and costly, and so feed more emigration. Government deficits to finance social-welfare type expenditures, between 1948 and 1955, had the merit of drawing on the virtually limitless credit of the Irish state. But it had the defect of stimulating imports without a commensurate growth in exports. By contrast, the economic policy introduced in 1958 appeared to be peculiarly appropriate to Ireland's unique position as a neighbor and a former capitalist colony.

Western nation-states had a chronic tendency to borrow, principally to finance wars. But the checks and balances inherent in the structure of individualist capitalist states, especially as these evolved following the rise to political dominance of "the cabin" curtailed that borrowing. Most western states increased their debt relative to GNP after the Second World war, in line with Keynesian ideas of stimulating demand and economic growth. But in none did the debt rise so rapidly relative to GNP as in Ireland; and in none except Belgium did interest on it become so great relative to GNP as in Ireland (see table 9.2).

Table 9.2. State Debt, Interest, and GNP, OECD Countries

	Debt/GNP Ratio		Interest Payments as a Percentage of GNP
	1972	1987	1987
US	44.1	52.9	4.9
Japan	17.5	74.4	4.4
Germany	18.8	44.0	2.9
France	26.4	47.3	2.8
UK	75.3	49.2	4.3
Italy	60.1	93.0	8.3
Canada	52.6	68.6	8.4
Australia	35.9	23.2	4.0
Austria	17.5	57.6	3.9
Belgium	71.4	131.7	10.8
Denmark	10.0	56.3	8.3
Finland	12.4	20.0	1.6
Greece	23.2	65.0	7.2
Ireland	60.8	135.2	9.3
Netherlands	46.6	75.2	6.4
Norway	50.3	42.3	4.3
Portugal	13.6	48.5	8.8
Spain	14.9	48.5	3.5
Sweden	30.7	59.3	6.5

Sources: 1972 figures from J. C. Chouraqui, B. Jones, and R. Montador, "Public Debt in a Medium-Term Context and its Implications for Fiscal Policy," OECD Department of Economics and Statistics, *Working Paper No. 30* (Paris: OECD, 1986); 1987 figures from OECD, *Economic Outlook,* 49 (Paris: OECD, July 1991), Table 31; Interest payments as a proportion of GDP calculated from OECD, *National Accounts,* Vol. II, ratio of Table 6, line 24 to Table 1, line 15.

The state in Ireland, as in all former capitalist colonies, was willing to borrow effectively without limit. The Irish state, however, also had the ability to borrow to an extent that was unique among these. State debt in none of the other former capitalist colonies is nearly so great, relative to GNP, as in Ireland. The Irish state had the Third World's willingness to borrow and the West's capacity to do so.

The Irish state's unique combination of ability and willingness to borrow was limited only by the leaking of public sector deficits into imports, which in the mid-1950s caused a depletion of foreign currency reserves. The new economic policy, by mobilizing the state's borrowing capacity to subsidize exports, offset the loss of foreign reserves by stimulating a counter inwards flow of foreign currency from exports and, to a less extent, from foreign investment in Ireland.[50] That countervailing inward flow of foreign currencies enabled the Irish state to borrow on a scale and over a duration that were unique among former capitalist colonies.

Ireland's neighbor status was critical for the state's capacity to stimulate exports as it was for its capacity to borrow. Because it was Britain's neighbor, it could, unlike other former capitalist colonies, complete in 1965 an Anglo-Irish free trade agreement with the former metropolitan power. Subsequently, because it was, uniquely amongst former capitalist colonies, located in Europe, it was able to join the EEC and secure unimpeded access to that market.

There were other aspects of the Irish situation stemming from its neighbor status and the emigration which that made possible and contributed to the feasibility of the emphasis on export stimulation. The country was politically stable and that stability was enhanced by the new economic policies, which brought substantial benefits but few costs to existing interests. Its population was well educated. Its public administration functioned well, and it was reasonably well served by its transport, communications, and other public utilities. As with all former capitalist colonies, its *lingua franca* was that of the former metropole English, the language most widely used in modern industry, commerce, and science.

The new economic policy stance of 1958, in drawing on the virtually limitless credit of the Irish state and in focusing on large markets to which Ireland had unique access among former capitalist colonies, was peculiarly appropriate to the place and time. As well as being appropriate, the new policies were peculiarly attractive. They threatened no established interest, but promised benefit to many. Leading academic economists predicted that, as firms found their protected home market under pressure from imports, they would switch to the new export opportunities opened by free trade.[51] If jobs were lost in the drive to free trade, they would be gained, with a bonus, in new, better jobs in exporting industries. Farmers could expect higher prices with closer integration into the UK economy, and subsequently the much higher prices available in the E.E.C.. Fund holders could expect ever higher interest rates as the state returned to the market to borrow more.

Concern about the long term consequences of state borrowing was silenced by a number of considerations. First, the policy was advanced by the Department of Finance, a bastion of financial rectitude. Second, the policy of public sector deficits to generate a Rostovian economic take off was enthusiastically supported by current economic thought and, as noted already, the Economic Research Institute lent its authority to the policy. Third, the policy promised immediate benefits; and, in the long run, as Keynes pointed out, "we are all dead." The future generations were like the emigrants, outsiders with no votes and incapable of influencing policy.

The remarkable appropriateness of the 1958 policy to Irish circumstances is demonstrated particularly by its success in stimulating exports, which was critical. These increased tenfold in volume between 1960 and 1990, a period during which world trade as a whole increased only threefold. The rate of increase was greater in the second decade than in the first; and greater in the third than in the second. Exports increased from the equivalent of 23 percent of GNP in 1960 to 75 percent in 1990.[52] Only Hong Kong, Singapore, and Belgium export as high a proportion of their product as Ireland;[53] but these countries have land communication with their principal markets or, in Hong Kong's case, is separated by a narrow strait. Irish export growth has been achieved although the country is separated from its markets by what has been described as the most expensive stretch of water in the world.

Such was the success of these policies that totally new economic constraints came into operation in the 1970s. Labor, half of which Ireland had exported since the mid-nineteenth century, became limiting, and net immigration, which had not occurred since the seventeenth century, took place on a substantial scale. In that decade also Ireland, which for over a century had been a relatively large exporter of savings, became a debtor country. Domestic savings ceased to meet the state's burgeoning borrowing requirements, which were instead met increasingly by foreign borrowing.

The economic policies of 1958 pioneered a new route to export expansion. The almost universal experience is that countries export products for which, for one reason or another, they have some production advantage. That advantage is established initially on the domestic market, in industries producing for that market which in time go on to produce for export also. The 1958 initiative bypassed this process. Ireland instead set about establishing industries that, from the beginning, were overwhelmingly or exclusively export-oriented. This, if sustainable, offered the prospect of limitless, painless economic growth.

Borrowing for Exports—The Flaw

There was, unfortunately, a fatal flaw in this promise of continuous, effortless progress. It was assumed that state expenditure would stimulate growth sufficiently for the size and cost of the debt, though increased absolutely, not to increase relative to GNP, and therefore become more onerous. It was a comforting assumption, but without empirical support. Whatever growth has been generated by public sector deficits in Ireland has been less than the increased interest payable on the state's debt. Interest on the state debt increased from 0.7 percent of GNP in 1948 to 2.5 percent in 1956. It increased further to 3.8 percent of GNP in 1969.[54] The relative cost of servicing the debt continued to rise until it peaked at the equivalent of 11.4 percent of current GNP in 1985. In only two years between 1948 to 1986 did interest on the debt grow less rapidly than GNP.[55]

Already in the 1970s, despite the phenomenal growth of exports and legal constraints on the export of funds by banks, insurance companies, and pension funds, the country's foreign currency reserves were under strain, as in the 1950s. But this time no senior civil servant had the unpleasant experience of having to importune foreign bankers for "a few million pounds." The shoe was on the other foot. The world of the 1970s was awash with Euro and petro-dollars. The world's bankers, keen to maintain their share of global business, had to make loans to match their burgeoning deposits. Anthony Sampson describes an assembly of these bankers at a meeting of the International Monetary Fund in the 1970s: "Many of them begin to look not so much like bankers as financial middle-men, contact men, or—could it really be ?—*salesmen*. As they pursue their prey down the escalators, up the elevators, along the upstairs corridors into the suites, they cannot conceal their anxiety to do business. For these men who look as if they might have been trained to say No from their childhood are actually trying to sell *loans*. 'I've good news for you,' I heard one eager contact man telling a group of American bankers: 'I think they'll be able to take your money.'"[56]

Lending to an Irish government was a most attractive proposition by the standards of the day. The country exported a higher proportion of its product than almost any other, and therefore earned the foreign currency to service foreign debts. It was politically stable and had recently joined the "rich man's club" of the EEC. When therefore in the 1970s, the country's desire for imports outstripped its ability to pay for these, from current export earnings or by liquidating external assets that no longer existed, there was no dearth of lenders of foreign currency. It was accordingly possible for the coalition government of Liam Cosgrave, which came into office in 1973, not only to continue incurring deficits, but to do so on an enhanced scale which, net of interest on existing debt, left the government with four times as much additional resources, relative to GNP, as its predecessor had. The average excess of net borrowing over interest payments during the four years of the Cosgrave coalition government was 6.2 percent of current GNP. It had been 1.6 percent during the preceding four years.[57]

The sustained borrowing of the 1960s and 1970s, which failed to generate GNP growth commensurate with the growth of state debt, was bound in time, through the logic of compound interest, to create a crisis, the severity of which would increase the longer its onset was delayed. To pay interest that rose to the equivalent of 11.4 percent of GNP in 1985 and to secure additional funds to finance encouragement to exports without raising taxes to unacceptable levels, state borrowing was raised to a record level of 15.7 percent of current GNP in 1982.[58] By then too the mood of the world's bankers, whom Keynes also has described as "the most romantic and least realistic of men," had changed. No longer awash with Euro and dollars-dollars, the world banking system was instead encumbered with enormous amounts of loans made to former capitalist colonies which it was clear these countries could not service, much less repay, and which threatened to bankrupt many of the world's leading banks.

The coalition government led by Garret FitzGerald, which took office at the end of 1982, had no option but to rein back on state borrowing, which had got out of hand and was no longer acceptable to the world's bankers. Borrowing, which had increased from the equivalent of 1.3 percent of GNP in 1948 to 15.7 percent in 1982, was cut back gradually to 2 percent of current GNP in 1990.[59] This was regarded as the maximum government deficit that could be sustained without undermining confidence in the entire public finance system. The net addition to demand (i.e., net borrowing minus interest on existing state debt) declined from 7.9 percent of GNP in 1981 to virtually zero in 1987 and to a negative 7.4 percent of GNP in 1990.[60] The state in 1990, with its credit exhausted, could borrow only the equivalent of 2 percent of current GNP, while interest payments on existing debt amounted to 9.4 percent of GNP. The state took from taxpayers in that year, to pay the rentier holders of state debt, £2,114 million, or the equivalent of 8.1 percent of GNP, more than it could now borrow.[61]

This was history repeating itself. A *Fine Gael*-led coalition government, hooked on Keynesianism, initiated sustained state deficit financing in 1948. In a subsequent term in office, in the mid-1950s, it reaped the whirlwind of the drain of the banking system's external assets, which precipitated a major economic recession. Another *Fine Gael*-led coalition, this time committed to the *"Just Society,"* [62] accelerated state borrowing in 1973 to secure four times as much "free" resources as previously, and reaped yet another whirlwind a decade later, when rapidly growing state debt threatened to swamp the country's financial system. Contractionary economic policies were again unavoidable. History was repeating itself, but as usual with a difference. For one thing, the 1950s crisis was generated by the loss of the banking system's sterling assets, which was equivalent to an individual becoming strapped for cash in the bank. The 1980s crisis was far more profound as it involved the exhaustion of the state's credit and not merely its foreign reserves.

The policies of the late 1950s were thought by some to have ushered in an age of Irish economic miracles, similar to that in contemporary Germany. GNP growth, which, from at least the mid-nineteenth century, had lagged far behind that in the rest of Europe,[63] accelerated. It rose to an average of 3 percent annually in the period 1948–1960 and over the 1960s and 1970s averaged 3.6 percent annually, placing it among the best performing economies in Europe. This performance was, however, much more mirage than miracle. As state borrowing was reined back, economic growth slowed to an average of 1.3 percent annually in the 1980s and came to a halt at the end of the decade. With population now growing, Ireland, for the first time since the Great Famine and in common with the other former colonies which comprise the Third World, experienced an increase in poverty. An ESRI study shows that the extent and severity of poverty increased in the period 1973 to 1987 and that the risk of poverty for families with four or more children more than doubled.[64]

The longest rope has an end. The Irish state, because of the country's unique neighbor and colony status, had been given and had taken a longer line of credit than any other. With that line of credit exhausted, the economy has become enmeshed in an unprecedentedly expensive state debt. And for what? Has Ireland under these policies succeeded in casting off its particular version of the legacy of undevelopment? Has the focus on export promotion increased the numbers of Irish people who can earn a living in Ireland?

Borrowing for Exports—The Impact on Jobs

Capitalist colonial undevelopment in the Third World takes the form of an increasing mass of people experiencing worse poverty. It has taken the distinctive form in Ireland, since the mid-nineteenth century, of the emigration of that part of the population which has failed to secure incomes that tended in time to approximate closer to those of Britain and the other destinations of Irish emigrants. The acid test of policy in Ireland is the extent to which people are enabled to secure there incomes that have been exogenously determined for 150 years. That, in turn, is determined in the medium and long term by the number of people at work. The impact of the Irish state's "borrowing for exports" policy on job creation is thus the acid test of its effectiveness.

There have been two blips in an otherwise unbroken decline since 1841 in the number of people at work in Ireland (twenty-six counties). The first was briefly in the 1930s, following the introduction of intensive protection. The second, slightly longer and greater, was in the 1970s. The number at work increased by almost 10 percent, from 1,055,000 in 1970 to a peak of 1,156,000 in 1980. The number at work, on an unchanged enumeration basis, has since declined to 1,083,000 in 1991. It would have reverted to the 1970 level but for various social employment and training schemes operated by the state agency FAS, which reduced these politically embarrassing unemployment figures by a further 20,000, to give a total which would otherwise have been 1,063,000.[65]

Table 9.3. Persons at Work in Ireland, 1960–1990 (in thousands)

	Agriculture	Manufacturing	Construction	Services	Total
1926	652	120	38	410	1220
1936	613	141	58	413	1225
1960	390	172	57	436	1055
1970	283	213	76	481	1055
1980	209	243	103	601	1156
1990	161	215	73	637	1086

Source: R. D. Crotty, *Maastricht: Time to Say No!* (Dublin: National Platform for Employment, Democracy and Neutrality, 1992), 5–6, Table 1.

Agricultural Jobs

Agriculture shed 230,000 jobs, or almost 60 percent of its workforce, between 1960 and 1990. Though in absolute numbers somewhat less than the decline of 260,000 in agricultural jobs from the state's first census in 1926 up to 1960, the *rate* of decline in the later period, at 3 percent annually, was twice as rapid as in the earlier period. This continued, not to say accelerated, decline in agricultural employment was not what most people had been led to expect from export promotion policies or from EEC membership and the much higher farm prices this brought in Ireland.

The composition of the agricultural job losses has also changed recently. The outflow, commencing in the mid-nineteenth century, which was a century earlier than in virtually any other country, was, until around 1970, principally of the non-landed, farm laborers, and relatives assisting on farms. Their number declined from around 380,000 in 1926 to 107,000 in 1970, or by over two-thirds. The number of farmers, on the other hand, declined by less than a third, from 272,000 to 182,000. Decline in both categories accelerated in the 1970s. But since then the number of farm laborers and relatives assisting has stabilized at around 60,000 while the number of farmers has continued to decline rapidly. Their number fell by 18,000, or 2.7 percent annually, between the census years 1981 and 1986 and has continued to do so.[66]

The accelerated loss of agricultural jobs in recent decades had causes that applied differently to the landed and the non-landed agricultural workforce. The accelerated GNP growth induced by government deficits created an exceptional demand for labor in the economy, as reflected by the very uncharacteristic 10 percent increase in total job numbers in the 1970s. The non-landed agricultural workforce, heirs to the medieval churl and the nineteenth century cottier and the lowest social class in the country, responded to the increased local demand for labor by quitting agriculture more rapidly. Their number, which had declined by 2.4 percent annually between 1926 and 1966, declined by 5.7 percent annually between then and 1981, when, as noted, it stabilized.

Push as well as pull factors probably operated on the non-land-owning agricultural workforce. Farm workers' wages increased almost twelvefold between 1960 and 1980. That was twice as rapid as the increase in farm gate prices over the same time. This gave an incentive to use some of the income, becoming more freely available to farmers through the operation of the EEC's Common Agricultural Policy, for more intensive substituting-substituting, capital formation. One manifestation of that process is that, in 1960, expenditure on fuel and on maintenance and depreciation of machinery, at £14 million, was slightly less than expenditure on farm workers' wages (which did not include payments made to the two-thirds of the non-landowning agricultural workforce who were relatives assisting). The former costs had risen to £516 million in 1990 when farm workers' wages were £146 million.[67] Furthermore, as explained more fully below, the operation of the EEC's Common Agricultural Policy (CAP) in Ireland favored increased pastoralism and seasonal production off grass, which is the lowest cost and most extensive-extensive type of farming.

The farmer lobby points to the accelerated decline in the number of farmers, or landed workforce, since the 1980s as evidence of the continuing poor incomes received by the majority of farmers. The opposite is closer to the truth. It is implausible that Irish farmers, with a record of holding on to their farms in difficult times, would abandon them in increasing numbers at a time of unprecedented agricultural prosperity, but which was also one of increasing unemployment when the alternative to farming was the dole queue or emigration. Bright city lights, whatever their impact on the non-landed agriculturists, were not responsible for the accelerating decline in the number of farmers. The problem was the increasing difficulty of becoming a farmer, which in turn was caused by Irish farming's exceptional prosperity. Irish agriculture prospered under the CAP on two scores. One was the high guaranteed prices paid for farm produce; the other was the manner of administration in Ireland of a CAP that was designed primarily for continental European agriculture.

A system of guaranteed prices designed for a crop-based continental agriculture has exceptional profit-making potential for Ireland's pastoral agriculture. Continental agriculture, which consists principally in converting harvested crops into livestock products, is characterized by fairly uniform, year-round output. Grass-based production is more seasonal but, being based on natural grass growth, is also much less costly. It is characterized by that succession of seasonal feasts and famines, gluts and scarcities which is also characteristic of steppe life and from which mankind largely escaped through the medium of individualist capitalism. Pastoralism replaced a crop-based agriculture in nineteenth century Ireland. This was so, notwithstanding the fact that production being seasonal, prices realized on the export market tended to be low. Producers attempted to counter seasonally low prices by producing out of season through such measures as supplementing seasonal pastoral dearth with crops and their by-products and by conserving grass. Nice judgment was required to determine the extent to which higher out-of-season prices warranted higher out-of-season production costs.

EEC intervention prices are available throughout the year, including periods of pastoral glut. Irish farmers responded to this opportunity by curtailing costly efforts to de-seasonalize production and concentrated instead on producing directly and most cheaply from pasture. The tillage area, which declined by 0.08 percent annually between 1901 and 1960, has since declined by 1.16 percent annually.[68] The long established trend towards pastoralism accelerated after 1972 and entry to the EEC.

Table 9.4. Proportions of Irish Agricultural Output: Cattle, Sheep, and Milk

Year	Cattle %	Sheep %	Milk %	Total %
1854	16.7	4.2	17.7	38.6
1926	23.1	4.9	23.5	51.5
1960	28.7	6.8	22.0	57.5
1972	32.5	4.0	23.7	60.2
1990	38.5	4.5	33.4	76.4

Sources: O'Grada, *Ireland Before and After the Famine*, 68; Industry and Commerce 1930; CSO 1976; CSO 1992.

Increasingly milk and cattle production has been concentrated into periods of seasonal glut. The coefficient of variation (c.v.) is the recognized, objective measure of variance or, in this case, of the month to month variation in the amount of milk delivered to creameries and of cattle to abattoirs. Table 9.5 shows that the seasonal variation in the supply of milk from Irish farms (0.5302) is almost five times greater and the seasonal variation in the supply of cattle (0.4118) is over four times greater than the overall EEC variations. The variation in the supply of milk or cattle is in no other EEC country half as great as in Ireland.

Table 9.5. Coefficients of Variation of Monthly Milk and Cattle Production

Country	Milk	Cattle
Belgium	.2055	.1095
Denmark	.0680	.0915
Germany	.0928	.1623
Greece	.1029	.0550
France	.1446	.0577
Ireland	.5302	.4118
Italy	.0843	.0607
Netherlands	.0834	.0979
Portugal	.1280	.1312
Spain	.1131	.0616
UK	.0868	.1861
EEC	.1103	.0962

Source: Eurostat, *Animal Production Quarterly Statistics*, No. 2 (Brussels: EEC, 1992).

The highly seasonal character of Irish pastoral production has meant that an exceptionally large proportion of it is sold into EEC intervention, for dumping ultimately in non-EEC markets. As a result, Irish agriculture, which accounts for 2 percent of EEC total production, absorbs 5 percent of the EEC Guarantee Funds which are used for buying up surpluses and dumping them in Third World countries.[69]

Pastoral production of a seasonal character is the simplest conceivable type of farming. Combined with high guaranteed prices, profitability is ensured through both high gross returns and low costs. Irish farmers were able to increase profits by shedding labor as their farming became increasingly pastoral and seasonal. One result of this is that output per person in agriculture in 1990 was 111 percent of the EEC average, although GNP per person in Ireland was only 62 percent of the EEC average in the same year.[70] A second result was the loss of farm jobs referred to above. A third result was exceptionally high farm profits. The gross margin, which includes both profit and returns to family labor, in Irish farming in 1990 was 41 percent of gross value added (GVA). It was 26 percent of GVA in the EEC as a whole. Only in Greece was the proportion higher, at 63 percent. But there the relatively high gross margin represents payment for the large amount of family labor used, with output per person only 40 percent of the EEC average, compared to Ireland's 111 percent.[71]

The exceptional profitability of Irish pastoral farming in the EEC, achieved partly through the rapid shedding of labor, attracted some of the money that a relaxed monetary regime made available. At the peak, in 1982, bank advances to farmers, at £1,008 million, were the equivalent of 93 percent of the value of net farm output that year. Bank advances had been the equivalent of 22 percent of output twenty years earlier.[72] The influx of credit fed the demand for farmland

and its price rose fivefold between 1950 and 1970, and tenfold between 1970 and 1977.[73] This was two and a half times the rate of inflation in the earlier period and four times the inflation rate in the later years.[74] Credit was not applied randomly; all agriculturists had not equal access to it. Generally it went to the most creditworthy, to those who had assets to offer as collateral. That is to say, credit went generally to large farmers, enabling them to become larger. They acquired, with credit, land that came on the market through the attrition of existing farmers, and, by adding pieces of land to their existing holdings, precluded others from acquiring those smaller holdings and becoming farmers on their own account. This process is reflected in the much higher cost now of servicing debt on large Irish farms than on smaller ones. Interest costs per hectare owned according to farm size in 1992 were: £2.87 on farms of 2–10 hectares; £16.28 on farms of 10–20 hectares; £36.45 on farms of 20–30 hectares; £38.13 on farms of 30–50 hectares; £52.87 on farms of 50–100 hectares; and £71.94 on farms over 100 hectares.[75]

The drive to pastoralism, which had dominated nineteenth century Irish society, had been slowed by various structural bottlenecks and immobilities. As a result, a degree of stability in the tillage acreage, cattle stocks and rural population had been achieved by the time of the state's formation. The operation of the CAP gave a fresh impetus to the drive towards pastoralism and rural depopulation. It also gave a new twist to rural depopulation.

Increasing relative profitability of cattle and sheep ruined the landless agricultural worker in nineteenth century Ireland. Those, however, who could acquire the price of a handful of sheep or cattle and pay a competitive rent, continued to have access to land as petty graziers and tillage farmers. The number of these who managed to cling to farming, as the only alternative to emigration, remained remarkably stable for more than a century following the Great Famine. But the CAP's operation, by greatly enlarging the barriers to entry to farming on a person's own account, has precipitated a rapid decline in the number of farmers, which previously had been a point of relative stability in a scene of otherwise rapid social disintegration. Those barriers to entry include a land price that today requires seventy-five days soldiering to pay for an acre, compared to one day in the Cromwellian era, and a battery of EEC land "extensification" and "set aside" regulations deliberately designed to reduce the number of people able to secure a livelihood in agriculture.

Manufacturing Jobs

The 1958 policies achieved an increase in manufacturing jobs of over 70,000, or 40 percent, between 1960 and the peak year, 1980. Manufacturing jobs subsequently declined to 215,000 in 1990, leaving a net gain of 43,000, or 25 percent over the thirty years, 1960–1990 (table 9.3).

All the manufacturing job increases were in foreign-owned firms. About 30,000 people worked in foreign-owned firms in 1960, which were then principally subsidiaries of British firms, producing for the still protected Irish market.

The number employed in foreign-owned manufacturing firms increased subsequently to a peak of 91,000 in 1981.[76]

Foreign owned manufacturing firms were attracted to Ireland, in the first instance, by the prospect of ready access to the UK market under the Anglo-Irish free trade agreement of 1965, and subsequently of access to the EEC market following Ireland's accession to that organization in 1973. They were additionally attracted by government grants, tax holidays, and low cost capital. Grants paid to manufacturing industry by the state organizations IDA and SFADCO doubled in real terms in the 1970s. Their cost amounted to £184.6 million, or 2 percent of GNP, in 1980.[77]

Corporate profits from manufacturing for export were for long tax free in Ireland. More recently they have been taxed at 10 percent, compared to a normal rate of 40–50 percent elsewhere. Foreign-owned, transnational firms, by practicing administered pricing and reporting small or zero profits on their upstream and downstream operations outside Ireland, could report all, or most, of the profit made from integrated, transnational operations as accruing in Ireland, where they were formerly tax-free and continue almost so. Because of double-taxation treaties between Ireland and the countries of origin of the foreign-owned firms, these profits remained untaxed when repatriated. Understandably, foreign firms operating in Ireland reported remarkably high profits (see table 9.6).

Table 9.6. Profitability of Irish Industry (profits before tax as a percent of sales)

	1984	1985	1986	1987	1988
Irish owned firms	2.1	2.0	2.4	3.1	3.9
Foreign owned firms	21.8	21.4	23.3	24.1	23.9

Source: Department of Industry & Commerce 1990, 38.

A large part of the reported profits of foreign firms were, no doubt, accounting profits that resulted from tax-avoiding transfer pricing. Nevertheless, the tax-avoiding possibilities were an important attraction of an Irish location. Thus, for example, the *Sunday Tribune*, (Dublin, January 12, 1986) reporting on the benefit of this arrangement for one of the largest foreign owned firms in Ireland stated:

> A saving of 143 million dollars has been made on Digital Equipment Corporation's tax-bill over the past four years as a result of locating in Ireland. . . . Last year alone the tax saving was $50.83 million and a similar amount was saved in the previous year. This makes Digital one of the most profitable companies in the country. It is, however, quite common for American companies to declare much of their profits in Ireland because of our nil tax rates on exports.

The *Sunday Press*, (Dublin, June 21, 1987) reported: "This Irish tax-free facility is immensely valuable to Cross and similar companies. Shareholders' funds amount to 103 million dollars, but the accumulated profits from Ireland indicate that half that sum originated in Ireland."

Foreign-owned firms locating in Ireland could borrow, locally and abroad, at favorable terms under so called "Section 84" legislation. A Section 84 loan derives its attraction to Irish resident companies from the fact that, for tax purposes, the interest paid on the loan is treated as a dividend and is therefore not taxed in the hands of the lender. Part of this benefit to the lender, which is typically a bank or other financial institution, is then passed to the borrower in the form of a reduced interest charge. The benefit to a company paying tax at 10 percent may be illustrated as follows:

	Ordinary Loan	Section 84 Loan
	IR£	IR£
Interest received by bank	100	57
Tax payable by bank	(50)	0
Stamp duty on S.84 loan	-	(7)
Bank's after-tax income	50	50
After-tax cost to borrowing company	90	57
Saving for borrowing company	33	

Source: Craig Gardiner Price Waterhouse, 1986, 36.

This reduction in the cost of borrowing secured by Section 84 loans was additional to the exceptionally low real interest rates that obtained in Ireland.

Continuous large public sector deficits, combined with a relaxed monetary stance, caused prices to rise rapidly in Ireland. Consumer prices rose by an average annual 5 percent in the 1960s and 14 percent in the 1970s, which was considerably faster than the EEC average or than in Britain, still Ireland's principal trading partner by far (see table 9.7).

Table 9.7. Average Price and Wage Inflation Rates, 1960s and 1970s: Percent

	Period	Ireland	EEC (12)	UK
Prices	1960s	5.1	3.8	3.9
	1970s	13.9	10.7	13.3
Wages	1960s	10.8	9.2	7.1
	1970s	18.1	14.3	16.0.
Real wage rate increase	1960–1980[1]	2.44	2.29	1.71

1. Wage inflation divided by price inflation
Source: EC, *European Economy*, No. 51 (Brussels: EEC, 1980), 204, 208.

Wages rose more rapidly than prices, by an average of 11 percent annually in the 1960s and by 18 percent annually in the 1970s. Over the twenty years, 1960–1980, they rose 2.44 times more rapidly than prices in Ireland, compared to an average of 2.29 times in the EEC and to 1.71 times in Britain (table 9.7).

Wage rates rose more rapidly in Ireland than export prices, which increased on average by 2 percent annually in the 1960s and 14 percent in the 1970s.[78] Only exporting firms with exceptionally high labor productivity or exceptionally lucrative markets could absorb indefinitely wages and other costs that rose more rapidly than the prices realized. Understandably there was much job attrition in the foreign-owned firms: "It appears that new foreign plants commonly experience rapid employment growth in the early years as they build up to the initial target size, followed by periods of slower growth, stagnation and eventual decline or closure."[79] For example, of 1810 jobs in 1973 in foreign owned electronics firms established in 1964 or earlier, only 807 remained in 1985.[80] However, a doubling of subsidies in real terms between 1972 and 1981, coupled with the other advantages of an Irish location, evidently offset the effects of rising wage and other costs so that the number of jobs in foreign-owned manufacturing firms increased during these years from 66,000 to 91,000.[81]

Employment in foreign-owned firms peaked at 91,000 in 1981 and thereafter declined to 85,000 in 1989.[82] Failure to attract sufficient new foreign firms to offset job attrition in existing ones was due, in part at least, to the inability of the state, under the straitened public finances of the 1980s, to maintain the level of subsidies given. The amount of subsidies, having doubled in real terms in the 1970s, was halved in the 1980s.[83] Further, as unemployment became a more pressing problem throughout the EEC, other countries sought to attract the footloose manufacturing firms that had been brought to Ireland by its exports support policy. They had the advantages over Ireland, where the state was now also strapped for cash, of larger domestic markets and a more central location. Additionally, all of them, including Britain by the end of this century when the Channel tunnel is completed, have, or will have, land links with the main EEC market. Ireland alone remains isolated from that market by "the most expensive stretch of water in the world."

Table 9.8. Labor Costs and Output in Irish Industry, 1989

	Average Wage per Person Engaged £000s/annum	Net Output per Person Engaged £000s/annum	Wage / Net Output percent
Irish Manufacturers			
Non-food	11.2	23.4	47.8
Food	11.2	30.7	24.1
Foreign Manufacturers	13.4	71.1	18.8

Source: CSO, *Census of Industrial Production* (Dublin: CSO, 1989).

Indigenous manufacturing companies had few, if any, opportunities for transfer pricing and therefore for the tax avoidance available to the transnational firms establishing in Ireland. They are much more labor intensive, especially those that are not engaged in the food industry.

The corollary of Ireland getting unimpeded entry, first to the UK and then to the EEC markets, was that its own market was opened to producers in the UK and the EEC. Its market was subsequently opened to producers further afield as the EEC sought more liberal worldwide trade and freed its trade in manufactured goods with Third World countries. These produced, for the most part, labor intensive, technologically less advanced goods which did not compete seriously with the products of the more technologically advanced EEC countries, but which did compete with the products of Ireland's less advanced, indigenous industry.

As costs rose and protection ended, large swaths of established manufacturing industry disappeared. Contrary to the somewhat facile predictions of academic theoreticians that, with increased competition on the home market, these industries would grasp the greater opportunities to export offered by free trade,[84] the firms involved, for the most part, simply ceased to exist. Foreign-owned, mainly British, firms that had subsidiaries manufacturing in Ireland for the protected market also ceased manufacturing and became simply warehouses, importing from the parent company. Irish owned manufacturing industry, which had increased employment from 120,000 at the state's first census in 1926, to a peak of around 170,000 in 1966,[85] thereafter declined and in 1990 employed no more than it did seventy years earlier. The decline would have been more severe but for an increase, between 1960 and 1990, in the number at work in the meat and dairy industries, from 13,000 to 17,500.[86] These industries had, however, become highly dependent on sales to EEC intervention by 1990.

The period 1960–1990 marked the onset of the post-industrial age in the more developed countries of the OECD. Industrial employment (defined as manufacturing, plus mining, plus public utilities) ceased to expand and declined in many countries. It reached a peak of some 37 percent of the workforce around 1970. Thereafter employment in the service sector became increasingly preponderant.[87] Irish experience was broadly in line, though industrial employment peaked later, around 1980, and at a lower level, 32 percent.

There were, however, two important differences between the Irish and the general OECD experience. First, the decline in Irish manufacturing jobs was the second such, the first having occurred in the latter half of the nineteenth century. Second, the recent decline in manufacturing jobs in Ireland was from a smaller peak than elsewhere. In the eight EEC countries—including Ireland—for which statistics of manufacturing jobs are available, their number peaked at 29,375,000 in 1970 when it was equivalent to 12.5 percent of the total population. At the peak of manufacturing employment in Ireland, at 231,000 in 1980, this was only 6.8 percent of the total population. Moreover, nearly half those in manufacturing in Ireland worked for foreign-owned firms producing overwhelmingly for export. This means that, at the peak of Irish industrialization, only about 4 percent of its total population was engaged in manufacturing goods primarily for domestic consumption, compared to over three times that proportion in other EEC countries, as well as in the United States and Japan.

Construction Jobs

Construction employment increased by 80 percent between 1960 and 1980, or twice the rate of increase in manufacturing and service employment (table 9.3). Much of the increased employment was in house-building where, in a few decades, major inroads were made into the shortfall in housing resulting from the virtual cessation of house-building in Ireland during the century prior to independence.

Demand conditions in Ireland peculiarly favored housing in these years. First, real incomes rose rapidly in the 1960s and 1970s, and demand for housing rose at least as rapidly as incomes. As people became better off, they spent a larger proportion of their greater incomes on housing. The 1987 Household Budget Survey reports that, while the poorer half of urban households spent on average 9.2 percent of total expenditure on housing, the wealthier half spent 10.3 percent.[88] Second, houses could not be imported and demand did not leak away into imports, as it did for manufactured goods. Finally, fiscal and monetary policy made house acquisition peculiarly attractive.

Average and especially marginal tax rates on salaries and wages are high in Ireland. Tax rates are high partly because of reliefs given for particular costs, including especially interest payments on home mortgages. This arrangement subsidizes house purchasing at the expense of taxpayers without house mortgages.

Table 9.9. Proportion of Homes Owner-Occupied in the 1980s

Country	%
Ireland	80
Spain	65
United Kingdom	62
Finland	61
Denmark	53
France	51
Austria	50
Norway	50
Netherlands	43
West Germany	42

Source: Private communication, Department of the Environment, January 24, 1990.

Real interest rates have been exceptionally low in Ireland until recently. Home mortgages that were incurred even at high nominal interest rates quickly declined in real terms as nominal incomes rose rapidly. This made the real cost of housing exceptionally low. While the all-items consumer price index, base 1968 = 100, rose to 709 in 1984, the housing cost component rose to only 421, which was the smallest increase among the ten components in the all-items index.[89] This position has been reversed since 1984, as state borrowing has been curtailed and real interest rates have risen, with housing costs rising more rapidly than any other.[90]

The low real cost of housing and the still lower real cost of mortgage interest, because of the tax relief on this, made home ownership particularly attractive in Ireland. Ireland consequently has the highest proportion of owner-occupied housing in western Europe.

House construction responded to these favorable demand conditions. The number of new houses built annually increased from 7,000 in 1961–1965 to 20,250 between 1970 and 1984 inclusive. It declined to 19,600 annually between 1985 and 1990, under less favorable demand conditions.[91] The expansion in house-building was a major factor in the increase in construction jobs from 57,000 in 1960 to 76,000 in 1970 and to the peak of 103,000 in 1980. The decline in house-building since the mid-1980s has, in turn, contributed to the reduction in construction jobs to 73,000 in 1990, or slightly less than the 1970 level.

Service Jobs

Service jobs include all those at work other than in agriculture, manufacturing, or construction, including the less than 1 percent normally employed in mining, quarrying, and peat production. The proportion of people at work in services increased from 34 percent in the 1926 census to 46 percent in 1970. An acceleration in the growth of service jobs between 1970 and 1983 contributed to the peak in the total number at work, which was reached in 1980 (table 9.3). That acceleration in service jobs was, in turn, largely attributable to the increase in jobs in state and semi-state bodies from 240,000 in 1970 to 325,000 in 1983.[92] The increase in public service employment was made possible by the greater state borrowing of the 1970s. The more straitened public finance conditions of the 1980s compelled the shedding of 42,000 public service jobs over the following decade and, as a result, there was little growth in service jobs from 1983 onwards.

The proportion of the workforce engaged in the service sector generally tends to increase with incomes. (This does not hold in the Third World, where much of the rapid growth of poor populations is concentrated in the "informal" service sector in urban areas, where they eke out a precarious existence.) Ireland, even after the shake-out in public service jobs, continues to have a larger proportion of service jobs than income levels would suggest. One contributing factor is a remarkable expansion in the number at work in banking and insurance. Only three of the ten EEC countries for which comparable data are available have a larger proportion of their service sector employment in these industries. While employment in these industries in the EEC grew by an un-weighted average of 31 percent in the period 1975–1985, it increased in Ireland by 79 percent, which was more rapidly than in any other country.

Table 9.10. Employees in Banking and Insurance in EEC Countries

	1975 (000s)	1985 (000s)	% Increase 1975/1985	B&I as % All Services
Belgium	188	237	26.1	11.6
Denmark	129	184	42.6	11.6
France	1189	1520	27.8	13.0
Germany	1146	1638	42.9	13.3
Greece	65	79	21.5	6.5
Ireland	38	68	78.9	13.0
Italy	391	619	58.3	7.4
Netherlands	321	485	51.1	15.1
Spain	383	391	2.1	9.2
United Kingdom	1462	1961	34.1	13.5

Sources: Eurostat, *Employment and Unemployment*, 1986; 1988,Tables II/12 and III.1

This rapid expansion owed much to activities related to securing the liberal grants, subsidies, and exemptions that the creation of debt allowed the state to make, or to avoiding the heavy taxation, necessitated in large measure by the state debt.

Jobs: Summary

The overall increase in the number at work between 1960 and 1990, though small by international standards, is not insignificant in Ireland, where the number at work now is about one-third as many as 150 years ago. The increase in jobs between 1960 and 1990 was greater than that in the last period of job growth, from 1,220,000 in 1926 to 1,225,000 in 1936. The significance, in both cases, was not the size of the increase, but that there was any increase in a situation of long term job decline. However, as the increase in jobs in the 1930s was an aberration that quickly disappeared with the exhaustion of the expedient of protection, the evidence suggests that the more recent increase in job numbers will also be temporary. Job numbers have already declined by 70,000 in the 1980s, which was a period of high worldwide unemployment and low emigration from Ireland, comparable to conditions in the 1930s, when there was an increase in jobs in Ireland.

A wedge of costs has been inserted between the price of labor to its supplier and its cost to its user by the policies of the post-1950s. Table 9.11 shows how this has been done.

The proportion of personal income and of consumption expenditure that the state takes in taxes says little about the impact on welfare and deterrence (column 1). If all the tax take were, for example, transferred back immediately as a poll grant, or poll tax in reverse, real incomes would be unaffected by high tax rates, apart from being made more equal. It is necessary also to consider state expenditure to assess the impact of fiscal policy on welfare and deterrence.

An extraordinarily high proportion of state revenue goes to service debt in

Ireland (column 3). This transfer to the rentier holders of debt is a straight loss to workers. Ireland has the highest dependency ratio in the OECD (see below). This implies that a large part of the tax take is preempted for welfare services. These, however commendable, absorb resources that might have been used to improve public services like medicine and transport for workers; or that workers might have kept to spend themselves.

Table 9.11. Making Low Income Irish Labor Expensive

	1 (%)	2 (%)	3 (%)	4 (%)	5
Belgium	42.1	4.0	26.4	17.7	66.0
Denmark	45.1	4.9	16.8	16.4	70.1
France	38.0	4.4	6.7	16.8	53.1
Germany, W.	34.5	3.1	9.9	12.7	50.8
Greece	34.2	2.7	3.2	33.0	53.9
Ireland	40.1	3.4	23.3	24.5	75.7
Italy	31.5	4.7	20.8	24.5	64.6
Luxembourg	33.1	10.5	1.0	14.9	41.6
Portugal	30.8	0.6	18.3	33.4	65.8
Spain	28.9	3.4	1.1	24.5	42.3
UK	28.6	9.0	11.5	13.6	46.9
Un-weighted averages	35.3	4.6	12.6	21.1	57.3

Sources: OECD 1989b; EEC 1989; IMF 1988
Col. 1: Tax revenue on personal incomes, goods and services, and social welfare contributions as a percent of GNP.
Col. 2: Tax revenue on property and corporate income as a percent of GNP.
Col. 3: Proportion of tax revenue required to service state debt.
Col. 4: Proportion of consumers' total expenditure on food.
Col. 5: An index of deterrence to labor.

Finally, as column 4 shows, Irish consumers spend an unusually high proportion of their smaller incomes on food, the cost of which the Common Agricultural Policy causes to be higher than necessary.

The state in these ways, either itself or through adherence to common EEC policies, depresses workers' real incomes. A rough indication of the extent to which it does so, or an "index of deterrence to labor" is given in column 5. This is the sum of columns 1 and 3 and half of column 4. Ireland, with a score of 75.7, is clear of the field, Denmark being next with a score of 70.1. That score takes no account of Ireland's low rate of taxation on property and corporate income (column 2) and its exceptionally high dependency ratio, both of which would place it still further ahead.

The Irish state can take a high proportion of workers' incomes and give workers a poor return in services. But it cannot determine workers' real incomes. These are determined by incomes in Britain and elsewhere and by workers' outward mobility. High taxes and poor services to workers in Ireland thus give rise either to high nominal wages which the users of labor must pay or to a reduction in the quantity and quality of labor available. The fiscal and other measures considered here are tantamount to a wedge of costs between the low incomes of the suppliers of labor and the much higher cost of that labor to users. This wedge of fiscal and policy costs between what the suppliers receive for their labor—and below which they remain idle or emigrate—and what users of that labor must pay for it has caused the wiping out of large swathes of indigenous traded manufacturing industry.

State borrowing, which in Ireland was undertaken on a scale that was unparalleled in amount and duration, was for the purpose of creating jobs. Yet Ireland's job-creating record for the period 1960–1990 was the poorest of the twenty-four countries comprising the OECD. (See table 9.12.) The number at work in Ireland increased by 6 percent compared to 39 percent for the OECD as a whole. Some 346,000 more people would have been at work in Ireland in 1990 had job numbers increased at the average OECD rate, which would have given virtually full employment and zero emigration.

Table 9.12. Labor Force Changes, OECD and Ireland, 1960–1990 (Base 1960=100)

	OECD	Ireland
Total population	131	125
Total labor force	143	117
Total at work	139	106
Agriculture	49	43
Industry	117	124
Services	206	154

Source: OECD, *Labor Force Statistics* 1962–1982; 1970–1990.

The slow growth in service jobs, the decline in manufacturing jobs after 1980 from a small base, and the slightly more rapid than normal decline in agricultural jobs resulted in Ireland's exceptionally small increase in total jobs. Because of the exceptionally slow growth in total jobs and notwithstanding an exceptionally small population increase, Ireland was one of only five OECD countries where the dependency ratio increased. (The dependency ratio is the total number of people per person working.) In the OECD as a whole that ratio declined from 2.38 in 1960 to 2.24 in 1990. In Ireland it increased from 2.58 to 3.13. It was higher in Ireland in 1990 than in any of the other 23 OECD countries. The comparable figure in 1926, at the state's first census, was 2.04.[93] While the dependency ratio has increased throughout the state's existence, that increase accelerated sharply after 1960, which was in direct contrast to the general OECD experience. The high and rising dependency ratio contributes to the wedge of costs between what the supplier receives and the user pays for labor.

Borrowing for Exports—The Winners

Post-1950s economic policy has re-created in the late twentieth century a phenomenon similar to that of the four remarkable successes of nineteenth century
Ireland. Capital formation was encouraged by IDA grants and by low cost Section 84 loans. But these were the tip of an iceberg of a policy structure whereby
the state made capital extraordinarily cheap at the cost of making labor dear. The
major, invisible part of the iceberg has been the state's monetary policy. Re-
trenchment was forced on the economy in the 1950s when the banks lost a substantial part of their external reserves. The state subsequently relaxed this foreign exchange constraint on bank lending by using borrowed funds to subsidize
exports and capital inflows, by restricting capital outflows, and, in the final
analysis, by borrowing abroad. With external reserves thus secured, the Irish
banking system could expand the money supply, while maintaining the exchange rate and currency convertibility under conditions of ever freer trade.

The Irish money supply was increased by an annual average 10.4 percent
between 1960 and 1970. Only France and Greece, of subsequent EEC members,
increased their money supply more rapidly.[94] Between 1963, when comparable
data become available, and 1970, the average annual increase in the money supply was 11.6 percent in Ireland and 10.6 percent in the EEC of ten (i.e., excluding Spain and Portugal). In the following twelve years (i.e., up to 1982 and the
advent to office of the second coalition government led by Dr. FitzGerald) the
Irish money supply was increased by an average annual 18.4 percent compared
to 14.0 percent for the EEC of twelve as a whole. Only Italy, Spain, and Greece
increased their money supply more rapidly.[95]

The fact that the Irish state raised money indirectly by selling bonds, rather
than directly by using the printing press like states in other former capitalist
colonies, had a number of consequences. Among these, more of the money was
saved. This was because the banks lent money only to creditworthy persons who
would maintain and add to the assets they already had by saving. Because the
increased money supply was not directed evenly, or randomly, over the population but towards savers, the value of the assets that savers prefer to have increased disproportionately. This was because, although trade in manufactured
goods was increasingly liberated, the purchase abroad of bonds and other capital
assets remained tightly circumscribed. Understandably then the price of bonds
and other claims to future income rose more than prices generally. While consumer prices rose fourteenfold between 1953 and 1990, prices of stocks and
shares on the Dublin stock exchange rose thirty-six times.[96] A similar situation
obtained with respect to agricultural land. Its price rose fifty-one times between
1950 and 1977, which was ten times more rapidly than the contemporary increase in farm product prices.[97] The buoyancy in farmland prices also owed
something to the abolition of local government taxes, which had been based on
real property.

Disproportionately high bond and capital asset prices implied low real interest rates, i.e., interest rates which, net of inflation, were low. Average real

interest rates in Ireland and other relevant countries over the period 1956–1985 were as in table 9.13.

Table 9.13. Average Real Interest Rates, 1956–1985

	%
Ireland	0.7
USA	1.8
UK	1.4
West Germany	3.9

Source: J. Fitzgerald, "The National Debt and Economic Policy in the Medium Term," *Policy Research Series,* No. 7 (Dublin: Economic and Social Research Institute, 1986), 11.

(These low interest rates were not, and are not, inconsistent with extremely high interest rates charged to the property-less and non-creditworthy masses on borrowing for consumption purposes.)

Ireland, uniquely among former capitalist colonies, thus combined a liberal money supply, free trade, currency convertibility, and low interest rates. It was able to do this by its unique capacity, among former capitalist colonies, in the first instance to borrow from its predominantly middle class citizens and then to use these borrowed funds to subsidize exports, for which it had unique access to metropolitan markets, and by its capacity subsequently to borrow abroad, on the basis of its rapidly growing, subsidized exports.

The state simultaneously made land free and extraordinarily valuable to its privileged possessors. It did so by combining with a relaxed monetary stance, the abolition of remaining land taxes and the securing of high prices for Irish agricultural produce, through the Anglo-Irish Free Trade Agreement with the UK and entry to the EEC. The cost of making land both valuable and free to its possessors and capital cheap was to make labor dear to its users. Labor was made dear by unnecessarily high food costs; by inflation induced by monetary expansion, combined with a fixed exchange rate and exchange controls; and by taxes to service the debt that made the entire process possible in the first place.

State monetary and fiscal policy reinforced the traditional capitalist colonial condition of cheap capital. It also reinforced a characteristic which, since the mid-nineteenth century, has been distinctive of Ireland among capitalist colonies: relatively high cost labor. In both respects, therefore, policy gave a new impetus to the traditional capitalist colonial process of substituting capital for labor. That process was exemplified in the nineteenth century by the substitution of cattle and sheep for people on the land, without any increase in agricultural output. More recently it has been profitable to substitute capital made cheap by policy for labor made dear by policy, without expanding total output, in those Irish industries which, for one reason or another, are only slightly, if at all, subject to international competition. In the process, job numbers in the industries concerned have collapsed and a handful of individuals have been made grotesquely wealthy, in a manner analogous to the creation of the four remarkable successes that coexisted with the otherwise pervasive socioeconomic decay of nineteenth century Ireland. The industries in question include banking, cement and building aggregates, newspapers, packing paper, processing agricultural produce for EEC intervention buying, and retailing. Individuals in these industries, simply by using capital made cheap by policy to replace labor made dear by policy, have made large fortunes without in the process adding anything to the quantity or quality of the total product.

Redundancy payments figured largely in the consolidation process. Financed with cheap capital, these made it attractive for workers to surrender well paid jobs without resisting unduly through industrial unrest. The profits of substituting capital for labor were thus shared by employers and the existing workforce. The losers were the outsider persons for whom in future there would be fewer jobs.

Limits to the replacement of dear labor by cheap capital were soon reached in a small domestic market that grew slowly, if at all. When those limits were reached by the take-over and amalgamation of all or most of the businesses in their field of operation, the entrepreneurs involved sought further expansion by acquiring foreign subsidiaries. The acquisition of foreign subsidiaries had particular attractions for Irish monopolies and conglomerates.

First, foreign assets with given earnings were of greater capital value to Irish than to foreign buyers, because of capital's low cost in Ireland. Second, investment in Irish firms that were profiting by amalgamations and the subsequent substitution of capital for labor and that were also actively acquiring foreign subsidiaries, provided a backdoor for Irish investors who were otherwise prevented by exchange and other controls from acquiring foreign assets. The demand for the shares of these companies was particularly strong and their price/earnings ratio accordingly high. That reduced still further the cost of capital to these firms, making the acquisition of foreign assets still more profitable. Third, Irish firms with foreign subsidiaries can reduce their total tax liabilities. They can do so by attributing to their foreign subsidiaries as much as possible of the firms' total overhead costs, thereby reducing the profits reported by the foreign subsidiaries, which are liable for taxation on these in the countries of operation; and they can ascribe instead more of the profits to their Irish operations, on which they paid no taxes until recently and now pay very little. Expansion through foreign acquisitions thus secured the tax advantages, without the production disadvantages, of an Irish location.

It is understandable therefore that, relative to their market value, Irish firms spend more on foreign acquisitions than those of any other country—14 percent compared to 6 percent for Britain, the next highest—and that 90 percent of acquisitions by value made by Irish firms in recent years were outside Ireland.[98] The Telesis report, *A Review of Industrial Policy*, commented on this in 1982: "Most of the largest and strongest companies are investing abroad in businesses only minimally related to Irish employment and exports. From the national point of view, this cannot be the best use of the managerial, financial and organiza-

tional capabilities of these companies."[99] The process has been taken much farther since Telesis, especially by firms in the food industry. The cost of these
foreign acquisitions accounted for part of the near £2 billion that Irish firms and
individuals have invested abroad annually since 1989. That foreign investment
is equivalent to nearly 12 percent of current national income and to half of current national savings.[100]

Borrowing for Exports—The Cost of Exporting

The outstanding achievement of thirty-five years of "outward looking" economic policy has been the expansion of exports. These increased tenfold in volume between 1960 and 1990. They increased in value from 23 percent to 62
percent of current GNP.[101] They increased more rapidly than exports from virtually every other country. However, even the greatest achievement can be a mis-
take if the cost is too great. Irish export expansion has been achieved at the cost
of an extraordinary degree of import dependence.

The Irish state has practiced two principal forms of economic intervention:
intensive protection in the 1930s and 1940s, and intensive export stimulation
since the late 1950s. The ability to replace imports with protected home products
had nothing to do with efficiency of production; it had all to do with the measures taken by the state to curtail imports. A much better perspective on the effect
of protection on economic efficiency is derived from the performance of exports
which, unlike production for the home market, had to compete on foreign markets. The volume of these exports declined by 24 percent between 1928, prior to
the introduction of protection, and 1952,[102] when, with both home and export
markets stagnating, protection was abandoned.

Ireland's remarkable export performance likewise has little to do with economic efficiency, but everything to do with the state's ability to borrow to
stimulate manufactured exports with grants, tax holidays, and cheap capital and
with its readiness to subordinate national sovereignty to the common policies of
the EEC in order to secure access to that body's high priced, guaranteed agricultural markets. The dependence of foreign-owned, exporting Irish manufacturing
industry on state subventions has been demonstrated repeatedly by the removal
from Ireland of those industries when the subventions have ceased to outweigh
the disadvantages inherent in an Irish industrial location. The growth of Irish
agricultural exports has been linked to the EEC's willingness to buy these at
high prices and subsequently to dump them at high cost in non-EEC countries.

The growth of imports is a better indicator of economic efficiency than the
growth of exports under "outward looking policies," just as the reduction in exports was a better indicator of economic efficiency than the reduction in imports
under protection in the 1930s and 1940s. The country's increased dependence on
imports is shown in table 9.14. Virtually all manufactured goods consumed in
Ireland now are imported. The only exceptions are products of peculiarly Irish
interest, like newspapers; or products like mineral waters and building aggregates that are very bulky relative to their value; or very perishable products like

bread.

Table 9.14. Non-Food Imports as a Proportion of Consumption, 1960, 1990

	Gross Output (£M)	Exports (£M)	Imports (£M)	Consumption (£M)	Cols.3/4 (%)
1960	434.2	59.2	188.3	563.3	33
1990	14,028.3	11,476.7	12,472.4	15,024.0	83

Source: CSO, *Review of Industrial Performance* (Dublin: CSO, 1990)
Note: Consumption = Gross output - exports + imports.

The continued ability to pay for manufactured goods that can no longer be produced competitively depends on manufactured exports, which the state can no longer stimulate with borrowed funds, and on agricultural exports which the EEC, under a reformed Common Agricultural Policy, is now actively discouraging. Meanwhile indigenous Irish exports, like pigs, poultry, eggs, stout, and whiskey, having been handicapped by protection in the 1930s, have never since expanded like similar enterprises in other countries. The share of Irish exports in these markets has dropped sharply since the 1930s.

The outward looking policy of subsidizing exports with borrowed funds was an expedient which, under Irish circumstances, could last longer than the earlier policy of protection. It had, on the other hand, a particular defect from which protection was free. As an island, Ireland has a natural protection which a protection policy complements. But an outward looking policy of subsidizing exports diverts resources from production for the home market into production for foreign ones, adding to the cost of goods consumed or invested in Ireland, the cost of shipping abroad the exports needed to pay for the imports which must then be shipped into Ireland, in both cases over "the most expensive stretch of water in the world."

Part 3:   An Assessment and Prognosis For the Irish Case

The Essential Continuity

A central theme of this work is that independence is sought and obtained in capitalist colonies only when the metropolitan-created, local elite has been sufficiently strengthened and the colonized mass sufficiently debilitated to ensure the perpetuation of a socioeconomic system that created the local elite in the first instance. In this sense, nationalism can be said to be the final phase of national destruction.

The Irish state which came into existence in 1922 was concerned, above all else, to uphold the existing socioeconomic framework, "to maintain law and order." The changes it contemplated were cosmetic only. This was so although Ireland had been more thoroughly capitalist colonized than anywhere else, so that its population expanded and contracted precisely in line with external market demand throughout the two centuries preceding independence. A commitment to minimalist government obtained, although independence, in important ways, exacerbated the underlying weaknesses of the Irish situation. This was because of the cessation of the transfers from the British core to the Irish periphery; the cessation of the pressures for political reform which Irish emigrants had previously exerted on UK governments; and the insulation through partition of the pastoral, Catholic south from the constructive tensions of the more industrialized, Protestant north. It is unsurprising therefore that the process of economic undevelopment, or retrogression, persisted in the post-independence era as it had under capitalist colonialism.

The 1920s dissipated the nationalist illusion that the transfer of the seat of government from London to Dublin would transform Irish life. Successive governments thereafter sought to effect change through a series of expedients: protection, deficit financing for welfare purposes, and deficit financing for export promotion. Each of these brought immediate gain to some, though at long term cost to the nation as a whole. Government, during seven decades of independence, was, in a sense, a replay of seven centuries of foreign rule.

The Normans, on the frontier of central western European individualist capitalism, built walled towns for their protection. Some of "the mere Irish" congregated outside the walls of these towns and outside the scope of Norman law. These Irishtowns, located for the most part in less salubrious areas and distinct from the Hightowns built within the walls, persist in most Irish cities and towns of medieval origin. With the Tudor conquest and the end of the frontier, means other than town walls were introduced to preserve the privileges of the colonizers and to enforce the disabilities of the colonized in order to maintain the dichotomy of Irish society into Hightowners and Irishtowners. The land of the clans was appropriated and bestowed on those who, in fee simple, undertook to uphold the law and implement the policy of the metropole; and titles to the land were protected by the colonial administration. The recusant Catholic Irish were excluded by the Penal Laws, of which the "declared object was to reduce the Catholics of Ireland to a miserable populace, without property, without estimation, without education. . . . They divided the nation into two distinct bodies, without common interest, sympathy or connection, one of which bodies was to possess all the franchise, all the property, all the education. The others were to be drawers of water and cutters of turf for them."[103]

The Penal Laws, like the Norman walls, in time too ceased to be the means of dichotomizing the Irish into privileged and disinherited. This was when a new form of property, in cattle and sheep, materialized in the nineteenth century. The owners of these livestock were for the most part Catholics, and they, with their co-religionists in the professional and commercial classes, now joined the privileged elements within the walls. But this access to privilege merely excluded the outsiders more firmly. As flocks and herds expanded, more and more of "the mere Irish" were forced from the land.

The series of expedients implemented by successive Irish governments has not fundamentally changed the structure of capitalist colonial privilege and disability that first found expression in the town walls that divided the colonizing Hightowners from the colonized Irishtowners. A handful of magnates have been made grotesquely wealthy; a minority of farmers have also grown extraordinarily rich; and some 400,000 trade unionists enjoy working conditions comparable to those in Britain. At one stage it even seemed as if the old walls had gone and that the Irish had been rid of their colonial disabilities. That was during the 1970s when there was not only full employment, but work also for many returning emigrants as Ireland, for the first time since the seventeenth century, experienced net immigration. But, as Winston Churchill remarked in another context, "as the tide of World War receded, the bleak spires of the Fermanagh chapels appeared again out of the mist,"[104] so too when the state's credit was exhausted by the end of the 1970s, the walls separating insiders from outsiders reappeared out of the miasma of the state's borrowed prosperity, only now they were enlarged and reinforced by massive debt.

Still outside the walls are the landless. They are now more firmly excluded from access to land, by high land prices and by quotas and "set-aside" provisions that are designed to maximize the profits of those who own land, than at any time since the confiscation of the clans' lands. Outside the walls too are those who cannot get employment, because a substantial part of their earnings is preempted in taxes to pay the rentier holders of state debt, which is the latter-day equivalent of the rent charged to the expropriated nation for the land's use. Because capital has been made cheap by making labor dear, outside the walls too are a substantial proportion of the 600,000 workers who are not in trade unions and the nature of whose work precludes collective action to get better terms. Also outside the walls are those who do not own their own homes and for whom housing costs, which for a favored generation rose less than other costs, now rise more rapidly than any other. Outside the walls too are the half-million Catholics resident in a north of Ireland statelet where their job prospects and housing conditions are systematically inferior to those of the Protestant majority, and whose young men and boys are more frequently questioned and arrested, by police and soldiers, than Protestants. Seventy years of independence have not removed the walls created by the colonizers to segregate the privileged from the disinherited. That more have been admitted within the walls over the centuries has made it possible to exclude more firmly those who are outside.

Given an Irish state committed to preserving the privileges, with their associated disabilities, of colonial rule and given a state with all its major offices located within a mile of Dublin Castle, the heart of colonial rule in Ireland, it is understandable that the main socioeconomic consequences of its seventy years rule should be remarkably similar to those of the preceding seventy years of capitalist colonialism. Trends in emigration, incomes and jobs changed little in the period 1920–1990 from what they were in 1850–1920.

Because population continued to decline over the later period, there were

fewer births and fewer potential emigrants. But the number of emigrants continued to be around 45 percent of births.[105] Incomes continued to rise at 1.6 percent
annually in the later period, as they did in the earlier. This was so although there
was a marked quickening in the mean rate of income growth in the rest of
Europe, from 1.1 percent annually in the earlier period to 2.1 percent in the later.
British incomes, however, which had been among the fastest growing in Europe
in the earlier period, accelerated less than other European incomes in the later
period, with the result that Irish incomes continued to increase more rapidly than
British incomes throughout the entire period.[106] (This long-term approach of
Irish incomes towards the higher British incomes has had important consequences for Irish emigration, the bulk of which has always been to Britain—a
point considered below.)

The number of people at work in Ireland declined by only 11 percent between 1926 and 1991, compared to 39 percent between 1851 and 1926.[107] But
this deceleration in job losses owed much to trends within agriculture that were
independent of government policy. The difficulties of increasing cattle stocks as
the tillage acreage declined, in pre-mechanized-silage-making days were noted
above. Those difficulties caused cattle stocks, which increased by 70 percent
between 1851 and 1911, to increase by only 9 percent over the following 40
years.[108] Because of the close negative correlation between people and cattle
numbers, the slower growth of cattle stocks contributed to the slower decline in
the number of people at work. In more recent years, with mechanized silage
making, increasing cattle stocks, and an associated decline in the agricultural
population, the overall decline in job numbers has been contained through the
expedient of public sector borrowing, which, however, has serious long-term
consequences for job numbers.

More stable cattle stocks up to 1951 and the expedient of state borrowing in
more recent decades would seem to account for most, if not all, of the slow-
down in the rate of job losses during the seventy years of independence compared to the preceding seventy years. But the Irish state, in its seventy years existence, has not rectified the failure of the economy to provide livelihoods for its
people; nor has it slowed the rate of emigration or quickened the growth of incomes. It has not demolished the walls built by the colonizers to dichotomize
Irish society into the privileged and the disinherited.

Responsibility

The highly deterministic character of this assessment of capitalist colonialism
narrows the area of individual and social responsibility. Societies that have been
capitalist colonized undevelop; those that have not, develop. Yet even in this
highly deterministic context, individuals and societies have some freedom of
choice. Other choices might have resulted in a less infelicitous outcome.

The baneful effects on Ireland of capitalist colonialism, at least down to
1922, are clearly attributable to Britain, the colonial power. Insofar as an inescapable heritage accompanied independence, Britain might also be held respon-

sible for Ireland's continuing undevelopment in the postcolonial era. Yet Ireland's location and the character of its indigenous society forced Britain, in the modern era of European expansion westwards, to colonize the island. To have left it uncolonized would have invited the competing Spanish, French, Dutch, or Germans to occupy it as a base for attack on Britain's western flank. As a capitalist colonized society, Ireland fared no worse or better than 140 other similarly circumstanced societies, apart from the fact that it was colonized longer and more thoroughly. Britain, on the other hand, profited little from an Irish connection that cost it dear, from the loss of Tudor wealth in the bogs and woods of sixteenth century Ireland to the £3 billion a year that retention of Northern Ireland within the UK now costs mainland Britain. Conditions for Britain over the past 500 years would have been easier had there been no pastoral, tribal Ireland on its western flank.

It can be said in mitigation of those who have directed Irish affairs since independence that, while Ireland's socioeconomic performance has lagged greatly behind that of other west European countries, its performance was no poorer than that of any of the other 140 former capitalist colonies, which between them contain half the world's population. Countries that performed better than Ireland were not capitalist colonized.

Yet those who, in pursuit of independence and the political power that gave them, agreed to the island's partition and to the abandonment of half a million Catholics to the sectarian Protestant Northern Ireland statelet, and who accepted the loss of transfer payments to the Irish grassroots from the British core, did have a moral responsibility to ensure, notwithstanding Burkean admonitions, that the results of their government would warrant those costs. The initiators and implementers of protection in the 1930s and 1940s, notwithstanding the peculiar unsuitability of that policy for Ireland, cannot escape responsibility for the enduring damage done by protection to indigenous exporting industries. Those who initiated and those who condoned sustained state borrowing in excess of GNP growth did so notwithstanding the warnings of Mr. Micawber and a thousand others of the consequences of sustained consumption in excess of production and in disregard of the entire history of individualist capitalism; they cannot escape responsibility for that.

Again, it might be said of those responsible for these policies through seventy years of independence, as of similarly positioned persons in the other former capitalist colonies, that had they not done as they did, others would have and with similar consequences. In that case, however, responsibility for the ineffective government of the former capitalist colony would have accrued to those others and not to the persons who did govern. It can be said of the latter that their desire to lead outweighed concern for where they led the nations. None of those who have led the peoples of the former capitalist colonies since independence was conscripted into presiding over their peoples' continued capitalist colonial undevelopment. All of them could have quit when they saw the results of misgovernment.

A Prognosis

Nothing in the Third World scene suggests that the process of capitalist colonial undevelopment will halt or be reversed. The poor populations of these countries seem destined to continue to expand, with ever more people experiencing ever worse poverty. This prognosis is reinforced by continued, increasing, Western intervention. Western people, rich in material wealth, acquire, along with their wealth, a sense of guilt, a need to intervene and to donate to the poor of the Third World which is as impelling as was that of their forebears of five centuries ago to intervene in order to confiscate the wealth of those countries. That need is catered for by a vast, sophisticated, rapidly expanding Third World aid industry, ranging from the World Bank at one extreme to the humblest, local non-governmental organization at the other. This industry, with an identity and interests of its own, provides for those engaged in it lucrative and well regarded careers in a Western world where careers become increasingly scarce.

The West's intervention now is through, or under the license of, the elites who govern the Third World. Its intervention therefore cannot undermine the elites' position, but must generally sustain it. This it does particularly by actions that reduce death rates and that therefore increase the size, poverty, and impotence of the Third World's population.

Though in Ireland, seventy years after independence, no one explicitly echoes the despairing observation of the head of the civil service made after thirty-five years of independence, similar sentiments underline public policy. Policy is directed primarily towards completing the transfer of the sovereignty won in 1922 to the EEC, which Ireland joined in 1972. Adherence by the political establishment to that policy was exemplified by the public appearance together, in 1992 in front of the Irish house of parliament, of the leaders of the four principal political parties to urge the people to vote for acceptance of the Maastricht Treaty in an imminent referendum. Those four parties secured 88 percent of the votes and won 90 percent of the seats in parliament in a subsequent general election. This readiness to surrender a sovereignty that has failed to realize popular expectations is echoed widely in the Third World, where people frequently yearn for the order and stability of colonial times.

Conceivably Irish sovereignty will be fully absorbed in time into a federal Europe which, if it materializes, seems likely to include also the countries of eastern and southeastern Europe, in what General de Gaulle once referred to as "a vast thingamajig." Conceivably too, Irish national identity may be lost in a larger European identity, as it never was in a British empire that spanned a major part of the globe. A separate Irish people, with its distinctive character and history, would in that event cease to exist, as very many other peoples have in the past. The world would be the poorer for the loss of an element of that heterogeneity which has been a main source of strength and wealth to Europe especially. It is more likely, however, that the offer of Irish sovereignty in return for continued monetary subventions to the elected representatives of the Irish people will be rejected by the EEC, as would an offer by Third World countries of reincorporation into new empires be unacceptable to the former capitalist colonial powers. A distinctive Irish polity seems destined to continue for the foreseeable future.

There are major internal inconsistencies in the continued undevelopment of Ireland which do not apply to the other former capitalist colonies comprising the Third World. Those inconsistencies arise in the first instance from Ireland's dual status as neighbor and colony, and, arising from that, the fact that Irish undevelopment takes the form of fewer people securing a livelihood at increasing incomes. That process, continued over 150 years, within an imposed, essentially unchanged institutional framework, has created, first, an Irish society with tastes and aspirations that it can not afford—that are beyond the capacity of its structurally unreformed capitalist colonial economy to satisfy. Second, it has seriously impaired the free working of the safety valve of emigration, which, for almost two centuries, has drained Ireland of social and political discontent and reconciled much that was otherwise irreconcilable. Finally, it has created in Northern Ireland a situation verging on civil war.

As acceptable standards have risen across the board with real incomes, the capacity of an unreformed, un-restructured, socioeconomic system to attain those standards has been impaired as a result of the expedients pursued through seventy years of independence. The conflict inherent in rising incomes and expectations, on the one hand, and the inability of an unreformed, un-restructured socioeconomic system to meet those expectations, on the other, has traditionally been resolved in Ireland by the emigration of almost half those born there. This conflict-resolving mechanism has ceased to operate as effectively as formerly.

Emigration has been reduced, on both the pull and push sides. First, with Irish incomes rising more rapidly than British incomes for 150 years, the disparity between those incomes is now much less, and the attraction of Britain, which has always been the main destination of Irish emigrants, has much declined. Second, the conditions which, for nearly two centuries, created a virtually limitless external demand, in Britain and the settler colonies, for Ireland's Caucasian labor, have terminated. There is now, in these countries an unprecedentedly high and growing incidence of unemployment. The frontier has disappeared in the New World. High incomes, which generate large savings, supply abundant capital which, with modern, computerized technology, readily replaces high cost labor. The capitalist colonies are no longer a captive market, while the noncapitalist-colonized Five Tigers of east Asia, in a reversal of roles, are now exporting to the West the unemployment that the West formerly exported to the colonies. The New World countries have reinforced the deterrent of an oversupply of labor with immigration restrictions.

On the push side, 150 years of 1.6 percent annual real income increases means that Irish incomes are now some eleven times higher than they were at the commencement of massive emigration. Not only have average incomes increased manifold, but, in line with the across-the-board raising of acceptable standards in public affairs, income disparities have, to an extent, narrowed. In particular, the incomes of those most likely to emigrate, the unemployed, have risen more than proportionately. The 50,000 unemployed in 1965 received on average that year £116, which was 32 percent of GNP per head.[109] The 219,000 who were unemployed in 1990 received on average £3,224, which was 49 percent of GNP per head.[110] The pressure on Ireland's surplus, unemployed people to leave has thus been much reduced at the same time as the opportunities abroad for them to do so have also declined. The escape valve of emigration, which has been the dominant feature of Irish life for 150 years, has, in this way, ceased to operate as freely and effectively as formerly. The Irishtowners, outside the system, no longer depart as readily, but congregate outside the walls in a swelling, unemployed mass. The number of persons registered as unemployed and drawing unemployment benefit/assistance, which previously fluctuated around fifty to sixty thousand, has, since 1970, increased fairly steadily to 300,000, or 20 percent of the workforce, in 1993.

This 300,000 may represent a new, equilibrium unemployment level. The pressures it generates may be sufficient to force enough people to emigrate so as to prevent any further rise in unemployment. That eventuality is the more likely because of a recent sharp decline in the Irish birthrate. That rate, having been reduced to one of the lowest in the world by the socioeconomic conditions that obtained in post-famine Ireland, remained around 22 per 1000 for a century or more. It then dropped from 21.5 per 1000 in the intercensal period 1979–1981 and to 14.6 per 1000 in 1992. The natural population increase, which was boosted to around 1 percent annually by the accelerated death rate decline after the Second World war, has, as a result of the recent birthrate fall, reverted to the long term rate of around 0.6 percent annually.[111]

However, while the reduced natural population increase will tend to reduce also the number entering the workforce, that tendency is likely to be offset by a counter one. This is a probable increase in the number of females entering the workforce. Women account for 30.9 percent of the Irish workforce, compared to 38.5 percent of the total EEC workforce. Only in Spain do women account for a lower proportion of the workforce than in Ireland.[112] It is to be expected, especially in light of the declining birthrate, that many more Irish women will seek to enter the workforce. Ireland's long-term labor surplus is therefore likely to continue in the future, though unrelieved by the freely flowing emigration of the past.

Given a continued, though smaller, natural increase in population but more women seeking to enter the labor force, and given no increase in total jobs, either unemployment must continue to rise or emigration must remove the excess labor supply. Given also a reduced external demand for Irish labor and reduced domestic pressure on the unemployed to leave, the character of Irish emigration will probably change. Unemployed Irish persons receiving over 50 percent of an average GNP/head that moves closer to that of the emigrant's country of destination will continue to be reluctant to emigrate to a situation where they will probably remain unemployed, with little income increase. On the other hand, skilled persons, in an over-supplied Irish labor market, paying high taxes, necessitated in part by the need to pay unemployment benefit/assistance to 20 percent or more of the workforce, are likely to leave. These people will continue to find work abroad, designing, making, and operating the automated capital equipment that replaces unskilled labor.

The character of Irish emigration, in response to the reduced pull and push, is thus likely to change in two respects. First, a greater pressure of numbers of unemployed persons will be required to force out sufficient emigrants to achieve equilibrium between a continuing excess supply and a continuing inadequate domestic demand for labor. Second, the people leaving are increasingly likely to be the more skilled, who are able to secure employment abroad, rather than, as heretofore, a cross-section of the oncoming population. In other words, Irish emigration is likely to acquire increasingly the character of the brain drain that exists from the Third World. Walsh reports on this as follows: "Whereas in the past most emigrants came from subsistence farming, unskilled and unemployed backgrounds, now the rate of emigration is highest among third-level graduates. Even within the third-level sector, the more highly qualified people are, the more likely they are to leave, with emigration rates of up to 30 percent being recorded in the 1980s for people with higher degrees."[113]

A less freely working emigration safety valve is likely therefore to cause unemployment to remain higher than heretofore and to filter out the more skilled, rather than a cross-section of the workforce. The economy's capacity to meet rising expectations engendered by continuously rising, exogenously determined incomes will thus be further impaired by the greater cost of the permanently expanded pool of unemployment and by the loss, through continuing emigration, of the most skilled and adaptable. These conditions have already generated unwonted political pressures, which have been reflected especially in the defeat of the government in every general election since 1969, when emigration declined under the impact of Whitakerism. These political pressures for change in the twenty-six counties are complemented by no less powerful pressures for change in the six counties that comprise Northern Ireland.

Northern Ireland

The planted, armed, Protestant garrison in Ulster had, from the beginning, a higher socioeconomic status than the disarmed Catholics of Ulster, whose land they appropriated, as well as the Catholics of the rest of the island. That privileged status resulted in greater economic growth in the eighteenth and nineteenth centuries and in higher incomes, especially for the Protestant majority, in northeastern Ireland. The Protestants of Northern Ireland wished to maintain the British connection, which had created and preserved their privileged minority status in a predominantly Catholic and hostile island. Accordingly six northeastern counties remained within the United Kingdom when the other twenty-six counties seceded in 1921.

Southern politicians, in their haste to secure independence, concurred in the island's partition. This generated considerably less opposition than the Oath of Allegiance to the British monarch, which was the core issue in the civil war that followed the signing of the Anglo-Irish Treaty of 1921.[114] The Oath of Allegiance threatened to circumscribe the new rulers' sovereignty whereas partition merely limited sovereignty to twenty-six out of thirty-two counties. Partition did involve the abandonment by the island's Catholic majority of their half million co-religionists resident in the six counties to the new, Protestant statelet established by the majority in that part of the island. That abandonment was the more readily acceptable because of the general perception of the temporary character of the partition. Southern nationalists believed that the six counties could not long survive as an entity and would soon agree to join the south. Northern unionists, for their part, discounted the ability of the southern nationalists to rule and expected them soon to seek reintegration into the United Kingdom. Both political entities have proved more durable than expected.

The economy of the new Northern Ireland statelet, which benefited from enhanced transfers from the British core, continued, after independence and partition, to expand more rapidly than the south's. Its population, which had ceased to decline by 1901, continued to grow while the south's continued to decline for a further sixty years. The north's share of the island's population, which had been 20 percent in 1841, had increased to 28 percent by 1901 and to 34 percent in 1961. Notwithstanding the disabilities imposed on them, the number of Catholics there increased by 18 percent between 1926 and 1961 while the south's Catholic population declined by 3 percent over the same period.

The better economic performance of Northern Ireland heightened rather than ameliorated political tensions. It heightened Protestant awareness of being a minority group in an island with an economically unsuccessful and seemingly hostile Catholic majority, which was manifested by the 55 percent reduction in the south's non-Catholic population between 1911 and 1961.[115] It was expressed in frequent official and non-official criticisms of partition, which seemed to gain in stridency in proportion as the south's economy faltered. The north's better economic performance raised the living standards of its disfavored Catholics more than those in the south and that caused Catholic numbers to increase in the north while they declined in the south. But improving living standards do not ensure political harmony. They sharpened Catholic perceptions of their continuing disabilities, which included a disproportionately smaller share of better jobs, disproportionately higher unemployment, poorer public housing, and the more frequent arrests and interrogation by the security forces of young Catholic men.[116] Moreover, rising living standards enhanced Catholic capacity, though higher education standards, increased articulateness and better political organization, to struggle against remaining disabilities.

Rising Catholic living standards were, of course, part of the broader economic development of the West. Integral to that economic development was increased democratization and the amelioration of harshness in public affairs, of which the abolition of the death penalty and the improved conditions in Irish (twenty-six county) jails were aspects. These conditions obtained in Britain as much as elsewhere, and by proxy in the north of Ireland, over which Britain had ultimate control. There has been, therefore, in Northern Ireland in the twentieth century no Cromwell who, 300 years earlier, purportedly massacred the population of Drogheda in order to impress upon the rest of Ireland the futility and danger of resistance. Thus, as living standards rise, perceptions of, and resistance to, outstanding disabilities increase; but readiness to suppress that resistance diminishes. Disability, under these circumstances, gives rise to strife that is directly proportionate to the level of incomes and indirectly proportionate to the scale of the disability.

There is no present prospect of Catholic disability disappearing in the north of Ireland, any more than of the barriers between Hightowners and Irishtowners disappearing in the rest of Ireland. The number getting a livelihood in the island of Ireland continues its 150 year decline, while the island's unemployed has reached a record 400,000, or 20 percent of the workforce. Northern Protestants can be expected, under the circumstances, to struggle to retain their privileged access to jobs, while northern Catholics will struggle to secure equal access to the declining job opportunities. Both Protestants and Catholics now resist absorption into an Irish Republic that is burdened with a massive state debt and that has an economy structurally weakened by the expedients of import discouragement in the 1930s and 1940s and of export encouragement in the 1960s, 1970s, and 1980s.

Ireland, reflecting its dual status of neighbor and colony, is itself split in two. The conflict inherent in rising incomes co-existing with an imposed, defective socioeconomic system which dichotomizes society into privileged Hightowners and disfavored Irishtowners, and into privileged Protestants and disfavored Catholics, heightens in both parts of the island. As the resulting pressures mount in both parts, there is a prospect of change which did not exist when the safety valve of emigration operated more freely in the south and when police suppression was more brutally effective in the north. One possible means of channeling the social pressures that are building up in Ireland, north and south, towards constructive change is considered in chapter 10.

Chapter 10

From Undevelopment to Development

We have been seeking to understand the causes of the undevelopment of nations. This ugly new word—"undevelopment"—has been introduced deliberately to differentiate under-developed countries, the nations whose states of socioeconomic development are simply relatively less advanced than those of the First World, from those nations of the world which experience absolute socioeconomic retrogression and which, given existing institutions, can be expected to continue to retrogress, or undevelop, indefinitely.

The emphasis has been placed not so much on the question of why some nations seem not to have developed, as on the other side of that coin: why have some—specifically Europe and its settler colonies—have been so phenomenally successful? The overriding importance of individualist capitalism and of the elaborate network of social institutions which, over millennia, co-evolved with it, have been emphasized throughout as being the engines of European success. The devastating effect of individualist capitalism, when it is imposed by external force, rather than cultivated internally, is proposed here as being the underlying cause of undevelopment.

The purpose here is to stimulate a re-examination of the problems and causes of undevelopment in the light of the insights and hypotheses presented. It is hoped that, on the basis of these ideas, further work that might more effectively trigger some form of sustainable reversal of the process of undevelopment might be undertaken.

Capitalist colonialism sets loose, out of context, forces of individualism which, once loosed, cannot be re-constrained. Specifically, it introduces the concept and institutions of individual property into societies that had previously been nonindividualist. Simultaneously, it introduces influences that reduce death rates below their long term equation with biologically determined birthrates, leading on the one hand to population growth and, on the other, to a degree of impoverishment that did not exist when higher death rates maintained homeostasis at higher nutritional levels.

Capital, in capitalist colonies from the beginning, has been provided either by the metropoles or by the local elites, unlike in the heartland of central western Europe, where it was supplied by the mass of small savers/investors. Because of its source, capital in the capitalist colonies has therefore been at all times much more competitive with labor than it has traditionally been in the West. The more competitive character of capital and the poverty of the masses in the capitalist colonies has meant that the use of capital there has been principally either to replace labor or, in conjunction with land, to produce for export. Capital, in either case, impoverishes the capitalist colonized nations, in the one case by replacing their labor and in the other by diverting their land from the nation's support to production for export.

The capitalist colonized peoples undevelop unceasingly because their masses, unlike those in developed countries who were the source of all developmental change, are debilitated by the excess of births over deaths which condemns them to deepening, swelling poverty. The process, which derives its momentum from the tendency of poor people to have biological birthrates, is reinforced by continued, western intervention that has the effect of holding death rates down. Under these circumstances an equilibrium may be achieved in the long term by a countervailing increase in death rates, forced up by a degree of poverty and immiseration that would have been inconceivable before the forces of individualism were set loose by capitalist colonialism.

The combination of the paradox of property, which leads to the inefficient use of natural resources, with investment that replaces labor or appropriates land for production for export, with death rates that are substantially below birthrates that tend to their biological limit offers little prospect of change in the established pattern of Third World capitalist colonial undevelopment.

It has been argued throughout this work that the forces that caused half the world's population to develop and the other half to undevelop have, for the most part, been outside human control. They were the forces that directed the evolution of life itself—the same forces that led to the early build up of human technical and social skills through the eons prior to the last Ice Age and, after that, to the discoveries of crop growing and animal husbandry. The subsequent development of lactose tolerance, the migrations of Indo-European pastoralists, the emergence of early European capitalist modes of agriculture, and the histories of societies that sprang from these processes are all part of the same interaction between geographically determined production capabilities and human innovation and adaptive response.

All of the responses discussed here and thousands of other critical tiny innovations were made by individuals who, for the most part, are unrecorded in history. And rightly so; for had they not innovated, given the conditions that obtained, others would surely have done so. There was no Plan in this, no Grand Design; simply the efforts of millions upon millions of individuals, over tens of thousands of years, groping more or less blindly towards something better, something lighter, warmer, more nutritious or whatever.

The result—at least today's state of affairs—is a situation in which one half of the world is embarked on a process of apparently permanent development: more people at any point in time better off than formerly and fewer worse off than before. The challenge that persists is the other half of the world: the half that appears to be engaged in a process of permanent undevelopment, with more people worse off than formerly, or fewer better off than before.

The initiative contemplated in the following pages is unprecedented; it can therefore be guided only by reason, informed by an inevitably imperfect understanding of the circumstances involved. Like Columbus at the opening of the era of capitalist colonialism, who sought a route to the East by sailing westwards, and who was guided in sailing into uncharted waters solely by the dawning appreciation of the global nature of the earth, those who would change undevelopment into development must rely on reason, guided by one or two key perceptions gleaned from existing knowledge.

One of the key perceptions, it has been argued here throughout, is that the source of undevelopment of nations was the imposition, out of context, through capitalist colonialism, of inappropriate institutions, basic laws, and technologies. Another key is recognition of the character of the capitalist colonial state, which retains those impositions in place, in favor of a local elite. Unlike states that emanate from within nations and are nation-states, capitalist colonial states are an extension of superimposed colonial administrations and are the enemies of the nations they govern.

These considerations suggest that the first step in transforming capitalist colonial undevelopment into development is to deprive the state, which is the enemy of the nation, of its control of the nation's resources, which has been its means of perpetuating capitalist colonial undevelopment. A second critical step towards transforming undevelopment into development is the recognition and effective implementation of the nation's title to these resources. The manner in which these two steps may be taken will vary from nation to nation according to the particular legacy bequeathed by the colonial powers.

It is at this point that the two strands of the discussion which parted after chapter 5 are re-united. The body of the book in chapters 6 and 7 discussed the history and impact of capitalist colonialism in the 140 or so countries which are conventionally described as comprising the Third World. Chapters 8 and 9 followed the same themes in much greater depth in a case study of the Irish experience. The aim in this approach is to draw out the features of Irish political and socioeconomic history which place the Irish people convincingly amongst the undeveloped nations of the world.

The first part of chapter 10 thus suggests a series of actions which the Irish people might take in order to re-gain control of their national resources; the second part of the chapter discusses the effects on factor prices; and the third section examines some of the wider results that might be expected to follow. The actions proposed are all perceived as being entirely consistent with the theory of the market economy; their thrust is towards the development of institutions that will align factor prices in a way that will ensure that Ireland's national resources are deployed to the maximum effective benefit of all the Irish people, rather than

to the exclusive benefit of the elite few who, in their control of the machinery of
the state, inherited and perpetuate the capitalist colonialist exploitation of Ireland, its people and their resources.

It is for others, in other countries and in the development industry, with
greater knowledge of the particular circumstances faced by other nations of the
Third World, to consider these suggestions and hopefully, to develop their own
appropriate versions of this model. The first and general objective must be the
re-alignment of factor prices towards the generation of a social dividend. The
mechanisms employed and the purposes to which the social dividend might be
put will, of necessity, be specific to the individual nation. However, given the
enormous obstacle to development presented by uncontrolled population
growth, this must take high priority.

Ireland—An Opportunity to Break the Mold

Though people are what they are because of forces over which they have had
little control, neither are they atoms enslaved to immutable laws of physics or
biology. Irish people, after 150 years of rising incomes, are no longer dominated
exclusively by physiological needs. They are freer than they have ever been to
contemplate their circumstances. They are free to recognize the existence of bad
order and to contemplate the origin and causes of it. They are free to contemplate the possibility of transforming bad into good order.

Ireland's national resources are the common heritage of all Irish people;
they are not attributable to the efforts of any individual or group. They include,
most especially, the nation's land and its money supply. That land, which was
valueless and produced no income when the first people arrived in Ireland a
mere 10,000 or so years ago, now has great value, as reflected in the £9.4 million paid recently for four acres located in the Ballsbridge suburb of Dublin or,
at the other end of the scale, the £1,500 an acre which Irish farmers pay on average for farmland.[1] These values are attributable to all the people who have lived
in Ireland since its original habitation and to all the actions outside Ireland
which have created the modern milieu in which Irish land has value. Those land
values are a major part of the national heritage.

Second only to land, in a modern market-dominated economy, is the nation's money supply, which has always been an attribute of sovereignty; monarchs have ever been jealous of their sovereign right to issue money and have
made forgery a capital offence. Beyond land and money, there is a range of
other resources which rightly belong to none, but to all, of which the natural
environment is probably the most important example.

The first step, it is suggested, in transforming capitalist colonial undevelopment into development is to deprive the state, which is the enemy of the nation, of its control of these resources, which has been its means of perpetuating
capitalist colonial undevelopment. The second critical step towards transforming
undevelopment into development is the recognition and effective implementa-

tion of the nation's title to these resources.

It is suggested that the nation's economic resources, in a democratic society, are most appropriately distributed equally to all resident citizens, as its political power is through universal adult suffrage. The means of effecting that distribution could be a national dividend, or citizen's income, or any other preferred title for the equal, unconditional, distribution of national resources to all resident citizens.

The collection on behalf of the nation and the distribution to the nation of the nation's resources would clearly necessitate an administrative organization. That administration would be the nucleus of a state reconstituted to serve the nation's needs, and hence a nation-state. There could be no objection in principle to further expansion of the role of a nation-state established to collect and distribute to the nation its resources. Expansion of the role of a reconstituted state, beyond collecting and distributing to citizens national resources, would imply a democratic choice to expend national resources collectively rather than individually. Conceptually the nation could decide to expend all its resources collectively, or redistribute all for individual expenditure, or opt for an intermediate position. The available options are illustrated diagrammatically in figure 10.1.

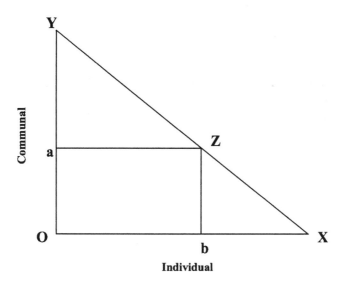

Figure 10.1. Society's Resource Allocation Choices

At one, collective, extreme, the nation would opt for a national administration, or state, to expend all its resources, OY, collectively on behalf of its citizens. At the opposite, individual, and anarchic extreme, the nation would opt to distribute all national resources, other than those required for collection and distribution, to its citizens for individual expenditure, OX. Citizens are likely, in practice, to opt for some intermediate position, such as Z, where Oa resources would be expended collectively and Ob individually. The nation's will on the matter could be ascertained by a "preferendum" procedure facilitated by computerized voting.

It is to be expected that the majority of citizens with less than average incomes would opt for the distribution of a large portion of the nation's resources for individual expenditure. On the other hand, the minority, with above average incomes and therefore less need for further cash income, would prefer to have more resources retained for a collective expenditure that would enhance those conditions that enables them to earn above average incomes.

To the question "how much are the nation's resources?" possibly the most sensible reply at this stage is "a lot." Any resources left in the control of a state that is the enemy of the nation and perpetuates undevelopment are excessive. They are the armory which enables the state to undevelop the nation for the benefit of an elite. They could be alternatively a treasure throve for the nation's enrichment and empowerment. The transfer of control from the state to the nation ought not to be delayed or impeded in order to make fine estimates of the amounts involved. This is especially so as any estimate is likely to be an underestimate because of the dynamic consequences of effecting the transfer. The transfer would set free productive capacities that now, because of inappropriate institutions and basic laws, are precluded from contributing to the national wealth. In Ireland's case they include that half of the nation's population which normally emigrates permanently, and the one-fifth of its workforce that is now unemployed.

For purposes of discussion and to indicate the broad order of the magnitudes involved, the following "guesstimates" of the nation's annual resources are offered:

	£M.
1. Irish State's exchequer revenue, 1992	9,806
2. Annual value of farmland	1,422
3. Annual value of urban land	3,367
4. Annual value of the money supply	2,083
5. Miscellaneous	1,668

Notes:

1. See Central Bank, *Annual Report* (Dublin: Stationery Office, 1992), Table D4.

2. The country has 14.077 million acres of farmland.[2] The average competitive rent, or conacre, paid by farmers in 1992 was £101 per acre.[3] Competitive rents are the annual value of land.

3. One quarter of other land, or approximately 500,000 acres, is assumed to be urban, and worth on average £100,000 an acre, or 66 times the value of farmland. The estimated corresponding annual value of urban land is £101 x 66, or £6,733 per acre; or £3,367 million in total.

4. The total money supply on 31 December 1992 was £20,834 million, having increased by an average annual 7.5 percent during the preceding decade.[4] An appropriate level of taxation on the money supply would prevent the financial system from usurping, and misusing, in the manner described above, the nation's prerogative of creating money.

A suggested appropriate average annual rate of taxation on the money supply is 2.5 percent, with more being levied on small and less on large amounts. Some such rate of taxation would be sufficient to make it unprofitable for the financial institutions to increase the money supply while at the same time being insufficient to induce depositors to incur the inconvenience and exchange rate risk of depositing their money outside the jurisdiction. The state could then proceed to increase the money supply annually by 7.5 percent without inducing greater inflation than that of the decade 1982–1992. These amounts, equivalent to 10 percent of the present money supply, sum to £2,083 million.

5. These are miscellaneous additional revenues, taken as 10 percent of the foregoing, which an administration, concerned to recover all the national wealth for the nation, might levy. The envisaged taxes would all seek to maximize revenue. They would embrace such items as (a) taxes on polluters, including noise polluters, in accordance with the principal that the polluter pays; (b) taxes on advertising to discourage producers from spending resources on convincing consumers of the merit of their products, other than through lower prices or higher quality and to make the media more dependent on, and accountable to, the public and less so to advertisers; (c) taxes on vendors of public transport and alcoholic liquor that are sufficiently high to ensure that all persons of good standing, with adequate facilities and willing to pay the appropriate tax, could provide these services; (d) scaled excise and/or VAT taxes to ensure that economies of scale are captured for the national benefit and are not siphoned off in monopoly profits.

The above are resources which accrue to the nation of Ireland because of its location off the coast of the longest developed, most fully developed and wealthiest region of the world, because of the extent and fertility of its land, and because of the quality of its people. None of this wealth is attributable to any individual or group of individuals. It would exist whether any individual or group of individuals ceased to exist in Ireland, because of either their death or emigration. Their place would be quickly and automatically filled by others. This national wealth is the equivalent of £5,200 per annum per person resident in Ireland (Republic) at the last, 1991 census. It is equivalent to £7,260 per annum per person registered as Dail (parliament) electors in that year.

The appropriation of that large share of GNP that properly accrues to national resources and its distribution by way of a national dividend to resident citizens implies a repudiation of the individualism which never worked in a socially beneficial manner in Ireland or other capitalist colonies and which, after millennia of successful operation in the metropolitan West, is there also now encountering increasing problems of a fundamental character. It implies the restoration, in a basic sense, of that ordering of society which obtained in pre-conquest Ireland and, indeed, throughout the pre-Columbian, non-European world. That is that people, because of their existence and membership of a society, had a right, strong or weak, effective or ineffective, to a share in the produce of the resources controlled by that society. It implies a rejection of the individualist view that "thou shalt earn thine bread by the sweat of thine brow," with its implicit threat to the individual of no bread without sweat.

The procedure suggested by no means abstracts from the monumental changes that have occurred in Ireland and throughout the world in the post-Columbian era. Rather it poses for the people of Ireland and other former capitalist colonies the possibility of a new approach, a fresh start towards coping with those changes, which include particularly the vast accumulation of capital, technological progress, and the ever closer integration of the world's economy. While, on the one hand, there are now, as there were 500 years ago in pre-Tudor Ireland, resources which clearly belonged to the clans then and which now belong to the nation, there are also now, thanks to the progress of 500 years of individualist capitalism, opportunities opened to individuals which did not exist then. The ability of the individual to add to his own or society's wealth was tightly circumscribed in the past. Total wealth was determined overwhelmingly by the extent and quality of the natural resources available to the society and by the state of the art. Now, thanks to the vast accumulation of capital and to technological progress, especially in relation to populations which, in one half of the world, have virtually ceased to expand, land no longer is a limiting factor and individuals have an unprecedented capacity to generate wealth, over and above the wealth that accrues to society as a whole.

More than one course is available to an Irish nation, freed of its heritage of capitalist colonialism, which would enable its citizens to avail of the opportunities opened by the global accumulation of capital and by technological progress. The course with which it is most familiar is market-led, individualist capitalism, which failed in Ireland because it operated within an institutional and legal framework that was imposed and inappropriate. There is no reason, however, why, with a different, appropriate institutional and legal framework, market-led, individualist capitalism cannot operate as successfully in Ireland as it has wherever it operated within an evolved, non-imposed, institutional and legal framework, viz. in the metropolitan West and in the settler colonies. The autocratic capitalism of Russia, first under the czars and later under the commissars, offers another model for an Ireland freed from the heritage of capitalist colonialism to exploit the enormous potential of modern capitalism and modern technology. The Japanese-Korean-Taiwanese blend of autocracy-cum-market determination offers a third model. China, now that it has rid itself of the intellectual imperialism of Marxism, appears to be successfully pioneering yet another route to development with the help of modern capital and technology. The point is not that any one of these models, or any combination of them, or any other ordering of society is the appropriate way for a nation to exploit the possibilities of modern capitalism and technology. The point rather is that there is more than one way of doing it.

However, the remainder of this section is concerned to delineate how the transfer of control of national resources from a state to the nation by means of a national dividend might affect Irish society and the Irish economy within the existing individualist capitalist, but decolonized, socioeconomic institutional and legal framework.

The Effect on Factor Prices

Capitalist colonialism ruins nations by making land free for its appropriators and capital cheap for its elites by raising the cost of labor. Ridding the former capitalist colonies of their heritage involves, above all, ridding them of the institutional mechanism by which this ordering of factor prices is achieved. This section considers the effect on the relative costs of labor, land and capital of distributing national resources recovered from the state, the nation's enemy, as a national dividend.

Labor Cost

The supply of Irish labor has been peculiarly elastic. Below a certain income, determined by current real incomes in the countries to which the Irish emigrate, labor leaves and ceases to be available in Ireland. A national dividend paid unconditionally to resident citizens (taken here and subsequently as those residents on the register of Dail electors) could increase substantially the real income of workers. A national dividend, which could be over £100 per week, would be equivalent to around 40 percent of the average gross earnings of all Irish industrial workers in 1991. It would also be approximately double the rate of unemployment assistance. An immediate effect of receipt of a national dividend would be to make its recipients more reluctant to leave Ireland. Fewer emigrants would imply a larger supply of labor and a tendency to depress wages. Many workers, rather than emigrating, would be likely to accept a lower wage which, together with the national dividend, would still leave them better off than formerly.

One fifth of the Irish workforce is now unemployed. A person receiving long term unemployment assistance got £57.20 in 1992, with additions for dependants. A single person forwent £20.70 of this assistance by working any time, and all of it by working twenty-four or more hours a week. This represented an effective tax of £2.38 per hour on the potential earnings of a single, unemployed person and much more on the earnings of a married person with dependants. Payment of a national dividend in excess of the rate of unemployment assistance would give an unemployed person, as well as a higher cash income, freedom to undertake socially useful and valuable work, without forgoing income, as an unemployed person does now when he/she works and loses unemployment assistance. Similar considerations would apply to other persons receiving means-tested social welfare, including widows and non-contributory-old age pensioners. All these would benefit by the excess cash value of the national dividend over their present means-tested social welfare receipts; and they would further benefit by being left free to undertake socially useful and valuable work, without losing any part of a national dividend paid unconditionally to all resident citizens. Some of these people, it can be safely assumed, would undertake work for less reward than is now necessary to compensate for the effort involved and the loss of means-tested welfare benefits.

A national dividend would, in these ways, increase the supply and lower the cost of labor in Ireland. It would do so while simultaneously raising the incomes of those supplying the labor at current rates of labor input, with any higher level of input representing a superior choice and greater welfare. Because workers' incomes would be increased, the quality of the labor supplied would also increase, if for no other reason than that fewer skilled workers, who now mostly emigrate, would do so in future. That is to say, a national dividend would increase the supply, raise the quality, and reduce the cost of labor.

The Cost of Land

Land would be taxed at the rate of its current value in its most productive legal use. Assuming that the average tax on farmland was £100/acre and that the national dividend was £100/week, an individual holder of fifty average acres would receive as much in national dividend as he/she would pay in land tax. A couple would receive as much in national dividend as they would pay in tax on 100 acres. Many present owners of land, especially occupiers of larger farms, are likely to find that the land is of less value to them than the land tax and so will relinquish their occupancy. Persons who are now unemployed and who are precluded from renting land on conacre because of the loss of means-tested welfare benefits will be free to take over the occupancy of this land. This will cause land which, because of the paradox of property, now yields a net return below its conacre/annual value, to be used more productively.

A revenue-maximizing tax on urban land would similarly secure the more productive use of this land, which probably represents two-thirds by value of all Irish land. Land that is now unproductively used, because of the paradox of property, or because it is held in anticipation of future capital appreciation, would be released and available to those willing and able to pay a tax equal to the land's annual value. This freed urban land would be a resource for the larger supply of better quality labor to work on in order to meet the demands for the whole range of non-agricultural goods and services of a nation enriched by a national dividend.

A land tax that raises the cost of land to users while reducing the cost of, and increasing the returns to, labor will cause land to be used more productively for two reasons. First, because those less competent to use it, and so unable to pay the tax, will be forced to surrender land to those who are more competent and able to pay the tax. Second, because at a given level of competence, with a given quantity of land, it will be profitable to use more labor that is both cheaper and better.

These are precisely the results which basic economic theory suggests follow from changing the cost of factors of production: raising its cost to users will cause land to be used more productively; lowering the cost of labor to users will cause more of it to be used on the more costly land.

Capital

The economic heritage of capitalist colonialism is that it makes labor costly to its users in order to make land free and capital cheap to the privileged. Removing the heritage of capitalist colonialism involves reducing the cost of labor to its users while increasing its return to its suppliers, which can be done by raising the cost of land and capital to users. A revenue maximizing tax, which would recover for the nation its annual value, is the appropriate way to proceed in the case of land. A revenue maximizing tax on deposits with the financial institutions, coupled with the ending of government grants and tax holidays on profits, is the way to proceed to recover for the nation its sovereign control of the money supply. These measures will procure for the nation resources which, via a national dividend, can reduce the cost of labor while simultaneously raising the returns to it. It will also increase the cost of capital, giving a trade off between lower labor and higher capital costs.

In the past, capital made cheap by making labor dear has made both capital and labor idle. Dear labor can no longer be profitably employed except in highly capital-intensive operations. Less capital intensive and more labor intensive farms, factories, workshops, public utilities, offices, and shops go out of production, leaving idle both the capital and labor they employed. There are inadequate savings available to employ all the labor made costly by policy and there is an inadequate market to absorb profitably the produce of the capital-intensive, labor-extensive production facilities.

Labor made cheap to its users by making capital dear will cause both more labor and more capital to be employed. Existing plant can be brought back into use, employing more of the labor which will be available and which will be of higher quality, because of the higher incomes of those supplying it. For example, hospital wards that have been closed because the operating authorities can no longer afford to pay the high cost labor required for their servicing could be brought back into use with lower cost labor, providing a needed service with resources that already exist.

Making labor cheaper as a result of making capital dearer will cause more labor to be employed and cause some existing capital that is now idle to be brought back into production, and other capital that is now used to be used more intensively. So much for the existing stock; but what of the future supply of capital? A preliminary point needs to be made before addressing that issue.

The overwhelming importance of capital formation has been fully recognized and emphasized here. Scarcely less emphasis has been given to the complexity and variability of the process of economic development that was triggered by the introduction of the new factor, individualist capital. That complexity and heterogeneity of circumstances certainly leaves scope for the possibility of development, under particular circumstances, in the absence of capital formation. Thus, economic development could stem from a simultaneous reduction in birth and death rates, so that fewer people were born but lived longer, healthier, and therefore better lives. Economic development might, and normally does, come from technological improvement, so that when a car, tractor, computer, or other piece of equipment is amortized and replaced by a new model of similar cost but involving no addition to the capital stock, it will generally be technically more advanced and have a greater output. Higher output and economic development might come, in the absence of capital formation, through the more efficient management of land, which would not necessarily require any additional capital; or—of particular relevance to Ireland—it might come from the fuller use of available labor, only half of which has ever been used there.

The link between capital formation and economic growth has been especially tenuous in Ireland. The rapid growth of the economy during the sixty year reign of George III involved very little capital formation. Output was increased by the extension, without capital, of the potato acreage. Nineteenth century capital formation in Ireland was principally in livestock. While this increased profits, it tended to reduce agricultural output and GNP. Likewise in more recent times, there has been little correlation between public sector borrowing and GNP growth. Indigenous private sector investment, as noted, has been largely concerned with establishing monopolies, while producing no more, no better, or cheaper products but doing so with less labor, for which there has been no alternative use.

For these reasons, the impact of the proposed measures on future capital formation should not be a primary concern. Much more important than the quantity of capital that will be available will be its productivity. Excess rather than inadequate saving has for long been characteristic of the Irish economy. Those excess savings, implying lower demand and lower output, in the nineteenth century were shipped to England, where they helped to finance British industry to compete with Ireland's declining cottage industry. Now they are transferred abroad in part by "most of the largest and strongest Irish companies which are investing abroad in businesses only minimally related to Irish employment and exports."[5] More are transferred abroad by the financial institutions. These private capital transfers are equivalent annually to around 8 percent of GNP.[6]

The proposed reforms will cause the existing, and any future, stock of capital to be used more productively. It will do so partly because labor of a given quality will be available at lower cost. But under the regime suggested, capital will also be used more efficiently for the same reason as a land tax will cause land to be used more efficiently. That is, the market value of productive assets will be reduced and proprietorial titles will provide less insulation against market forces. Only proprietors responsive to those forces will retain title and remain in control of the assets. If simultaneously the incomes of the assets' operators (i.e., management and workers) are increased, they will be better able to acquire the assets and thereafter to manage them more efficiently than non-executive directors representing shareholders and financial institutions.

Three aspects of the proposed regime would tend to raise the cost of savings, reduce the return to capital, and so discourage capital formation. First, increases in the nation's money supply would no longer be directed by the financial institutions selectively to savers. They would instead be directed through a national dividend equally to consumers and savers alike; more funds would be consumed and less saved. Second, the funds now used as capital grants to industry would be similarly distributed. Finally, it is unlikely, under the proposed regime, that tax holidays would continue to be available on the profits from capital-intensive manufacturing.

Other considerations, however, point to the likelihood of increased capital formation. First, the overwhelmingly important determinant of total savings is the level of GNP. The proposed changes, by bringing idle resources into production and by making resources now working more productive, would cause a marked increase in GNP. That in turn, through the economies of scale captured by the Verdoorn Law[7] would induce further GNP expansion. While it is probable that, under the circumstances envisaged, a higher proportion than now would be consumed and correspondingly less saved, it is hardly conceivable that all the incremental GNP would be consumed and none saved. Almost certainly, therefore, there would be more savings available for capital formation.

Second, Ireland, like other capitalist colonies, has normally had a surplus of savings, which were attracted to the metropoles to finance the development of secondary and tertiary economic sectors there. Investment opportunities, other than for export, or to improve the links between the metropole and the colony, or to replace labor, have been limited in the capitalist colonies because of poor domestic demand. That has generally been because of low incomes, aggravated in Ireland's case by emigration. Local savings have been inadequate in the capitalist colonies only when the state has intervened, itself to invest or to subsidize investment by others, as the Irish state has done notably since the 1950s. Under the envisaged circumstances of higher incomes and zero net emigration, inadequate domestic demand would no longer be a deterrent to investment. Further, with abundant, high quality, low cost labor available, a good return on capital formation, involving the use of this labor to expand output to meet a growing domestic demand, would make investment more profitable than it has normally been in undeveloping capitalist colonies. The envisaged reforms would, to summaries, end the competitive relationship of capital with labor, which is normal in capitalist colonial situations, and replace it with the complementary capital/labor relationship that was the norm, in the past, in individualist capitalist, central western Europe.

Other Effects

Irish society, like society in other capitalist colonies, has been dominated by the market in a manner, and to a degree, that is scarcely conceivable by noncapitalist colonized societies. Irish society, seventy years after independence, continues to be ill-served by the market, because of the manner in which the state rigs factor prices and because of the emphasis given by government policy to exporting at the expense of production for the home market. It is understandable that most former capitalist colonies, including Ireland to an extent under the protectionism of the 1930s and 1940s, have at various stages turned their backs on a market system that has served them so poorly. Most of them, to a greater or less degree, have resorted to command economics, with central state planning attempting to control economic activity. Invariably these efforts have led to results even worse than those secured by the market in capitalist colonized countries.

The market is the most effective means of organizing economies that have progressed beyond the most primitive subsistence stage. That market forces have yielded wretched results in capitalist colonized countries is not the fault of the market, but of the conditions under which people resort to the market. Stripped of resources, especially of the land on which their economies have been based, capitalist colonized peoples have gone to the market with only their labor to offer. As Karl Marx pointed out, thus naked, they could not escape without getting "a tanning" from the market.

There is in Ireland a particularly strong case for preferring the market to any alternative, command system of economic organization. That is, the determination of Irish incomes by income levels in the countries to which Irish labor emigrates. This factor made protection peculiarly inappropriate in Ireland. The emphasis here, therefore, is not on replacing the market, but on changing the conditions under which the nation resorts to it, to ensure that the nation no longer does so, stripped by its enemy the state of the resources that rightly belong to it. That can be achieved most effectively by some form of national dividend which would cause the prices of labor, land, and capital to reflect more closely politico-economic realities rather than as now, the consequences of a centuries old conquest.

One fairly predictable consequence of restoring its resources to the nation and the change in relative factor prices that would ensue is that relatively fewer resources would be used for producing for foreign markets, which are costly to access, and more would be used for production for the close-to-hand domestic market. Conceivably economic growth would occur with little or no increase in foreign trade. The value of Ireland's foreign trade in 1992 was 136 percent of the country's GNP.[8] A doubling of GNP, with no further increase in foreign trade, would still leave the latter at a still high 68 percent of GNP.

How the main sectors of the Irish economy might respond to the changes in relative factor prices that a national dividend would cause is considered below.

Agriculture

One person family farms are likely to become universal in the absence of major economies of scale in farming or of economies of scale that cannot be secured by intelligent cooperation by farmers selected by their ability to pay revenue maximizing land taxes rather than by accident of birth. It will require extraordinary management ability to pay a land tax equivalent to competitive rent on sufficient land to make it worthwhile to employ a farm worker who could instead acquire a farm for virtually no cost other than paying the appropriate land tax. Or put another way: most people prefer to hoe their own row and to milk their own cow; with equal opportunities for doing so, only a combination of exceptional ability on the one hand and exceptional dependence on the other, will cause anyone to hoe another's row or milk another's cow.

Land intensive enterprises, like cattle and sheep, are likely to give way to labor intensive ones like crops and free range poultry. Exports of beef and lamb may contract as well as imports of grain for human and animal consumption. Some imports of fruit and vegetables are also likely to be replaced by home production.

With more livestock feed produced on one-person farms and with more labor of higher caliber at work on those farms, it is likely to be profitable to revert to a more dispersed form of livestock production. The concentration of livestock production into larger, factory-like units, which has occurred in recent years in response to measures by the state which have made capital cheap and labor dear to users, is likely to be reversed. With production taking place in larger numbers of smaller units, disease and its control will be less of a problem, making possible the production of higher quality products, including such items as free range poultry and eggs and antibiotic-free pig meat. Also with more dispersed and smaller scale livestock production units, there will be less likelihood of pollution from by-products like silage effluent and pig slurry.

More generally, farms that are more efficiently operated by farmers paying land taxes equivalent to competitive rents are likely to use more of their own lower cost, but better rewarded and therefore higher quality, labor to replace inputs that are now purchased. These purchased inputs, or direct costs, now equal one-third of the value of gross farm output.[9] They include, along with feeding stuffs, such items as artificial fertilizers, chemicals for crop protection and drugs for livestock. Farmers' incomes and agriculture's contribution to GNP could both be increased by almost 30 percent without any increase in gross farm output by halving the level of purchased inputs. Better rewarded, more skilled labor would, in this way, produce superior commodities, under aesthetically and hygienically superior conditions.

There should be interesting possibilities for developing export markets for these high quality, labor intensive products. There is an increasing demand for superior foods in an increasingly wealthy Europe, which has a growing aversion to poorer quality, unhealthy, mass produced, livestock products. There would be interesting possibilities for economies of scale in marketing products of this sort. It should be possible, for example, with a thriving, high quality poultry industry to get eggs on to the shelves of the better class stores of London, Paris, Frankfurt, and other continental cities, within about three days of being laid in Irish fields, when they would be at peak condition.

The price of farm produce will be less important than now for both producers and consumers. Higher prices will be reflected in correspondingly higher land taxes. These will leave the producer of average intensity per unit of land no better or worse off, though producers of less intensity will be worse off and those of higher intensity will be better off. Consumers, including those on farms, though losing from higher food prices, will benefit from a higher national dividend, a part of which will come from the higher prices paid by foreigners for

Irish agricultural exports. Lower agricultural prices will operate similarly, *mutatis mutandi*.

Industry

Higher capital and lower labor costs will make Irish manufacturing more efficient and productive. Much of the greater output is likely to be used to replace imported staples, which account for 86 percent of total domestic consumption of manufactured goods.

If manufacturing, in an Irish economy that is freed from the heritage of capital colonialism and so developing, follows the classical pattern of the non-capitalist-colonized and developing countries, then, through a process of organic growth, from the base of a sound, expanding home market, exports of selected products will develop. The important factors that will influence that selection will be: (i) high Irish incomes; (ii) correspondingly high skills; (iii) low labor costs; (iv) distance from foreign markets; (v) a small local market.

The type of product likely to be exported will be (a) crafted rather than mass produced and (b) of high quality, well designed, distinctive, and embodying much research and development. Quality food products from soundly operated farms which, with lower cost labor, more highly processed than now, are an obvious possibility. Quality clothes, footwear, household utensils, and furniture are others, along with computer software and specialist equipment of all sorts including the tools to make the tools to make the tools that are used in mass production. Harland and Wolfe used Belfast's innovative and skilled labor in the nineteenth century to build for a limited number of customers ships which could be sailed to those customers and thus circumvented the disadvantage of an isolated location. An export oriented aircraft industry might be the appropriate equivalent for an expanding Irish economy in the twenty-first century.

Production of goods for mass markets is never likely to be profitable in a small, isolated Irish economy. It may, nevertheless, be possible to acquire products supplied to that market more cheaply than by purchase at list price. A wide range of mass produced durable consumer and capital goods are quickly amortized because of wear and tear. These include especially cars, tractors, trucks, and aircraft. Highly skilled, but low cost, Irish labor would have a pronounced competitive advantage in reconditioning items of this sort. Thus, for example, BMW cars sold in continental Europe after three years for half the list price of a comparable new Ford might be reconditioned and sold in Ireland for the price of a new Ford, or for less. In this way, by incorporating skilled, but low cost/high income, Irish labor into mass market products, Irish consumers could have higher quality goods for the same price as lower quality goods are available to consumers elsewhere.

Conceivably an Irish industry that reconditioned for the domestic market the mass products of a Europe with high labor costs might go on to re-export some of these reconditioned goods. Markets exist, particularly in Third World countries, for completely reconditioned goods selling below the price of the same goods new. An Ireland with low cost/high income, skilled labor might, with profit to itself and benefit to the Third World, supply these markets.

Services

People have only one stomach to feed and only one back to clothe. When their stomachs are filled and their backs clothed, they have little need for more food or clothes. In the noncapitalist-colonized, developing world, incomes by and large have reached, or are close to, the level where people require little additional food and comparatively little additional clothing, footwear, and other manufactured goods. As incomes nevertheless continue almost inexorably to rise, more and more of them are spent on buildings (including dwelling houses), fuel, power, and especially services. Reflecting this trend, the value of agricultural and manufactured output in the EEC declined from 49 percent of total output in 1975 to 37 percent in 1990. The numbers employed in these sectors declined from 50 percent to 39 percent over the same period.[10] The proportions of output and employment accounted for by the other, mainly service sectors, increased correspondingly.

People's demand for services, unlike for food or manufactured goods, is virtually insatiable. This is so from the womb to the tomb—from the moment of their conception when they need monitoring and fostering with ante-natal medical services to the moment of departure from this life with dignity and ease. In an age of automation and abundant capital, the supply of goods is virtually potentially limitless; more can be produced with very little more than the abundant, growing stock of capital and technological innovation. While capital and technology can increase the quantity and improve the quality of services provided, ultimately that supply depends mainly on the quantity and quality of labor available. Ireland, under the envisaged dispensation of high incomes and therefore high quality labor, available at low cost, would be exceptionally well circumstanced to meet the growing, worldwide demand for services.

Ireland's location and its capitalist colonial undevelopment which, in various ways, have handicapped and will continue to handicap, agricultural and manufacturing output, confer distinct competitive advantages in the services and building sectors. Distance from major centers of population, which handicaps imports of raw materials and exports of agricultural and manufactured goods, can be an advantage to a service sector. This is especially so in an age of rapid, cheap and safe travel and communication. A relatively sparsely inhabited and isolated island has obvious potential attractions for people wishing to get "far from the maddening crowd" for holidays or retirement. That attractiveness is now marred by the prevalence of crime in a society where the half of the population who are denied a livelihood are alienated and react in the only way open to them. Crimes of violence could be expected to diminish greatly in a restructured, efficient and equitable society. That would help to realize the potential of the service industries in Ireland.

Education, research and development, and medicine are all service industries in which a restructured Irish economy, offering low cost but high income, and therefore high quality, labor would have major comparative advantages. Not least of these advantages would be Ireland's use as its *lingua franca* of English, which becomes increasingly the language of universal communication in commerce, science, education, and research. That the services were being produced in a small, relatively isolated location would add to their attractiveness for many of both the producers and the consumers of the services.

The ultimate consumers of many of the services would come to Ireland to receive them. Marketing the services would, therefore, not have the cost of transport which is now borne by agricultural and manufactured exports. They would be the more willing to come if, in addition to remoteness, Ireland could offer an environment that was distinctive and not battered and forced into a common mold, spoiled by polluting factory farming and manufacturing industries, and by juggernaut trucks hauling massive amounts of goods to and from continental Europe.

The services not consumed *in situ* in Ireland can nowadays readily and cheaply be transported to distant markets. Aircraft can fly out the bulkier specifications, computer software, plans, and drawings. Others can be exported by telecommunications, for which an insular location is no handicap.

For these reasons, an efficient, equitable Irish economy, freed from the heritage of capitalist colonialism, could expect to secure for its members, through servicing their own needs and those of the world at large, as good a life as is available to them outside Ireland.

Political Implications

The earlier sections of this chapter have attempted to show that change which would transform Irish undevelopment into development is economically feasible. That transformation would be of great intrinsic importance to the Irish people. But it gains immeasurably in significance because it would provide a precedent, now missing, for transforming capitalist colonial undevelopment into development for the 140 or so countries which together comprise the Third World and which contain half the world's population. This section considers how a political will might be mobilized to effect in Ireland an economically feasible transformation of undevelopment into development.

It is argued in chapter 9 that the forces for change that are endemic in societies are no longer being dissipated in Ireland by emigration; they gather there now both in the south and the north of the island. They are manifested in the south by disaffection with the established political system, as reflected in the failure of any government since 1969 to secure re-election, as well as by opinion polls. Pressure for change is manifested in the north by the IRA's "armed struggle" and by its forcible containment. Direction might be given to these forces for change by a two-pronged approach. One of these is to emphasize the inefficiency and inequity of the existing socioeconomic system, which is the heritage of capitalist colonialism and which is sustained by a state that is the enemy of the nation. The other is to show the economic feasibility of creating a restructured system, free of the heritage of capitalist colonialism and able to secure for all an acceptable livelihood in Ireland on a sustainable basis. That approach needs to be pursued in the Republic, in the north of Ireland and Britain, among Irish emigrants, and within the EEC.

Within the Republic

Capitalist colonialism universally creates local elites, who are its agents and collaborators. These elites, in time, win the colonies' independence, which they then use to secure and enhance their own privileged position. Third World elites cling to their privileges in large measure because the alternative would be submergence in the broadening, deepening morass of poverty that is the corollary of expanding elitism. Because of emigration, there is not now a yawning gap in Ireland between the privileged and the disinherited, between the Hightowners and the Irishtowners. Any substantial improvement in economic performance resulting from discarding the privileges of an inefficient and inequitable capitalist colonial heritage would leave the majority of the privileged better off. Only a few—but an influential few—would still be worse off.

The present may be a peculiarly favorable time for change in Ireland. Emigration no longer operates as freely and pressures for change that were formerly dissipated now mount. But there is evidence of a reaction by the privileged to these pressures. That reaction would involve a reversal of the long term relative increase in the lowest incomes, effected by the reinstatement of the disabilities of the disprivileged. The most common and vocal form of this reaction is the advocacy of various types of "workfare" in place of welfare. "Workfare" involves imposing more stringent conditions for receiving unemployment assistance, including requiring recipients to undertake some form of community service and withdrawing the individual's entitlement altogether after a specified time. These changes would reduce the cost of welfare and force unemployed persons to accept low-paid employment or emigrate. If implemented, they would reduce the prospect of change, first, by driving out of Ireland persons who would otherwise favor change and, second, as a result of widening the gap between the privileged and the disprivileged, by increasing the former's motivation for maintaining the status quo.

The conditions favoring now in Ireland a change that has been unprecedented in the history of capitalist colonialism may be summarized as: (i) the continued long-term increase in incomes and the greater expectations, including those pertaining to the public sector, associated with those rising incomes; (ii) the deepening problems of government resulting from the structural defects of an inherited capitalist colonialism, which defects have been exacerbated by an exhausted series of expedients; and (iii) the possibility of an elitist reaction aimed at reducing unemployment costs.

The United Kingdom

Much of the cost of perpetuating capitalist colonial undevelopment in the twenty-six counties has been externalized to the people of the six counties. The creation of the latter as a separate polity resulted from the secession of twenty-six counties from the United Kingdom of Great Britain and Ireland, under a leadership that was more concerned about the constraints on their sovereignty from an Oath of Allegiance to the king of England than about the partition of Ireland. The perpetuation of a six county statelet has been a consequence of the continued capitalist colonial undevelopment of the twenty-six counties. Had the latter area developed, in the sense of eliminating mass unemployment and emigration and securing living standards at least as high as those in Britain, it is inconceivable that the six county statelet would still exist. The *raison d'etre* of that statelet is to preserve Protestant privilege against Catholic disprivilege in the north and against absorption into an overwhelmingly Catholic Republic that has failed to transform undevelopment into development.

The political choices made in the Republic, which created and now sustain the partition of Ireland, are the real, the ultimate cause of the mayhem that virtually inescapably follows from partition. Part of the cost of those choices is thus externalized to the people of the six counties and to the people of Britain, who pay some £3 billion annually to contain the violence of the six counties. The clearer this point is made to the people of Northern Ireland and Britain, the more pressure is likely to be directed towards securing radical reform in the Republic, which alone can eliminate mass unemployment, mass emigration and mass poverty, which in turn alone can eliminate partition and the evils consequent on it.

The Emigrants

The half of the population stream which for almost 200 years has emigrated permanently has nevertheless played a dominant role in the evolution of Irish society. For 150 years, their departure has been the means by which, notwithstanding superimposed socioeconomic institutions and basic laws, living standards in Ireland have risen more or less in line with those of the West. Beyond that, their influence, directly as voters in Britain and indirectly through financial support and pressure on the governments of the former settler colonies where many settled, has been critical in determining UK policy in Ireland. One of the major costs of independence has been that that influence for beneficial change has ceased to operate on the affairs of the Republic.

Emigrants easily recognized the malign character of British rule in Ireland and did not hesitate to put pressure on the UK state to reform those circumstances which forced them to emigrate. It has been less easy for Irish emigrants, as for others, to recognize the true character of the post capitalist colonial Irish state which, no less than the colonial administration from which it sprang, is the enemy of the nation. So far, therefore, from continuing to press on government in Ireland for beneficial reform, emigrants have been generally benign towards an Irish state that continues, like the colonial administration that proceeded it, to force half the Irish to emigrate. An awareness among emigrants of the true character of the Irish state should generate a more critical attitude, leading, it might be hoped, to action, as in pre-independence, designed to force change in the course of Irish government.

The export promoting policy of the 1950s, with its emphasis on expanding exports, has given hostage to fortune and made government in Ireland no less vulnerable to emigrant pressure now than in the past. Irish emigrants, in a number of ways, could bring irresistible pressure to bear for reform in Ireland. That reform might well include granting votes in Irish parliamentary elections to emigrants, as is the case with the emigrant citizens of many countries. Emigrants who, *ipso facto*, are the most dissatisfied, would be likely to vote in favor of change in those circumstances that caused them to emigrate.

The European Community

EEC membership is doubly conducive to maintaining the status quo in Ireland. First, unlike the UK, prior to Ireland's independence, which transferred resources from the center directly to the people and thereby strengthened the latter, the EEC transfers resources to Ireland via the state and its nominees. This strengthens the state and its elite supporters and debilitates the nation. This is especially the case with the Common Agricultural Policy, which raises the cost of food unnecessarily and accentuates all the inefficiencies associated with the paradox of property.

Second, as Ireland, in common with the other member states, becomes increasingly enmeshed in a web of common EEC laws and policies, it is more plausibly insisted that any exercise of sovereignty that threatened to tangle the web would result in expulsion from the EEC and isolation as a pariah among the nations. Essential radical reform is thus discouraged.

It is desirable to alert public opinion in the EEC to the fact that Irish membership, on present terms, is neither in the EEC's nor the Irish nation's interest. An unreformed Ireland will be a persistent sore in the body politic of the EEC, comparable in many ways to Northern Ireland within the UK during the past seventy years. An economy that continues to undevelop will require continuous transfers from the EEC and these, because they are effected through the state and not via the people, will continue to strengthen the state and weaken the nation. Because the economy will continue to undevelop, partition will also persist and, with it, the scandal of Protestants and Catholics contending murderously for livelihoods in an island where the number of these continues their 150 year decline. Injecting resources will not rectify this situation any more than giving aid to the Third World can alleviate conditions there. The status quo in both cases is consolidated and the possibility of necessary reform is reduced. It is important therefore, in the EEC's and Ireland's long term interest, to create a public opinion critical of the transfer of resources within the EEC to Ireland.

Of vastly greater significance than any of these immediate motives, reform in Ireland could create the precedent of transforming capitalist colonial undevelopment into development, without which it is doubtful if the Third World will ever develop. The countries of the EEC, as an integral part of their own individualist, capitalist development, capitalist colonized most of the non-European world and thereby created the Third World, with its heritage of perpetual undevelopment. Recognition of responsibility for that condition is a major consideration underlying the substantial aid which the EEC now gives to the Third World. That aid, however, so far from alleviating, accentuates the Third World's socioeconomic problems. Far and away the best—possibly the only—atonement the EEC member states can make to the Third World for inflicting on it the heritage of capitalist colonial undevelopment is to encourage that one of its own members which, in its dual capacity of neighbor and colony, shares that heritage, to rid itself of it, and, in doing so, provide the essential precedent for similar reform throughout the Third World.

Third World Population

The similarities of experience between Ireland and the countries of the Third World make a transformation of Irish undevelopment into development a relevant and helpful precedent for the those countries. This is so notwithstanding the different demographic and income situations in Ireland and in the Third World. It is those differences which raise the possibility of spontaneous, radical change in Ireland, alone of the former capitalist colonies. No similar prospect of radical change exists within the countries of the Third World. Worsening poverty may indeed terminate population growth and achieve equilibrium in the long term; but it will be by causing death rates to rise, despite continuing western intervention, to equate with biologically determined birthrates, under a degree of immiseration that hardly bears contemplation.

The successful transformation of Ireland's capitalist colonial undevelopment into development depends critically on the nation recovering from the state resources now used by the latter to perpetuate the undevelopment of the former. Development, in Ireland's case, requires those resources, which the state now uses to make land free and capital cheap to the privileged, to be used instead to raise the returns to labor while simultaneously reducing its cost, all with a view to reducing and, if possible, ending net emigration.

A *sine qua non* of Third World development must also be the recovery from the state of national resources now used to undevelop the nations and their use instead for the nations' development. But whereas in Ireland the primary use of the recovered resources is perceived as being directed towards simultaneously raising returns to, and lowering the cost of, labor, in order to stem the emigration that has perpetuated undevelopment, in the Third World the primary use of the recovered national resources would seem to be to re-establish the balance, disrupted by capitalist colonialism, between birth and death rates, otherwise than through rising death rates. That means reducing Third World birthrates.

There is now, of course, a close negative correlation between incomes and birthrates. People with high incomes tend to have low birthrates and vice versa. While recovering national resources for national benefit from the state may raise real incomes, birthrates are unlikely to be lowered sufficiently to equate with death rates made low by western intervention. Indeed, higher Third World incomes may aggravate the imbalance between birth and death rates by causing further, temporary declines in the latter as a result of improved nutrition. A more closely focused use of Third World national resources appears called for in order to escape from the trap of undevelopment set by the introduction of western individualism into Third World communalism. The Third World's primary need must be to counter the western influences that enable individuals to have low death rates while their societies continue to tend to have biologically determined birthrates. That is to say, the recovered national resources might best be used to secure lower birthrates.

The lack of empathy on the part of those who speak and write of population pressure is matched only by that of those who seek for poor people's motives for having numerous children. Poor people have children for the same biological reason that birds and bees have offspring. The question that needs to be asked is not "why do poor people have so many children?" but "why do people who are not poor not have children, or have few of them?" The answer to this, as suggested above, seems clear-cut: people above the subsistence level can contemplate the future; their rate of time discount declines and future costs acquire immediate significance. Specifically, the cost of children, through pregnancy, parturition, infancy, and child dependency acquires, with low time discount rates, a present significance sufficient to induce better-off people to use available means of avoiding conceiving children. That is to say, the present discounted cost of children for better-off people is sufficient to warrant avoiding having children.

Poor people's rates of discount are high. A person who is hungry today and is likely to be hungry again tomorrow and all the tomorrows cannot contemplate the future. A person like that may well exchange the certainty of £5 in a week's time for a penny to assuage today's hunger pains. For such persons the cost of a child to be born in nine months time has no present significance. Of even less significance are the costs or benefits to the parents of that child subsequently. Because the present cost of children for poor people, and especially for people made poorer by capitalist colonialism, with their very high rates of time discount, is virtually zero; they understandably take no measures to offset the future consequences of their biologically and psychologically induced mating.

The lack of empathy suggested above has more recently given rise to the concept of the value of children for poor people, or VOC. Poor people, according to this perception, breed and rear children as a long term investment, to supply them with cheap labor in later childhood and to provide them with the equivalent of old age pensions later still. It should be obvious, with a moment's reflection, that it is the present discounted cost of children (COC) and not VOC which causes poor people to have birthrates tending to their biological limit. Poor people have many children because their COC is effectively zero, not because the future value of children, VOC, is high.

Conceptually birthrates can be reduced to any level, including zero, by raising COC sufficiently. The People's Republic of China has reduced birthrates below their reproduction level, opening the prospect of a declining population early in the next century. It has done so by what western observers regard as harassing young people to induce them to refrain from having children when they are very young and to induce them to have no more than one child subsequently. This harassment in effect raises COC and makes it worthwhile to avoid having more than one child. Some years ago, when Indira Gandhi's government attempted a similar approach to reducing birthrates in India, the forces of individualism in the former capitalist colony brought about the demise of the government, largely on this issue. It is unlikely, in view of this experience, that governments in former capitalist colonies will attempt similarly to reduce birthrates.

Because any conceivable increase in living standards or any conceivable compulsion is unlikely to reduce Third World birthrates sufficiently, it is worth considering the possibility of using the national resources recovered from the state, which are now used to perpetuate the undevelopment of the former capitalist colonies, for the purpose of raising COC. That could be done by using some or all of the resources in question to pay fecund women for remaining non-pregnant.

Women in the fecund age group, fifteen to forty-five years, wishing to qualify for non-pregnancy payments would take a pregnancy test, say every six months. If proven non-pregnant, they would receive a dated certificate, valid for six months, to that effect. The certificate would entitle them to receive, at a local post office or its equivalent, weekly payments. Women wishing to continue to receive non-pregnancy payments would undertake further pregnancy tests as desired. The poorer the women, and therefore the more likely they are now to have biologically determined birthrates, the more eager they are likely to be to earn non-pregnancy payments of any given level. The higher the level of the non-pregnancy payments, the more women who will try harder to avoid pregnancy and the more sharply birthrates will fall.

The stabilization or reduction of Third World populations, secured by paying women not to become pregnant, would bring more benefit to more poor people than anything else. The women who would receive the payments are the world's poorest and weakest and would be made immediately better off. The most money would be received by the poorest women who suffer most. Resources that are now pre-empted in poor societies for rearing and supporting the rapid growth of populations that are economically excessive would be freed for physical capital formation. Capital formation per person would increase because populations would be smaller and the amount available for physical capital formation would be larger. Poor countries and poor people would secure quick relief from the inefficiency, inequity, and corruption that are the inescapable consequence of the rapid growth of poor populations and the degradation of individuals implicit in that situation.

Conclusion

This book has sought explanations for a problem that has been foremost since the end of the Second World war, half a century ago: that is, the poverty that enmeshes ever deeper the half of the world's population living in the Third World. The explanation for that poverty proffered here is that it is the result of the superimposition, through the process of capitalist colonization, of the institutions, technologies, and basic laws of the individualist, capitalist West on societies that were neither individualist nor capitalist and the retention, after colonialism, of that superimposition by states that are extensions of capitalist colonial administrations, and, so far from being nation-states, are the enemies of the nations that they rule.

The transformation of the economic undevelopment of the former capitalist colonies into the economic development that is characteristic of countries that have not been capitalist colonized depends, it has been argued, on recognizing the malign character of the state in former capitalist colonies and recovering for the nations the resources which those states now command and which they use for the undevelopment of the nations and the profit of the elites who control them. There is now in Ireland, because of that country's unique status of neighbor and colony, a prospect of breaking the mold of hitherto unceasing capitalist colonial undevelopment, thereby providing for the Third World the critical precedent, which it now lacks, for progressing from capitalist colonial undevelopment to development.

The realization of that prospect of radical change depends, as always in history, on initiatives taken by ordinary people, and not by elites who invariably seek to preserve a status quo that made them elites. The critical initiative in the present case is the recognition by the people of Ireland of the malign character of the Irish state and the need to claw back for the nation the resources and powers confiscated by conquest and transferred, at independence, to a state that is heir to the colonial administration, that is the enemy of the nation and that perpetuates the nation's undevelopment.

The people of Ireland can be assisted and encouraged by the many who have an interest in transforming capitalist colonial undevelopment into development. First among these are the almost half of those born in Ireland who now live abroad and who wish for change in the conditions that forced them and half of six earlier generations to emigrate. Next are the British people, who are embarrassed and taxed by the running sore of Northern Ireland. They can be relieved of this last vestige of empire only by the ending of capitalist colonial undevelopment in Ireland, which is a precondition for ending partition and all that follows from that. The peoples of the European Community who, insofar as they are cognizant of Ireland, are most likely to be irritated by the unceasing rattling of the Irish state's begging bowl, have an interest of a far higher order in Ireland. The community owes it to the Third World, which is the creation of the nations of the community to provide it with a precedent, which alone seems possible in

Ireland, for transforming capitalist colonial undevelopment into development.

Notes

Foreword

1. To the extent he himself uses the term "Third World," Crotty equates it with former capitalist colonized countries, as we shall also do in the following. For the distinction between underdevelopment and undevelopment, see note 32 below.

2. All references to the present book in the following are given in brackets in the text.

3. Barney Glaser and Anselm Strauss, *The Discovery of Grounded Theory* (New York: Aldine de Gruyter, 1967).

4. Raymond D. Crotty, *A Radical's Response* (Dublin: Poolbeg Press, 1988), 32.

5. Crotty, *A Radical's Response*, 6.

6. Crotty, *A Radical's Response*, 10.

7. Crotty, *A Radical's Response*, 18.

8. Crotty, *A Radical's Response*, 16. Henry George, *Progress and Poverty* (New York: Appleton, 1880). Henry George, *The Irish Land Question* (Glasgow: Dunn and Wright, 1881).

9. Crotty, *A Radical's Response*, 17.

10. Crotty, *A Radical's Response*, 19.

11. Raymond D. Crotty, *Irish Agricultural Production: Its Volume and Structure* (Cork: Cork University Press, 1966). Cf. also his later pamphlet: Raymond D. Crotty, *The Cattle Crisis and the Small Farmer* (Mullingar, Ireland: The National Land League, 1974).

12. George, *Progress and Poverty*, 341.

13. George, *Progress and Poverty*, 413.

14. In the following, all the references to steps refer to the list in the third section above.

15. Crotty, *A Radical's Response*, 36.

16. From this time stems his first effort to link the study of Ireland to the study of colonialism elsewhere, Raymond D. Crotty, "Capitalist Colonialism and Peripheraliza-

tion: The Irish Case," in *Underdeveloped Europe,* ed., Dudley Seers, Bernard Schaffer, and Marja-Liisa Kiljunen (Hassocks, Sussex: Harvester, 1979), 225–37.

17. Raymond D. Crotty, *Cattle, Economics and Development* (Slough, England: The Commonwealth Agricultural Bureaux, 1980).

18. Crotty, *A Radical's Response,* 56.

19. Raymond D. Crotty, *Ireland in Crisis: A Study in Capitalist Colonial Undevelopment* (Dingle, County Cork: Brandon, 1986).

20. His last pamphlet on Irish development was Raymond D. Crotty, *Farming Collapse: National Opportunity* (Dublin: Amárach-Ireland 2000, 1990).

21. Crotty, *A Radical's Response,* 1.

22. The philosophical and ethical arguments here have been provided by Jürgen Habermas. For feminist standpoint theory, see, e.g., Dorothy E. Smith, *The Everyday World as Problematic: A Feminist Sociology* (Milton Keynes, Bedfordshire: Open University Press, 1987).

23. It is not possible within the context of this introduction to consider the relation between Crotty's analyses and the specialized literature, e.g., on agrarian history.

24. Paul Costello, *World Historians and Their Goals* (DeKalb, Ill.: Northern Illinois University Press, 1993).

25. W. H. McNeill, *The Rise of the West* (Chicago: University of Chicago Press, 1963).

26. E. L. Jones, *The European Miracle* (Cambridge: Cambridge University Press, 1981).

27. R. D. Crotty, "The European Miracle," book review, *Irish Journal of Agricultural Economics and Rural Sociology* 9, no. 2 (1983): 193–95.

28. Perry Anderson, *Passages from Antiquity to Feudalism* (London: New Left Books, 1974); Perry Anderson, *Lineages of the Absolutist State* (London: New Left Books, 1974).

29. Michael Mann, *The Sources of Social Power,* vols. I and II (Cambridge: Cambridge University Press, 1986 and 1993).

30. Also with the work of Charles Tilly, *Coercion, Capital and European States AD 990-1990* (Oxford: Blackwell, 1992).

31. Immanuel Wallerstein, *The Modern World System,* vols. I-III (New York: Academic Press, 1974, 1980, 1989).

32. This is seen directly from the title of one of the last analyses of Ireland that Crotty himself published: Raymond D. Crotty, "Ireland—a Case of Peripheral Underdevelopment or Capitalist Colonial Undevelopment?" in *Regions, Nations and European Integration: Remaking the Celtic Periphery,* ed. Graham Day and Gareth Rees (Cardiff: University of Wales Press, 1991), 265–74.

33. Eric R. Wolf, *Europe and the People without History* (Berkeley: University of California Press, 1982).

34. The term is also used in Crotty, *A Radical's Response,* 57. The titles of the various drafts of *When Histories Collide* shifted. In 1992, his title was *Colonialism and Undevelopment;* in 1993, he used the title *Our Enemy the State.*

35. Immanuel Wallerstein and Terence K. Hopkins (coordinators), "Cyclical Rhythms and Secular Trends of the Capitalist World-Economy: Some Premises, Hypotheses, and Questions," *Review II,* no. 4 (Spring 1979).

36. André Gunder Frank and Barry K. Gills, "The Cumulation of Accumulation: Theses and Research Agenda for 5000 Years of World System History," *Dialectical Anthropology* 15 (1990); Frank, "A Theoretical Introduction to World System History,"

Review 13 (1990); Frank, "A Plea for World System History," *Journal of World History* 2 (1991).

37. Douglass C. North and Robert Paul Thomas, *The Rise of the Western World* (Cambridge: Cambridge University Press, 1973).

38. A comparison with the analysis of Robert Brenner, "The Agrarian Roots of European Capitalism," *Past and Present*, no. 97, November 1982 would be relevant, but cannot be pursued here.

39. Walt W. Rostow, *How It All Began* (New York: McGraw-Hill, 1975).

40. Alfred W. Crosby, *The Columbian Exchange* (Westport, Conn.: Greenwood, 1972); Alfred W. Crosby, *Ecological Imperialism* (Cambridge: Cambridge University Press, 1986); Alfred W. Crosby, *Germs, Seeds and Animals: Studies in Ecological History* (Armonk, N.Y.: M.E. Sharpe, 1994).

41. William H. McNeill, *Plagues and Peoples* (Harmondsworth: Penguin, 1976), 54. Also W. H. McNeill, *The Human Condition* (Princeton, N.J.: Princeton University Press, 1980), and Jared Diamond, *Guns, Germs, and Steel* (New York: Norton, 1997).

42. Edward Said, *Orientalism* (New York: Pantheon Books, 1978); Bart Moore-Gilbert, *Postcolonial Theory* (London: Verso, 1997).

43. Dieter Senghaas, *The European Experience* (Leamington Spa, Warwickshire: 1985 (German original 1979); Ulrich Menzel and Dieter Senghaas, *Europas Entwicklung und die Dritte Welt* (Frankfurt am Main: Suhrkamp, 1986). For a summary and overview, see Lars Mjøset, "Comparative Typologies of Development Patterns: the Menzel / Senghaas Framework," in *Contributions to the Comparative Study of Development*, Report 92: 2, ed. Lars Mjøset (Oslo: Institute for Social Research, 1992).

44. Senghaas borrowed these notions from Samir Amin, *L'accumulation à l'echelle mondiale* (Paris: Editions Anthropos, 1970); cf. also Samir Amin, "Accumulation and Development: A Theoretical Model," in *Review of African Political Economy* 1 (1972).

45. Empirically, in the early nineteenth century, land distribution in Ireland was not more skewed than that of the Nordic country Denmark, cf. Lars Mjøset, *The Irish Economy in a Comparative Institutional Perspective* (Dublin: National Economic and Social Council, 1992), 210.

46. This is in contrast with Senghaas, as discussed in the preceding section. The same point is made in Crotty's contribution to a review symposium on Eoin O'Malley's study of Irish industrialization, cf. *The Economic and Social Review*, 12:2, January 1990, 239–40.

47. This explanation may be questioned: an alternative one would emphasize different political economic alliances and compromises, in line with the analysis of Barrington Moore, *Social Origins of Democracy and Dictatorship* (Boston: Beacon Press, 1966). In the United States, industrializing elites allied with mid-west family farmers, in Latin America, the alliances were more like that alliance that was blocked by the northern state's victory in the Civil War: an alliance between quasi-feudal estate-owners and industrial-urban elites.

48. Carlota Perez, "Microelectronics, Long Waves and World Structural Change: New Perspectives for Developing Countries," *World Development*, 13:3 (1985); Carlota Perez, "Structural Change and Assimilation of New Technologies in the Economic and Social Systems," *Futures*, 15:5 (1983): 357–75.

49. Marcel Mazoyer & Laurence Roudart, *Histoire des Agricultures de Monde* (Paris: Seuil, 1997), 18.

50. Peter B. Evans, "Predatory, Developmental, and Other Apparatuses: A Comparative Political Economy Perspective on the Third World State," *Sociological Forum*,

4:4 (1989); Peter B. Evans, *Embedded Autonomy* (Princeton, N.J.: Princeton University Press, 1995).

51. Often Crotty cannot resist the temptation to draw lines directly from ancient history to the present situation. Some examples in *When Histories Collide* are his remarks on the problems of the Middle East (25), on Russia/China (21), on conscription in England during World War 2 (91), and on the high income per capita in the Nordic countries (86).

Chapter One: Introduction and Background

1. *Editor's Note*. This definition of *development* is derived from the work of Gunner Myrdal. It is not clear that Myrdal ever actually defined *development* in this way; this should therefore be treated perhaps as RDC's interpretation of Myrdal's intent.

2. Crotty, *Irish Agricultural Production*; Crotty, *Ireland in Crisis*.

3. World Bank, *World Development Report* (Washington, D.C.: World Bank, 1992), Table 1.

4. World Bank, *World Development Report*, Table 26

5. World Bank, *World Development Report*, Table 26.

6. World Bank, *World Development Report*, Table 26.

7. World Bank, *World Development Report*, Table 26.

8. R. Sundrum, *Growth and Income Distribution in India: Policy and Performance since Independence* (London: Sage, 1987), 44.

9. M. Lipton and J. Toye, *Does Aid Work in India?* (London: Routledge, 1990), 43.

10. N. Alexandratos, ed., *World Agriculture: Toward 2000* (London: Belhaven Press, 1988), Table 3.4; also S. Reutlinger and M. Selowsky, *Malnutrition and Poverty: Magnitude and Policy Options* (Baltimore: Johns Hopkins Press, 1976).

11. F. S. L. Lyons, *Ireland Since the Famine* (London: Collins/Fontana, 1973), 34–44.

12. Lyons, *Ireland Since the Famine*.

13. Department of Health, *Report on Vital Statistics* (Dublin: Stationery Office,1966), Table 4; Central Statistical Office, *Statistical Abstract* (Dublin, Stationery Office: 1991), Tables 2.1 and 2.2.

14. CSO, *Statistical Abstract*, Table 2.2.

15. For 1841 population: Department of Industry and Commerce, *Census of Population of Irish Free State—Preliminary Report* (Dublin: Stationery Office, 1926), Appendix Table 1. For 1991 population: CSO, *Statistical Abstract* (Dublin: Stationery Office, 1991), Table 2.2.

16. For 1841 figure see Crotty, *Irish Agricultural Production*, 2; NIEC, *Report on Full Employment, Report No. 18* (Dublin: Stationery Office, 1967), Table 2; CSO, *Statistical Abstract*, Table 2.28.

17. K. H. Connell, *The Population of Ireland 1750-1845* (Oxford: Clarendon Press, 1950), 4, Table 1.

18. Crotty, *Irish Agricultural Production*, 43; CSO, *Statistical Abstract,* 382.

19. FAO, *Production Yearbook 1990; Vol. 44* (Rome: FAO, 1991), Table 3.

20. C. McEvedy and R. Jones, *Atlas of World Population History* (Harmondsworth: Penguin, 1978), 348–49.

21. T. Kennedy, T. Giblin, and D. McHugh, *The Economic Development of Ireland in the Twentieth Century* (London: Routledge, 1988), 18, Table 1.2.

22. FAO, *Production Yearbook 1990*, Table 3.

23. World Bank, *World Development Report*, Table 26.

24. Among many studies, see: R. F. Dernberger, *Chinese Development Experience in Comparative Perspective* (Cambridge, Mass.: Harvard University Press, 1980).

25. World Bank, *World Development Report*, Table 26.

26. FAO, *Production Yearbook* 1990; *Vol. 44;* 19, 29, 30 Table 3.

27. World Bank, *World Bank Atlas—25th Anniversary Edition* (Washington, D.C.: World Bank, 1992), 18–19.

28. World Bank, *World Bank Atlas*.

29. Crotty, *Cattle, Economics and Development*, 150–51.

30. A. Crotty, *The Problems of Smallholder Agriculture in South-West Perak State, Malaysia,* (BA dissertation, unpublished) University of Dublin, 1978, 27.

31. A. Macfarlane, "The Cradle of Capitalism: The Case of England," in *Europe and the Rise of Capitalism*, ed. J. Baechler, J. Hall, and M. Mann (Oxford: Basil Blackwell, 1988), 185.

32. FAO, *Production Yearbook* 1990; *Vol. 44,* Table 3.

Chapter Two: Early Agriculture

1. J. Woodburn, "Hunters and Gatherers Today and Reconstruction of the Past," in *Soviet and Western Anthropology*, ed. E. Gellner (London: Duckworth, 1980).

2. A. Sheratt, "Interpretation and Synthesis," in *Cambridge Encyclopedia of Archaeology* (Cambridge: Cambridge University Press, 1980, 404).

3. C. McEvedy and R. Jones, *Atlas of World Population History* (London: Penguin, 1978), 4.

4. McEvedy and Jones, *Atlas of World Population History*, 343.

5. J. A. Hall, *Powers and Liberties* (London: Penguin, 1986), 27.

6. S. Piggott, *Ancient Europe from the Beginning of Agriculture to Classical Antiquity* (Edinburgh: Edinburgh University Press, 1965), 37–38.

7. The term is taken from C. Geertz, *Agricultural Involution* (Los Angeles: University of California Press, 1968).

8. F. J. Simoons, "The Geographical Hypothesis and Lactose Malabsorption: A Weighing of the Evidence," *American Journal of Digestive Diseases* 23 (1978): 963–80.

9. D. A. Sturdy, "The Exploitation Patterns of a Modern Reindeer Economy in West Greenland," in *Papers in Economic Prehistory*, ed. E. S. Higgs (Cambridge: Cambridge University Press, 1972).

10. R. Elphick, *Kraal and Castle: Khoikhoi and the Founding of White South Africa* (New Haven, Conn.: Yale University Press, 1977).

11. J. Middleton, ed., *Peoples of Africa* (London: Marshall Cavendish, 1978), 180–83.

12. P. K. Hitti, *The Near East in History: A 5,000 Year Story* (Princeton, N.J.: Van Nostrand, 1961), 14.

13. Simoons, *The Geographical Hypothesis*.

14. D. N. Levine, *Wax and Gold: Tradition and Innovation in Ethiopian Culture* (Chicago: University of Chicago Press, 1965), 103–4.

15. Simoons, *The Geographical Hypothesis*.

16. J. D. Clarke, *The Prehistory of Africa* (London: Thames and Hudson, 1970), 216; R. Oliver, "The Problem of Bantu Expansion," *Journal of African History*, VII,

(1966): 203; and R. Oliver and B. M. Fagan, *Africa in the Iron Age* (Cambridge: Cambridge University Press, 1975).

17. Elphick, *Kraal and Castle.*

18. P. Rigby, *Cattle and Kinship among the Gogo* (Ithaca, N.Y.: Cornell University Press, 1969), 45.

19. B. A. L. Cranstons, "Animal Husbandry: the Evidence from Ethnography," in *The Domestication of Plants and Animals,* ed. Ucko & Dimbleby (London: Duckworth, 1969), 21.

20. Oliver and Fagan, *Africa in the Iron Age,* 30.

21. R. R. Inskeep, *The Peopling of Southern Africa* (London: David Philip, 1978).

22. Middleton, *Peoples of Africa.*

23. Judaic monotheism appears to have been part of the defensive mechanism of the lactose malabsorbent, cropgrowing Israelites who sought to preserve their identity by isolating themselves on the windward, rain fed western side of the Lebanese mountains from the Bedouin pastoralists of the surrounding Middle Eastern desert. Being lactose malabsorbent, it is unlikely that the tribes of Abraham were ever the shepherds that tradition would have it. Like the peoples of Mesopotamia and Egypt, they probably descended directly from hunter-gatherers.

24. *The Times Atlas of World History* has surely got it wrong in stating that the domestication of the horse made pastoralism possible in the Eurasian steppes. G. Barraclough, ed., *The Times Atlas of World History* (London: Times Books, 1978), 60. Only in the New World of the Americas and Oceania, where there is no indigenous pastoral tradition, are horses relied upon principally for herding stock. In the Old World, where pastoralism has been practiced for millennia, stock for the most part are either led by the pastoralists, or are controlled by collie dogs that have been guarding and working domesticated ruminants from the beginning. Rather then, successful adaptation by the northern pastoralists, including especially their acquisition of lactose tolerance, enabled them to domesticate the wild horses that were indigenous to the northern steppes; and by doing so, enabled them further to develop their capability.

25. R. Lattimore, *Inner Asian Frontiers of China* (Irvington-on-Hudson, N.Y.: Capital, 1951), 440–43.

26. Crotty, *Cattle, Economics and Development,* 165.

27. J. H. Hutton, *Caste in India: Its Nature, Function and Origins* (Oxford: Oxford University Press, 1963).

28. Simoons, *The Geographical Hypothesis.*

29. Central Statistical Office, *Statistical Abstract* (Dublin: Stationery Office,1936), 48.

30. M. Lal, "Cow Cult in India," in *Cow Slaughter: Horns of a Dilemma,* ed. A. B. Shaw (Bombay: Lalvani, 1967).

31. The diversion of Indian resources to the production of livestock products for the few instead of food grains for the many, which was averted in the past by the apotheosis of the cow and the tabooing of beef consumption, is now occurring in large measure as a result of the dumping of EEC dairy surpluses as food aid in India.

32. Hitti, *The Near East in History,* 30.

33. H. Frankfort, *The Birth of Civilisation in the Near East* (London: Williams and Norgate, 1951), 75.

34. G. Daniel, *A Hundred and Fifty Years of Archaeology* (London: Duckworth, 1975), 190–227.

35. C. Clark, *Population Growth and Land Use* (London: Macmillan, 1965), 64.

36. FAO, *Production Yearbook 1990* (Rome: FAO, 1991), Tables 1, 3, 106.

Chapter Three: The Emergence of Individualism in Europe

1. R. Oliver, "The Problem of Bantu Expansion," *Journal of African History*, Vol. VII (1966): 64.

2. R. de Vaux, *Ancient Israel: Its Life and Institutions,* trans. J. McHugh (London: Darton, Longman & Todd, 1961), 145.

3. M. A. Cook, ed., *Studies in the Economic History of the Middle East* (Oxford: Oxford University Press, 1970), 78.

4. Hitti, *The Near East in History*, 14.

5. R. Dawson, *The Chinese Experience* (London: Weidenfeld & Nicolson, 1978), 12, 43.

6. E. O. Reischauer, *The Japanese* (London: Harvard University Press, 1977), 237.

7. C. A. Burland, *Peru Under the Incas* (London: Evans Brothers, 1967), 41.

8. Cook, *Studies in the Economic History of the Middle East,* 35–36.

9. A. Toynbee, *Mankind and Mother Earth* (Oxford: Oxford University Press, 1976), 119.

10. E. D. Lambert, "The Role of Climate in the Economic Development of Nations," *Land Economics* 47 (1971): 334–44.

11. F. Barth, *Nomads of South Persia: The Baseri Tribe of the Khamseh Confederacy* (Oslo: Oslo University Press, 1975).

12. Sturdy, "The Exploitation Patterns of a Modern Reindeer Economy in Western Greenland."

13. P. Farb, *Man's Rise to Civilisation* (London: Paladin, 1971), 39–60.

14. FAO, *Production Yearbook 1990* (Rome: FAO, 1991).

15. B. H. S. von Bath, *The Agrarian History of Western Europe, AD 500–1850* (London: Arnold, 1963), 18. Also, G. Duby, *The Early Growth of the European Economy: Warriors and Peasants from the Seventh to the Twelfth Century,* trans. H. B. Clark (London: Weidenfeld and Nicholson, 1974), 28.

16. R. Duncan-Jones, *The Economy of the Roman Empire: Quantitative Studies* (Cambridge: Cambridge University Press, 1982), 49.

17. A. H. M. Jones, *The Later Roman Empire, 284-602 AD: A Social and Administrative Survey, Vol. 2* (Oxford: Oxford University Press, 1964), 767.

18. FAO, *Production Yearbook 1990,* 19.

19. R. Oliver, *The Problem of Bantu Expansion.*

20. M. I. Rostovtzeff, *The Social and Economic History of the Hellenistic World* (Oxford: Clarendon Press, 1953), 272–80.

21. Duncan-Jones, *The Economy of the Roman Empire,* 3. Also M. I. Findley, *Aspects of Antiquity* (London: Penguin Books, 1968).

22. O. Murray, *Early Greece* (Brighton, Sussex: Harvester, 1980), 80.

23. F. J. Simoons, "The Geographical Hypothesis and Lactose Malabsorption: A Weighting of the Evidence," *American Journal of Digestive Diseases,* Vol. 23 (1978): 963–80.

24. C. Tacitus, *The Agricola and Germania,* trans. S. A. Handford (London: Penguin Books, 1970), 102, 116.

25. M. Herity and G. Eogan, *Ireland in Prehistory* (London: Routledge and Kegan Paul, 1977), 3.

26. M. I. Finley, "Was Greek Civilisation Based on Slavery?" in *Slavery in Classical Antiquity: Views and Controversies,* ed. M. I. Finley (London: Heffer, 1960), 54.

27. A. H. M. Jones, "The Roman Economy." In *Studies in Ancient Economic and Administrative History,* ed. P. A. Brunt (Oxford: Blackwell, 1974), 138; M.I. Finley, *The Ancient Economy* (London: Chatto and Windus, 1975), 109.

28. J. Mokyr, *The Lever of Riches* (Oxford: Oxford University Press, 1992), 174.

29. A. H. M. Jones, *Athenian Democracy* (Oxford: Blackwell, 1960), 99–133.

30. W. H. McNeill, *Europe's Steppe Frontier 1500–1800* (Chicago: University of Chicago Press, 1964), 27.

31. R. S. Sharma, "Class Formation and Its Material Basis in the Upper Gangetic Basin (C1000–500)," *Indian Historical Review,* Vol. 2 (1975): 1–13.

32. N. Deer, *The History of Sugar, Vol. 2* (London: Chapman and Hall, 1950), 278.

33. M. Cratan and J. Walvin, *A Jamaican Plantation—The History of Worthy Park: 1670-1970* (London: Allen, 1970), 130.

34. M. Weber, "The Social Causes of the Decay of Ancient Civilizations," in *The Slave Economies,* ed. E. D. Genovese.

35. U.S. Department of Commerce, *Historical Statistics of the United States: Colonial Times to 1957* (Washington, D.C.: U.S. Department of Commerce, 1960), 9.

36. P. A. Brunt, *Social Conflicts in the Roman Republic* (London: Chatto and Windus, 1971).

37. E. Gibbon, *The Decline and Fall of the Roman Empire, Vol. 1* (London: Everyman, 1905), 93.

38. M. P. Todaro, *Economics for a Developing World* (London: Longman, 1982), 236.

39. P. H. Gulliver, ed., *The Family Herds: A Study of Two Pastoral Tribes in East Africa* (London: Rutledge, 1955), 247.

40. A. Crotty, *The Problems of Smallholder Agriculture in Southwest Perak State, Malaysia,* BA Dissertation unpublished (Dublin: Dublin University, 1978), 27.

41. Crotty, *Ireland in Crisis,* 236.

42. B. Bradshaw, *The Irish Constitutional Revolution of the Sixteenth Century* (Cambridge: Cambridge University Press, 1979), 28.

43. J. Blum, *The End of the Old Order in Rural Europe* (Princeton: Princeton University Press, 1978), 252–57.

44. E. Gellner, *Nations and Nationalism* (Oxford: Blackwell, 1983), 3.

45. Crotty, *Cattle, Economics and Development,* 117–44.

Chapter Four: The Growth of Individualist Capitalism

1. Tacitus, *The Agricola and Germania,* 102, 116.

2. R. Koebner, "The Settlement and Colonisation of Europe," in *The Cambridge Economic History of Europe, Vol. 1, The Agrarian Life of the Middle Ages,* ed. J. H. Chapman and E. Power (Cambridge: Cambridge University Press, 1941), 13.

3. FAO, *Production Yearbook—1990* (Rome: FAO, 1991), Table 15.

4. R. Brenner, "Agrarian Class Structure and Economic Development," in *The Brenner Debate,* ed. T. H. Aston and C. H. E. Philpin (Cambridge: Cambridge University Press, 1985), 33.

5. Koebner, *Settlement of Europe,* 20.

6. The alluvium also denied anchorage to trees, so that these richest parts of the ancient world had to import all their tree product requirements, including timber, charcoal, olive oil, and wine.

7. J. M. Roberts, *The Hutchinson History of the World* (London: Penguin, 1976), 183–85.

8. J. D. Bernal, *Science in History, Vol. 1: The Emergence of Science* (London: Penguin, 1969), 147.

9. M. Todd, *The Northern Barbarians: 100 BC to AD 300* (Oxford: Basil Blackwood, 1987), 77.

10. Crotty, *Cattle, Economics and Development*, 166.

11. Mokyr, *The Lever of Riches*, 55–56.

12. Mokyr, *Lever of Riches*, 44.

13. J. Hajnal, "European Marriage Patterns in Perspective," in *Population in History: Essays in Historical Demography*, ed. D. V. Glass and D. E. C. Eversley (London: Arnold, 1965), 101–43.

14. E. H. P. Brown and S. V. Hopkins, "Seven Centuries of the Prices of Consumables," in *Essays in Economic History, Vol. 2*, ed. E. M. Carus-Wilson (London: Arnold, 1962).

15. A. Maddisen, *Class Structure and Economic Growth: India and Pakistan Since the Mughals* (New York: Norton, 1971).

16. McNeill, *Europe's Steppe Frontier*, 66.

17. P. Anderson, *Lineages of the Absolutist State* (London: New Left Books, 1974), 417.

18. R. H. Hilton, "A Crisis of Feudalism," in *The Brenner Debate*, ed. T. H. Aston and C. H. E. Philpin (Cambridge: Cambridge University Press, 1985), 123.

19. G. Duby, *The Early Growth of the European Economy: Warriors and Peasants From the Seventh to the Twelfth Century*, trans. H. B. Clark (London: Weidenfeld and Nicholson, 1974), 178.

20. J. R. Strayer and R. Coulborn, "The Idea of Feudalism," in *Feudalism in History*, ed. R. Coulborn (Princeton: Princeton University Press, 1956), 3.

21. M. Davitt, *The Fall of Feudalism in Ireland; or The Story of the Land League Revolution* (London and New York: Harper Bros., 1904).

22. H. S. Klein, *Parties and Political Change in Bolivia: 1880-1952* (Cambridge: Cambridge University Press, 1969), 403.

23. M. Morishima, *Why Has Japan Succeeded?* (Cambridge: Cambridge University Press, 1982), 45; Reischauer, *The Japanese*, 57.

24. Morishima, *Why Has Japan Succeeded?* 57, 64.

25. N. Machiavelli, *The Prince*, trans. W. K. Marriott (London: Dent and Sons, 1908), 79.

26. M. Mann, *The Sources of Social Power, Vol. 1: A History of Power from the Beginning to AD 1760* (Cambridge: Cambridge University Press, 1986).

27. G. Ardant, "Financial Policy and Economic Infrastructure of Modern States and Nations," in *The Formation of the National States in Western Europe*, ed. C. Tilley (Princeton: Princeton University Press, 1975), 104.

28. E. L. Jones, *The European Miracle* (Cambridge: Cambridge University Press, 1981), 106.

29. Jones, *The European Miracle*, 132.

30. Ardant, *Financial Policy and Infrastructure*, 194.

31. McNeill, *Europe's Steppe Frontier*, 109.

32. J. F. Bosher, *French Finance 1770–1795* (Cambridge: Cambridge University Press, 1970), 304.

33. G. Rude, *Revolutionary Europe 1783–1815* (London: Collins, 1967), 76.

34. R. Forster, *The House of Saulx-Tavannes, Versailles and Burgundy 1700-1830* (Baltimore: Johns Hopkins University Press, 1971).

35. P. M. Pilbeam, *The Middle Classes in Europe,1789–1914* (London: Macmillan, 1990).

36. R. W. Southern, *Western Society and the Church in the Middle Ages* (London: Penguin, 1979).

37. Crotty, *Cattle, Economics and Development,*118–19.

38. Roberts, *Hutchinson History of the World,* 46.

39. Toynbee, *Mankind and Mother Earth.*

Chapter Five: Europe of the Regions

1. M. Bolch, *French Rural History: An Essay on its Basic Characteristics*, trans. J. Sondheimer (London: Routledge, 1966), 274.

2. FAO, *Production Yearbook:* Vol. 40 (Rome: FAO, 1986), 68.

3. McEvedy and Jones, *Atlas of World Population History*, 28.

4. P. Farb, *Man's Rise to Civilization* (London: Palladin, 1971), 39–40.

5. F. D. Logan, *The Vikings in History* (London: Hutchinson, 1983), 13.

6. P. Anderson, *Passages from Antiquity to Feudalism* (London: New Left Books, 1974), 176.

7. P. Foote and D. M. Wilson, *The Viking Achievement* (London: Sidgwick & Jackson, 1970), 69.

8. R. G. Popperwell, *Norway* (London: Ernest Benn, 1972), 69.

9. J. Blum, *Lord and Peasant in Russia from the Ninth to the Nineteenth Century* (Princeton: Princeton University Press, 1972), 21.

10. Blum, *Lord and Peasant in Russia,* 23; N. V. Riasonovsky, *A History of Russia* (Oxford: Oxford University Press, 1977), 51.

11. Blum, *Lord and Peasant in Russia,* 128.

12. Hitti, *The Near East in History,* 330.

13. V. J. Parry, "Materials of War in the Ottoman Empire," in *Studies in the Economic History of the Middle East,* ed. M. A. Cook (Oxford: Oxford University Press, 1970), 225–57.

14. S. Shaw, *History of the Ottoman Empire and Modern Turkey, Vol. 1, Empire of the Ghazis: 1280–1808* (Cambridge: Cambridge University Press, 1976); McNeill, *Europe's Steppe Frontier.*

15. Commission of the European Community, *Agricultural Situation in the Community, 1992 Report* (Brussels: EEC, 1992), Tables 258, 269.

16. McEvedy and Jones, *Atlas of World Population History,* 28.

17. Crotty, *Cattle, Economics and Development,* 23.

18. M. J. Tucker, *The Life of Thomas Howard* (The Hague: Mouton & Co, 1964), 37; G. Carter, *Outlines of English History: Dates, Facts, Events, People* (London: Ward Lock, 1984), 181.

19. G. R. Elton, *England Under the Tudors* (London: Methuen, 1955), 232.

20. L. Stone, *The Causes of the English Revolution 1529-1642* (London: Routledge and Keegan Paul, 1972), 154.

21. T. B. Macauley, *The Works of Lord Macauley: Essays and Biographies, Vol. II* (London: Longman Green, 1898), 190–91.

22. J. Blum, *The End of the Old Order in Rural Europe* (Princeton: Princeton University Press, 1978), 252-257.

23. Popperwell, *Norway,* 94–95; N. Davies, *God's Playground: A History of Poland, Vols. 1 & 2* (Oxford: Oxford University Press, 1981), 33; M. N. Pokrovsky, *A Brief History of Russia, Vol. 1,* trans. D. S. Mirsky (London: Martin Lawrence, 1933), 70.

24. See, e.g., J. Klein, *The Mesta: A Study of Spanish Economic History, 1273–1836* (Cambridge, Mass.: Harvard University Press, 1920).

25. E. H. P. Brown and S. V. Hopkins, "Seven Centuries of the Prices of Consumables," in *Essays in Economic History, Vol. 2,* ed. E.M. Carus-Wilson (London: Arnold, 1962).

26. von Bath, *The Agrarian History of Western Europe,* 80–81; P. Laslett, "Introduction: The Numerical Study of Society," in *An Introduction to English Historical Demography,* ed. E. A. Wrigley (London: Weidenfeld and Nicholson, 1966), 6; E. A. Wrigley, *Population in History* (London: Weidenfeld and Nicholson, 1969), 13.

27. R. B. Smith, *Land and Politics in the England of Henry VIII* (Oxford: Oxford University Press, 1970), 49.

28. Author's field research. Based on particulars of wine establishment in South Africa now, supplied by Professor A. Kassier, Department of Agricultural Economics, University of Stellenbosch, South Africa, March 1983.

29. B. Moore, *The Social Origins of Dictatorship and Democracy* (London: Penguin, 1967), 46–48.

30. I. Wallerstein, *The Modern World System: Mercantilism and the Consolidation of the European World Economy 1600–1750* (London: Academic Press, 1980), 85.

31. G. F. Mitchell, *The Irish Landscape* (London: Collins, 1976).

32. F. Bacon, *The Works of Francis Bacon, Vol. IV* (London: Millar, 1711), 280.

33. The Venerable Bede, *A History of the English Church and People,* trans. and intro. by L. Sherly-Price (Edinburgh: Penguin, 1956), 39.

34. Giraldus Cambrensis, *Topographia Hibernica,* translated as *The History and Topography of Ireland,* by J. J. O'Meara (London: Penguin, 1982), 53.

35. A. T. Lucas, "Cattle in Ancient and Medieval Irish Society," in *The O'Connell School Record 1937-58* (Dublin: O'Connell School, 1958), 75–85.

36. Lucas, *Cattle in Ancient and Medieval Irish Society.*

37. A. T. Lucas, *Irish Food Before the Famine* (Peterston super Ely, South Wales: Gwerin Publications, 1960), 14.

38. Crotty, *Cattle, Economics and Development,* 117–27.

39. F. McCormick, *Livestock Husbandry in Early Christian Ireland,* Ph.D. Thesis, (Belfast: Queen's University Belfast, 1988), 52.

40. C. Litton Falkiner, ed., "The Itinerary of Fynes Moryson," in *Illustration of Irish History and Topography Mainly of the Seventeenth Century* (London: Longman Green, 1904), 230, 321.

41. J. Kirwan, *Earl of Ormonde* (Dublin: Dublin University, 1991).

42. England, Departments of State and Official Bodies, Public Record Office, *Calendar of State Papers, Foreign Series, of the Reign of Elizabeth* (London: Longman, 1863), 269.

43. K. Hughes, "Introduction," in *A History of Medieval Ireland,* ed. A. A. Otway Ruthvan (Cambridge: Cambridge University Press, 1968), 9.

44. B. Bradshaw, *The Irish Constitutional Revolution of the Sixteenth Century* (Cambridge: Cambridge University Press, 1979), 28.

45. M. McCurtain, *Tudor and Stuart Ireland* (Dublin: Gill and Macmillan, 1972), 117.

46. T. C. Smout, *A History of the Scottish People, 1560–1830* (London: Collins, 1969).

47. R. Koebner, "The Settlement and Colonisation of Europe," in *The Cambridge Economic History of Europe from the Decline of the Roman Empire, Vol. 1: The Agrarian Life of the Middle Ages* (Cambridge: Cambridge University Press, 1941), 18.

Chapter Six: Capitalist Colonialism

1. M. M. Postan, "Medieval Agrarian Society in its Prime," in *Cambridge Economic History of Europe, Vol. 1* (Cambridge: Cambridge University Press, 1966), 548–623.

2. J. Z. Titow, *English Rural Society 1200–1350* (London: Allen and Unwin, 1969), 53.

3. D. Denoon, *Settler Capitalism: The Dynamics of Dependent Development in the Southern Hemisphere* (Oxford: Oxford University Press, 1983), 25.

4. E. Burke, *Speeches and Letters on American Affairs* (London: Dent, 1908), 89.

5. Denoon, *Settler Capitalism,* 27.

6. J. H. Parry, *Europe and a Wider World* (London: Hutchinson, 1949), 61–64.

7. N. Deerr, *The History of Sugar, Vol. 1* (London: Chapman and Hall, 1950), 379; A. Burns, *A History of the British West Indies* (London: Dent, 1965), 216–17.

8. E. Williams, *From Columbus to Castro: The History of the Caribbean 1492–1969* (London: Andre Deutch, 1970), 162; R. Pares, *Yankees and Creoles* (London: Longmans Green, 1956), 86.

9. R. B. Sheridan, *Sugar and Slavery: An Economic History of the British West Indies* (Barbados: Caribbean University Press, 1974), 313; Williams, *From Columbus to Castro;* Pares, *Yankees and Creoles.*

10. J. H. Elliot, "The Decline of Spain," in *Past & Present*, No. 20, 1961.

11. M. E. Chamberlain, *Britain and India* (Newton Abbott, Devon: David and Charles, 1974), 23.

12. J. Lynch, *Spain Under the Hapsburgs*, Vol. II (Oxford: Basil Blackwell, 1964), 11.

13. See, for example, McNeill, *Europe's Steppe Frontier.*

14. H. S. Klein, *Parties and Political Change in Bolivia: 1880–1952* (Cambridge: Cambridge University Press, 1969), 379.

15. McEvedy and Jones, *Atlas of World Population History*, 277, 280.

16. U.S. Department of Commerce, *Historical Statistics of the United States: Colonial Times to 1957* (Washington, D.C.: U.S. Department of Commerce, 1960), 9.

17. See, for example, Morison, Commager and Leuchtenberg, *The Growth of the American Republic*, Vol. 1 (Oxford: Oxford University Press, 1969), 590 *et seq.*

18. There was, however, a return to conditions of land abundance and labor scarcity in Africa in the late nineteenth and early twentieth centuries. A variant of the *encomienda* system and the slavery that were practiced in the western hemisphere was then introduced to Africa. That was a poll tax which compelled adult male Africans to sell their labor, either to the colonial authority or to western estates, in order to earn enough to

pay the tax, failure to pay which was punished by imprisonment with hard labor. A poll tax is retained in several postcolonial African countries. It may also be recalled that serfdom, which as practiced in eastern Europe had much in common with slavery, was retained in Russia until 1861 and in Poland until 1864.

19. C. M. Andrews, *The Colonial Period of American History*, Vol. 2 (New Haven: Yale University Press, 1936), 197.

20. R. C. Mills, *The Colonisation of Australia: 1824–42* (London: Sidgwick and Jackson, 1915), 63–64.

21. Mills, *The Colonisation of Australia*, 205–17.

22. U.S. Department of Agriculture Economic Research Service, *Major Uses of Land in the USA* (Washington, D.C.: USDA, 1969); European Communities Commission, *Memorandum on the Reform of Agriculture in the EEC* (Brussels: EEC, 1968).

23. McEvedy and Jones, *Atlas of World Population History*, 272.

24. Crotty, *Ireland in Crisis*, 232–41.

25. J. A. Schumpeter, *History of Economic Analysis* (Oxford: Oxford University Press, 1955), 998–1026.

26. Chamberlain, *Britain and India*, 114.

27. C. Furtado, *Economic Development of Latin America* (Cambridge: Cambridge University Press, 1970), 30.

28. C. Barlow, *The Natural Rubber Industry: Its Development, Technology and Economy in Malaysia* (Kuala Lumpur: Oxford University Press, 1978).

29. Crotty, *The Problems of Smallholder Agriculture in South West Perak State, Malaysia*, Table 5.

30. Food and Agricultural Organisation of the United Nations, *Production Yearbook 1966; Ditto 1981* (Rome: FAO, 1966 & 1981).

31. See, for example, Bank for International Settlements, *10th Annual Report* (Basle: Bank for International Settlements, 1940), 89.

32. McEvedy and Jones, *Atlas of World Population History*, 343.

33. McEvedy and Jones, *Atlas of World Population History*, 344.

34. E. L. Jones, *The European Miracle* (Cambridge: Cambridge University Press, 1981), 198.

35. McEvedy and Jones, *Atlas of World Population History*, 43.

36. C. M. Cipolla, *The Economic History of World Population* (London: Penguin, 1965), 82.

37. N. V. Riasonovsky, *A History of Russia* (Oxford: Oxford University Press, 1977), 331.

38. Cipolla, *The Economic History of World Population*, 80.

39. C. Clark, *Population Growth and Land Use* (London: Macmillan, 1977), 108.

40. Based on:

a.)	Increase in national income	£232M (1801) >	£1,643M (1901)
b.)	Fall in general price index (Base 1865/85 = 100)	167 (1800-4) >	80 (1896-1900)
c.)	Increase in population	10.7m (1800) >	36.7m (1900)

Source: B. R. Mitchell and P. Deane, *British Historical Statistics* (Cambridge: Cambridge University Press, 1962).

41. A. M. Carr-Saunders, *World Population: Past Growth and Present Trends* (Oxford: Oxford University Press, 1936), 61–68.

42. D. W. Fryer and J. C. Jackson, *Indonesia* (London: Benn, 1977), 58.

43. Jones, *The European Miracle*, 197.

44. P. Laslett, "The European Family and Industrialization," in *Europe and the Rise of Capitalism,* ed. Bachelor, Hall, and Mann (Oxford: Blackwell, 1988), 235.

45. *The Ecologist,* December 1980.

46. Cipolla, *The Economic History of World Population,* 105.

47. K. G. Myrdal, *An International Economy: Problems and Prospects* (New York: Harper and Brothers, 1956), quoted in G. Barraclough, *An Introduction to Contemporary History* (London: Penguin, 1966), 231.

48. FAO, *Production Yearbook,* Vol 44 (Rome: FAO, 1990).

49. Crotty, *Cattle, Economics and Development,* 117–44.

50. Crotty, *Cattle, Economics and Development,* 138.

51. Crotty, *Cattle, Economics and Development,* 104–49.

52. Crotty, *Cattle, Economics and Development,* 149–55.

53. L. M. Cullen, *The Emergence of Modern Ireland* (London: Batsford, 1981), 87.

Chapter Seven: Political Independence

1. T. B. Macauley, *The Works of Lord Macaulay, Vol. II, Essays and Biographies* (London: Longmans, 1898), 178–212.

2. A. Toynbee, *A Study of History* (London: Oxford University Press, 1954).

3. Mann, *The Sources of Social Power, Vol. 1,* 166–68.

4. McEvedy and Jones, *Atlas of World Population History,* 349.

5. World Bank, *World Bank Atlas* (Washington, D.C.: World Bank, 1989), 11.

6. E. Burke, *Letter to Sir Hercules Langrishe* (London: Debrett, 1792), 8.

7. C. Furtado, *Economic Development of Latin America* (Cambridge: Cambridge University Press, 1970), 17–18.

8. R. H. Morse, "The Heritage of Latin America," in *The Founding of New Societies,* ed. L. Hartz (New York: Harcourt Brace and World, 1964), 160.

9. D. E. Worcester and W. G. Schaeffer, *The Growth and Culture of Latin America,* Vol. 1 (London: Oxford University Press, 1971), 387–89.

10. R. F. Foster, *Modern Ireland: 1600-1972* (London: Allen Lane, 1988), 251.

11. O. MacDonagh, *The Hereditary Bondsman: Daniel O'Connell, 1775–1829* (London: Weidenfeld and Nicholson, 1988), 273.

12. Crotty, *Irish Agricultural Production,* 277; British Parliamentary Papers BPP XCI (C.6524), 1891, *Agricultural Returns of Great Britain* (London: HMSO, 1891), 78–79.

13. T. W. Moody, "The Irish University Question of the Nineteenth Century," *History* XLIII, 1958.

14. That equilibrium has been disturbed in recent decades by the introduction of mechanized grass silage making, which enables Irish farmers to conserve as much winter fodder as desired, though at considerable cost. Cow and cattle numbers have accordingly been increased, while the number engaged declines and tillage contracts.

15. BPP 1902 (285) LV (London: HMSO, 1902); BPP 1914 (387) L, *Returns Relating to Imperial Revenue (Great Britain and Ireland) for 1914* (London: HMSO, 1914).

16. Crotty, *The Cattle Crisis and the Small Farmer,* 14.

17. G. Dangerfield, *The Damnable Question: A Study in Anglo-Irish Relations* (London: Constable, 1977), 133.

18. Dangerfield, *The Damnable Question,* 251, 192–300.

19. J. M. Curran, *The Birth of the Irish Free State* (Tuscaloosa: University of Alabama Press, 1923), 157.

20. Curran, *The Birth of the Irish Free State,* 222.

21. Chamberlain, *Britain and India*, 171.

22. A. Seal, *The Emergence of Indian Nationalism* (Cambridge: Cambridge University Press, 1968), 195.

23. Seal, *The Emergence of Indian Nationalism*, 193.

24. J. Breuilly, *Nationalism and the State* (Manchester: Manchester University Press, 1982), 141.

25. Chamberlain, *Britain and India*, 111.

26. Bannarjee, *Under Two Flags*, 126.

27. McEvedy and Jones, *Atlas of World Population History*, 154.

28. W. A. Dando, *The Geography of Famine* (London: Edward Arnold, 1980), 81.

29. C. M. Cipolla, *The Economic History of World Population* (London: Penguin, 1965), 105.

30. J. Strachey, *The End of Empire* (London: Victor Gollancz, 1959), 124.

31. Barraclough, *An Introduction to Contemporary History*, 154.

32. A. D. Smith, *State and Nation in the Third World* (Brighton, Sussex: Wheatsheaf, 1983), 74–75.

Chapter Eight: The Capitalist Colonisation of Ireland

1. M. Dolley, *Anglo-Norman Ireland* (Dublin: Gill and Macmillan,1972).

2. Central Statistics Office of Ireland (henceforth CSO), *Census of Agriculture— June 1991* (Dublin: Government Stationery Office, 1992), Table 2.

3. F. Bacon, "The Works of Sir Francis Bacon, Vol. IV," quoted by P. Anderson, in *Lineages of the Absolutist State* (London: New Left Books, 1975), 131.

4. L. M. Cullen, *The Emergence of Modern Ireland, 1600–1900* (London: Batsford Academic, 1981), 11.

5. C. Barlow, *The Natural Rubber Industry: Its Development, Technology and Economy in Malaysia* (Kuala Lumpur: Oxford University Press, 1978), 201.

6. H. S. Wilson, *The Imperial Experience in Sub-Saharan Africa Since 1870* (Minneapolis: University of Minnesota Press, 1977), 155.

7. M. MacCurtain, *Tudor and Stuart Ireland* (Dublin: Gill and Macmillan, 1972), 102.

8. R. F. Foster, *Modern Ireland: 1600-1972* (London: Penguin, 1988), 14.

9. MacCurtain, *Tudor and Stuart Ireland,* 127.

10. S. J. Connolly, *Priests and People in Pre-Famine Ireland: 1780–1845* (Dublin: Gill and Macmillan, 1982), 75.

11. Another was that between the Muslim religion of the Ottoman rulers and the Christianity of many of their Balkan subjects.

12. J. H. Hutton, *Caste in India: Its Nature, Function and Origins* (Oxford: Oxford University Press, 1963), 149.

13. L. Meir, *Primitive Government* (London: Penguin, 1962), 135; D. W. Philippson, *The Later Pre-History of Southern Africa* (London: Heinemann Educational, 1977), 16.

14. J. H. Hexter, *Reappraisals in History* (London: University of Chicago Press, 1979), 109.

15. G. de Beaumont, *Ireland: Social, Political and Religious,* ed. W. C. Taylor, (London, 1839), 282–83.

16. K. S. Boteigheimer, *English Money and Irish Land* (Oxford: Oxford University Press, 1971), 142–63.

17. D. Woodward, "The Anglo-Irish Livestock Trade in the Seventeenth Century," *Irish Historical Studies,* Vol. 18 (Dublin: 1973), 489–523.

18. D. V. Glass and D. E. C. Eversley, eds., *Population in History* (London: Arnold, 1965); E. H. P. Brown and S. V. Hopkins, "Seven Centuries of the Prices of Consumables," in *Essays in Economic History,* Vol. 2, ed. E. M. Carus-Wilson (London: Arnold, 1962).

19. E. Strauss, *Sir William Petty: Portrait of a Genius* (London: Bodley Head, 1954), 226.

20. W. Petty, "A Treatise of Ireland," in *The Economic Writings of Sir William Petty,* Vol. 2, ed. CH Hull (Cambridge: Cambridge University Press, 1899).

21. J. Sheppard, *The Redlegs of Barbados* (Milwood, N.Y.: KTO Press, 1977), 34.

22. Sheppard, *The Redlegs of Barbados,* 35.

23. C. V. Wedgwood, *Thomas Wentworth, First Earl of Strafford 1593–1641—A Revaluation* (London: Jonathan Cape, 1961).

24. C. A. Edie, "The Irish Cattle Bills," in *Transactions of the American Philosophical Society,* Vol. 60, Part 2 (1970).

25. Crotty, *Irish Agricultural Production: Its Volume and Structure,* 10.

26. CSO, *Statistical Abstract* (Dublin: Government Stationery Office, 1936), 33.

27. J. O'Donovan, *Economic History of Live Stock in Ireland* (Cork: Cork University Press, 1940), 109.

28. von Bath, *The Agrarian History of Western Europe,* 326–27.

29. R. Pares, *Yankees and Creoles* (London: Longmans, Green, 1956), 86.

30. K. H. Connell, *The Population of Ireland, 1750–1854* (Oxford: Oxford University Press, 1950).

31. C. O'Grada, *Ireland Before and After the Famine* (Manchester: Manchester University Press, 1988), 109.

32. Crotty, *Irish Agricultural Production,* 277.

33. W. Tighe, *Statistical Observations Relative to the County of Kilkenny, Made in the Years 1800 and 1801* (Dublin: 1802), 216, 473.

34. Crotty, *Ireland in Crisis,* 42–43.

35. Crotty, *Irish Agricultural Production,* 283.

36. CSO, *Statistical Astract,* 1969.

37. Connell, *The Population of Ireland,* 25.

38. British Parliamentary Papers (henceforth BPP) 1890/91 (C.6542) XCI, *Agricultural Returns of Great Britain* (London: HMSO, 1891), 78–79.

39. Crotty, *Irish Agricultural Production,* 35–51.

40. E. Strauss, *Irish Nationalism and British Democracy* (London: Methuen, 1951), 81.

41. Crotty, *Irish Agricultural Production,* 279.

42. R. Kane, *The Industrial Resources of Ireland* (Dublin, 1845).

43. CSO, *Statistical Abstract* (1936), 6–7.

44. BPP, Vols. XIX, XX, XXL, *Devon Commission Report "...Into the State of the Law and Practice in Respect of the Occupation of Land in Ireland"* (London: HMSO, 1845), 440.

45. Crotty, *Irish Agricultural Production*, 289–93.

46. CSO, *Statistical Abstract* (1936), 168.

47. Crotty, *Irish Agricultural Production*, 85–88.

48. Commission of Enquiry into Banking, Currency and Credit (henceforth BCC), *Reports* (Dublin: Government Stationery Office, 1938), 6.

49. J. Lee, *The Modernisation of Ireland* (Dublin: Gill and Macmillan, 1973), 16.

50. BCC, *Reports*, 9.

51. R. Orsingher, *Banks of the World* (New York: Walker & Co., 1967).

52. M. Moynihan, *Currency and Central Banking in Ireland, 1922–60* (Dublin: Gill and Macmillan, 1975), 41.

53. Department of Foreign Affairs, *Facts About Ireland* (Dublin: Department of Foreign Affairs, 1985), 21.

54. Crotty, *Cattle, Economics and Development*, 123–24.

55. O'Donovan, *Economic History of Live Stock in Ireland*, 60-73.

56. CSO, *Statistical Abstract* (1936), 168–69.

57. BCC, *Reports*, 437.

58. Crotty, *Irish Agricultural Production*, 83.

59. Crotty, *Irish Agricultural Production*, 84–92; CSO, *Statistical Abstract*, 46–47.

60. McEvedy and Jones, *Atlas of World Population History*, 32.

61. Connell, *The Population of Ireland*, 27.

62. C. O'Grada, *The Great Irish Famine* (Dublin: Gill and Macmillan, 1989), 14.

63. P. Lynch and J. Vaizey, *Guinness's Brewery in the Irish Economy 1759-1876* (Cambridge: Cambridge University Press. 1960).

64. BPP. (17) XXXI, *Report to the Commissioners of Enquiry into the Excise Establishment; Malt. Appendix No 61* (London: HMSO, 1835).

65. BPP. (155) LV through (242) LXIII, *Return of the number of Persons in each of the Collections of the United Kingdom Licenced as Brewers* (London: HMSO, 1856—1860).

66. BPP. (C82.1) XX, *Report to the Commissioner of Inland Revenue on the Duties Under their Management for the Years 1856 to 1869* (London: HMSO, 1870).

67. J. E. Vaizey, *The Brewing Industry 1886–1951: An Economic Study* (London: Pitman, 1958), 6.

68. R. D. C. Black, "The Process of Industrialisation, 1850–1920," in *Ulster Since 1800*, ed. T. W. Moody and J. C. Beckett (London: BBC, 1955), 59.

69. R. D. Crotty, "Modernisation and Land Reform: Real of Cosmetic? The Irish Case," in *Journal of Peasant Studies*, Vol. 11, No. 1 (London: Cass & Co., 1983), 105; Crotty, *Cattle, Economics and Development*, 15–22.

70. Crotty, *Ireland in Crisis*, 268, n62.

71. Crotty, *Ireland in Crisis*, 268, n62.

72. Crotty, *Ireland in Crisis*, 268, n63.

73. Crotty, *Ireland in Crisis*, 268, n64.

74. Ireland has an exceptionally large number of persons in mental hospitals. See D Walsh, "Hospitalised Psychiatric Morbidity in the Republic of Ireland," *British Journal of Psychiatry* Vol. 114 (1968): 11–14.

75. *Census for Ireland 1841,* BPP. 1843 (459) XXIV; *Census of Population of England and Wales. Occupation Abstract* BPP. 1845 (606) XIX; *Census of Ireland 1911. General Report* BPP. 192/13 (Cd 6663) XVIII; *Census of England and Wales 1911. Occupations and Industries* BPP. 1913 (Cd. 7018) LXXVIII.

76. Crotty, *Irish Agricultural Production,* 354.

77. Crotty, *Irish Agricultural Production,* 353.

78. Crotty, *Irish Agricultural Production,* 358.

79. Crotty, *Irish Agricultural Production,* 356.

80. J. C. Beckett, *The Making of Modern Ireland* (London: Faber and Faber, 1966), 359.

81. Tighe, *Statistical Observations.*

82. See for example, T. W. Moody, "Introduction," in *A New History of Ireland: Early Modern Ireland,* ed. T. W. Moody, F. X. Martin, F. J. Byrne (Oxford: Clarendon, 1976).

83. See, for example, R. F. Foster, *Modern Ireland 1600–1972* (London: Allen Lane, 1988), 376.

84. BCC, *Reports,* 9.

85. CSO, *Statistical Abstract* (1936), 6.

86. Crotty, *Irish Agricultural Production,* 356.

87. Crotty, *Irish Agricultural Production.*

88. F. Callavan, *The Parnell Split* (Cork: Cork University Press, 1992), 4.

Chapter Nine: The Aftermath of Capitalist Colonialism

1. K. Kennedy and B. Dowling, *Economic Growth in Ireland: The Experience Since 1947* (Dublin: Gill & Macmillan, 1975), 14.

2. Kennedy and Dowling, *Economic Growth in Ireland,* 18.

3. Central Statistics Office of Ireland (henceforth CSO), *Statistical Abstract* (Dublin: Stationery Office, 1931), Tab 25; CSO, *Statistical Abstract* (1933), Tab 2.32.

4. London and Cambridge Economic Service (henceforth LCES), *The British Economy: Key Statistics 1900–1970* (London: Times Newspapers, 1974), 9, Tab F; OECD, *Quarterly Labor Force Statistics,* No. 4 (Paris: OECD, 1990), 65.

5. OECD, *Labor Force Statistics, 1971–1991* (Paris: OECD, 1993), Tab 4.0; 1926 figure estimated by back projection of later growth rates.

6. FAO, *Production Yearbook 1992* (Rome: FAO, 1993), Tab 3; 1926 figure estimated by back projection of later growth rates.

7. Commission on Agriculture, *Saorstat Report* (Dublin: Stationery Office, 1923), 5.

8. CSO, *Statistical Abstract* (1933), Tab 172, 124; *Statistical Abstract* (1936), Tab 172, 126; Commission of Enquiry into Banking, Currency and Credit (henceforth BCC), *Report* (Dublin: Stationery Office, 1938), 452.

9. Public Services Organization Review Group 1966-1969, *Report: Parliamentary Paper 792* (Dublin: Stationery Office, 1969), 11.

10. Department of Industry and Commerce, *Irish Trade Journal,* Feb. 1926 (Dublin: Stationery Office, 1926), 97; CSO, *Statistical Abstract* (1934), Tab 260.

11. Department of Health, *Report on Vital Statistics* (Dublin: Stationery Office, 1966).

12. Department of Health, *Report on Vital Statistics,* 2, Tab 1.

13. CSO, *Statistical Abstract* (1933), Tab 1.

14. CSO, *Statistical Abstract* (1936), Tab 172.

15. National Industrial Economic Council (henceforth NIEC), *Report on Full Employment* (Dublin: Stationery Office, 1967), 15, Tab 2.

16. W. J. L. Ryan, "Measurement of Tariff Levels in Ireland," *Journal of the Statistical and Social Enquiry Society of Ireland,* Vol. XVIII (Dublin, 1949): 130. See also, Crotty, *Irish Agricultural Production*, 135.

17. CSO, *Statistical Abstract* (1936), 6–7, Tab 8.

18. CSO, *Statistical Abstract* (1936), 166–67, Tab 237.

19. CSO, *Statistical Abstract,* (1936), 168, Tab 239.

20. CSO, *Statistical Abstract* (1936), 60, Tab 78.

21. NIEC, *Report on Full Employment.*

22. For state expenditure, CSO, *Statistical Abstract* (1940), Tab 165; for GNP figures, J. Meenam, *The Irish Economy Since 1922* (Liverpool: Liverpool University Press, 1970), 58–59.

23. BCC, *Report,* 300.

24. Kennedy and Dowling, *Economic Growth in Ireland,* 18.

25. LCES, *The British Economy,* 5, Tab B (For UK Figures); BCC, *Report,* 78 (For Irish GDP growth 1929–33).

26. LCES, The British Economy, 8, Tab E; Department of Health, Report on Vital *Statistics* (Dublin: Stationery Office, 1966), 2, Tab 1.

27. CSO, *Statistical Abstract* (1939), Tab 83; CSO, *Statistical Abstract* (1942), Tab 82.

28. CSO, *Statistical Abstract* (1938), Tab 110; CSO, *Statistical Abstract* (1942), Tab 87.

29. CSO, *Statistical Abstract* (1942), Tab 46; CSO, *Statistical Abstract* (1958), Tab 53.

30. Meenan, *The Irish Economy Since 1922,* 58–59.

31. F. List, *The Natural System of Political Economy* (1837), trans. and ed. W. O. Henderson (London: Cassell, 1983).

32. Department of Health, *Report on Vital Statistics,* 2, Tab 1; E. Nevin, *Public Debt and Economic Development.* Paper No 11 (Dublin: Economic Research Institute, 1962).

33. Quoted in M. Moynihan, *Currency and Central Banking in Ireland 1922-60* (Dublin: Gill and Macmillan, 1975), 41.

34. CSO, *Statistical Abstract* (1952), Tab 200; LCES, *The British Economy,* Tab A.

35. CSO, *Statistical Abstract,* (1952), Tab 200; LCES, *The British Economy,* Tab A.

36. Maddison, *Economic Growth in the West,* 28, Tab 1-1.

37. NIEC, *Report on Full Employment,* 15,Tab 2.

38. CSO, *Statistical Abstract* (1956): 130, Tab110; 131, Tab111; 232, Tab239.

39. CSO, *Statistical Abstract* (1956): 130, Tab110; (1957): 239, Tab 230.

40. T. K. Whitaker, *Interests* (Dublin: Institute of Public Administration, 1983), 89.

41. CSO, *Statistical Abstract* (1957): 239, Tab230.

42. CSO, *Statistical Abstract* (1960): Tab 272, for data on Banks' assets within the State; CSO, *Statistical Abstract* (1962): 318, Tab 338, for price rise calculations.

43. CSO, *Statistical Abstract* (1957): Tab 219.

44. NIEC, *Report on Full Employment* 15, Tab 2.

45. Department of Health, *Report on Vital Statistics* (1966): 2, Tab 1.

46. Department of Finance, *Economic Development* (Dublin: Stationery Office, 1958), 5.

47. W. W. Rostow, "The Take-off into Self-Sustained Growth," *Economic Journal*, Vol. LXVI (March, 1956): 25–48.

48. Department of Finance, *Economic Development*, 7.

49. Whitaker, *Interests*, 53.

50. A. Foley and D. McAleese, *Overseas Industry In Ireland* (Dublin: Gill and Macmillan, 1991), 106.

51. D. McAleese, *Effective Tariffs and the Structure of Industrial Protection in Ireland* (Dublin: ESRI., 1971), 50.

52. CSO, *Statistical Abstract* (1961):151, Tab 126; 261, Tab 245; for 1960 data. CSO, *Statistical Abstract* (1992): 166, Tab 6.3; p273, Tab 11.3 for 1990 data.

53. World Bank, *World Development Report* (Washington, D.C.: World Bank, 1992), Tabs. 1,14.

54. CSO, *Statistical Abstracts*. Various years

55. CSO, *Statistical Abstracts*. Various years

56. A. Sampson, *The Money Lenders* (London: Hodder and Stoughton, 1981), 12-13.

57. CSO, *National Income and Expenditure*. Various years.

58. National Economic and Social Council, (enceforth NESC), *A Strategy for Development 1986–1990*. Report No. 83 (Dublin: Stationery Office, 1986), Tab 3.1.

59. NESC, *A Strategy for the Nineties*. Report No. 89 (Dublin: Stationery Office, 1990), Tab A1.6.

60. CSO, *National Income and Expenditure,* Various years.

61. CSO, *Statistical Abstract* (1992), Tabs 11.4 and 11.23.

62. Fine Gael, *The Just Society* (Dublin: Fine Gael, 1965).

63. Kennedy and Dowling, *Economic Growth in Ireland*, 18.

64. T. Callan, B. Nolan, B. J. Whelan, D. F. Hannan, with S. Creighton, *Poverty, Incomes and Welfare in Ireland* (Dublin: Economic and Social Research Institute, 1990), 74, 96.

65. R. D. Crotty, *Maastricht: Time to Say No* (Dublin: National Platform for Employment, Democracy and Neutrality, 1992), 5–6.

66. CSO, *Census of Population; Vol 7, Occupations* (Dublin: Stationery Office, 1981), 4, Tab 2; CSO, *Summary Population Report* (1986), 49, Tab 21.

67. CSO, *Statistical Abstract* (1962), Tab 68; CSO, *Statistical Abstract* (1992), Tab 3.16.

68. CSO, *Statistical Abstract* (1931), Tab 38; *Statistical Abstract,* (1961), Tab 33; *Statistical Abstract,* (1991), Tab 3.2.

69. Commission of the European Community (henceforth EC), *The Agricultural Situation in the Community*. Various issues, various years (Brussels: EC), Tabs 3.1.2, 3.4.2.

70. EC, *The Agricultural Situation in the Community* (1990), Tab 2.0.1, for Agricultural output per head; A. Matthews, *Managing the EU Structural Funds* (Cork: Cork University Press, 1994), for GNP per head.

71. EC, *The Agricultural Situation in the Community* (1991), Tabs 3.1.13, 2.01.

72. Central Bank, *Quarterly Bulletins,* (Dublin: Central Bank, Autumn 1962, November 1982), for bank advances to agriculture; CSO, *Statistical Abstract* (1982–85): Tabs 64, 67, for value of net agricultural output.

73. R, O'Connor and F. Conlon, *Agricultural and Forestry Land Prices in Ireland* (Dublin: Economic and Social Research Institute, 1993), 1.

74. CSO, *Irish Statistical Bulletin* (March 1954), 24; CSO, *Irish Statistical Bulletin* (March, 1972), 28; CSO, *Irish Statistical Bulletin* (March, 1978), 37.

75. Teagasc, *National Farm Survey* (Dublin: 1992), 51,54.

76. E. O'Malley, *Industry and Economic Development: The Challenge for the Late-Comer* (Dublin: Gill and Macmillan, 1989), 101, Tab 6.2.

77. NESC, *A Review of Industrial Policy* (Dublin: Stationery Office, 1982), 388.

78. EC, *European Economy:* No 51 (Brussels: Commission of the EC, 1992), 79.

79. O'Malley, *Industry and Economic Development,* 184, 205.

80. O'Malley, *Industry and Economic Development,* 187.

81. O'Malley, *Industry and Economic Development,* 101.

82. CSO, *Census of Industrial Production* (Dublin: Stationery Office, 1989), 68, Tab 5.

83. Foley and McAleese, *Overseas Industry In Ireland,* 63.

84. McAleese, *Effective Tariffs,* 50.

85. O'Malley, *Industry and Economic Development,* 101; CSO, *Statistical Abstract* (1931), Tab 29.

86. CSO, *Statistical Abstract* (1962), Tab 122; CSO, *Statistical Abstract* (1992), Tab 4.14.

87. OECD, *Labor Force Statistics 1962–1982; 1970–1990* (Paris: OECD, 1982 and 1990).

88. CSO, *Household Budget Survey 1987* (Dublin: Stationery Office, 1987), 20–21, 26–27.

89. CSO, *Statistical Abstract* (1976), Tab 310; CSO, *Statistical Abstract* (1986), Tab 13.1.

90. CSO, *Statistical Bulletin Dec 1992* (Dublin: Stationery Office, 1992), 508.

91. CSO, *Statistical Abstract* (1977), Tab 130; CSO, *Statistical Abstract* (1986), Tab 5.10; CSO, *Statistical Abstract* (1992), Tab 5.7.

92. P. Humphreys, *Public Service Employment: An Examination of Strategies in Ireland and Other European Countries* (Dublin: Institute of Public Administration, 1983), 14, 88, Tab 11.11.

93. CSO, *Statistical Abstract* (1931), 14, Tab 24.

94. EC, *European Economy* No 51 (Brussels: EC, May 1992), 225, Tab 46.

95. EC, *European Economy* No 51 (Brussels: EC, May 1992), 225, Tab 46.

96. CSO, *Statistical Abstract—Various Years.*

97. CSO, *Statistical Abstract* (1954), Tab 290; CSO, *Statistical Abstract* (1977), Tab 316.

98. *Sunday Tribune,* 5 Nov 1989, Dublin.

99. NESC / Telesis Consultancy Group, *A Review of Industrial Policy.* Report No 64 (Dublin: Stationery Office, 1982), 111.

100. CSO, *Statistical Abstract* (1992), Tabs 11.1, 11.5.

101. CSO, *Statistical Abstract* (1965), Tab 237; CSO, *Statistical Abstract* (1992), Tabs 6.3, 11.3.

102. CSO, *Statistical Abstract* (1932), Tabs 83, 239; CSO, *Statistical Abstract* (1955), Tabs 105, 304.

103. E. Burke, *Letter to Sir Hercules Langrishe* (London: Debrett, 1792), 8.

104. W. S. Churchill, *The Aftermath: Being a Sequel to the Last Crisis* (London: Macmillan, 1929), 319.

105. CSO, *Statistical Abstract* (1992), Tab 2.1.

106. Kennedy and Dowling, *Economic Growth in Ireland,* 18.

107. Census of Population, *General Report* (Dublin: Stationery Office, 1851), 634–36; CSO, *Statistical Abstract* (1931), Tab 24; CSO, *Statistical Abstract* (1992), Tab 2.32.

108. CSO, *Statistical Abstract* (1931), Tab 50; CSO, *Statistical Abstract* (1954), Tab 54.

109. CSO, *Statistical Abstract* (1969), Tabs 159, 169, for calculation of Unemployment payment; CSO, *Statistical Abstract. Summary of Principal Statistics* (1966), Tab 238, for GNP / head.

110. CSO, *Statistical Abstract* (1992), Tab 8.27; CSO, *Statistical Abstract* (1992), Tab 11.3; Crotty, *Maastricht: Time to Say No,* Tab 1.

111. CSO, *Statistical Abstract* (1992), 23, Tab 2.2.

112. Eurostat, *Employment and Unemployment.* Theme 3, Series C (Brussels: Eurostat, 1988), 89.

113. *Irish Times,* 17 Sept. 1993, Dublin.

114. F. S. L. Lyons, *Ireland Since the Famine* (London: Fontana, 1985), 442–43.

115. CSO, *Statistical Abstract* (1964), Tab 42.

116. L. De Paor, *Divided Ulster* (London: Penguin, 1971).

Chapter Ten: From Undevelopment to Development

1. R. O'Connor and F. Conlon, *Agricultural and Forestry Land Prices in Ireland* (Dublin: Economic and Social Research Institute, 1993), Tab S.1.

2. Commission of the EC, *The Agricultural Situation in the Community* (Brussels: Commission of the EC, 1993), Table 105.

3. Teagasc, *National Farm Survey* (Dublin: Stationery Office, 1992), Tables 26b, 26d.

4. Central Bank of Ireland, *Annual Report* (Dublin: Central Bank of Ireland, 1992), Table D4.

5. National Economic and Social Council, *A Review of Industrial Policy Report No 64* (Dublin: Stationery Office, 1981), 111.

6. Central Bank of Ireland, *Annual Report,* 24, Table D4.

7. For a discussion of the Verdoorn Law, see K. A. Kennedy and B. Dowling, *Economic Growth in Ireland: The Experience Since 1947* (Dublin: Gill and Macmillan, 1975), 72-4.

8. Central Bank of Ireland, *Annual Report,* 14.

9. Teagasc, *National Farm Survey,* 47.

10. Eurostat, *Basic Statistics of the Community* (Brussels: EC Commission, 1977), Tab 9; Ditto (1978), Tab 18; Ditto (1992), Tabs 2.5, 3.18.

Index

About the Author

Raymond D. Crotty started his adult life as a farmer in Kilkenny, Ireland. He subsequently lectured in Agricultural Economics at the University of Wales. He went on to work as a consultant in several Third World countries with the UK International Development Agency, the World Bank, and the Food and Agriculture Organization of the United Nations. He is the author of *Irish Agricultural Production: Its Volume and Structure* (Cork, Ireland: Cork University Press, 1966), and of *Cattle, Economics and Development* (Slough, England: Commonwealth Agricultural Bureaux, 1980). He died in January 1994, soon after completing the manuscript of the present book.